Living & W[o

LONDON

● A Survival Handbook ●

Edited by

Graeme Chesters & David Hampshire

Survival Books ● London ● England

First published 2000
Second Edition 2004
Third Edition 2007
Fourth Edition 2008

Survival Books Limited
26 York Street, London W1U 6PZ, United Kingdom
☎ +44 (0)20-7788 7644, 🖷 +44 (0)870-762 3212
✉ info@survivalbooks.net
🖳 www.survivalbooks.net

British Library Cataloguing in Publication Data
A CIP record for this book is available
from the British Library.
ISBN: 978-1-905303-69-4

Printed and bound in India by Ajanta Offset

Acknowledgements

Our sincere thanks to those who contributed to the successful publication of this, the 4th edition of Living and Working in London, and the previous editions of this book. They include Graeme Chesters & David Hampshire (updating and editing this edition); Joe and Kerry Laredo (editing); Lilac Johnston, Peter Read and Grania Rogers (proofreading); Di Tolland (research and DTP); plus Clare O'Brien, Elizabeth Opalka, Dougal Robertson, Kerry Laredo, Sian Astrop, Valerie Baxter, Tamsin Gregory, Jason Grimsley, Susan Hardcastle, Sandra Horniman, Charlie Masson Smith, Mill Millward and Nick Williams. Finally, a special thank you to Jim Watson for the cover design, illustrations and maps, and to the many photographers (listed on page 350), whose beautiful images add colour and bring the city to life.

What readers & reviewers have said about Survival Books:

'If you need to find out how France works then this book is indispensable. Native French people probably have a less thorough understanding of how their country functions.'

Living France

'It's everything you always wanted to ask but didn't for fear of the contemptuous put down. The best English-language guide. Its pages are stuffed with practical information on everyday subjects and are designed to compliment the traditional guidebook.'

Swiss News

'Rarely has a 'survival guide' contained such useful advice – This book dispels doubts for first-time travellers, yet is also useful for seasoned globetrotters – In a word, if you're planning to move to the US or go there for a long-term stay, then buy this book both for general reading and as a ready-reference.'

American Citizens Abroad

'Let's say it at once. David Hampshire's Living and Working in France is the best handbook ever produced for visitors and foreign residents in this country; indeed, my discussion with locals showed that it has much to teach even those born and bred in l'Hexagone – It is Hampshire's meticulous detail which lifts his work way beyond the range of other books with similar titles. Often you think of a supplementary question and search for the answer in vain. With Hampshire this is rarely the case. – He writes with great clarity (and gives French equivalents of all key terms), a touch of humour and a ready eye for the odd (and often illuminating) fact. – This book is absolutely indispensable.'

The Riviera Reporter

'A must for all future expats. I invested in several books but this is the only one you need. Every issue and concern is covered, every daft question you have but are frightened to ask is answered honestly without pulling any punches. Highly recommended.'

Reader

'In answer to the desert island question about the one how-to book on France, this book would be it.'

The Recorder

'The ultimate reference book. Every subject imaginable is exhaustively explained in simple terms. An excellent introduction to fully enjoy all that this fine country has to offer and save time and money in the process.'

American Club of Zurich

'The amount of information covered is not short of incredible. I thought I knew enough about my birth country. This book has proved me wrong. Don't go to France without it. Big mistake if you do. Absolutely priceless!'

Reader

'When you buy a model plane for your child, a video recorder, or some new computer gizmo, you get with it a leaflet or booklet pleading 'Read Me First', or bearing large friendly letters or bold type saying 'IMPORTANT - follow the instructions carefully'. This book should be similarly supplied to all those entering France with anything more durable than a 5-day return ticket. – It is worth reading even if you are just visiting briefly, or if you have lived here for years and feel totally knowledgeable and secure. But if you need to find out how France works then it is indispensable. Native French people probably have a less thorough understanding of how their country functions. – Where it is most essential, the book is most up to the minute.

Living France

A comprehensive guide to all things French, written in a highly readable and amusing style, for anyone planning to live, work or retire in France.

The Times

Covers every conceivable question that might be asked concerning everyday life – I know of no other book that could take the place of this one.

France in Print

A concise, thorough account of the Do's and DONT's for a foreigner in Switzerland – Crammed with useful information and lightened with humorous quips which make the facts more readable.

American Citizens Abroad

'I found this a wonderful book crammed with facts and figures, with a straightforward approach to the problems and pitfalls you are likely to encounter. The whole laced with humour and a thorough understanding of what's involved. Gets my vote!'

Reader

'A vital tool in the war against real estate sharks; don't even think of buying without reading this book first!'

Everything Spain

'We would like to congratulate you on this work: it is really super! We hand it out to our expatriates and they read it with great interest and pleasure.'

ICI (Switzerland) AG

Important Note

London is a huge city with many faces, a huge variety of ethnic groups, religions and customs, added to which the UK has continuously changing laws, rules, regulations, interest rates and prices. We cannot recommend too strongly that you check with an official and reliable source (not always the same) before making any major decisions or taking an irreversible course of action. However, don't believe everything you're told or read – even, dare we say it, herein!

Useful addresses, websites and references to other sources of information have been included in all chapters and in **Appendices A, B** and **C** to help you obtain further information and verify details with official sources. Important points have been emphasised **in bold print**, some of which it would be expensive, or even dangerous, to disregard. **Ignore them at your peril or cost.**

Note

Unless specifically stated, the reference to any company, organisation or product in this book doesn't constitute an endorsement or recommendation. None of the businesses, products or individuals mentioned in this book have paid to be mentioned.

Contents

Editors' Notes

♦ Times are shown using am for before noon and pm for after noon. All times are local – you should check the time difference when making international telephone calls (see **Time Difference on** page 292).

♦ Unless otherwise stated, prices shown include VAT (at 17.5%) and should be taken as estimates only, although they were correct at the time of publication.

♦ His/he/him also means her/she/her (please forgive us ladies). This is done to make life easier for both the reader and the editors, and isn't intended to be sexist.

♦ References are made in this book to the European Union (EU), which comprises Austria, Belgium, Bulgaria, Cyprus, the Czech Republic, Denmark, Estonia, Finland, France, Germany, Greece, Hungary, Ireland, Italy, Latvia, Lithuania, Luxembourg, Malta, the Netherlands, Poland, Portugal, Romania, the Slovak Republic, Slovenia, Spain, Sweden and the UK, and to the European Economic Area (EEA), which includes the EU countries plus Iceland, Liechtenstein and Norway.

♦ All spelling is (or should be) British English and not American English. American English equivalents are shown in brackets where these differ significantly from British English words.

♦ Warnings and important points are shown in **bold** type.

♦ The following symbols are used in this book: ☎ (telephone), 🖹 (fax), 💻 (Internet) and ✉ (email).

♦ Lists of **Useful Addresses**, **Further Reading** and **Useful Websites** are contained in **Appendices A**, **B** and **C** respectively.

♦ For those unfamiliar with the American system of **Weights and Measures,** conversion tables (Imperial/metric) are included in **Appendix D**.

♦ Useful tables are included in **Appendix E** and a Glossary of rhyming Cockney slang in **Appendix F**.

♦ A map of London's 32 boroughs and the City of London is shown inside the front cover and a map of the London underground network inside the back cover.

Beefeaters, Tower of London

Introduction

L ondon is one of the world's great cities, but it can be a confusing and daunting place for newcomers – it isn't only vast and labyrinthine, but also chaotic. However, fear not, whether you're already living or working in London or just thinking about it – this book is for you. Forget about those glossy guide books, excellent though they are for tourists; *Living and Working in London* was written especially with you in mind and is worth its weight in whelks. The 4th edition has been completely updated, enlarged and redesigned - and furthermore, it's printed in colour.

This book is designed to meet the needs of anyone who wants to know the essentials of London life, whether you're an immigrant, temporary worker, transferee, business person, student, retiree or long-stay visitor. However long your intended stay, you'll find the information contained in *Living and Working in London* invaluable.

General information isn't difficult to find in the UK; however, reliable and up-to-date information specifically intended for newcomers living or working in London isn't easy to find. Our aim in publishing this book was to help fill this void and provide the practical information necessary for a relatively trouble-free life. You may have visited London as a tourist, but living and working there is a different matter altogether. Adjusting to a different environment and culture and making a home in any foreign city can be a traumatic and stressful experience, and London is no exception.

Living and Working in London is a comprehensive handbook on a wide range of everyday subjects and represents the most up-to-date source of general information available to foreigners in London. It isn't, however, simply a monologue of dry facts and figures, but a practical and entertaining look at life in London.

Adapting to life in a new country is a continuous process and this book will reduce your novice phase, minimise the frustrations and help you make informed decisions and calculated judgements, instead of uneducated guesses and costly mistakes. **Most important of all, it will help save you time, trouble, and money and repay your investment many times over.**

Although you may find some of the information a bit daunting, don't be discouraged – most problems occur only once and fade into insignificance after a short time (as you face the next half dozen!). However, although foreigners in the UK may occasionally complain about the government, traffic wardens and the weather, most love living there. A period spent in London is a wonderful way to enrich your life, broaden your horizons, make friends and, with any luck (and some hard work), make your fortune. We trust this book will help you avoid the pitfalls of life in London and smooth your way to a happy and rewarding future in your new home.

Good luck!

Graeme Chestersa & David Hampshire

August 2008

London Eye & the River Thames

1.
WELCOME TO LONDON

London is one of the world's great cities and Europe's largest; Greater London covers over 610mi² (1,580km²) and has a population of around 7.5m. It's Britain's seat of government, the home of the British royal family, the UK's commercial, cultural and sporting centre, Europe's leading financial market, the 'capital' of the English-speaking world, and a world leader in architecture, art, fashion, food, music, publishing, film and television.

London is also Europe's most racially and culturally diverse city, and one of the most cosmopolitan in the world; one in three Londoners (2.5m people) were born outside the UK and between them they speak over 300 languages. Greater London is home to almost half of the ethnic minority population of the UK. Londoners hail from all corners of the globe, particularly Europe and the Commonwealth countries of Africa, Asia and the West Indies – it has some 60 communities of over 10,000 people born outside the UK. To add to this cultural potpourri, a phenomenal 25m visitors swell London's population each year, not to mention the hundreds of thousands of commuters who flock there daily from the surrounding (home) counties and further afield to work.

London is the UK's main employment centre, with a huge variety of job opportunities and an unemployment rate well below the national average. However, in common with most capital cities, the cost of living is high – property in particular is among the most expensive in the world – although higher salaries compensate to some extent. Like all large cities, London displays stark contrasts of wealth and poverty, and few places offer such endless opportunities to make or lose your fortune.

London's failings include pollution, an ageing and over-burdened public transport system, traffic congestion, substandard housing and homelessness, over-crowding, high crime (in some areas) and racial tension. However, it's the people – the good, the bad and the ugly – who make London what it is and give the city its unique character. Although the British can be infuriating at times, they will invariably charm and delight you with their sense of humour and idiosyncrasies.

The sheer size of London can be daunting – it isn't only vast and labyrinthine, but also chaotic. Central London was originally an assortment of villages and some 250 years ago there were wide spaces between them, although today they've merged into an almost seamless metropolis. The surrounding areas of London developed mainly in the Victorian period, when the 'suburbs' were at least partly planned. Outer London has more open space and the population density is generally below 2,750 people per mi² (7,000 per km²) – half of what it is in the city centre.

Any attempt to divide London into manageable and comprehensible chunks can be only partially successful. The task is made difficult by the overlap between the various artificial divisions that have been created over the years – geographical, cultural, historical, administrative and postal. A customary dividing line is the River Thames, which flows from west to east through London's centre. There's widespread belief that the areas north of the river are more pleasant than those to the south, just as it's generally believed that the West End is superior to the East End, but those generalisations often don't stand up when you look at areas in more detail.

GREATER LONDON AUTHORITY (GLA)

The Greater London Authority (GLA) was formed in 2000 to govern London and replaced the Greater London Council (GLC), which was abolished in 1986. It's the London-wide body responsible for coordinating the boroughs, strategic planning, and operating some of Greater London's services such as the Metropolitan Police Service (note: the City of London has its own police force), the London Fire Service and public transport. The GLA consists of the Mayor of London (Boris Johnson, elected in 2008) and the London Assembly, who are elected by Londoners every four years (the next elections are due in 2012).

When the GLC was abolished, most of its functions were taken over by the London boroughs, while others became the responsibility of joint-boards and other unelected bodies. The boroughs thus enjoyed a high degree of autonomy and although they lost some of their powers when the GLA was formed, they still retain many responsibilities which they didn't have under the GLC.

The Greater London Authority's site (💻 www.london.gov.uk) provides information about the 14 constituencies (see below), and the UpMyStreet site (💻 www.upmystreet.com), run in conjunction with Thomson Directories, is a mine of information about each postcode area.

CONSTITUENCIES

The creation of the GLA grouped the boroughs into 14 constituencies (listed below). There are other more or less arbitrary divisions: 16 health authority areas, five police regions, four ambulance service zones and three fire brigade sectors.

Officially, each borough is also divided into 'wards' (an administrative district of a parliamentary constituency), although most

Greater London Authority Constituencies

Constituency	Boroughs
Barnet and Camden	Barnet, Camden
Bexley and Bromley	Bexley, Bromley
Brent and Harrow	Brent, Harrow
City and East London	Barking and Dagenham, City of London, Newham, Tower Hamlets
Croydon and Sutton	Croydon, Sutton
Ealing and Hillingdon	Ealing, Hillingdon
Enfield and Haringey	Enfield, Haringey
Greenwich and Lewisham	Greenwich, Lewisham
Havering and Redbridge	Havering, Redbridge
Lambeth and Southwark	Lambeth, Southwark
Merton and Wandsworth	Merton, Wandsworth
North East	Hackney, Islington, Waltham Forest
South West	Hounslow, Kingston-upon-Thames, Richmond-upon-Thames
West Central	Hammersmith and Fulham, Kensington and Chelsea, Westminster

residents don't know their ward names. Most people refer instead to districts, which in some cases don't appear on maps, but which either are named after places long since swallowed by the outward sprawl of the city or derive from contemporary 'estate agent speak' (e.g. 'Blythe Village' and 'Brackenbury Village' in the borough of Hammersmith & Fulham and 'Limehouse Village' in Docklands). In many cases, these districts straddle borough or county boundaries.

POSTCODES

The most perplexing of London's various partitions is its division into postal areas, each with a different 'postcode' (the equivalent of US zip codes) that seldom bears any relationship to counties, boroughs or districts.

The postcode is the most important part of any address when sending mail, which, together with the house number, uniquely identifies an individual building or dwelling. The system was designed at a time when the official London boundary was restricted to the square mile of the City of London. The area has continually expanded over the centuries and in 1965, when Greater London was created, its boundaries extended far beyond the London postal districts. The boroughs with a London postal district are shown in the table below.

Areas in central London (an area stretching in some cases to the borders of Greater London) have postcodes beginning with W (for west), NW (north-west), N (north), E (east), SE (south-east) and SW (south-west) – there are no NE or S postcodes, which were abolished between 1866 and 1868. Those in outer London have codes relating to the nearest town where there's a main sorting office, which is in some cases a 'borough' town (e.g. BR for Bromley, CR for Croydon, EN for Enfield, HA for Harrow, KT for Kingston and SM for Sutton – although there's no M in Sutton!) and in other cases isn't (e.g. DA for

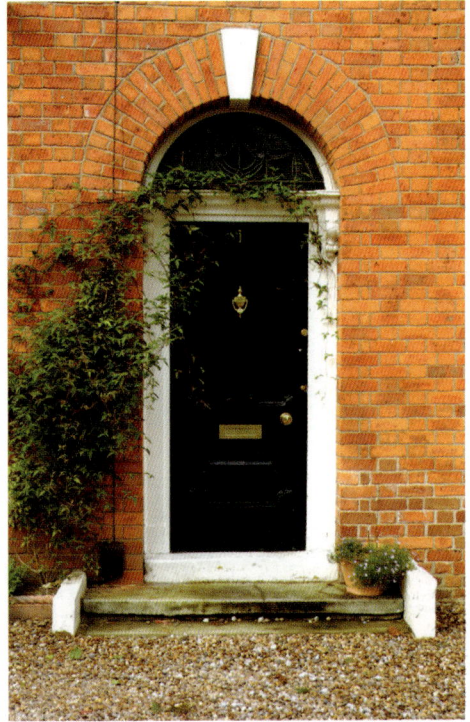

London Postcode Areas	
Included	**Boroughs**
Entirely	City of London, Camden, Hackney, Hammersmith & Fulham, Haringey, Islington, Kensington & Chelsea, Lambeth, Southwark, Tower Hamlets, Wandsworth, Westminster
Mostly	Greenwich, Lewisham, Newham, Waltham Forest
Partly	Barnet, Bexley, Brent, Bromley, Croydon, Ealing, Enfield, Harrow, Hounslow, Kingston-upon-Thames, Merton, Redbridge, Richmond-upon-Thames
Excluded	Barking & Dagenham, Havering, Hillingdon, Sutton

Outer London Postcodes

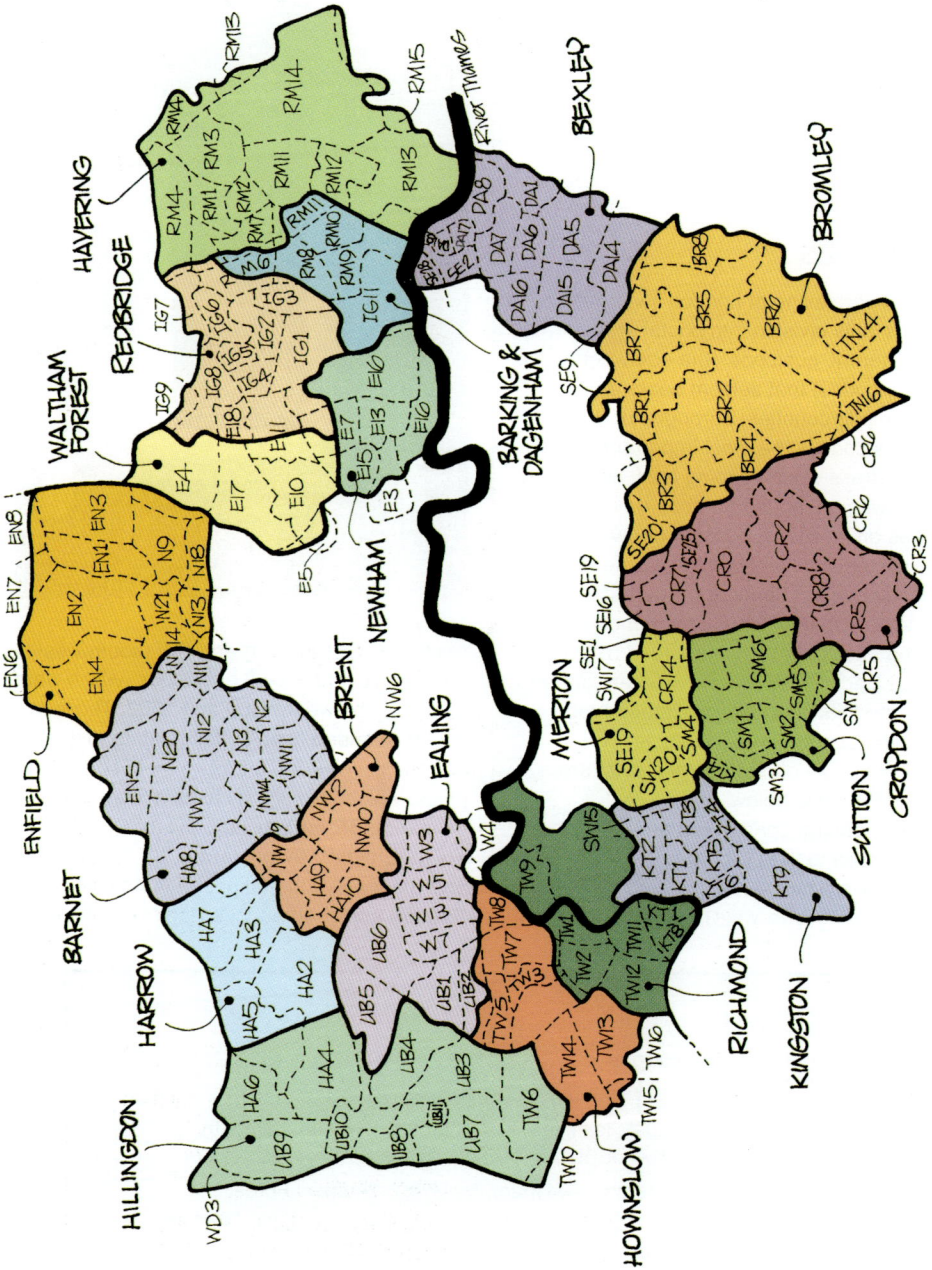

Inner London Postcodes

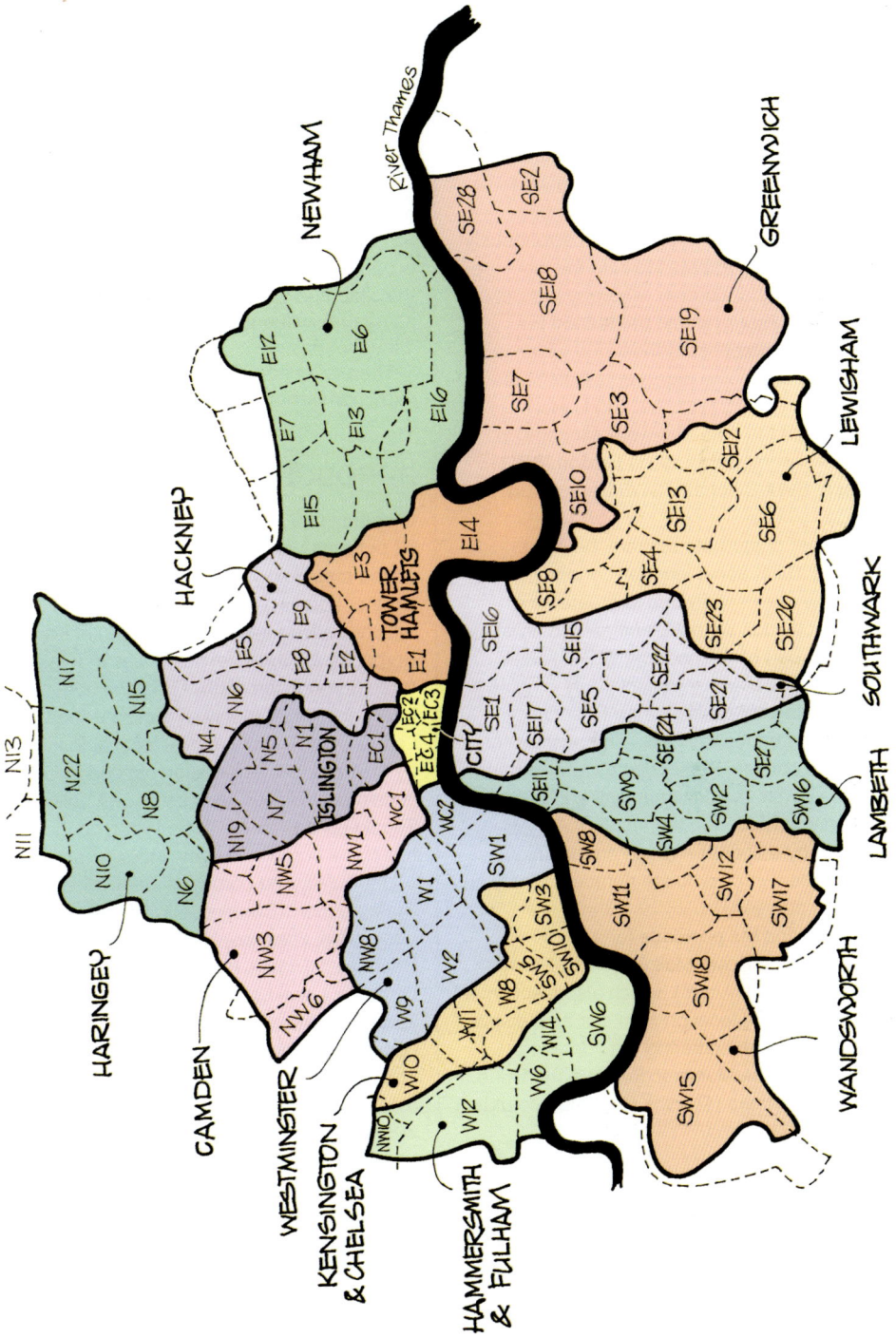

Dagenham in Bexley, IG for Ilford in Redbridge, RM for Romford in Havering, TW for Twickenham in Richmond and UB for Uxbridge in Hillingdon).

As if all this weren't confusing enough, the numbers following the initial letter or letters of postcodes can also be misleading. Originally, the system was based on the initial letter of each sub-district in the alphabet; a district beginning with the letter 'A' was given the number 1 and so on. Many people erroneously believe that the numbers indicate the distance from the centre of London, whereby logically the lowest numbers would be nearest the centre and the highest furthest out, which isn't usually the case. The most central districts were allocated a '1' (W1, N1, SW1, etc.) but after that the numbers were allocated in alphabetical order, so SW2 is Brixton, SW3 Chelsea, SW4 Clapham, SW5 Earls Court, and so on.

To further complicate matters, between 1968 and 1971, some 'central' London postcodes were subdivided to create new, smaller postcode districts, and gained an extra letter, e.g. part of W1 become W1H. These letters have changed in recent years – no doubt making life easier for the Post Office but costing London residents and businesses millions of pounds. Postcodes have also been 'extended' with an additional digit and two letters (separated from the first 3 or 4 'digit' postcode by a space) – which are all unique and together with the house number identify an individual address.

You can find the postcode for any UK address via the Royal Mail website (💻 www.postcode.royalmail.com), which also displays a map showing the location (you can also display and print a map by entering the address or postcode into the Multimap (💻 www.multimap.com) or Streetmap (💻 www.streetmap.co.uk) websites.

> House prices in London are mainly defined by location and some people are willing to pay above the odds to acquire a home with a desirable postcode, which can inflate or reduce the value of a property.

TELEPHONE NUMBERS

London telephone numbers were changed (unnecessarily) in 1995 and again in 1999 (to rectify the mistake made in 1995). All London numbers now have the code 020, followed by eight digits, the first of which is 7 for numbers in inner London – an area which, needless to say, doesn't correspond with the geographical concept of inner London – and 8 for outer London. It's widely believed, even by Londoners, that the code for inner London is 0207 and for outer London 0208. This isn't the case and you can dial a number within the same area without using the 020 code, but not if the 7 or 8 is omitted.

There's a certain snob appeal in having an 0207 number rather than an 0208 number.

BOROUGHS

Created in 1965, Greater London is divided into 32 boroughs and the City of London (as shown on the map below) – the administrative areas of Greater London – which in turn is one of the 45 administrative regions (or counties) of England. Boroughs are the local authorities that raise taxes (through the council tax) and administer local services. The only exception is the City of London, which isn't run by a local authority but by the historical Corporation of London, and has certain peculiarities such as its own police force. The so-called City of Westminster, on the other hand, is a borough like any other.

Unofficially, the boroughs are divided between 'inner London' (Camden, City of London, Greenwich, Hackney, Hammersmith & Fulham, Haringey, Islington, Kensington & Chelsea, Lambeth, Lewisham, Newham, Southwark, Tower Hamlets and Wandsworth) and 'outer London' (the remaining 19 boroughs). Inner London boroughs tend to be characterised by a huge gulf between rich and poor, and a wide racial and cultural mix. Outer London boroughs are more suburban, with swathes of green belt (areas in which building is restricted) and a predominantly white (and 'white-collar') population.

Many people still consider only the central areas to be 'proper' London, the outer areas belonging to the surrounding ('home') counties – e.g. Kingston was previously part of Surrey and Bromley was in Kent, although both towns have given their names to London boroughs. The boroughs vary considerably in size but each has a population of between 150,000 and 350,000, with the exception of the City of London, which has just 7,800 residents.

Each London borough has its own website containing a wealth of information, which can be accessed via 🖳 www.london.gov.uk/london/links.jsp. The addresses of individual sites are www.[borough name].gov.uk (e.g. 🖳 www.brent.gov.uk or 🖳 www.barking-dagenham.gov.uk), with the exception of Hammersmith & Fulham (🖳 www.lbhf.gov.uk), Kensington & Chelsea (🖳 www.rbkc.gov.uk) and Waltham Forest (🖳 www.lbwf.gov.uk).

Vital statistics for the 32 boroughs and the City of London – in alphabetical order – are provided on the following pages.

Barking & Dagenham

The east London borough of Barking and Dagenham is more deprived than average. It was once marshland and much of it consists of terraced council houses (public housing owned by the local authority), some of which are now privately owned. The Barking Barrage has enabled development to take place along the River Roding in the south-west and there are plans to reclaim more marshland along the north bank of the River Thames over the next two decades, providing space for some 4,000 new homes.

Property

The borough's largest housing estate (a development that often refers to council or public housing), Becontree, was built in the '20s and '30s for East End workers. It consists of some 27,000 homes, mostly two- and three-bedroom red brick houses. Other council estates were subsequently built to its north, and there's a relatively small amount of private housing in the borough, although it's among the cheapest in London. Barking town offers small Victorian (1836-1901) terraced houses and some larger Edwardian (1901-1910) and '20s and '30s properties. The slightly more upmarket Chadwell Heath has some semi-detached houses (semis), but over two-thirds of properties in Barking & Dagenham are in terraces (the highest proportion in London) and a further quarter are flats, most purpose built. The southern part of the borough will be affected by the Thames Gateway housing scheme (see page 115).

Costs

Average house prices and rents are among the lowest in London (see pages 325 and 326), while council taxes are just below the London average (see page 329).

Communications

Public transport is good in most areas, particularly for commuting into central London. The tube's District Line runs through Barking, Becontree and Dagenham, and there are three Overground lines: one running into London's Liverpool Street station,

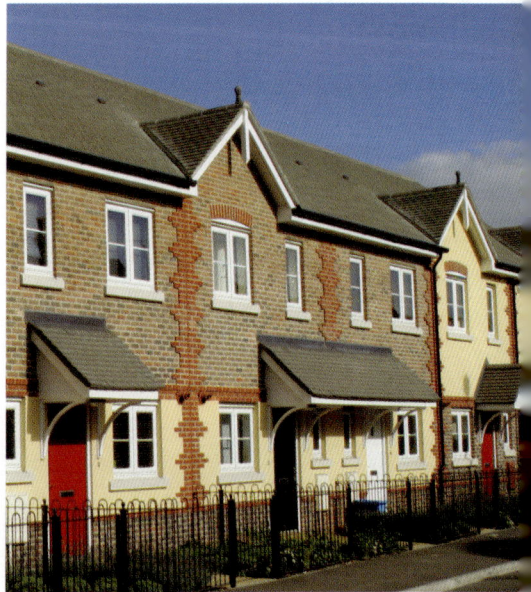

one to Fenchurch Street, and another from Barking to Gospel Oak near Hampstead Heath (Camden). Buses are a better bet for travelling north/south and there are good services between the towns of Barking and Dagenham. The main A13 road to Essex cuts across the southern part of the borough, while the A406, known as the 'North Circular Road', forms Barking and Dagenham's western boundary.

Leisure Facilities

There's plenty of open space in Barking and Dagenham but it tends to be flat and rather dull. The largest of the borough's 16 parks, Eastbrookend Country Park in the east, boasts a lake and its own Millennium Centre, and the government is creating attractive walks along the River Roding and landscaping the A13. The borough is well supplied with cinemas and leisure centres, although there's only one museum, one theatre and one main library (in Barking).

If you're looking for an area with plenty of good restaurants, Barking and Dagenham isn't for you!

Schools

Barking & Dagenham's state secondary schools are among the fastest-improving in London and its Education Authority has been described by the Office for Standards in Education (OFSTED) as 'a model of clarity', whatever that means. There are no private schools in the borough.

Shopping

Barking is the best place for shopping, with the recent Vicarage Fields centre and a pedestrian precinct. Chadwell Heath has reasonable shops, but Dagenham is poorly served.

Barking & Dagenham

Council offices: Civic Centre, Rainham Road North, Dagenham RM10 7BN (☎ 020-8515 3000, 🖥 www.lbbd.gov.uk).
Postcodes: IG11, RM6 (part), RM7 (part), RM8, RM9 (part) and RM10.
Population: 165,000, with a high proportion of people under 20. Barking and Dagenham has a predominantly 'white' population, just 14 per cent belonging to ethnic minorities, although that percentage looks set to increase as immigration into the UK continues.
Unemployment: Around 8.5 per cent.
Crime rate: Barking and Dagenham's crime rates are lower than the London average (see table in **Appendix F**).

Barnet

The outer London borough of Barnet is one of the city's largest. Much of its housing sprang up along the Northern Line tube route, which was built in the early part of the last century. The town of Barnet is at the far northern end of the line and retains a market town character. In the centre, Totteridge and Mill Hill offer some attractive properties, while to the west, Edgware is solid but dull and Burnt Oak has a lot of rather soulless council property. Hendon in the south is a better bet, with distant echoes of its rural past. Finchley and Friern Barnet in the east are more upmarket, while Hampstead Garden Suburb in the south-east corner of the borough is home to the rich and famous. In the extreme south-west are Golders Green (noted for its large Jewish population), Cricklewood and Brent Cross, the last two (with West Hendon) being the site of London's largest current housing development, not due for completion until 2020.

Other areas being developed are Grahame Park and Stonegrove in the north-west of the borough and Dollis Valley in the north-east.

Property

Property in the borough is divided between flats (38 per cent), semi-detached (31 per cent), terraces (20 per cent) and detached houses (11 per cent), and ranges from the affordable (in Edgware, Brent Cross and parts of Finchley) to the outrageously expensive (in Hampstead Garden Suburb, where London's 'Millionaires' Row', Bishops Avenue, is found) and includes every style from modern apartment blocks and ex-council houses to Georgian and Edwardian mansions.

Costs

House prices and rents are just above the London average (see pages 325 and 326), as are council taxes (see page 329).

Communications

The Northern Line remains the borough's main public transport artery, but trains can be infrequent, slow and crowded. Barnet isn't well served by mainline trains, although one of London's two trans-Thames routes, appropriately named Thameslink, links Mill Hill, Hendon and Cricklewood to Wimbledon and Sutton via Blackfriars station in the City. Buses run to central London but there are few east/ west routes.

The UK's oldest motorway, the M1, begins in Barnet and other main roads (e.g. the A1 and A41) cut through the borough from north to south. The A5 runs along the boundary between Barnet and Brent, and the North Circular Road (A406) joins the M1 at the busy Brent Cross intersection. Most areas have resident parking zones.

Leisure Facilities

There's plenty of open space in Barnet, particularly towards the border with Hertfordshire, where there are several golf courses. There are also plenty of museums (including the RAF Museum at Hendon and the Jewish Museum in Finchley), cinemas, leisure centres and libraries, and a major arts and leisure centre in North Finchley, which includes a theatre. There's also the Bull Theatre in Barnet town.

Schools

A high proportion of Barnet's state secondary schools provide an above-average education. There are also plenty of private schools in the borough.

Shopping

Barnet is second only to Westminster in the number of its retailers. Shops range from small specialist Jewish shops (and restaurants) in Golders Green to London's only Eastern shopping centre in West Hendon and the huge 'mall' at Brent Cross. Edgware, Finchley, Hendon and Barnet town all offer reasonable shopping.

Barnet

Council offices: North London Business Park, Oakleigh Road South, London N11 1NP (☎ 020-8359 2000, 🖳 www.barnet.gov.uk).

Postcodes: N2, N3, N10 (part), N11 (part), N12, N20, NW2 (part), NW4, NW7, NW9 (part), NW11, EN4 (part), EN5 (part), EN6 (part) and HA8 (part).

Population: 329,000 – London's second most populous borough. Barnet is mainly prosperous, with a high proportion of middle-class families. Almost 26 per cent of its population belongs to ethnic minorities, including London's largest Gujerati community, while Golders Green is home to the capital's biggest Jewish community.

Unemployment: Around 4.5 per cent.

Crime rate: Barnet has an average crime rate, with something of a burglary problem (see table in **Appendix F**).

Bexley

The south-east London borough of Bexley (meaning 'clearing in the box wood') is mainly suburban and often rather dull, although there are smarter areas towards its southern end and the boundary with Bromley.

Property

A large proportion of Bexley's property is semi-detached (44 per cent – the highest in London), with 30 per cent terraced, 20 per cent flats (almost all purpose built) and only 6 per cent detached.

Most properties date from the '20s and '30s, and vary from the smart (around Sidcup and Blackfen in the south-west) to the shabby (around Erith in the north-east, which is in line for a 'government improvement scheme'). In the centre of the borough, the town of Bexley itself (called Bexley Village) is attractive with something of a village feel, while neighbouring Bexleyheath and Welling consist mainly of solid but unremarkable '20s and '30s terraces and semis. In the flat marshland to the north-west, Thamesmead offers some modern properties, and there are bargains to be found among the tower blocks in the north of the borough. This northern part of Bexley will be affected by the Thames Gateway housing scheme (see page 115).

Costs

House prices are among London's lowest (see pages 325 and 326) and council taxes just above average (see page 329).

Communications

The underground doesn't reach Bexley, but it's particularly well served by Overground trains: Belvedere, Bexley, Bexleyheath, Erith, Falconwood, Sidcup and Welling are linked to various central London terminals (Blackfriars, Cannon Street, Charing Cross, London Bridge, Victoria and Waterloo) and to all parts of Kent in the other direction. Bexley also has reasonable bus services.

The main A2 and A20 roads linking London with the Channel ports slice through the borough and offer escape routes into rural Kent, although they're inevitably heavy with traffic. Parking is increasingly controlled (and charged for) through resident permit zones.

Leisure Facilities

There are a number of hills in Bexley, as well as woods, parks and other open spaces, with golf courses in the centre of the borough and walks along the Rivers Cray and Thames. Restaurants are scarce and shopping is adequate rather than inspiring. Sports facilities are good and there are four theatres, several museums and two cinemas.

Schools

Bexley's state secondary schools, which unusually include grammar schools, are mostly high performing and over-subscribed; to have

a chance of admission, a child must usually live within two miles of a school. There are no private secondary schools in the borough.

Shopping

The best shops are in Bexleyheath and the most limited in Erith (although it has a popular twice weekly street market); there are hardly any shops in Thamesmead.

Bexley

Council offices: Bexley Civic Offices, Broadway, Bexleyheath DA6 7LB (☎ 020-8303 7777, 🖳 www.bexley.gov.uk).
   Postcodes: SE2, SE28 (part), DA1 (part), DA5 (part), DA6, DA7, DA8, DA14, DA15, DA16, DA17 and DA18.
   Population: 222,000. Bexley has a largely well-to-do, predominantly white population (92 per cent), with a small Asian community centred in Belvedere.
   Unemployment: Around 4.1 per cent.
   Crime rate: Bexley has less crime than most of London (see table in **Appendix F**).

Brent

Brent takes its name from the river that runs through it and is a borough of various characters, neither a typically 'inner' nor a typically 'outer' London borough. The North Circular, London's inner orbital road, splits the borough in half, each half having distinct economic and social characteristics. In the south, areas such as Harlesden, South Kilburn and Stonebridge suffer inner-city levels of social deprivation, while parts of the more affluent, leafy, suburban north (Brondesbury, Willesden Green, Dollis Hill, Kingsbury and areas bordering Harrow) boast tree-lined streets and a conservation area modelled on a picture-postcard English village (there's even a castle and a thatched cottage!).

   Wembley is home to one of the world's most famous sporting stadiums (recently rebuilt), as well as the Arena and Conference Centre, which attract tens of thousands of visitors every week. Further east, Neasden has a partly deserved reputation for dullness (and the largest Hindu temple outside India), while Queens Park and Kilburn in Brent's south-east corner are among the capital's upwardly mobile areas.

Property

Brent has a high proportion of flats (48 per cent), over a third of them conversions, 24 per cent each of terraces and semis, and a mere 4 per cent of detached houses.

   The flats around Queens Park are particularly attractive, mostly in spacious, converted houses and close to central London.

Costs

House prices (see pages 325 and 326) are generally below average but vary widely, and council taxes are just above average (see page 329).

Communications

Public transport in Brent is generally good. The Bakerloo and Jubilee tube lines serve most areas, but Wembley is one of the few places in the borough with Overground railway services: a mainline link to Marylebone and Euston stations, and one of London's trans-Thames rail services, serving Clapham Junction, Croydon and places south.

   The A406 North Circular Road, which cuts the borough in half, has recently been widened but is still prey to traffic jams at peak times. The A5 runs along the boundary with Barnet. Residents' parking permits have been widely introduced and there are high fees for second and third cars.

Leisure Facilities

Wembley Arena hosts world-class musicians and other performers, and there are good theatres and cinemas and reasonable sports facilities (including two boules rinks) in Brent.

The borough has around 1,000 acres of open space, including Queens Park in the south, Gladstone Park with its exotic plants in the east, Roundwood Park (venue of the largest Irish festival outside Ireland), Fryent Country Park in the north and the Brent Reservoir (known as the Welsh Harp because of its shape) on the border with Barnet.

Wembley is noted for its Indian restaurants and a major Asian street market in Ealing Road.

Schools

Brent has 17 secondary schools, two of them private. Most of the state schools are grant maintained and most have good educational standards, despite the culturally diverse population; many children's first language isn't English, and over 120 languages are spoken in the borough. There are three schools for religious groups – Hindus, Jews and Muslims – and two colleges of technology, an arts college and a language college.

Shopping

Shopping in Brent tends to be functional, although there's a variety of ethnic shops in Kilburn, Willesden and Wembley. Nearby Brent Cross shopping centre (in Barnet) is one of London's largest.

Brent

Council offices: Forty Lane, Wembley HA9 9HD (☎ 020-8937 1200, 🖳 www. brent.gov.uk).

Postcodes: NW2 (part), NW6 (part), NW9 (part), NW10, HA3 (part), HA9 and HA0.

Population: 272,000. Brent has the most multi-cultural population in London, the majority of its inhabitants belonging to ethnic minorities (55 per cent of residents are non-'white'), consisting mainly of people of Asian origin (almost 28 per cent of the total population, mostly in the north and west) and Afro-Caribbeans (20 per cent); over 70 languages are spoken in Brent. The borough also has the highest proportion of Irish-born inhabitants in London (9 per cent), mostly around Kilburn in the south-east. Poverty is a significant problem in the south of the borough and the number of low-income households is increasing. Some 70 per cent of people in Harlesden are officially 'poor'.

Unemployment: Around 7.3 per cent.

Crime rate: Average (see table in **Appendix F**).

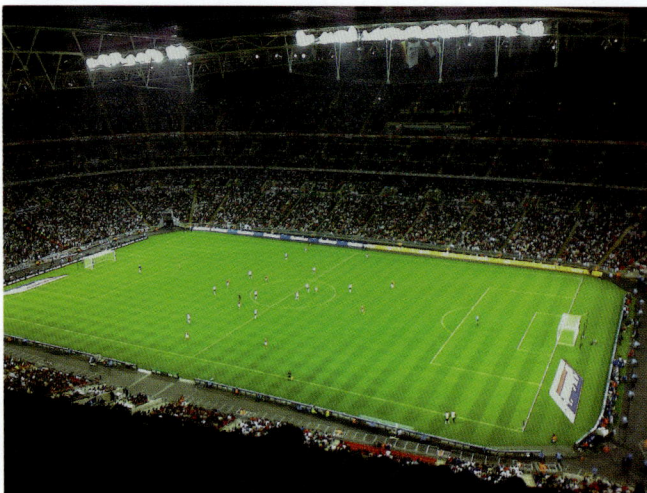

Wembley Stadium

Bromley

The largest of London's boroughs, Bromley is often regarded as being part of Kent – particularly by its inhabitants. There are almost rural villages like Keston and Farnborough in the south, but plenty of typical London suburbia elsewhere. Bromley's north-west corner, which borders Lambeth, Southwark and Lewisham, has a rather depressed, inner city feel, although the government is committed to regenerating the areas around Penge, Anerley and Crystal Palace (once one of London's major attractions and the site of several aborted development projects). As you move east, to Beckenham, Bromley town, Hayes and West Wickham, standards (and prices) rise, the most expensive parts of the borough being the decidedly upmarket Chislehurst and Petts Wood in the north-east.

Property

Bromley has the highest percentage of detached houses in London (18 per cent), reflecting its high number of well-heeled residents. Most of these houses were built during the first third of the 20th century. The remainder of properties are fairly evenly divided between semi-detached (29 per cent), terraces (25 per cent) and flats (28 per cent).

Costs

Average property prices and rents in Bromley are below the London average (see pages 325 and 326). Council taxes are also relatively low (see page 329).

Communications

Bromley isn't served by the underground, but Overground rail stations are plentiful and services are good. Anerley, Beckenham, Bromley, Chislehurst, Crystal Palace, Hayes, Orpington, Penge, Petts Wood and West Wickham are variously linked to Blackfriars, Cannon Street, Charing Cross, London Bridge, Victoria and Waterloo stations, and the East London line is expected to be extended as far as Crystal Palace. Buses are also plentiful, but most don't travel to the city centre. The roads are particularly busy around Crystal Palace, where parking can be

a problem; otherwise the borough is mostly permit free.

Leisure Facilities

There's plenty of open space in Bromley, as well as a selection of theatres, concert halls, libraries and museums, but just two cinemas. There are several sports centres – and the famous Athletics Stadium at Crystal Palace – and half a dozen golf courses. Chislehurst has a reasonable selection of restaurants.

Schools

Bromley has only one Local Education Authority-run secondary school, the rest being foundation, private or voluntary-aided schools.

Shopping

There's excellent shopping in Bromley town and good shops in Orpington; other towns are less well served.

Bromley

Council offices: Bromley Civic Centre, Stockwell Close, Bromley BR1 3UH (☎ 020-8464 3333, 🖥 bromley.gov.uk)

Postcodes: SE20, BR1 (part), BR2, BR3, BR4, BR5, BR6, BR7, BR8 (part), CR6 (part), TN14 (part) and TN16 (part).

Population: 300,000, with the second-highest proportion of over 50s in the 33 boroughs. Bromley has a generally affluent, predominantly white population – less than 10 per cent of the population is non-white.

Unemployment: Around 5.5 per cent.

Crime rate: In contrast to its northern neighbours, Bromley boasts a generally low crime rate, although burglary rates are above average (see table in **Appendix F**).

Camden

Camden contains some of London's smartest areas – notably around Regent's Park in the south-west and Hampstead in the north-east – as well as some of its

seediest, around King's Cross station in the south-east, one of the capital's unofficial red light districts (but which is part of a multi-million pound regeneration project expected take at least ten years). A smaller development – of shops, offices and homes, to be called 'Regent's Quarter' – is under way in the area surrounding the Pentonville Road.

In the centre of the borough, Camden Town, with its colourful markets, is one of the most 'in' places in London. Bloomsbury and Fitzrovia in the south are almost as trendy, while further west Primrose Hill and Belsize Park are attractive areas and are popular with affluent 'creative' types.

Property

The vast majority of Camden's properties are flats (86 per cent), of which over a third are conversions (i.e. large houses divided into flats); 10 per cent are terraced houses and just 4 per cent detached and semi-detached houses. Property varies from drab council blocks (in Somers Town) to elegant Georgian terraces (Camden Town) and Italianate villas (Belsize Park and Primrose Hill). The King's Cross development (see above) will create 'affordable' housing on the 60-acre site behind King's Cross and St Pancras stations.

Costs

Property prices and rents vary enormously in Camden: reasonably priced houses can be found in some areas but in others you must pay over £1m for a three-bedroom flat or house (see pages 325 and 326); council tax rates are also high (see page 329).

Communications

In most parts of Camden you're spoilt for choice with public transport – which is just as well, because the council is waging war on the use of cars, and parking is a problem throughout the borough. The tube's Northern Line serves Belsize Park, Hampstead, Tufnell Park and Kentish Town, which is also on an Overground line running through Blackfriars and across the river to Wimbledon and Sutton, as well as on a route linking Richmond with east London. A cross-river tram scheme linking Camden Town with Waterloo, Brixton and Peckham is being considered. King's Cross, St Pancras and Euston stations are all in the borough of Camden. King's Cross has been given a facelift and St Pancras has recently become the London terminal for Eurostar trains (formerly Waterloo), making it possible for Londoners to reach Paris by train in just two-and-a-quarter hours.

Leisure Facilities

There's no shortage of leisure facilities in Camden, which includes part of London's 'theatreland', as well as the British Museum

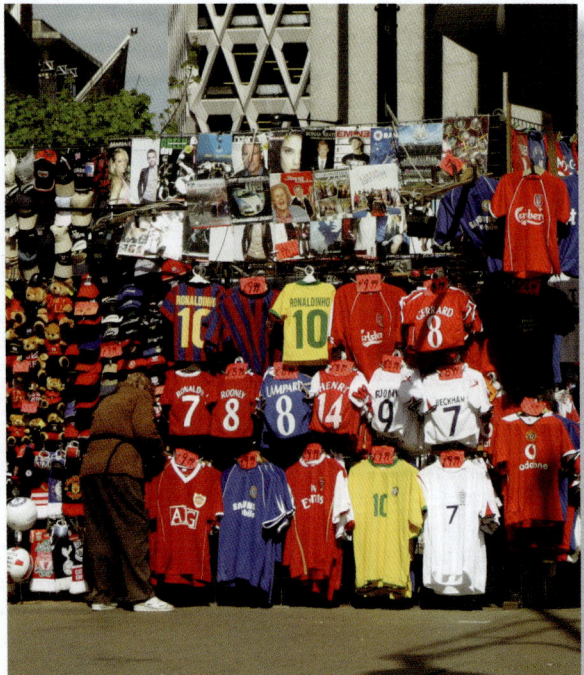

and the British Library in its new home at St Pancras. Hampstead Heath lies within the borough as does part of Regent's Park, and there are plenty of other green spaces, including Primrose Hill, Parliament Hill and Kenwood. Camden has a vast choice of excellent restaurants.

Schools

Camden's state schools are 'excellent' – according to the government's latest performance review, which awarded the borough a three-star rating – and include no fewer than eight 'beacon' schools (boasting extremely high standards). As a result, a large number of pupils 'commute' from neighbouring boroughs. There's also a good choice of private schools in and near Hampstead, while Camden houses much of the University of London.

Shopping

For shoppers, Camden boasts everything from 'crafty' Covent Garden and ethnic Camden Market (actually five separate markets with a total of over 1,000 stalls) to the techies' heaven of Tottenham Court Road.

Camden

Council offices: Judd Street, London WC1H 9JE (☎ 020-7278 4444, 🖥 www.camden.gov.uk).

Postcodes: N6 (part), NW1 (part), NW3, NW5, NW6 (part) and WC1.

Population: 228,000. On the one hand, Camden is one of the more deprived areas of England, on the other, many super-rich live there. The non-white population is 27 per cent.

Unemployment: Around 8.9 per cent. The King's Cross development (see above) is expected to create 20,000 jobs in the borough by 2020.

Crime rate: Camden has some of London's highest crime rates (see table in **Appendix F**). But figures for car theft and violence are distorted by the large influx of visitors to the borough, particularly to London's West End.

City of London

The most ancient part of London, dating back to Roman times, 'the City' measures just one mile by one mile and is therefore often referred to as 'The Square Mile'. This is the financial heart of London and, until quite recently, it consisted of almost nothing but banks, brokers and office buildings. Even today, outside working hours, it's a quiet place, with many shops, pubs and restaurants closed in the evenings.

Property

Virtually all the property (99 per cent) in the City of London is purpose-built flats. The largest development is the Barbican, dating from the '70s – a concrete maze broken up by occasional green spaces and ponds – and there are luxury flats around St Paul's cathedral and Fleet Street (now deserted by the newspaper industry in favour of Docklands).

Costs

Not surprisingly, the City's few properties are among the most expensive in London to buy or rent (see pages 325 and 326), although council tax rates are among the capital's lowest (see page 329).

Communications

Being in the centre of London, the City is well served by public transport and has eleven tube stations and four Overground terminals: Blackfriars (serving north London, the Midlands and the north of England, as well as south London, Sussex, Hampshire and Dorset), Cannon Street (serving south-east London and Kent), Fenchurch Street (serving the East End and Essex) and Liverpool Street (serving Essex and East Anglia).

The City isn't a place where cars are welcome; access to the City is subject to a charge of £8 per day (see **Congestion Charge** on page 103), there's no resident parking and car parks can cost £12 or more per day.

Leisure Facilities

The Barbican has its own Arts Centre (incorporating a theatre, concert hall, museum, art galleries and cinemas) and is home to the Guildhall School of Music and Drama. The City is also the site of the Museum of London, but there's only one public leisure centre in the borough, although there are umpteen private 'health clubs' for those who can afford them. Green spaces are few and small. Like its shops, the City's restaurants cater mainly for the local office population and choice is limited in the evening.

Schools

There are three private schools in the City but only one state school, a primary school.

Shopping

Shops cater mostly for the working population, with the exception of the famous Petticoat Lane market (actually in Middlesex Street on the border with Tower Hamlets).

City of London

Council offices: The Guildhall London, The Corporation of London, PO Box 270, London EC2P 2EJ (☎ 020-7606 3030, 🖥 www.cityoflondon.gov.uk). The City of London is unlike the other 32 boroughs because it's governed by a corporation, which has existed since the Middle Ages, and has its own police force – the City of London Police.

Postcodes: EC2 (part), EC3 and EC4.

Population: Although some 350,000 people work in the City, its resident population is a mere 7,800 – most of them wealthy. The proportion of people under 20 is by far the lowest of any London borough, and the proportion of people between 20 and 35 is among the highest.

Unemployment: Almost zero.

Crime rate: Low, with property theft the most common crime, but the risk of terrorist attack is one of the highest in London (see table in **Appendix F**).

The City & East London

Croydon

The outer London borough of Croydon has more than its fair share of drab areas – particularly the town of Croydon in the centre of the borough – but there are smarter suburbs in the south.

Property

Croydon has a mixture of flats (31 per cent), terraces (34 per cent) and semi-detached or detached houses (35 per cent). Large Victorian properties predominate around Upper Norwood and South Norwood in the north, many converted into flats. Thornton Heath and Norbury in the north-west are mainly flats. Shirley Hills, south-east of Croydon town, is one of the borough's smartest areas, and there are attractive semi-detached and detached houses around Coulsdon, Purley and Selsdon in the south. The best parts of Croydon town are the east and south.

Costs

House prices and rents vary greatly but overall are around the London average (see pages 325 and 326), and council tax rates just above average (see page 329).

Communications

There are no tube stations but excellent rail services from Croydon town, north to central London and south to Gatwick airport. A 'railway' system called Tramlink runs across Croydon from New Addington (on the border with Bromley) in the east to Mitcham and Wimbledon (in Merton) in the west. Most bus routes stop short of the city centre. The A23, which becomes the M23 south of Croydon, runs south into Surrey and Sussex.

Leisure Facilities

There are lots of parks in the borough, including Lloyd Park near Croydon town, South Norwood Country Park and Happy Valley Park near Coulsdon, and the North Downs in the south of the borough. There's a fine house and garden at Norwood Grove near Upper Norwood, which offers splendid views. The borough has a reasonable selection of

cinemas, libraries, museums and leisure centres, and Croydon town boasts the new Clocktower arts centre and Fairfield Halls – one of the major concert halls outside central London.

Croydon boasts more golf courses than any other London borough.

There are some interesting restaurants in Crystal Palace and Upper Norwood, but Croydon town isn't a particularly exciting place for eating out.

Schools

Croydon has a variety of secondary schools, including state, private, voluntary-aided and foundation schools, and the country's only school of performing arts. Standards vary widely.

Shopping

A great deal of money has being spent on Croydon town's shopping centres, which are among the best outside central London. Otherwise, shopping in the borough is rather uninspiring.

Croydon

Council offices: Taberner House, Park Lane, Croydon CR9 3JS (☎ 020-8726 6000, 🖳 www.croydon.gov.uk).

Postcodes: SE19, SE25, SW16 (part), CR0, CR2, CR3 (part), CR5, CR7 and CR8.

Population: 337,000 – London's most populated borough. Almost 30 per cent of Croydon's population are members of ethnic minorities, mostly Asian and Afro-Caribbean.

Unemployment: Around 6.3 per cent.

Crime rate: Croydon has slightly higher crime rates than its outer London neighbours, but they're below the London average (see table in **Appendix F**). Croydon town centre is a particular trouble spot.

Ealing

Ealing boasts interesting buildings, good shops, plenty of open space and efficient public transport, and the borough is being promoted as a tourist and business destination. Ealing town in the centre is much sought-after, but Bedford Park in the south-east corner is the most expensive area. Acton in the east is less smart but up-and-coming.

Property

Some 42 per cent of properties in Ealing are flats, 35 per cent are terraces, 19 per cent are semi-detached houses and just 4 per cent are detached houses. Property in Ealing town is largely Victorian, as it is in Acton, where there are some attractive converted flats. West Acton has mock Tudor houses and flats, and North Ealing is mainly Edwardian. Near the A40 (Great West Road), Southall in the west and Greenford and Northolt in the north comprise rather uninteresting '30s semis. West Ealing and Hanwell are among the borough's cheapest areas.

Costs

House prices and rents are around or slightly above the London average (see pages 325 and 326), as are council taxes (see page 329).

Communications

One of Ealing's main attractions is its excellent train and tube links. The Central Line runs east/west across the middle of the borough and the Piccadilly Line runs north/south. Acton and Ealing are on an Overground route into London Paddington, and Acton is also linked by rail to Richmond and the City Airport in Docklands. The A40 runs across the north of the borough, linking it to central London and Birmingham, but, like all London's arterial roads, it's often badly clogged. The A406 North Circular Road, which cuts through Ealing from north to south, is notoriously busy at Hanger Lane (which is a bottleneck).

Leisure Facilities

There are plenty of theatres, cinemas and leisure centres in the borough, but poor library provision. There's also lots of open space, particularly in the north, where there are fine views from Horsenden Hill, and a surprising number of golf courses. Attractive walks can be had along the River Brent and the Grand Union Canal in the south-west of the borough. Shops are good in Ealing, but dull in Acton. Southall has many excellent Indian restaurants and there's a wide range of restaurants in Acton and Ealing.

Schools

There's a variety of secondary schools, both state and private, including the Greek School of London and the Japanese School. St Augustine's is one of the country's best-performing private schools.

Shopping

There's a large choice of shops in Ealing, including the usual high street names. Most of the rest of the borough has uninspiring shopping, with the exception of Southall, which has a wealth of Indian shops selling everything from spices to saris, and excellent indoor and outdoor markets.

Ealing

Council offices: Perceval House, 14/16 Uxbridge Road, Ealing W5 2HL (☎ 020-8825 5000, 🖥 ealing.gov.uk).

Postcodes: W3, W5, W7, W13, UB1, UB2, UB5 and UB6.

Population: 306,500, mostly middle class. Around 40 per cent of residents belong to ethnic minorities and the borough has London's largest Indian population (centred in Southall, where there's also a significant Afro-Caribbean community).

Unemployment: Around 5.8 per cent.

Crime rate: Ealing's crime rates are around average for London, but burglary numbers are above average (see table in **Appendix F**).

Enfield

Enfield is London's most northerly borough and a mixture of salubrious suburbs in the west and grim council estates in the east, although the industrial areas around Edmonton and Ponders End are being regenerated. The smart parts are Palmers Green, Oakwood, the rather twee village of Winchmore Hill, and Hadley Wood – the most expensive part of Enfield, where the odd celebrity may be spotted. In the centre is Enfield town itself, which is more of a county town than a London suburb.

Property

There's everything from grand detached houses in the north-west to grim tower blocks in the east. But even Edmonton and Ponders End have some attractive Victorian terraces

and '30s semis. Terraces make up 42 per cent of properties in Enfield, flats (which are mostly purpose-built) 32 per cent, semi-detached houses 20 per cent and detached houses the remaining 6 per cent.

Costs

House prices and rents are around the London average, similar to those of neighbouring Brent (see pages 325 and 326), but council taxes are higher than in Brent – just above the London average (see page 329).

Communications

Only the west of the borough is served by the tube: the Piccadilly Line stops at Southgate and Oakwood. There are Overground rail services to Moorgate and Liverpool Street stations from most parts of the borough, but few buses make the slow journey to central London. The main A10 bisects Enfield north/south and the A406 North Circular Road cuts east/west across its southern end.

Leisure Facilities

Enfield has a reasonable selection of theatres, cinemas and leisure centres as well as several parks: Trent Park Country Park in the west, Whitewebbs Park and Forty Hall Country Park in the north, and Lee Valley Park (as well as the River Lee and a chain of reservoirs) in the east. Towards the Hertfordshire border is the vast open space of Enfield Chase. Enfield has a rather unexciting choice of restaurants.

Schools

The borough has a selection of good private and selective state secondary schools.

Shopping

Enfield town has good shops and there are a number of antiques shops in Winchmore Hill. Southgate's shopping is uninspiring, however, and Edmonton Green has some of the worst shopping facilities in London.

Enfield

Council offices: Civic Centre, Silver Street, Enfield EN1 3XY (☎ 020-8379 1000, 🖥 www.enfield.gov.uk).
   Postcodes: N9, N13, N14 (part), N21, EN1, EN2 (part), EN3, EN4 (part) and EN7 (part).
   Population: 285,500. Enfield's population is mainly white (24 per cent belong to ethnic minorities), with a significant Indian and Afro-Caribbean community in Enfield town.
   Unemployment: Around 5.9 per cent.
   Crime rate: The borough's crime rates are just below the London averages (see table in **Appendix F**).

Greenwich

Greenwich is a curious mixture of the historic and the futuristic, the grand and the derelict. Despite Greenwich town being one of London's principal tourist attractions, with its Observatory, National Maritime Museum, Royal Naval College and park (collectively declared a World Heritage Site in 1997 – see 🖥 www.greenwichwhs.org.uk), the borough as a whole is among the most deprived areas in England.

The government is addressing the problem through a number of regeneration projects, including those at the Royal Arsenal in Woolwich, Kidbrooke, Thamesmead and Greenwich Peninsula.

Greenwich Peninsula is the site of the ill-fated Millennium Dome, now rebranded as the 'O2 Arena', which offers a concert hall, 11-screen cinema, exhibition and theatre spaces, bars and restaurants. It will host the Artistic Gymnastics World Championships in 2009 and will be an Olympic venue in 2012, hosting gymnastics and basketball. The Peninsula development will provide 10,000 new homes – almost 40 per cent of them 'affordable' – and create an estimated 24,000 jobs.

Property

Property ranges from grand Victorian and Georgian houses in Blackheath and West Greenwich to small Victorian terraces in East Greenwich, Shooters Hill and Plumstead, to grim '60s tower blocks in Thamesmead. Some of the cheapest properties in London are on the council estates of Abbey Wood in the south. Some 42 per cent of properties in Greenwich are flats (the great majority purpose built), 39 per cent are terraced houses, 16 per cent are semi-detached and just 3 per cent are detached houses. Most detached properties are to be found in Kidbrooke (centre) and Charlton (north), the latter enjoying good views across the River Thames to Docklands.

There's a considerable amount of new development in Greenwich, including up to 1,500 homes in the Millennium Village on Greenwich's so-called peninsula (its north-west corner, which protrudes into a bend in the River Thames) near the Dome. The development commenced in 2000 (around 1,000 homes had been built by 2008) and is expected to be completed in 2015.

Greenwich Peninsula extends to 300acres (121ha) with 1.6m (2.6km) of river frontage, equivalent to the distance from Waterloo to London Bridge. Around £200 million will be invested to make

Greenwich, Royal Observatory

it into a real community with schools, health and childcare facilities, and create almost 50acres (20ha) of green space and parkland. The project is expected to create some 30,000 jobs (including 5,000 during the construction phase) and will eventually include 10,000 homes (including 3,800 for key workers and those on a range of incomes), 3.5m ft² (325,000m²) of office space and over 350,000ft²/32,500m² of retail space plus 150 shops and restaurants.

There are also plans for 2,500 more homes along Gallions Reach to add to the recently built 'starter' homes at Thamesmead North. The northern part of Greenwich will be affected by the Thames Gateway housing scheme (see page 115). Several interesting buildings in and around Woolwich are also being renovated and converted into housing.

Costs

Property prices and rents in Greenwich are below the London average (see pages 325 and 326), as are council taxes (see page 329). The cheapest accommodation is in the east of the borough, in Plumstead, Thamesmead and Woolwich.

Communications

The Docklands Light Railway (DLR) has been extended to Greenwich, with two stops in the borough – Cutty Sark and Greenwich town – and a further extension, from City Airport to Woolwich, is under construction. The Jubilee Line serves North Greenwich, which is a 15-minute journey from the City. Overground train services are better in some areas than others; Thamesmead, for example, is more than two miles from a station. Bus services are little better, although there are routes across the river to the city centre and river taxi services have recently been revived.

The A2, the main road from northern Kent, runs through the borough to central London and is bisected by the A204 'South Circular Road', which connects with the North Circular north of the river via the free Woolwich ferry (see). A new bridge from Thamesmead to Beckton has been approved, although it will take many years to build. Parking is virtually impossible around tourist-thronged Greenwich town, particularly at weekends.

Leisure Facilities

As well as the attractions of Greenwich town (see above), the borough has many parks, woods and open spaces: Oxleas Woods in the east, Greenwich Park and Blackheath in the west, and Avery Hill near Eltham in the south-west (Eltham also boasts the splendid Eltham Palace). There are numerous leisure centres but few theatres and cinemas, although a 14-screen cinema has recently opened on the Greenwich Peninsula. The Blackheath Concert Halls do their best to rival those in Croydon and central London, and the new Laban Dance Centre in Deptford offers classes and performances. The Royal Arsenal site in Woolwich incorporates the national museum of the Royal Artillery as well as the borough museum. Most of the borough's best restaurants are in Eltham and Greenwich town.

Schools

With the exception of two 'beacon' schools, Greenwich's secondary schools generally perform poorly and truancy levels are high, although standards are improving. Its primary schools, on the other hand, are among the best in the country. There are some good private schools in the borough and six centres offering vocational and academic training for children over 16.

Shopping

There are some interesting shops in Eltham and Greenwich town, and the latter has lively covered and open-air markets. The Greenwich Peninsula development (see above) incorporates a shopping centre, there's a new retail park in Charlton, and the shopping facilities in Woolwich town centre are being revamped.

Greenwich

Council offices: 29–37 Wellington Street, Woolwich, London SE18 6PQ (☎ 020-8854 8888, 🖳 www.greenwich. gov.uk).

Postcodes: SE3, SE7, SE9, SE10, SE18 and SE28 (part).

Population: 223,000. Some 23 per cent belong to ethnic minorities.

Unemployment: Around 8.9 per cent.

Crime rate: Greenwich's crime rates are around average for London (see table in **Appendix F**).

Hackney

Hackney stretches from the City to Haringey and shares with neighbouring Islington inner city problems such as high unemployment and crime rates and poor schools. In response to these, the government is injecting money into Dalston, Haggerston, Hackney Wick and Hackney town.

Property

The borough has a lot of council property, including ugly tower blocks, some of which are due to be demolished. Some of the best property is by the Regent's Canal in the south, bordering Victoria Park (which is in Tower Hamlets) in the east and in De Beauvoir Town in the west. There are some large Victorian houses around Stamford Hill in the north and Clapton in the east. Warehouses and factories are being converted into flats in Shoreditch and Hoxton in the south. Flats account for the vast majority of properties in Hackney (77 per cent), while around 20 per cent are terraced houses. Just 2 per cent of properties are semi-detached and fewer than 0.5 per cent are detached houses, most of them in and around Stoke Newington.

Costs

Hackney has some of the cheaper property in London (see pages 325 and 326), while council taxes are around average (see page 329).

Communications

Incredibly, there's only one tube station in Hackney – Old Street on the Northern Line, on the Islington boundary, but the borough has reasonable rail links into Liverpool Street, except in the south-west corner. There's also an Overground route running east/west through Dalston, Hackney and Homerton. Bus services are good, although most roads are clogged with traffic.

Leisure Facilities

The inhabitants of Hackney have access to the lovely Victoria Park in Tower Hamlets and to the Regent's Canal. Clissold Park, near Stoke Newington, boasts deer, while Hackney Marsh consists mostly of football pitches. Other entertainment facilities in Hackney include live circus, art cinemas and the famous Hackney Empire theatre. There are also plenty of art galleries, and many resident artists open their studios to the public. Hackney has four leisure centres and other sports facilities,

and the Stoke Newington West Reservoir is a watersports centre. Stoke Newington is the best place to eat out in the borough, and there are plenty of restaurants in Shoreditch and a number of Turkish restaurants elsewhere.

Schools

Hackney has 16 secondary schools, including six private schools, several of which are run by the local Jewish community.

Shopping

Shopping facilities are adequate, the most interesting shops being near Victoria Park (arts and crafts), Stamford Hill (Jewish) and Stoke Newington (ethnic).

Hackney

Council offices: Town Hall, Mare Street, London E8 1EA (☎ 020-8356 3000, 🖥 www.hackney.gov.uk).

Postcodes: E5, E8, E9, EC2 (part), N1 and N16.

Population: 208,500, with a high proportion of people under 20. Hackney is one of the country's most deprived areas, although it's trying to revive itself and attract artists and small businesses as well as middle-class homebuyers. Almost half of the population lives in council houses, but some parts – particularly adjacent to Islington – have recently become quite trendy, particularly Stoke Newington. Around 40 per cent of the borough's residents are non-white. There's a substantial Turkish population in Hackney and a large Orthodox Jewish community around Stamford Hill and Clapton.

Unemployment: Around 9.9 per cent.

Crime rate: Hackney has some of London's higher crime rates (see table in **Appendix F**).

Hammersmith & Fulham

Hammersmith & Fulham began to become fashionable in the '80s and is now

solidly respectable. The smarter areas – Hammersmith, Fulham, Parsons Green, Hurlingham, Sands End and the exclusive Chelsea Harbour – are in the south near the river and in the east along the border with Kensington & Chelsea. The further north you go, through Shepherds Bush towards White City and Wormwood Scrubs, the scruffier the borough becomes – as a result, these three areas are the centre of a multi-million pound government regeneration scheme.

Property

Hammersmith & Fulham has a similar property mix to Hackney, with just 3 per cent detached and semi-detached houses, 24 per cent terraces and 72 per cent flats, though almost half of these are conversions (compared with just a fifth in Hackney). West Kensington and Barons Court in the centre of the borough have mostly flats, as do Sands End in the south-east, although there the buildings are modern. Nearby Chelsea Harbour is an '80s development of exclusive flats, shops, restaurants and a five-star hotel surrounding a small marina with access to the River Thames. In the south-west around Fulham and Parsons Green the properties are mostly Victorian terraces – those along the river at Hurlingham having distinctive terracotta facings. All this is in stark contrast to the unsightly council estate at White City in the north of the borough.

Costs

There's a huge range of property prices and rents across the borough, but the averages are above the London average (see pages 325 and 326), while council taxes are below it (see page 329).

Communications

The Central, District, Hammersmith & City/Metropolitan and Piccadilly tube lines run through the borough, but Overground services are limited to two lines running along the boundary with Kensington & Chelsea, stopping at West Brompton. Bus services are generally good, but there's invariably heavy traffic on and around the A4, which cuts across the centre of the borough.

Hammersmith & Fulham is home to three major football clubs (Chelsea, Fulham and Queen's Park Rangers) as well as the Olympia Exhibition and Conference Centre, all of which can cause severe transport congestion.

Leisure Facilities

The borough boasts several well known theatres (notably the Apollo Hammersmith, Lyric and Riverside Studios), but only one mainstream cinema. There aren't many museums either, although the 'museum borough', Kensington & Chelsea, is next-door. There are few open spaces and the largest, Wormwood Scrubs (adjacent to the eponymous prison), is uninteresting. By way of compensation, there are attractive walks along the River Thames and three leisure centres.

Fulham, Parsons Green, Hammersmith and Shepherds Bush all have a reasonable selection of restaurants, pubs and wine bars.

Schools

Hammersmith & Fulham's 14 secondary schools include three private schools, a theatre school and a school (Twynholm) offering a curriculum leading to the National Christian Education Certificate. Standards vary considerably, although the Local Education Authority has been highly praised for its efforts to improve them.

Shopping

The smartest shops are along the New Kings Road in Fulham and at Chelsea Harbour. Hammersmith and Shepherds Bush have extensive but not very user-friendly shopping centres. There are markets in the North End Road east of Hammersmith and in Goldhawk Road in Shepherds Bush.

Hammersmith & Fulham

Council offices: Town Hall, King Street, London W6 9JU (☎ 020-8748 3020, 🖥 www.lbhf.gov.uk).
   Postcodes: NW10 (part), SW6, W6, W12 and W14 (part).
   Population: 172,000, with a low percentage of people under 20. Despite the 'yuppie-land' reputation of parts of the borough (particularly Fulham), Hammersmith & Fulham is one of the more deprived areas of England. 22 per cent of its residents are non-white.
   Unemployment: Around 7.9 per cent.
   Crime rate: Crime rates are around or below the London averages (see table in **Appendix F**).

Haringey

Haringey is generally considered to be part of inner London, lying north of Camden and Islington. It's a borough of extremes: some of London's wealthiest citizens can be found in Highgate in the south-west, while some of its poorest live in Tottenham in the north-east. The government is pouring money into new housing, shops and leisure facilities in Tottenham.

Property

Haringey's property is 52 per cent flats (almost half of which are conversions), 41 per cent terraced, 5 per cent semi-detached and just 2 per cent detached. There are some lovely Georgian residences in Highgate, which is marginally less expensive than Hampstead in neighbouring Camden, and splendid Edwardian properties in Muswell Hill, Alexandra Palace and Crouch End in the west. In the north, Wood Green, Noel Park and their more upmarket neighbour Hornsey offer Victorian terraces, while up-and-coming Finsbury Park in the south-east has plenty of large conversion flats. Property in Tottenham in the north-east consists mostly of drab council estates, but there are also some Victorian and Edwardian terraces. The cheapest properties are around White Hart Lane, where Tottenham Hotspur football club has its ground.

Costs

House prices in Haringey are near the average for London (see pages 325 and 326), but council taxes are quite high (see page 329).

Communications

The Victoria and Piccadilly tube lines run through the borough, but some parts (e.g. Muswell Hill) are a long walk from a station. Two Overground rail routes run north/south through the borough – one centrally, the other down the eastern side – and one runs east/west across the southern part of the borough. There are good bus services to central London. The A1 cuts across the south-west corner of

Haringey and the A10 forces its way up through the east end. There's only one controlled parking area, in Wood Green.

Leisure Facilities

Haringey is reasonably well provided with theatres, cinemas, museums and sports facilities, and boasts the recently rebuilt Alexandra Palace exhibition centre in Alexandra Park, which provides fabulous views over London. Haringey's many other open spaces include Finsbury Park in the south, Highgate Woods in the south-west and the River Lea on the border with Waltham Forest. There's a reasonable choice of restaurants, particularly Turkish and Greek, around Finsbury Park, Hornsey and Wood Green.

Schools

Haringey's secondary schools, two of which are private, have varying standards.

Shopping

There's a large mall at Wood Green and reasonable shopping in Highgate, Hornsey and Finsbury Park, but the best shops are in Muswell Hill and Crouch End. A new retail centre is planned for Tottenham, where there are several interesting Afro-Caribbean shops.

Haringey

Council offices: Civic Centre, High Road, Wood Green, London N22 8LE (☎ 020-8489 0000, 🖳 www.haringey. gov.uk).

Postcodes: E5, E8, E9, N4, N6 (part), N8, N10 and N16.

Population: 226,000. Around 35 per cent of the borough's inhabitants belong to ethnic minorities, with significant Afro-Caribbean, Asian, Greek and Turkish communities.

Unemployment: Around 7.2 per cent.

Crime rate: Haringey's crime rates are generally just above the London average (see table in **Appendix F**). Finsbury Park station has long been a trouble spot, although improved CCTV monitoring is helping.

Harrow

Many people in Harrow consider that they live in the county of Middlesex, even though Middlesex ceased to exist in 1965 and isn't marked on any current map. Harrow is famous for its public school, which is in Harrow-on-the-Hill, the smartest part of the borough. Much of the rest is dull '20s and '30s suburbia, which stretches from South Harrow in the south through Harrow town and Wealdstone to Harrow Weald in the north. Further out, around Stanmore in the north-east and Pinner in the north-west, are more open areas.

Property

Harrow boasts one of the highest levels of owner-occupied property in the UK.

Harrow-on-the-Hill in the south-east of the borough has mostly Victorian and Edwardian properties, many converted into flats. There are some attractive modern flats among the '30s semis in and around Harrow town just to the north, and bargain buys in South Harrow (south-west) and Wealdstone (centre). In the north-west, Pinner and Hatch End offer semi-detached and detached '30s Tudor-style houses, as well as modern townhouses. Stanmore in the north-east boasts some of the borough's grandest properties as well as modest semis and detached houses. Harrow has a high proportion of semi-detached houses (39 per cent), 27 per cent flats, 23 per cent terraced houses and 11 per cent detached.

Costs

Harrow has lower than average house prices and rents for London (see pages 325 and 326), but higher than average council tax rates (see page 329).

Communications

The Bakerloo, Jubilee and Metropolitan tube lines run through the western and eastern parts of the borough. In the centre, Harrow and Wealdstone are linked to London Euston by Overground trains, as well as being on the trans-Thames route to Clapham Junction and places south, while Harrow-on-the-Hill is linked to London Marylebone. Local bus services are good but don't go into central London. There are no major roads through Harrow, but plenty of traffic, and there's controlled parking in most areas.

Leisure Facilities

Harrow has an underwhelming selection of theatres, cinemas, museums and galleries, just one leisure centre – although it's the largest in north London – and few golf courses. There's plenty of open space, however, with more than 50 parks, including Bentley Priory Nature Reserve and woodland at Stanmore and Harrow Weald on the edge of Hertfordshire, as well as one of London's few working farms, at Pinner. There are fine views from Harrow-on-the-Hill and a reasonable selection of

restaurants in Harrow town, Harrow-on-the-Hill and Pinner.

Schools

Harrow has an unusual state school structure, with secondary schooling starting at the age of 12 instead of 11, and pupils moving to one of two tertiary colleges (there's also a Roman Catholic sixth-form college) at the age of 16. The famous Harrow School caters only for boys (boys whose parents are **very** wealthy).

Shopping

The new shopping centre in Harrow town is claimed to be one of London's 'top ten'. Otherwise, Harrow-on-the-Hill and Pinner have attractive shops, but Wealdstone and Stanmore are a disappointment.

Harrow

Council offices: Civic Centre, PO Box 57, Station Road, Harrow HA1 2XF (☎ 020-8863 5611, 🖳 www.harrow. gov.uk).

Postcodes: HA1, HA2, HA3, HA5 (part), HA7 and HA8 (part).

Population: 215,000. Harrow's population is 42 per cent ethnic, with a large Indian community and a Jewish community centred on Stanmore. The majority of the borough's inhabitants are white-collar workers who commute into the city centre.

Unemployment: Around 9 per cent.

Crime rate: Harrow has some of the capital's lowest crime rates (see table in **Appendix F**).

Havering

London's easternmost borough and the only one with a border outside the M25 orbital motorway, Havering offers more space between its houses than any other borough. Havering Atte Bower in the far north is more or less in the country, and there are marshes in the south around industrial Rainham by the River Thames. The main towns are in the

centre and west: Hornchurch and Upminster, which grew up around the District tube line, and Romford (on the border with Barking & Dagenham), which is Havering's commercial and administrative centre.

Property

Havering has the lowest percentage of flats of any borough (just 18 per cent – almost all purpose built), 32 per cent terraces, 40 per cent semi-detached houses and 10 per cent detached. There's a mixture of Victorian and '30s terraces, and converted and modern flats in Romford. Gidea Park to the east is one of London's garden suburbs, dating from the early 20th century, and boasts some elegant Edwardian houses.

The '50s council estate at Harold Hill in the north-east is now more than half privately owned and there are bargains to be found there.

Hornchurch and Upminster offer attractive properties in a variety of styles. The southern part of Havering will be affected by the Thames Gateway housing scheme (see page 115).

Costs

Havering's property prices are among the lowest in London (see pages 325 and 326) but council tax rates are quite high (see page 329).

Communications

Elm Park, Hornchurch and Upminster are on the District tube line. Upminster is also served by Overground trains into Liverpool Street (as are Romford, Gidea Park and Harold Wood in the north) and Fenchurch Street (as is Rainham in the south). Elsewhere, cars are the order of the day, as few bus services reach the city centre. The A12 cuts through the northern part of the borough, the A13 through the southern part, and the M25 makes a brief appearance in the east.

Leisure Facilities

There are two cinemas and two leisure centres in the borough, but just one theatre and no public museums or galleries. There's compensation for this by way of the amount of open space, including several parks and golf courses, and the attractive River Ingrebourne virtually bisects the borough from north to south. Havering is something of a culinary desert.

Schools

Havering has 22 secondary schools, none of which are private, and standards are mixed. Since 1995, all pupils over 16 have been educated in two sixth-form colleges.

Shopping

There isn't much in the way of shops except in Romford, which wouldn't itself claim to have the most exciting range.

Havering

Council offices: Town Hall, Main Road, Romford RM1 3BB (☎ 01708-434343, 🖥 www.havering.gov.uk).

Postcodes: CM14 (part), RM1, RM2, RM3, RM4 (part), RM5, RM7, RM9 (part), RM11, RM12, RM13, RM14 and RM15 (part).

Population: 227,500, with the lowest proportion of people between 20 and 35 among the 33 London boroughs and the highest proportion of people over 50. Havering has one of the lowest percentages of ethnic minorities of any London borough, 5 per cent.

Unemployment: Around 4.6 per cent.

Crime rate: Havering has below-average crime rates for London (see table in **Appendix F**).

Hillingdon

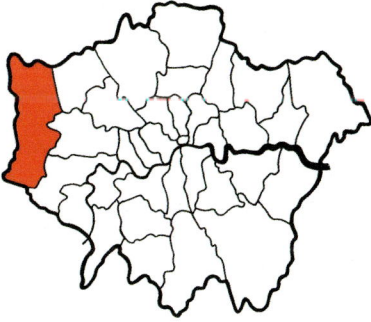

London's second-largest borough, Hillingdon covers the western border of the capital, and is generally more like the Home Counties than London, with swathes of green belt and expanses of suburbia. (Like the inhabitants of Harrow and Hounslow, most Hillingdon residents think they still live in now-defunct Middlesex.) London's first airport, Heathrow (see page 82), is entirely within the borough. Hillingdon also boasts a growing high-tech business centre at Stockley Park (between Uxbridge and Heathrow).

Property

Hillingdon's smartest areas are in the north-east: Eastcote, Ruislip, Northwood and Northwood Hills. This is 'Metroland', so-called because it grew up around the Metropolitan Line 'underground' (although it runs mostly above ground here) and memorably satirised by poet John Betjeman. The borough becomes progressively less salubrious as you move south, through Ickenham village, Uxbridge (the borough's administrative capital) to Hillingdon, Hayes and West Drayton. But government spending is revitalising these areas, particularly Uxbridge, where a massive new shopping and entertainment centre has recently been built (see below). Hillingdon boasts the second-highest proportion of detached houses (14 per cent) in London. Of the rest, 34 per cent are semi-detached, 28 per cent terraced houses and 24 per cent flats (almost all purpose built). Much of the property is in the '30s suburban style – if it can be called a style. Victorian terraces can be found in Uxbridge in the west and Hayes in the south-east.

Costs

Average property prices and rents in Hillingdon are below the London average (see pages 325 and 326), while council taxes are slightly above average (see page 329).

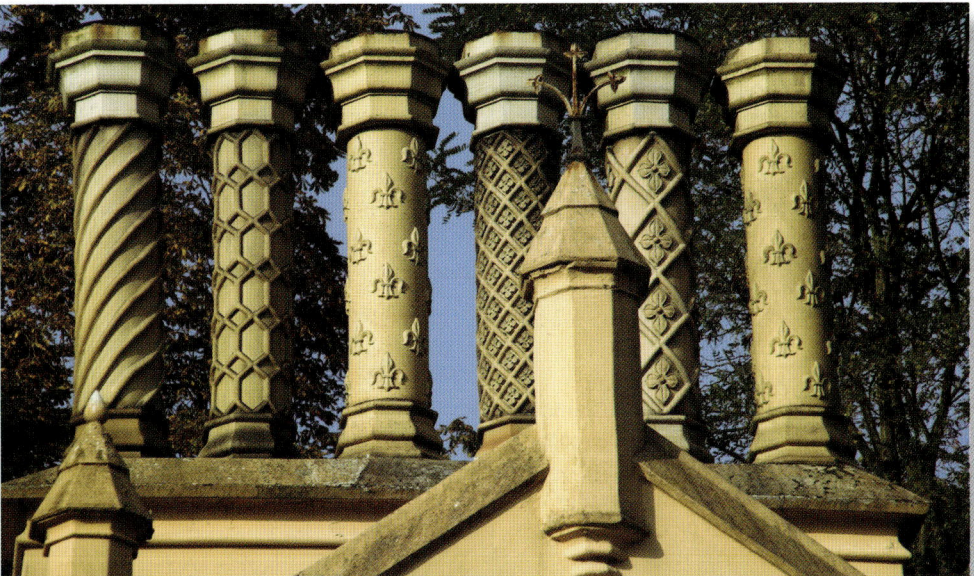

Communications

Hillingdon is well served by underground and Overground trains. The northern half of the borough has three tube lines (Central, Hammersmith & City/Metropolitan and Piccadilly) and an Overground line through Northolt Park and Ruislip. The southern half has two train lines running into London Paddington and another branch of the Piccadilly tube line. Heathrow airport is served by the non-stop Heathrow Express from Paddington (see page 82). Three major roads cut across Hillingdon from east to west – the A4 and M4 in the south and the A40 in the centre – so it's a good place from which to escape the city (although the three roads are often jammed with traffic!).

Leisure Facilities

Hillingdon's new shopping centre houses a nine-screen cinema – the only cinema in the borough – as well as a number of restaurants. Hillingdon has a good supply of leisure centres and other sports facilities (Uxbridge even has a dry ski slope), as well as several theatres, museums and galleries.

The borough is well endowed with open space and borders the Chiltern hills to the west and Ruislip Woods, which is claimed to be the largest uninterrupted stretch of woodland in London.

The Grand Union Canal, which runs across the borough between the M4 and A40 through mostly industrial areas, isn't as picturesque as it sounds.

Schools

There are no selective state secondary schools in Hillingdon, where there are 17 comprehensives and two private schools, as well as colleges of languages, performing arts and technology. Standards are mixed.

Shopping

Uxbridge is Hillingdon's main shopping area, including the recently opened Chimes centre. Windsor Road offers the borough's most upmarket shopping facilities, and interesting shops can be found in Ruislip and Northwood. Hillingdon has been voted one of Greater London's ten best shopping areas.

Hillingdon

Council offices: Civic Centre, High Street, Uxbridge UB8 1UW (☎ 01895-250111, 💻 www.hillingdon.gov.uk).

Postcodes: HA4, HA5 (part), HA6 (part), TW6, UB3, UB4, UB7, UB8, UB9 (part), UB10, UB11 and WD3 (part).

Population: 250,000. Hillingdon is very much part of the commuter belt, with a high proportion of white-collar workers and a 20 per cent non-white population.

Unemployment: Around 4.3 per cent.

Crime rate: Crime rates are around average for London (see table in **Appendix F**).

Hounslow

Hounslow stretches all the way from Hammersmith & Fulham to Surrey. Like those of Hillingdon and Harrow, many of Hounslow's inhabitants believe they live in Middlesex. Parts of the borough are unfortunate enough to lie directly under the path of aircraft landing at or (if the wind is from the east, as it occasionally is) taking off from Heathrow airport, and much of the rest of it is affected by constant aircraft noise. Hounslow has some attractive areas, particularly at its eastern end (around Chiswick and Bedford Park), which borders the River Thames and boasts some of London's most picturesque riverside views.

Brentford in the north-east has recently experienced the second-fastest property price

rises of any town in the UK as it undergoes a multi-million pound transformation from sleepy backwater to trendy enclave, complete with luxury riverside flats, hotels, restaurants, shops and offices. Other areas in line for development include Feltham High Street, where work on new flats, shops and leisure facilities began in 2004, and Hounslow High Street, which is to undergo a major facelift.

Property

Hounslow has 33 per cent detached and semi-detached houses, 31 per cent terraces and 36 per cent flats (mostly purpose built). Like neighbouring Hillingdon, Hounslow has more than its fair share of '30s developments, the worst of which are found around Feltham, Hanworth and Heston in the west. In the north, around Osterley Park, are more interesting properties. Chiswick in the east has attractive, expensive Victorian and Edwardian terraces, as well as Victorian semis and detached houses. The centre of Hounslow town also boasts Victorian terraces. Near the river in Isleworth are some interesting properties, a few dating back to the 16th century.

Costs

Hounslow has average property prices (see page 325) and council taxes (see page 329), but rents are on the high side (see page 326).

Communications

Only the north-east of the borough is served by the tube – the Piccadilly and District Lines, while other parts are well served by the South West Trains network. As in many outer London boroughs, there are no regular bus services into central London. Running east/west through much of Hounslow are the A30, the A4 and (often directly above it) the M4.

Leisure Facilities

Hounslow is home to several stately homes, including Chiswick, Gunnersbury, Osterley Park and Syon Houses with their accompanying parks and gardens. Bedfont Lakes Country Park and Cranford Countryside Park by the River Crane, both of which feature wetland, woodland and meadows, have recently won Civic Trust Green Flag awards – indicating the highest possible standards. More open space is provided by Hounslow Heath between Hounslow town and Hanworth. The borough has no shortage of leisure centres, plus two cinemas and two theatres. Upmarket Chiswick is the borough's restaurant capital.

Schools

Hounslow has 16 secondary schools, two of which are private, one voluntary controlled and four voluntary aided. The Local Education Authority has been awarded 'beacon' status, which means that education is a priority of the borough council, and Hounslow's schools were recently ranked fourth in the government's 'value added' tables.

Shopping

Hounslow town is the main shopping centre, with an airy indoor mall, and there are attractive and unusual shops in Chiswick. Brentford's transformation has greatly improved its shopping facilities, and Feltham High Street is in the process of revitalisation (see above).

Hounslow

Council offices: The Civic Centre, Lampton Road, Hounslow TW3 4DN (☎ 020-8583 2000, 🖳 www.hounslow.gov.uk).

Postcodes: W4, TW3, TW4, TW5, TW7, TW8, TW13 and TW14.

Population: 219,000. Hounslow has a significant Indian population, 35 per cent of the borough's residents belong to ethnic minorities and it's primarily a white-collar area.

Unemployment: Around 6.3 per cent.

Crime rate: Hounslow's crime rates are generally below average for London, (see table in **Appendix F**).

Islington

Until 30 years ago, Islington was run down and undesirable. Today it's one of London's trendiest boroughs – and property prices have risen accordingly. There remain very poor areas, although the council is investing to revitalise the worst of them.

Property

Islington has the second-lowest proportion of detached and semi-detached houses in London (less than 1.5 per cent), after the City. Some 16 per cent of properties are terraced houses, the remaining 82 per cent being flats (more than a third of them are conversions). In the extreme south of the borough, on the City border, are converted warehouses, council blocks and Georgian terraces in Clerkenwell and Finsbury (not to be confused with Finsbury Park, a few miles further north in Haringey). Highbury and Islington in the centre are the borough's smartest areas, with attractive Georgian and Victorian terraces, although property becomes less desirable the further east you go. In the north of the borough, Tufnell Park and Upper Holloway offer a mixture of council property, Victorian terraces and grander detached houses.

Costs

Islington has some of London's highest property prices and rents, although the range is wide (see pages 325 and 326), and council taxes are below average (see page 329).

Communications

Islington is poorly served by tubes and trains: the Northern Line (tube) barely touches the south-west corner of the borough and the Piccadilly Line cuts across the north-west corner only. The railway line from the north of England into Moorgate makes just three stops in the borough. Bus services, on the other hand, are good. The A1 cuts the borough in half vertically and traffic is particularly bad around Archway.

At £95 per year, residents' parking permits are around average for central London.

Leisure Facilities

If you like open space, Islington isn't for you, as it has less than any other London borough. Only the Regent's Canal, which runs across the centre of the borough, and Highbury Fields in the north-east offer any escape from concrete, bricks and mortar. On the other hand, Islington is one of the best places in the capital for fringe theatre. It's also the home of Sadlers Wells, famous for opera and ballet, and the theatres and cinemas of London's West End are nearby. There are seven leisure centres in Islington, as well as other sports facilities, and there are plenty of restaurants, particularly in Clerkenwell, Holloway and Islington town, where Upper Street has almost nothing but eateries.

Schools

Islington's secondary schools have traditionally performed worse than those of any other

London borough. However, since the school system was privatised in 2000, there has been considerable improvement. There's only one private school in the borough.

Shopping

Shopping facilities are generally no better than average, although Islington town has some interesting, unusual shops.

Islington

Council offices: 222 Upper Street, London N1 1XR (☎ 020-7527 2000, 🖥 www.islington.gov.uk).

Postcodes: EC1, N1 (part), N5, N7 and N19.

Population: 185,500. Around 25 per cent of Islington's population belongs to an ethnic minority and there's a large Italian community around Clerkenwell. The borough is known for its fashionable population, including left-wing media types.

Unemployment: Around 8.1 per cent.

Crime rate: Overall, Islington has one of the capital's higher crime rates (see table in **Appendix F**).

Kensington & Chelsea

Kensington & Chelsea is the most affluent part not only of London but of the UK. Over two-thirds of the borough is a conservation area and Kensington & Chelsea boasts some of the most attractive buildings in London. Not surprisingly, they're also some of the most expensive to buy. Kensington & Chelsea is crowded, particularly in summer when tourists flock to its museums and galleries. Colville is London's most densely populated area, with 20,000 residents per km². Recent development projects include a major redesign of Exhibition Road, Sloane Square and the area around South Kensington tube station, and further tidying-up of Earls Court (where a drinking ban has been introduced in an effort to combat problems caused by alcoholics).

Property

Some 84 per cent of properties in Kensington & Chelsea are flats, and it's the only borough in London where the number of conversions exceeds the number of purpose-built flats. Of the remaining 16 per cent of property, 14 per cent are terraced houses and just 2 per cent semi-detached or detached. Elegant properties in Chelsea (south), South Kensington (centre) and Knightsbridge (east) contrast with shabby Earls Court (west) and North Kensington (north). In between, Notting Hill has become one of London's trendiest areas and property prices have risen accordingly.

Costs

Not surprisingly, average house prices in Kensington & Chelsea are among the highest in London (see pages 325 and 326).

If you want a large house in Holland Park, you'll need a cool £10m or more; a three-bedroom Chelsea flat is a snip at a million or two!

On the other hand, the borough has some of the lowest council tax rates in London (see page 329).

Communications

The Central, Circle, District and Piccadilly tube lines all run through the borough. Only Chelsea is a long way from a tube stop (though if you can afford to live there you can afford to travel by taxi). Kensington/Olympia is also served by an Overground rail route between Clapham Junction to the south and Willesden Junction to the north, as well as by a trans-Thames line linking the north and south of England. New stations on the West London line are planned. Bus connections to the city centre are good and the A4 and M40 'Westway' run east/west through the borough. Parking, however, can be a problem, even outside your own home.

Leisure Facilities

If Westminster is London's 'theatreland', Kensington & Chelsea is its 'museumland'. The Science Museum, Natural History Museum and Victoria & Albert Museum are all crowded into a small area between Earls Court and Knightsbridge. There are also plenty of cinemas, although fewer theatres and leisure centres. Open space includes Kensington Gardens and Holland Park, as well as numerous 'garden squares', to which access is usually for residents only. If there isn't a restaurant to suit you in Kensington & Chelsea, you're extremely hard to please.

Schools

There are just five state secondary schools in the borough (although more are planned) and 13 private schools, and over 50 per cent of children are educated privately. Several schools (particularly Holland Park) have pupils of a wide variety of nationalities.

Shopping

Kensington & Chelsea is something of a shoppers' paradise, having the Kings Road, Kensington High Street (recently redesigned) and the Portobello Road within its boundaries, plus many interesting shops in Notting Hill and along the Fulham and Old Brompton Roads.

Kensington & Chelsea

Council offices: Town Hall, Hornton Street, London W8 7NX (☎ 020-7361 3000, 🖥 www.rbkc.gov.uk).

Postcodes: SW3, SW5, SW7, W8, W10, W11 and W14 (part).

Population: 178,000 – London's second least populous borough (after Kingston), with a high proportion of people under 20 and between 50 and 65. The population of Kensington & Chelsea is among London's most affluent, although it has its share of deprived areas. Around 21 per cent of people are from ethnic minorities – a lower proportion than in most of inner London – and there's a significant Afro-Caribbean community in North Kensington and Notting Hill, scene of an annual carnival over the August Bank Holiday weekend (if you choose to live there, you'll either have to join in the 'fun' or get out of town).

Unemployment: Around 7 per cent.

Crime rate: Crime rates are around average for London (see table in **Appendix F**), although some figures are distorted by the influx of non-residents to the borough. Kensington & Chelsea was the first London borough to introduce Police Community Support Officers in an effort to improve public safety and reduce crime.

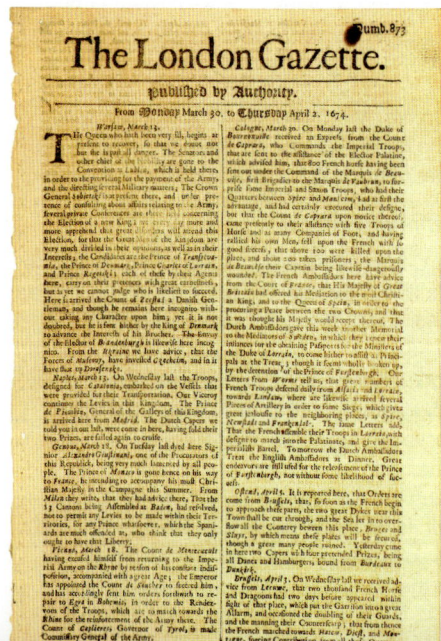

Kingston-upon-Thames

The borough of Kingston-upon-Thames protrudes deep into Surrey along its southern border. Indeed, to most people, Kingston is in Surrey rather than London. Kingston town in the north-west dominates the borough. Once an attractive market town and still boasting the best-preserved medieval street plan in Greater London, Kingston has been

The London Gazette.

of England with London Waterloo. The A3 cuts across the middle of the borough on its way to Portsmouth on the south coast. As in most outer London boroughs, bus routes stop short of the city centre, although there are good services to Hampton, Kew, Richmond and parts of Surrey; services are also good within Kingston itself and there are coach links with both Heathrow and Gatwick airports.

Leisure Facilities

There's a fair amount of open space, particularly in the south, including Canbury Gardens on the river Thames, Fishponds, Queen's Promenade, Trapps Lane and the War Memorial Gardens; larger parks – Richmond, Bushy, Hampton Court and Wimbledon Common – are to be found in neighbouring boroughs. Kingston has just one cinema (a 14-screen Odeon in Kingston town) and one theatre (part of a new complex, also in Kingston town). By way of compensation, there are two ten-pin bowling centres and four leisure centres, as well as numerous sports clubs.

Chessington World of Adventures – Surrey's answer to Disneyland and the most popular theme park in the south of England – Thorpe Park (another theme park), The All England Tennis Club, Twickenham rugby stadium and Sandown Park racecourse are all nearby.

Kingston town boasts several nightclubs and is the best place for eating out, although for the adventurous there are one or two Korean restaurants in New Malden. There are a number of art galleries and annual arts festivals in spring and autumn in Kingston town. Kingston Parish Church is a popular venue for classical music concerts.

Schools

Kingston has some of the best-performing schools in the country and many pupils live outside the borough. There are 14 secondary schools, of which four are private. Kingston College and Kingston University are near the centre of Kingston town.

Shopping

Kingston town is a Mecca for shoppers, with one of the major shopping centres outside central London (the UK's seventh-largest) with its unique Bentalls department store and centre, containing branches of most

developed almost out of recognition – and more developments are planned. New Malden has retained its 'village' atmosphere and Surbiton, once dubbed 'Queen of the suburbs' on account of its rail link with central London, is reasonably attractive.

Property

Kingston has the third highest proportion of detached houses in London (13 per cent). Around 32 per cent of its property is semi-detached, 21 per cent is terraced and 34 per cent is flats. The northern half of the borough is mostly a mass of '30s housing, with some Victorian and Edwardian properties to add a little variety. South of the A3, the housing thins out into fields as London gives way to Surrey. The borough's most attractive properties are found in the north-east around Coombe, where large detached houses predominate. In Kingston town, there are some attractive (and very expensive) riverside properties. The least attractive areas are Tolworth and Chessington in the south.

Costs

Average house prices and rents in Kingston are around the London average (see pages 325 and 326), although there are some very expensive properties by the river (up to £20,000 per month to rent!) and council tax rates are high (see page 329).

Communications

No tube lines reach as far as Kingston, the nearest tube stations being Richmond and Wimbledon (both a 15-minute bus ride from Kingston town). The borough is reasonably well served by the Overground rail network (with ten stations), linking the south and south-west leading chains. There are ten car parks in the town (although at peak times it can still be impossible to find a space) and the council operates a 'Shopmobility' service for the disabled and people with limited mobility. More relaxed shopping 'experiences' are offered by Chessington, Hook, New Malden and Surbiton. Tolworth, whose two shopping centres bestride the busy A3, has recently enjoyed a facelift.

Kingston-upon-Thames

Council offices: Guildhall, High Street, Kingston-upon-Thames, Surrey KT1 1EU (☎ 020-8547 5757, 🖥 www.kingston. gov.uk).

Postcodes: KT1, KT2, KT3, KT5, KT6 and KT9.

Population: 156,000 – London's least populous borough. Kingston is inhabited mostly by middle-class, white-collar workers and just 15 per cent of the population belongs to an ethnic minority. The largest of these is Indian and there's a significant Korean population around New Malden. Kingston town has a large student population.

Unemployment: Around 2.7 per cent.

Crime rate: Crime rates in Kingston are some of the lowest in the capital (see table in **Appendix F**).

Lambeth

Lambeth is in the process of recovering from years of inefficient local government, and an ongoing regeneration programme has been successful in many parts of the borough, although there remain significant areas of poverty and deprivation. Scene of rioting in 1981, Brixton (in the centre of the borough) is becoming one of the newly trendy areas of London, joining neighbouring Clapham to the west. Nearby Stockwell Park and Tulse Hill in the east are doing their best to catch up.

Property

Some 70 per cent of properties in Lambeth are flats (22 per cent are conversions), 22 per

cent are terraces, 6 per cent are semi-detached and 2 per cent are detached houses. The few properties along the River Thames in the north enjoy views of the Houses of Parliament. Most of the properties in Kennington in the north-east (where ex-council flats are found), Stockwell in the north-west, Brixton and Clapham are Victorian. Clapham – Lambeth's most expensive area – also boasts attractive Georgian houses. There are Victorian terraces in West Norwood and Gipsy Hill in the south-east and typical '30s semis around Streatham in the south.

Costs

There are some cheap properties in Lambeth, although there's a huge variation in costs; overall prices and rents are average for London (see pages 325 and 326). Council tax rates are below average (see page 329).

Communications

Only the north and 4west of the borough are served by the underground (Northern and Victoria Lines). Other parts are catered to by various Overground services: Brixton, Denmark Hill, Streatham, Tulse Hill and Norwood by services out of Victoria; and Vauxhall and Clapham from Waterloo (which is in the far north-east of the borough). Clapham is also linked to Willesden Junction north of the River Thames, while Streatham and Tulse Hill are on the trans-Thames line running through Blackfriars to the north.

Clapham Junction station is in the neighbouring borough of Wandsworth.

The Cross River Tram, due for completion in 2011, will link Brixton and Waterloo with Kings Cross, Euston and Camden in north London. Bus services are generally good, but roads are busy, particularly around Clapham (where the A3 'Portsmouth Road' meets the A205 South Circular) and Vauxhall in the north-west.

Leisure Facilities

Lambeth is home to London's largest arts complex, now called the South Bank Centre, comprising three concert halls, three theatres, a gallery, the National Film Theatre and the Museum of the Moving Image. As if that wasn't enough, there are cinemas in Waterloo, Clapham, Brixton and Streatham, the Imperial War Museum, the Old and Young Vic theatres, four leisure centres, four swimming pools, an ice rink and the Oval cricket ground. Brixton has a large number of excellent bars and clubs and, with Clapham, is increasingly a 24-hour entertainment venue. Clapham Common is one of the largest open spaces in London, but elsewhere a few small parks (Kennington Park, Brockwell Park and Streatham Common) are the best Lambeth can offer in the way of greenery, although West Norwood and Gipsy Hill in the south-east enjoy superb views. Clapham is the best place for eating out and the area around Waterloo station and the South Bank is fast improving. Brixton has a selection of Caribbean restaurants, Streatham has a diverse range of eateries and Stockwell is becoming known for its Portuguese cafes and restaurants.

Schools

There are 11 secondary schools in Lambeth, only one of which is private, and standards are generally below the national average, although improving. There are no private primary schools.

Shopping

Shopping in the borough is generally unexciting. The biggest choice of shops, and the most unusual, are in Brixton. Streatham High Road is Europe's longest shopping street and plans for a new shopping centre will transform the area. Clapham has a growing number of specialist shops, mainly catering to its 'yuppiefied' population.

Lambeth

Council offices: Town Hall, Brixton Hill, London SW2 1RW (☎ 020-7926 1000, 🖳 www.lambeth.gov.uk).

Postcodes: SE11, SE24 (part), SE27, SW1 (part), SW2, SW4, SW8 (part), SW9 and SW16 (part).

Population: 272,000. Around 37 per cent of its inhabitants belong to an ethnic minority, with a large Afro-Caribbean population centred on Brixton and a substantial Portuguese community in Stockwell and Vauxhall. Streatham has a growing Somali community.

Unemployment: Around 9.5 per cent.

Crime rate: Lambeth has some of London's highest crime rates (see table in **Appendix F**), although matters have greatly improved in recent years thanks to concerted efforts by the police and local authorities (a successful 'zero tolerance' policy has been implemented in Brixton).

Lewisham

Many parts of Lewisham are somewhat down-at-heel, but it does have some smart areas, notably elegant, expensive Blackheath in the north-east, and the worst areas (Deptford and Lewisham town centre) are being regenerated by government money. Like Lambeth, Lewisham has only a short stretch of River Thames frontage, along its northern boundary.

Property

Just 2 per cent of properties in Lewisham are detached houses, 9 per cent are semi-detached, 37 per cent are terraced and 52 per cent are flats (a third of these are conversions). Deptford, by the river, was once an industrial area and is overshadowed by ugly '60s tower blocks. However, there are also inexpensive ex-council properties and some attractive Victorian houses. Large (and affordable) Victorian properties are also to be found in Brockley, New Cross and Lewisham town to the south, as well as around Forest Hill and Sydenham in the south-west corner of the

borough. In the centre, Catford and Hither Green offer modest Victorian and Edwardian terraces. At Grove Park in the south-east, these have given way to the ubiquitous '30s semis of outer London.

Costs

Average house prices and rents are low in Lewisham, although the range of prices is greater than in many parts of the capital (see pages 325 and 326). Council taxes are around average (see page 329).

Communications

The tube barely touches Lewisham, the East London Line reaching only as far south as New Cross, but the DLR extends to Lewisham town. The rest of the borough is served by Overground trains only: a line running north/south through the extreme west of the borough links Sydenham, Forest Hill and Honor Oak Park to London Bridge and Charing Cross stations. A few buses venture to the city centre, while others link the borough with neighbouring Bromley. Lewisham is criss-crossed by main roads: the A2 and A20, which link central London with Kent, converge in the northern part of Lewisham; the A205 South Circular Road cuts across the southern part of the borough; and the A21 splits it from north to south.

Leisure Facilities

Lewisham has over 40 parks and gardens, although all are small except Blackheath; there are fine views from the hills around Crystal Palace in the south-west corner of the borough. Lewisham has only one cinema and one museum but boasts four leisure centres and several theatres. The widest selection of

restaurants is to be found in Deptford and Blackheath.

Schools

There are 15 secondary schools in the borough, only one of which is private. Standards are generally above average for inner London, but below the national average.

Shopping

As the borough's 'capital', Lewisham town should be the best place for shopping, but the shops in Deptford and Blackheath are more varied and interesting.

Lewisham

Council offices: Lewisham Town Hall, Catford, London SE6 4RU (☎ 020-8314 6000, 🖥 www.lewisham.gov.uk).

Postcodes: SE4, SE6, SE8, SE12 (part), SE13, SE14, SE23, SE26 and BR1 (part).

Population: 256,000. Around 34 per cent of Lewisham's population belongs to an ethnic minority, the largest communities being Afro-Caribbean (around Deptford and Lewisham) and Turkish.

Unemployment: Around 10 per cent.

Crime rate: Lewisham's crime rates are above the London average (see table in **Appendix F**). Drug offences are a particular problem.

Merton

Merton's most sought-after areas (and many of its open spaces) are in the north of the borough, nearest central London. Wimbledon, famous for its annual tennis tournament in late June/early July, and Wimbledon Village are the smartest parts, and Merton Park in the south is attractive.

Property

Merton has 4 per cent detached houses, 13 per cent semi-detached, 48 per cent terraced and 35 per cent flats. Most properties in

Wimbledon and South Wimbledon in the northern part of the borough are Victorian. Raynes Park in the south-west offers Edwardian terraces, while Morden in the south is mostly '30s semis, with inexpensive houses on the St Helier Estate.

Costs

Property prices and rental rates are mixed, high for detached houses but relatively low for other types of property (see pages 325 and 326). Council tax rates are quite high (see page 329).

Communications

Two tube lines reach into Merton: the District Line, which terminates at Wimbledon in the west of the borough, and the Northern Line, ending at Morden in the south. Wimbledon and Raynes Park are on an Overground line into Waterloo, while other parts of Merton are served by Thameslink trains to the City and Hertfordshire.

The new Tramlink service (see page 98) connects Wimbledon, Merton, Morden and Mitcham with various parts of the borough of Croydon.

The A24 is the borough's major road, cutting through Merton on its way to Surrey.

Leisure Facilities

Most of Wimbledon Common is within the borough of Merton, as are Wimbledon Park, Merton Park and Mitcham Common, and there are pleasant walks along the river Wandle. The world-famous All England Lawn Tennis Club, home of the annual Wimbledon tournament, is in Merton. There's a reasonable selection of theatres (including the New Wimbledon Theatre), concert venues, museums and leisure centres, but the 12-screen cinema in Wimbledon is the borough's only cinema. There are plenty of restaurants throughout the borough, the widest choice being in Wimbledon Village, the 'in' place to eat out in Merton.

Schools

Until 2003, Merton had a three-tier state education system, but it has changed to the usual primary/secondary structure. There are five state secondary schools, two voluntary-aided schools and three private schools. Some of them have received excellent government performance reports and Merton also boasts London's best selection of nursery schools, both state and private.

Shopping

Wimbledon has an attractive, upmarket retail centre (appropriately called 'Centre Court') and exclusive boutiques in the Village, but shopping in the rest of Merton is an underwhelming experience.

Andy Murray

Merton

Council offices: Merton Civic Centre, London Road, Morden SM4 5DX, (☎ 020-8274 4901, 💻 www.merton. gov.uk).
    Postcodes: SW19 (part), SW20, CR4 and SM4.
    Population: 198,000. Around 25 per cent of the population belongs to an ethnic minority, most of them Indian or Afro-Caribbean.
    Unemployment: Around 8.5 per cent.
    Crime rate: Merton has some of London's lowest crime rates (see table in **Appendix F**).

Newham

Newham is one of London's fastest-changing boroughs: it was once one of England's most deprived areas but is now the centre of the capital's 2012 Olympics regeneration scheme. Large-scale redevelopment of the Stratford and Royal Docks is under way, incorporating a Channel Tunnel Rail Link station (see page 87) and a major exhibition centre (see **Leisure Facilities** below). Ten new hotels (eight of them in the Royal Docks) have brought the borough's total to 13. Newham is also home to the University of East London Docklands Campus, which opened in 1999 and accommodates some 7,500 students.

Property

Newham has the second-highest proportion of terraced houses in London (57 per cent), with 39 per cent flats, 3 per cent semi-detached and just 1 per cent detached houses. There are some unusual Victorian properties between the docks and the river, while new housing is appearing around Beckton just north of the docks. Otherwise, the borough is architecturally rather dull, with long rows of late-19th and early-20th century terraces. There are some larger Victorian houses in East Ham in the centre of the borough, Stratford in the north-west and around Forest Gate in the north – probably the best part of Newham. Five residential developments have recently been completed in the Royal Docks, over 400 new homes are being built on Royal Quay (to be called Furlong City) and imaginative warehouse conversions are in progress in Stratford. Further developments under consideration include Stratford City, which would incorporate 4,500 homes, shopping, leisure and commercial developments, schools and hotels; and Silvertown Quays, which would comprise 5,000 homes and retail and entertainment facilities, including a National Aquarium.

Costs

Newham has relatively low house prices and rents (see pages 325 and 326). Council tax rates are below the London average (see page 329).

Communications

Newham boasts an international airport – London City Airport, whose runway occupies a strip of land between two huge docks. The north of the borough is served by the Hammersmith & City/Metropolitan and District Lines, the lower part and Stratford by the DLR and the Jubilee Line, and Stratford by the Central Line. A further DLR extension is due to link City Airport and North Woolwich. Two Overground lines run through Newham from east to west: one crossing the top of the borough en route to Liverpool Street station, the other running into Fenchurch Street station but stopping at West Ham only. A third Overground service links London City Airport with Richmond via north London, and the Stratford Channel Tunnel Rail Link station is due to open in 2009 (see page 87). A few bus services connect the borough with central

London. The main road through Newham is the A13, which cuts across from east to west.

Leisure Facilities

Newham has a limited amount of open space: most of its 24 parks are small, although there are attractive walks along the River Lea and Bow Creek in the west, and the 22-acre Thames Barrier Park provides a green oasis by the river. The borough has three cinemas, including the 14-screen Showcase Cinema in Beckton, as well as the Theatre Royal Stratford East and Stratford Circus, a high-tech performing arts centre. Newham also has good sporting facilities, including four leisure centres and watersports in the Royal Docks, and the borough is home to West Ham United football club. A major new conference and exhibition centre, ExCeL, opened in 2000 and is the new home of the prestigious London International Boat Show.

Traditional East End entertainment can be enjoyed at the Old Time Music Hall (formerly St Mark's Church) in Woolwich.

Schools

Newham has the country's highest proportion of children with special needs, but since 2000 the borough has been one of the fastest improving in terms of educational standards. There are 16 state secondary schools and no private schools.

Shopping

Newham isn't renowned for its shopping, although Stratford's shopping centre was refurbished in 2001 and the New Gallions Reach development, completed in 2003, has brought the number of retail parks in the borough to three. Green Street in Upton Park, home to 400 retailers of Asian clothing, jewellery and food, was given a major facelift a couple of years ago, and there are lively street markets in Canning Town, East Ham and Stratford.

Newham

Council offices: Town Hall, Barking Road, East Ham, London E6 2RP, (☎ 020-8430 2000, 🖥 www.newham.gov.uk).

Postcodes: E3 (part), E6, E7, E13, E15 and E16.

Population: 248,500, with the highest proportion of people under 20 and the lowest proportion of people over 65 of all the London boroughs. Newham has a higher proportion (around 62 per cent) of inhabitants from ethnic minorities than almost anywhere in London, with particularly large Afro-Caribbean and Asian populations.

Unemployment: Around 9.5 per cent.

Crime rate: Newham has generally high crime rates (see table in **Appendix F**). 'Safer Neighbourhood' initiatives are being introduced to try to improve the situation.

Redbridge

There's no town of Redbridge – the borough's 'capital' is Ilford in the south (curiously, it has IG postcodes) – and the borough takes its name from the brick bridge linking Ilford with Wanstead and Woodford.

Redbridge is neither deprived nor affluent, although it has several smart areas. The

River Thames

east of the borough tends to be working class and the west middle class, with particularly well-to-do areas around Woodford and Wanstead. Ilford Council is undertaking an ambitious regeneration programme that will create a new town square and high-quality housing and shopping facilities in the town centre.

Property

Property in Redbridge consists of 6 per cent detached houses, 27 per cent semi-detached, 40 per cent terraces and 27 per cent flats (a quarter of them conversions). Properties in the south around Ilford are mainly Victorian and Edwardian terraces, as they are in Goodmayes and Seven Kings to the east. Further north, around Gants Hill and Clayhall, are the usual '30s suburban semis, while the Hainault area in the north-east consists mainly of council estates. The west boasts larger, semi-detached and detached properties.

Costs

Redbridge's property prices and rents are around the average for London (see pages 325 and 326) and its council taxes just above average (see page 329).

Communications

Redbridge is served by the Central tube line, which goes to Epping in Essex. The only Overground service runs across the south of the borough, through Goodmayes, Ilford and Seven Kings, linking them with Liverpool Street station. A few buses go to the city centre. The M11 (Redbridge's main escape route to the country) touches the north-west corner of the borough. The other main roads are the A12, which cuts the borough in half from west to east, and the A406 North Circular in the west

Kew Gardens

and south-west. Most of Redbridge still has permit-free parking.

Leisure Facilities

The borough has three leisure centres, two cinemas, a theatre and a museum (in Ilford). Known as the 'leafy suburb', Redbridge also has plenty of open space (a third of the borough is green belt land), particularly in the north-east, where Hainault Forest offers wildlife and attractive views. Nearby are two golf courses, riding facilities and watersports on Fairlop Water. There's a vast selection of restaurants in Ilford but dining in the rest of the borough is rather limited.

Schools

Redbridge's 20 state secondary schools (including two grammar schools, Ilford County High and Woodford County High, and two private schools) rank in the top ten in England according to the percentage of high-grade GCSE passes achieved by their pupils (over 65 per cent compared with the English average of under 55 per cent).

Shopping

The borough's main shopping centre is Ilford, with smaller centres in Barkingside, Gants Hill, South Woodford, Wanstead and Woodford, and some interesting shops in Woodford Green and Wanstead.

Richmond-upon-Thames

Richmond-upon-Thames is the only borough divided by the River Thames. One of London's greenest areas, it includes Hampton Court Park, Bushy Park, Old Deer Park, Kew Gardens and Richmond Park (the capital's largest, complete with herds of deer). Like neighbouring Hounslow, however, northern parts of Richmond suffer from the continual drone of aircraft landing at Heathrow.

Property

Richmond's mix of properties is close to the outer-London average, with 8 per cent detached houses, 23 per cent semi-detached, 31 per cent terraces and 38 per cent flats. A high proportion of buildings are Victorian, from Castlenau and Barnes in the north-east corner, past East Sheen and Richmond Hill (the borough's most desirable area) and across the river to Hampton Wick and Teddington. There are also many attractive Georgian properties; the inevitable '30s semis don't start until Hampton and Whitton (the cheapest part of Richmond) in the extreme south-west. Kew in the far north offers everything from turn-of-the-20th-century to contemporary property.

Costs

Richmond has high property prices (see pages 325 and 326) and some of London's highest council tax rates (see page 329).

Communications

Richmond town is at the end of the rail route to the East End via north London and the District tube line. There are no bus services to the centre of London, but you can travel to Westminster by boat. The A205 South Circular Road cuts across the north-east of the borough and the A316 (an extension of the M3) runs across the top to join it. Several parts of the borough have controlled parking.

Leisure Facilities

Richmond is richly endowed with parks (see above) and historic houses, most notably Hampton Court Palace on the Surrey border (one of the country's royal palaces, which is open to visitors, except when the Queen is in residence), while Kew Gardens in the north-west incorporates the internationally renowned Royal Botanical Gardens. The borough also has three leisure centres and other sports facilities, including several golf courses, and there are three cinemas and two theatres in Richmond town.

Schools

Richmond's 13 secondary schools, which include two private schools, have generally high standards. There's also a German School and a Swedish School, which teach the curricula of those countries, and Richmond is home to the Royal Ballet School.

Shopping

Richmond has many interesting, small shopping centres and plenty of restaurants (and Kingston is nearby).

Richmond-upon-Thames

Council offices: Civic Centre, 44 York Street, Twickenham TW1 3BZ (☎ 020- 8891 1411, 🖥 www. richmond.gov.uk).
   Postcodes: SW14, KT8, TW1, TW2, TW10, TW11 and TW12.
   Population: 179,500. Just 8 per cent of the population belongs to an ethnic minority in this largely white-collar borough.
   Unemployment: Around 4.2 per cent.
   Crime rate: Richmond has one of the lowest crime rates in London (see table in **Appendix F**).

Southwark

Southwark is a borough of contrasts: in the north-east, the once industrial areas of Bermondsey and Rotherhithe have undergone a transformation over the last decade or so, including the construction of some 3,000 homes; in the west, formerly run-down Camberwell is fast becoming the borough's answer to Brixton or Notting Hill; in the centre, Peckham's grim tower blocks are being pulled down as part of a multi-million pound facelift; and in the south is the smart village of Dulwich. Despite this redevelopment, however, multicultural Camberwell, Peckham and Newington are among the country's most deprived areas, albeit with oases of affluence, and even Dulwich has its pockets of deprivation.

Property

Some 76 per cent of properties in Southwark are flats and a further 19 per cent terraced houses, with just 4 per cent semi-detached and 1 per cent detached houses.

Over half of Southwark's housing is publicly owned (compared with the London average of around 27 per cent). Bermondsey in the north consists mostly of council estates, but former warehouses are gradually being converted into flats (or 'lofts', as they're known).

There are new houses in Rotherhithe in the north-east, while The Borough in the north-west and The Elephant & Castle, Camberwell, Peckham and Nunhead in the centre and Dulwich in the south offer Victorian, Edwardian and Georgian properties – varying enormously in price!

Costs

Like many other inner city boroughs, Southwark has a huge range of property prices and rents (see pages 325 and 326). Council tax rates are below the London average (see page 329).

Communications

Only northern Southwark is served by the tube network, the Bakerloo and Northern Lines extending to the Elephant & Castle and the Oval, and the Jubilee Line with stations at Southwark, London Bridge and Bermondsey. Overground trains run from various parts of the borough into London Bridge, Blackfriars and Charing Cross. Bus services into central London are also good, although invariably slow due to the volume of traffic. The A205 South Circular passes through Dulwich.

Leisure Facilities

Government and National Lottery money has allowed Southwark to regenerate its stretch of River Thames frontage, with the reconstruction of the Globe theatre, the creation of a hugely successful modern art gallery (the Tate Modern) in the old Bankside power station, and a new footbridge across the river to the City. Elsewhere, there are two cinemas, five leisure centres and numerous museums and galleries (including the world's first wine museum, at Vinopolis near Borough Market!). Most of Southwark's open space is in the south, in and around Dulwich, and there are a few parks and gardens in the north. There's a variety of restaurants in Southwark, particularly in Dulwich, East Dulwich and along the river.

Schools

Over a third of Southwark's schoolchildren speak English as a second language. Nevertheless, educational standards are generally reasonable in the borough's 17 secondary schools, of which three are private (including the renowned Dulwich College).

Shopping

Southwark's main shopping centre is the unsightly complex at The Elephant & Castle. Elsewhere, shopping facilities are mostly uninspiring.

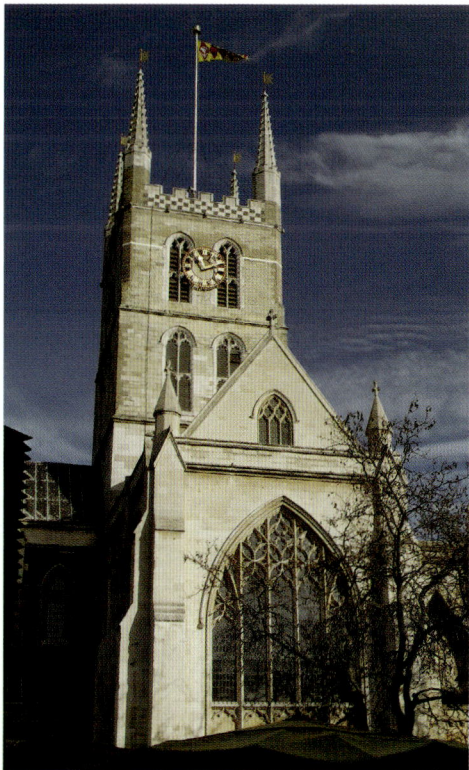
Southwark Cathedral

Southwark

Council offices: Town Hall, Peckham Road, London SE5 8UB (☎ 020-7525 5000, 🖥 www.southwark.gov.uk).

Postcodes: SE1, SE5, SE15, SE16, SE17, SE21, SE22 and SE24 (part).

Population: 270,000. Around 37 per cent of Southwark's population belongs to ethnic minority groups, the largest being Afro-Caribbean, Turkish and Vietnamese. Camberwell, Peckham and Newington have high ethnic minority populations. The borough is home to a lot of people dependent on state support, including asylum seekers.

Unemployment: Around 13.9 per cent, one of the highest rates in London.

Crime rate: Southwark's crime record has improved considerably in recent years, although it's still well above the London average (see table in **Appendix F**). The current focus is on tackling drug abuse and 'hate crime', including racist and homophobic attacks.

Sutton

Sutton calls itself the 'greener, cleaner borough' and is one of London's most affluent boroughs, having more in common with neighbouring Surrey than London 'proper'. The smartest areas are Carshalton Beeches (centre), North Cheam (north-west), South Sutton town (west) and Belmont (south-west). Cheaper parts include St Helier in the north and Beddington in the east.

Property

Sutton has 11 per cent detached houses, 27 per cent semi-detached, 29 per cent terraces and 33 per cent flats (the great majority purpose built). Properties built in the '20s and '30s predominate in the south, although there are some Victorian and Edwardian houses in Sutton town as well as on the large council estate in St Helier to the north, where bargains can be found. Victorian terraces can also be found in Wallington and Beddington in the east and in the 'village' of Carshalton in the

centre. There and in North Cheam are some 16th-century properties, while Beddington and Sutton town offer modern homes.

Costs

Average property prices in Sutton are surprisingly low, around the same as in neighbouring Croydon (see pages 325 and 326). Council tax rates are roughly average for London (see page 329).

Communications

Sutton is beyond the reach of the tube network but has good Overground rail services. Buses will take you to the shopping centres of Kingston or Croydon but not to central London. Main roads include the A24 and A217, both running north/south, and traffic is generally slow.

Leisure Facilities

Sutton's leisure facilities are limited to one cinema, two theatres, two leisure centres and a smattering of historic houses. But there's plenty of open space, including Beddington Park in the east and Cheam Park in the west, the latter adjoining Nonsuch Park just across the Surrey border. Cheam and Carshalton are the best bet for eating out.

Schools

After Kingston, Sutton has the best-performing state secondary schools (there are 14) in London, although the highest performers are selective schools. There are also two private schools.

Shopping

The borough's main shopping centre is Sutton town, although it offers little competition to

nearby Croydon. There are some attractive shops in Cheam and Carshalton.

Sutton

Council offices: Civic Offices, St Nicholas Way, Sutton SM1 1EA (☎ 020-8770 5000, 💻 www.sutton.gov. uk).

Postcodes: CR0 (part), CR4, KT4, SM1, SM2 (part), SM3, SM5 and SM6.

Population: 185,000. Around 11 per cent of Sutton's inhabitants belong to ethnic minorities and most of the population are reasonably well off.

Unemployment: Around 4.1 per cent.

Crime rate: Sutton has some of the lowest crime rates in the capital (see table in **Appendix F**).

Tower Hamlets

Taking its name from the historical association between the Tower of London and the riverside hamlets that once surrounded it, Tower Hamlets claims to be 'the fastest-changing place in the UK'. Financial and media businesses are moving there from the City, the Jubilee Line extension is set to link the East End to the West End, and the Spitalfields area (traditionally the centre of London's wholesale clothing industry) is fast establishing itself as an artistic quarter. At the centre of this transformation is Docklands, previously an area of disused docks and

derelict warehouses and now a thriving business centre.

Property

Tower Hamlets has the smallest proportion of detached and semi-detached houses outside the City of London (1 per cent). Some 14 per cent of properties are terraces and the remaining 85 per cent are flats (almost all of them purpose built), many council owned, with bargains around, particularly in Spitalfields and Whitechapel in the west and in Bethnal Green in the north-west.

Stepney in the centre of the borough is almost entirely council property, and there are some particularly unsightly council blocks in Bromley (not to be confused with Bromley town in the borough of Bromley) and Poplar in the east. In the north-east, Bow offers attractive Victorian and Georgian houses and the Spitalfields/Whitechapel area is spawning 'loft' conversions, which are already common in Wapping and Limehouse in the south-west. There and on the Isle of Dogs (not an island at all, merely a bend in the river) construction is ongoing.

Costs

Tower Hamlets has surprisingly high property prices and rents (see pages 325 and 326), but council tax rates are among the lowest in London (see page 329).

Communications

Tower Hamlets has some of the best rail connections of any London borough. No fewer than six tube lines (Central, District, East London, Hammersmith & City/Metropolitan, Jubilee and the DLR) run in various directions through the borough. The Overground line from Fenchurch Street station to parts of Essex also crosses the borough, and the service from Liverpool Street station to Cambridge cuts across its north-west corner. Bus services are better in the north than the south, and Tower Hamlets is an expensive area for car owners: there's no free parking, even outside residential property.

Leisure Facilities

Good sports facilities (including five leisure centres) compensate for the borough's lack

Tower of London

of theatres (one) and cinemas (none). The London Arena on the Isle of Dogs hosts pop concerts and exhibitions, and the capital's top tourist attraction, the Tower of London, is just within the borough's boundary (in the extreme west). Apart from Victoria Park in the north-east, Tower Hamlets has little green space to offer. What it does have in abundance is water – not only the River Thames, but the River Lea, the Regent's and Hertford Union Canals, and the old docks. Tower Hamlets isn't noted for its restaurants, although there are some good ethnic eateries.

Schools

Tower Hamlets' previously poor education standards are rising. Only one of its 16 secondary schools is private. It has more state nurseries for the under-fives than any other borough.

Shopping

Tower Hamlets' shopping facilities are rather patchy, but it has some colourful markets, including Brick Lane (Shoreditch), Roman Road (Bow) and the famous Petticoat Lane (which is actually in Middlesex Street on the border with the City).

Tower Hamlets

Council offices: Mulberry Place, 5 Clove Crescent, London E14 2BG (☎ 020-7364 5000, 🖥 www.towerhamlets.gov.uk).

Postcodes: E1, E2, E3 (part) and E14.

Population: 213,000. Tower Hamlets has the UK's largest Bangladeshi community – around 33 per cent of its inhabitants – as well as a lot of Vietnamese and Somali newcomers (the borough is 50 per cent non-white).

Unemployment: Around 12.5 per cent, one of London's highest rates.

Crime rate: High, although the burglary rate is quite low (see table in **Appendix F**).

Waltham Forest

Waltham Forest is one of London's 'in-between' boroughs – neither affluent nor impoverished, neither fashionable nor dull. One of its major attractions is the woodland and parkland of historic Epping Forest. The borough's administrative and geographical centre is Walthamstow, which is undergoing a massive regeneration project promising to bring state-of-the-art shopping and leisure facilities, including a library, to the town centre, along with modern transport links. In the south of the borough are the former working-class areas of Leyton and Leytonstone, and in the north the smart suburb of Highams Park. Standard outer London suburban blandness takes

over in the far north around Chingford near the Essex border.

Property

Around 48 per cent of properties are terraced houses, 11 per cent are semi-detached and 2 per cent are detached. The remaining 39 per cent are flats. Leyton and Leytonstone in the south offer mainly Victorian terraces, as does Walthamstow, where conversion flats are plentiful. In the north are Chingford's '30s semis and some attractive Victorian and Edwardian properties. There's a similar mix in Highams Park, the borough's most sought-after area.

Costs

Waltham Forest offers some of London's cheapest property (see pages 325 and 326), but its council tax rates are high (see page 329).

Communications

Waltham Forest's tube services are limited. The Central Line serves only Leyton and Leytonstone, and the Victoria Line terminates at Walthamstow. The Barking to Richmond Overground line passes through Leyton and Walthamstow, while northern parts of the borough are served by a line from Liverpool Street terminating at Chingford. The M11 link road provides quick access to Hackney and the borough's other major roads include the A406 North Circular, which cuts across the centre, and the A11/A12 in the south-east corner. There are residents' parking permit systems in Walthamstow and Chingford.

Leisure Facilities

There's just one cinema in the borough, but live entertainment is available at Chingford's and Walthamstow's Assembly Halls, and there are five leisure centres. Walthamstow is home to London's premier greyhound racing venue and the Village has some good pubs and restaurants. Nearby Lloyd Park is the site of the William Morris Gallery, but is otherwise uninspiring. There are a number of attractive parks, the most impressive open space being what's left of Epping Forest in the east. The west of the borough has a chain of reservoirs. Highams Park has an attractive lake surrounded by woodland, and the Whipps Cross boating lake and park are popular. Outside Walthamstow Village the borough's choice of restaurants is uninspiring.

Schools

Standards are improving in Waltham Forest's 19 secondary schools, two of which are private, although they're still below the national average.

Shopping

Walthamstow is the borough's shopping centre, with a shopping 'mall' and a daily High Street market (selling clothing, household goods and food) that claims to be the longest in Europe.

Waltham Forest

Council offices: Town Hall, Forest Road, Walthamstow E17 4JF (☎ 020-8496 3000, 🖥 www.walthamforest.gov.uk).

Postcodes: E4, E10, E11 (part) and E17.

Population: 222,000. Unusually for an outer-London borough, Waltham Forest has a high proportion (over 35 per cent) of residents from ethnic minorities, particularly Afro-Caribbean and Pakistani.

Unemployment: Around 8.6 per cent.

Crime rate: Crime rates in Waltham Forest are around the London average (see table in **Appendix F**).

Wandsworth

Wandsworth is one of London's most 'upwardly mobile' boroughs. Once working class, Battersea – where the council has spent millions on regeneration and the developers have moved in – has recently become a trendy place to live.

The borough council is one of the dozen best-performing in the country, according to the Audit Commission, and has won more

awards for the quality of its services than any other UK local authority.

Property

Typically for an inner London borough, Wandsworth has a mere 2 per cent detached houses, 5 per cent semi-detached, 30 per cent terraced and 63 per cent flats (almost a third of which are conversions). Most of the detached houses are in Putney in the south-west, Southfields in the centre and Wandsworth Common in the north-east, while most of the semis are in Tooting in the south-east, where much of the property is Edwardian (as it is in Putney and Earlsfield in the south).

Costs

Average house prices and rents are high, with some very expensive properties in the smartest areas (see pages 325 and 326), but Wandsworth boasts London's lowest council tax rates, around half those of most boroughs (see page 329).

Communications

Two tube lines run through Wandsworth: the District Line, slicing north/south through the centre of the borough, and the Northern Line, cutting across its south-eastern corner. The UK's busiest railway station, Clapham Junction, is also in Wandsworth, providing Overground rail links with much of the south of England and parts of the north. Wandsworth isn't the best place to live for car owners, however, as the A3 and A205 South Circular merge in an almost constant traffic jam right in the centre of the borough, and parking is restricted in many areas.

Leisure Facilities

Wandsworth is poorly supplied with entertainment facilities: one theatre, two cinemas and a small museum. The borough's majestic landmark, Battersea Power Station (which ceased to be used decades ago), still stands empty despite several attempts to transform it into an entertainment centre. However, Wandsworth boasts over 70 parks, gardens and open spaces, which account for almost 20 per cent of its area – the largest proportion of any London borough. Most popular are Battersea Park, recently given an £11m facelift, and Wandsworth Common in the north-east, Tooting Common in the south-east, and Putney Heath and Putney Common in the south-west, as well as parts of Clapham and Wimbledon Commons (see **Lambeth** and **Merton**). Beautiful Richmond Park is just next door. When it comes to eating out, Wandsworth residents are spoilt for choice, with a wide range of restaurants in Battersea, Putney, Tooting and Wandsworth town.

Schools

Like Southwark, Wandsworth has a high proportion of schoolchildren for whom English is a second language. Nevertheless, exam results in Wandsworth's schools have improved faster than anywhere else in the country in recent years, and its schools are now the most sought-after in London after Westminster's. There are 15 secondary schools, of which three are private. There's also a good choice of nursery schools, both state and private.

Shopping

Shopping facilities are improving, thanks mainly to the £70m refurbishment of the Arndale Centre (now called Southside) in Wandsworth town, and a new centre in Putney, with another planned in Wandsworth town. Putney and Clapham Junction have good shops, and there are some unusual shops in Tooting.

Wandsworth

Council offices: Town Hall, Wandsworth High Street, London SW18 2PU (☎ 020-8871 6000, 💻 www.wandsworth.gov.uk).

Postcodes: SW8 (part), SW11, SW12, SW15, SW17, SW18 and SW19 (part).

Population: 279,000, with the highest proportion of people aged between 20 and 35 of all the London boroughs. Wandsworth has an increasingly middle-class population and 22 per cent of its inhabitants are members of an ethnic minority.

Unemployment: Around 5.8 per cent.

Crime rate: Wandsworth's crime rates have dropped in recent years and are now around the London average (see table in **Appendix F**).

Houses of Parliament

Westminster

The City of Westminster, as it's properly called (although it's a borough like any other), contains most of London's most frequently visited attractions: Buckingham Palace, the Houses of Parliament, Leicester Square, Piccadilly Circus and Trafalgar Square, to name but a few. These areas are among the capital's most expensive, although Westminster also has its less salubrious parts. These are mainly in the north-west around Paddington, where redevelopment is in the pipeline, but also (for different reasons) in Soho in the east, traditionally London's sleaze centre but also an 'in' place to live and increasingly sanitised. In fact, Westminster is one of the country's most diverse boroughs and has an exceptionally wide gulf between rich and poor. The council's ambitious Civic Renewal programme aims to regenerate the more deprived areas.

Property

Some 90 per cent of properties in Westminster are flats (a third of them conversions), with 8 per cent terraces and just 1 per cent each of detached and semi-detached houses. There are flats of various styles (and prices) in Soho, Covent Garden (east), Marylebone (north-east), Pimlico (south) and Westminster itself (south-east). Maida Vale (north) and St John's Wood (north-east) offer some attractive properties near the Regent's Canal.

The crème de la crème addresses are in Mayfair (centre) and Knightsbridge and Belgravia (south-west), where Eaton Square is reputed to be London's smartest address.

Apart from Paddington, the cheapest properties are in Bayswater (west) and West Kilburn (north-west).

Costs

Unsurprisingly, Westminster has some of the capital's most expensive property (see pages 325 and 326): a three-bedroom flat in Knightsbridge can set you back £2m and a large house in St John's Wood five times as much! As a small compensation, council tax rates are the second-lowest in the capital, around half those in most boroughs (see page 329).

Communications

Westminster is at the heart of the tube network, so getting around is easy. With Paddington, Charing Cross and Victoria stations also in the borough, escaping from London (in a westerly or southerly direction) is equally straightforward, while the Heathrow Express route out of Paddington is handy for those wanting to flee to the country! There are also plenty of bus routes (including open-top city tour buses), but traffic often crawls and parking is a nightmare.

Leisure Facilities

Westminster is home to London Zoo, Madame Tussaud's, the Planetarium, the National and National Portrait Galleries, the Tate Gallery, the Royal Opera House, the Royal Albert Hall and the Wigmore Hall, not to mention over 40 theatres and more cinemas than you can shake a stick at (Leicester Square is the cinema-goer's Mecca, where new releases are often shown first). London's four most famous parks – Hyde Park, Regent's Park, Green Park and St James's Park – and the most attractive reaches of the Regent's Canal are also found within the borough. As if all that wasn't enough to keep its residents (and millions of visitors) entertained, Westminster has four leisure centres and the best-used libraries in the capital. Westminster is also blessed with some of London's most exclusive eating places.

Schools

Westminster has 20 secondary schools, of which 12 are private (including The American School in London, The International

Community School and a ballet and a theatre school). Standards vary and some of the state schools have suffered problems with pupil violence.

Shopping

Westminster offers shoppers a feast, its retailing shrines including Harrods, Oxford and Regent Streets, and Covent Garden.

Westminster

Council offices: City Hall, 64 Victoria Street, London SW1E 6QP (☎ 020-7641 6000, 🖳 www.westminster.gov.uk).

Postcodes: NW8, SW1, W1, W2 and W9.

Population: 232,000, with the lowest proportion of people aged under 20 outside the City of London and one of the highest proportions of people aged between 20 and 35 of all the boroughs. Around 27 per cent of Westminster's population belongs to an ethnic minority. There's also a large Jewish community in the north of the borough and London's greatest concentration of Chinese residents, in Soho.

Unemployment: Around 7.8 per cent.

Crime rate: Westminster has the highest crime rate in London, (see table in **Appendix F**), mainly because of the large number of non-residents (particularly foreign tourists) falling victim to petty crime in the borough.

Tower Bridge

12:30pm On Time
1:00pm On Time
4:09pm On Time
4:35pm On Time
15pm On Time
5pm On Time
pm Delayed
9, 2008

2.

ARRIVAL & SETTLING IN

Before making any plans to live or work in London, you must ensure that you have the appropriate entry documentation (e.g. a visa); without it, you won't be allowed into the country. If you're a national of a non-EEA country, you may need to obtain entry clearance (see page 71).

If you're in any doubt as to whether you require clearance to enter the UK, enquire at a British Diplomatic Post overseas before making plans to travel to the UK.

Permit infringements are taken seriously by the authorities and there are penalties for breaches of regulations, including fines and even deportation for flagrant abuses. The police and immigration authorities have the right to arrest anyone 'reasonably suspected' of being an illegal alien and can obtain search warrants to enter homes or places of employment. The penalties for harbouring illegal aliens are severe and prison sentences of up to seven years and heavy fines can be imposed on offenders.

The Home Office has the final decision on all matters relating to immigration. The latest information about immigration and permits can be obtained from its Border and Immigration Agency (💻 www.bia.homeoffice. gov.uk) and from local law centres, Citizens' Advice Bureaux and community relations councils. Further information is provided in our sister publication, *Living and Working in Britain* (Survival Books).

The Immigration Enquiry Bureau (IEB) operates a telephone information service (☎ 0870-606 7766) which deals with general enquiries about immigration rules and procedures, and queries about specific cases. Its lines are open from 9am to 4.45pm, Mondays to Fridays, although you may have to wait a long time to speak to an official. The busiest days are Mondays,

Tuesdays and Wednesdays (it's easier to get through towards the end of the week and in the afternoon). You can also use the following email address: ✉ indpublicenquiries@ind. homeoffice.qsi.gov.uk.

> ☑ **SURVIVAL TIP**
>
> You shouldn't base any decisions or actions on the information contained in this chapter without confirming it with an official and reliable source, such as a British embassy.

IMMIGRATION

The last few years have seen growing unease among increasing numbers of (generally tolerant and welcoming) Britons about the scale and pace of immigration to the UK in the 21st century. These concerns have been aroused by the fact that net immigration to the UK, i.e. the number by which immigrants outnumber emigrants, of whom there are also increasing quantities, is currently around 300,000 per year. The government estimated that no more than 13,000 people a year would arrive in the UK from the eight East European countries which joined the EU in 2004, although the actual number is thought to be at least 150,000 a year!

European migrants are now returning home or moving to other European countries where they can get better-paid jobs. Nevertheless, it seems likely that the criteria for allowing people entry into the UK will be tightened in the coming years and that the number of people allowed in each year might be capped.

Immigration is a complex subject and the information in this chapter is intended only as a general guide.

VISAS & PERMITS

The organisation responsible for issuing visas and providing information about who requires one is UK Visas (a joint undertaking of the Foreign and Commonwealth Office and the Home Office). UK Visas is represented at British Embassies, High Commissions and other British Diplomatic Missions (collectively known as British Diplomatic Posts) abroad, a complete list of which can be found at 🖥 www.fco.gov.uk. UK Visas can also be contacted by post at the Foreign and Commonwealth Office, King Charles Street, London SW1A 2AH, by phone (☎ 020-7008 1500, between 9am and 5pm Mondays to Fridays) or via its website (🖥 www.ukvisas.gov.uk).

Apart from those who are exempt, such as the citizens of EU and EEA countries, UK Visas plans to make a visa compulsory for anyone wishing to remain in the UK for over six months, which will be done in stages over the next few years. If you're in doubt whether you require a visa, check the latest situation with your nearest British Diplomatic Post before making any travel plans.

Visas & 'Visa Nationals'

Currently, nationals of certain countries, officially called 'visa nationals', require a visa (an official stamp in their passport) to enter the UK, irrespective of the purpose of their visit, e.g. holiday, residence or employment. If you need a visa and arrive without one, you'll be sent back to your home country at your own expense. Visitors' visas are issued for a

As well as the almost inevitable pressures on education, health and social services and utilities from large volumes of newcomers, as well as cultural and religious friction, there's a growing feeling that the UK has become overcrowded: it's now nearly twice as crowded as Germany and four times as crowded as France. Many Britons also feel that the UK has become a soft touch for asylum seekers, too many falsely claiming problems in their home country in order to gain entry to the UK and access to its generous social security handouts. These concerns are supported by the fact that, at present, only around a quarter of those who are refused asylum are actually removed from the country.

On the other hand, many businesses in London and elsewhere couldn't survive without migrant workers – particularly those in the hospitality sector and farming (especially crop-picking). Many such businesses are suffering from a shortage of workers, as many Eastern maximum stay of six months and are never extended beyond this period. If you want to stay longer, you must leave and apply for a new visa. Visa nationals aren't permitted to change their status.

Visa requirements for those planning to remain in the UK for more than six months are in a state of flux, as over the next few years, the visa requirement will gradually be applied to all nationalities previously exempt. The first group of countries to be included in the visa requirement consists of Australia, Canada, Hong Kong, Japan, Malaysia, New Zealand, Singapore, South Africa, South Korea and the USA. Nationals of these countries travelling to the UK for a stay of over six months now require a visa.

Entry Clearance

With the exception of European Economic Area (EEA) nationals, foreigners entering the UK may need to obtain 'entry clearance' from the Home Office or a British Diplomatic Post in their country of residence, before arrival in the UK. Entry clearance (in the form of a visa or entry certificate) also applies to returning residents who have been abroad for over two years, and is usually issued for a single entry but may also allow multiple entries over two or more years. A fee is payable depending on the type of entry clearance issued – contact your nearest British Diplomatic Post for details.

An entry certificate, which, like a visa, consists of an official stamp in your passport, is required by non-visa nationals, such as Commonwealth citizens coming to work or settle in the UK. If you're refused entry to the UK for any reason, an entry certificate gives you the right to an immediate appeal in the same way as a visa. A letter of consent is required by non-visa, non-Commonwealth citizens wishing to enter the UK for certain reasons.

⚠ Caution

Note that applications for entry clearance made in some countries can take some time to be processed due to the large number of applications received.

Work Permits

Work permits are issued to UK-based employers wanting to employ a worker from outside the EEA. Each permit is issued for a specific individual to work in a specific job, usually only when the employer has been unable to recruit a suitable employee from within the EEA. There are six types of work permit, detailed under the sub-headings below. Some work permits are only for short-term residents, while others provide a route to permanent residence in the UK.

Work permit applications can be downloaded from the Border and Immigration website (🖳 www.bia.homeoffice.gov.uk/workingintheuk).

Business & Commercial

Business and commercial permits are issued for a maximum of five years. To qualify for a Business and Commercial work permit, the position that an employer wants to fill must require one of the following:

♦ a UK degree level qualification;

♦ a higher national diploma (HND) level qualification which is relevant to the post;

♦ an HND-level qualification which isn't relevant to the post, plus one year of relevant full-time work experience.

Training & Work Experience Scheme

Employers can make a TWES application provided that:

♦ the post is additional to their normal staffing requirements;

♦ the person is going to be doing work experience or training for a minimum of 30 hours per week;

♦ the person speaks good English;

♦ the person leaves the UK at the end of the agreed period.

Sports & Entertainment

There are 25 sub-categories of this type of work permit, covering occupations as diverse as acting, boxing, classical music and pantomime production. Full details are provided on the Border and Immigration Agency website (🖳 www.bia.homeoffice.gov.uk).

Student Internships

These allow students from outside the EEA who are studying for a first or higher degree course overseas to undertake an internship with an employer in the UK. Students are allowed only one internship, for a maximum of three months.

General Agreement on Trade in Services (GATS)

GATS allows employees of companies based outside the EU to work in the UK on a service contract awarded to their employer by a UK-based organisation. Service contracts are for no longer than three months.

Sectors Based Scheme (SBS)

SBS allows UK-based employers to recruit low-skilled workers from outside the EEA to fill vacancies that cannot be filled by resident workers. However, since 1st January 2007 the SBS has been closed to new applications other than those from Bulgaria and Romania, who can only work in the food manufacturing sector (but existing SBS permit holders may apply for an extension or change of employment).

There are fears in 2008 that the restrictions on SBS visas will result in farmers being unable to recruit the workers necessary to harvest crops.

Working Holidaymakers

The working holidaymaker scheme is an arrangement whereby (primarily) single people between 17 and 30 can come to the UK for a maximum of two years. To qualify you must be a Commonwealth, British Dependent Territories, British Overseas or British National (Overseas) citizen. During the two-year period, you may work for a total of up to 12 months, but not in professional sport and entertaining, for which you need a work permit (see above). Whatever work you do, you'll be expected to take a holiday for part of your stay.

> ☑ SURVIVAL TIP
>
> Entry clearance (see above) must be obtained from a British Diplomatic Post before travelling to the UK, as it isn't possible to arrive as a visitor and change your status to that of a working holidaymaker.

Points-based System

February 2008 saw the unveiling of what the Border and Immigration Agency describes as 'the biggest shake-up of the immigration system in 45 years', with the introduction of an Australian-style points system. This is designed to attract only the most talented people to the UK and to address public concerns about the scale of immigration.

Full details of the proposed time scale, language requirements, schemes covered and other details see the UK Border and Immigration website (⌨ www.ukba.homeoffice.gov.uk).

Residence

'Settlement' (also known as 'indefinite leave to remain' or ILR) is the official name given to permanent residence in the UK and means that you can stay in the UK indefinitely, without any restrictions on working or the need for a work permit. A foreigner married to a UK citizen is granted settlement status after two years. Foreign nationals who have held a residence permit for between two and five years and who have been in continuous employment or self-employment or running a business in the UK, can apply for settlement. Work permit holders and Highly Skilled Migrant Programme workers must wait five years, unless they're also married to a British national, in which case it's two years. Five years applies to most other categories.

If you speak English to a reasonable standard, you will need to pass the Life in the UK test (see our sister publication **Life in the UK Test & Study Guide**). If you aren't an English speaker or your English is assessed as being below a certain level, you will need to take and pass a course in English and citizenship. For more information contact the 'Life in the UK Test' helpline (☎ 0800-0154 245). Applications for permanent residence cost approximately £750 (for postal applications).

If you've stayed in the UK legally for ten years (or 14 years if you weren't a legal resident), you can apply for settlement irrespective of your employment history. In this case your success will depend on a number of factors, including whether you've established a way of life in the UK and have strong ties with the country, and whether you have a criminal record or have spent long periods abroad.

For more information on how to apply for UK residence, see 🖳 www.ind.homeoffice.gov.uk/ukresidency.

Retirement

Pensioners who are EEA nationals have the right of residence in any EEA country but must make an application for a residence permit before they've spent six months in the UK. Non-EEA nationals who wish to live but not work in the UK require entry clearance in the form of a letter of consent (see page 71) before arrival in the UK.

To retire in the UK you must be aged at least 60 and have under your control and disposal in the UK an income of not less than £25,000 a year. You must also be able to show that:

◆ you're able to support and accommodate yourself and your dependants indefinitely without working and without recourse to public funds;

◆ you have private health insurance (if you're ineligible for cover under the National Health Service);

◆ your presence is 'in the best interests of the UK' (whatever that means!) or you have close ties with the UK, e.g. close relatives, children attending school there or periods of previous residence in the UK.

If you're prohibited from working in the UK, this also applies to members of your family and any dependants.

People of independent means (i.e. rich) are usually admitted for an initial period of one year and qualify for settlement after four years' continuous residence.

IMMIGRATION & CUSTOMS

If you come to London from abroad, your first task on arrival in the UK will be to negotiate immigration and customs, which, provided you have the necessary visa or entry clearance document (see above), should present no problems. Non-EEA nationals must complete a landing card on arrival, which are distributed on international flights and available from the information or purser's office on ferries.

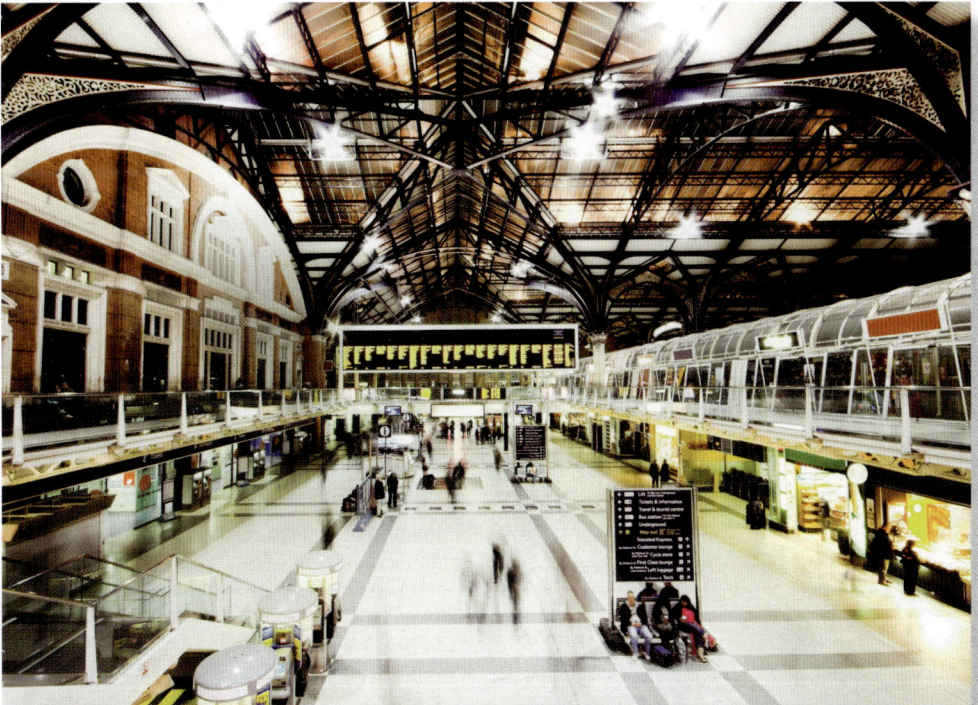

Liverpool Street Station

British customs and immigration officials are usually polite and efficient, although they may occasionally be a trifle 'over-zealous' in their attempts to detect smugglers, illegal immigrants and terrorists.

The UK isn't a signatory to the 1995 Schengen agreement (named after the Luxembourg village on the Moselle River where it was signed), which introduced an open-border policy between certain EU member countries. These now comprise 31 countries (27 EU states and four non-EU members, Iceland, Liechtenstein, Norway and Switzerland). The UK has no plans to join, ostensibly because of fears of increased illegal immigration and cross-border crime such as drug smuggling. Therefore, anyone arriving in the UK from one of the Schengen countries must go through the normal passport and immigration controls (the same applies when you enter a Schengen country from the UK).

When you land on British soil, the first thing you must do is go through Passport Control, which is usually divided into two areas: 'EU/ EEA Nationals' and 'All Other Passports'. Make sure you join the right queue. Passport Control is staffed by immigration officers who have the task of deciding whether or not you're entitled to enter the UK. You must satisfy the immigration officer that you meet whatever rules apply to the category of immigrant relevant to you. Present your passport to the immigration officer with any other documentation required.

The immigration officer may decide to send you for a routine (and random) health check before allowing you to enter the UK. After the health check you must return to immigration to have your passport stamped.

⚠ Caution

Generally the onus is on anyone entering the UK to prove that he is who and what he claims to be and that he won't infringe the immigration laws. The immigration authorities aren't required to prove that you've violated the immigration laws and can refuse your entry on the grounds of suspicion only.

Customs

The belongings you're allowed to bring into the UK duty and tax free depend on your status, where you've come from, where you purchased the goods and how long you've owned them, and whether duty and tax have already been paid in another country, as detailed below. There are no restrictions on the importation of goods purchased tax and duty paid in an EU country, although there are limits for certain goods, e.g. tobacco, beer and wine.

Your belongings may be imported up to six months in advance of your arrival in the UK, but no more than a year after your arrival.

Visitors & Students Resident Abroad

If you're a visitor, you can bring your belongings to the UK free of duty and tax provided that:

♦ all belongings are brought in with you and are for your use alone;
♦ they're kept in the UK for no longer than 24 months;
♦ you don't sell, lend, hire out or otherwise dispose of them in the UK.

If you're unable to export your belongings within 24 months, you must apply to the nearest Customs and Excise Advice Centre for an extension.

Students attending a full-time course of study in the UK can import their clothing and household linen, study articles and household effects for furnishing their accommodation.

People Moving or Returning to the UK

If you're moving or returning to the UK from outside the EU (including British subjects), you can import your belongings free of duty and tax provided that:

♦ you've lived for at least 12 months outside the EU;
♦ your possessions have been used for at least six months outside the EU;
♦ tax and duty have been paid on all items being imported (this requirement isn't applicable to diplomats, members of officially recognised international organisations, members of NATO or British forces, and their spouses and any civilian staff accompanying them);

◆ articles are for your personal use, are declared to customs, and aren't sold, lent, hired out or otherwise disposed of in the UK (or elsewhere in the EU) within 12 months, without customs authorisation.

People with Second Homes in the UK

If you're setting up a second home in the UK, you can bring normal household furnishings and appliances with you free of duty and tax if you usually live in another EU country. If you've lived outside the EU for at least 12 months, you can import household furnishings and equipment for setting up a second home free of duty but not free of value added tax (VAT), which is levied at 17.5 per cent.

To qualify, you must either own or be renting a home in the UK for a minimum of two years, and your household furnishings and equipment must have been owned and used for at least six months. Articles must be for your personal use,

be declared to customs, and mustn't be sold, lent, hired out, or otherwise disposed of in the UK (or elsewhere in the EU) within 24 months without authorisation from Customs and Excise. If furnishings and effects for a second home in the EU are imported unaccompanied, customs form C3 must be completed.

Procedure

If you need to pay duty or tax, it must be paid at the time the goods are brought into the country. Customs accept cash (sterling only), personal cheques supported by a cheque guarantee card, credit cards such as MasterCard and Visa, and, at some ports and airports, Switch debit cards. If you're unable to pay on the spot, customs will keep your belongings until you pay the sum due, which must be paid within the period noted on the back of your receipt. Postage or freight charges must be paid if you want the goods sent on to you.

All ports and airports in the UK use a system of red and green 'channels'. Red means you have something to declare and green that you have nothing to declare, i.e. no more than the customs allowances, no goods to sell and no prohibited or restricted goods. If you're sure that you have nothing to declare, go through the 'green channel'; otherwise go through the red channel. Customs officers make random checks on people going through the green channel and there are stiff penalties for smuggling. A list of all items you're bringing in is useful, although the customs officer may still want to examine your belongings. If you're arriving by ferry with a motor vehicle, random checks can be rigorous – even to the point of dismantling the vehicle in search of undeclared or prohibited items!

If you're shipping your belongings (which includes anything for your family's use, such as clothing, cameras, televisions and stereos, furniture and other household goods) unaccompanied to the UK, you must complete (and sign) customs form C3, obtainable from your shipping agent or HM Revenue and Customs (at the address below or via their website, 🖥 www.hmrc.gov.uk), and attach a detailed packing list. If you employ an international removal company, it will handle the customs clearance and associated paperwork for you.

Further Information

Information about customs regulations is contained in a number of booklets, called *Notices*. These cover belongings, household effects, private motor vehicles and people moving to the UK after marriage (*Notice 3*); pleasure craft or boats (*Notice 8*); inherited goods and vehicles (*Notice 368*); antiques (*Notice 362*); and motor vehicles, boats or aircraft imported from elsewhere in the EU (*Notice 728*). Revenue and Customs can provide information regarding the importation of items not covered by any *Notice*.

Copies of the *Notices* listed above can be obtained from customs offices or downloaded from 🖳 www.hmrc.gov.uk. The primary source of information is the Revenue and Customs national advice line (☎ 0845-010 9000 or, if phoning from abroad, ☎ +44-2920-501 261). Email and postal enquiry addresses for your local area can be found on the website. The principal address for written enquiries is HM Revenue and Customs, Crownhill Court, Tailyour Road, Plymouth PL6 5BZ.

REGISTRATION

Police Registration

Nationals from certain countries may be required to register with the police within seven days of their arrival in the UK, even when staying in temporary accommodation. This depends on the type of entry clearance granted and the length of stay. When applicable, the requirement to register with the police is stamped in your passport, either on entry or by the Immigration and Nationality Directorate (IND) of the Home Office when granting an extension of stay. In the case of an extension, you will have seven days to comply.

Those who may be required to register include nationals from the following countries: Afghanistan, Algeria, Argentina, Armenia, Azerbaijan, Bahrain, Belarus, Bolivia, Brazil, China, Columbia, Cuba, Egypt, Georgia, Iran, Iraq, Israel, Jordan, Kazakhstan, Kuwait, Kyrgyzstan, Lebanon, Libya, Moldova, Morocco, North Korea, Oman, Palestine, Peru, Qatar, Russia, Saudi Arabia, Sudan, Syria, Tajikistan, Tunisia, Turkey, Turkmenistan, United Arab Emirates, Ukraine, Uzbekistan or Yemen, and those who are stateless.

Police registration applies to nationals of any of the above countries, who have been given limited permission to enter or stay in the UK (confusingly called 'leave to enter' or 'leave to remain') for longer than six months. If your stay is less than six months' duration, it doesn't apply – travellers on short-duration visit visas aren't required to register with the police. In particular, it applies to:

♦ employees and au pairs

♦ students

♦ businessmen and investors

♦ the self-employed

♦ people of independent means

♦ creative artists

The spouse or partner and dependents aged 16 or over of someone required to register with the police, must also register. Exceptions include children aged 16 and under, seasonal workers at agricultural work camps, the private servants of diplomatic households, clergymen, spouses, civil and unmarried partners of people settled in the UK, a person exercising access rights to a child resident in the United Kingdom, the parent of a child at school in the UK who have 'leave to remain' to visit their child, or those formally granted asylum.

If you've been granted settlement or residency in the UK (usually stamped as 'indefinite leave to remain' or 'indefinite leave to enter'), then police registration isn't required.

In the Metropolitan Police area (Greater London), you must register at the Overseas Visitors Record Office (OVRO), Brandon House, 180 Borough High Street, London SE1 1LH (☎ 020-7230 1208). Business hours are 9am to 4pm, Mondays to Fridays, and you should expect to wait a long time (unless you're first in the queue). Bear in mind that the office may close early (e.g. 2.30pm) during busy periods.

You'll require your passport, work permit if you have one, any letters from the Home Office or documents from the Overseas Visitors Record Office, two passport-size photographs (black and white or colour) and the fee (currently £34). It's also wise to take a copy of your marriage certificate (if applicable) and birth certificate with you; students require a letter from the educational institution where they are studying confirming that they're enrolled there.

Details, such as your name, address, occupation, nationality, marital status and the date your permission expires, are entered in a green booklet called a Police Registration Certificate. If the police registration certificate isn't given to you on the spot, you may need to surrender your passport, which will be returned to you later with your certificate. Make a photocopy or a note of the certificate's number, date, and place of issue in case you lose it (in which case the fee must be paid again).

It's recommended that you take your Police Registration Certificate with you when travelling abroad, as this will make re-entry into the UK easier, although it should be surrendered to an immigration officer if you're travelling abroad for longer than two months.

Re-registration is required within seven days of changing your address and within eight days of changing any other details, including the issue of a new visa.

Council Tax Registration

All residents or temporary residents of the UK are required to register with their local authority or council for council tax soon after moving into a new home, either in the same council area or a new area. For information about council tax see page 77.

Embassy Registration

Nationals of some countries are required or requested to register with their local embassy or consulate as soon as possible after arrival in the UK. Even if registration isn't mandatory, most embassies like to keep a record of their nationals resident in the UK and it may help to expedite passport renewal or replacement. For a list of embassies and consulates in London, see **Appendix A**.

FINDING HELP

One of the biggest difficulties facing new arrivals in London is how and where to obtain help with day-to-day problems. This book was written in response to that need. However, in addition to the comprehensive general information you'll find here, you'll also require detailed local information. How successful you are at finding help will depend on your employer, the borough or area where you live, your nationality and your English proficiency.

Obtaining information isn't a problem, as there's a wealth of data available in London on every conceivable subject. But much of it isn't intended for foreigners and their particular needs. Your local council offices, library, tourist information centre and Citizens' Advice Bureau are excellent sources of reliable information on almost any subject. Some large employers may have a department or staff whose job is to help new

☑ SURVIVAL TIP

You're required to carry your Police Registration Certificate with you at all times, but not your passport.

arrivals, or they may contract this job out to a relocation consultant (see page 124).

There are expatriate clubs and organisations for nationals of many countries in most areas, many of which provide detailed local information regarding all aspects of living in the UK, including housing costs, school details, names of doctors and dentists, shopping information and much more. Clubs may produce data sheets, booklets and newsletters and organise a variety of social events, which may include day and evening classes ranging from local cooking to English-language classes. One of the best ways to get to know local people is to join a social club, of which there are hundreds in all areas of London (look under 'Clubs and Associations' in your local Yellow Pages).

Embassies and consulates usually provide information bulletin boards (jobs, accommodation, travel) and maintain lists of social clubs for their nationals. Many businesses (e.g. banks and building societies) produce books and leaflets containing valuable information for newcomers. Local libraries and bookshops usually have books about their areas (see also **Appendix B**).

⚠ Caution

You may find that friends, colleagues and acquaintances proffer advice based on their own experiences and mistakes. However, although they invariably mean well, bear in mind that their advice may be invalid for your particular area or situation).

CHECKLISTS

Before Arrival

The following checklist contains a summary of the tasks that should (if possible) be completed before your arrival in London:

♦ Obtain a visa, if necessary, for all your family members. Obviously, this must be done before arriving in the UK.

♦ Visit London to compare communities and schools and arrange schooling for your children.

♦ Find temporary or permanent accommodation and buy a car (if necessary). If you purchase a car in the UK, register it and arrange insurance.

♦ Arrange for shipment of your personal effects to the UK.

♦ Obtain an international credit or charge card if you don't have one, which will prove invaluable during your first few months in the UK.

♦ Arrange health insurance for your family. This is essential if you won't be covered by the National Health Service on your arrival in the UK.

♦ Open a bank account in the UK and transfer funds (you can open an account with many British banks from overseas).

♦ Obtain some British currency, as this will save your having to change money on arrival.

♦ Obtain an international driving permit, if necessary.

♦ Collect and, if appropriate, update your (and your family's) records, including birth certificates, driving licences, marriage certificate, divorce papers, death certificate (if a widow or widower), educational diplomas and professional certificates, professional and employment history (including job references), student identity cards, medical and dental records, bank account and credit card details, insurance policies and receipts for any valuables you're bringing with you. You'll also need the documents necessary to obtain a residence or work permit, plus certified copies, official translations and numerous passport-size photographs.

After Arrival

The following checklist contains a summary of tasks to be completed after arrival in London (if not done before):

♦ On arrival at a UK airport or port, have your visa cancelled and passport stamped, as applicable.

◆ If you don't own a car, you may wish to hire (rent) one for a week or two until you can buy one. Note that it's difficult to get around in some areas without a car.

◆ Register with the police (if applicable).

◆ Register for council tax at your local town hall.

◆ Register with your local consulate or embassy.

◆ Register with your local social security and tax offices.

◆ Open an account at a local bank and give the details to your employer (if applicable).

◆ Arrange schooling for your children.

◆ Find a local doctor and dentist.

◆ Arrange whatever insurance is necessary, including health, car, home contents and personal liability insurance.

UNDERGROUND
CARNABY STREET W1
CITY OF WESTMINSTER
NO SMOKING
PRIVATE
NO ENTRY
UNDERGROUND
NO SMOKING
WAY OUT
ABBEY ROAD NW8
CARNABY STREET W1
DRUG FREE ZONE
OXFORD STREET W1
CITY OF WESTMINSTER
WAY OUT
LADIES
BUCKINGHAM PALACE SW1
PICCADILLY CIRCUS W1
NOTTING HILL GATE W11
TOILET
OXFORD STREET W1
COVENT GARDEN WC2
ARSENAL
NO BEGGING
City of Westminster
LADIES
City of Westminster
GENTLEMEN
9.99
LONDON
UNDERGROUND
MIND THE GAP
ENTRY
City of Westminster
DRUG FREE ZONE
2.99
MIND THE GAP
NO SMOKING
ARNABY
TREET W1
Y OF WESTMINSTER
ABBEY ROAD NW8
CITY OF WESTMINSTER
AY OUT
City of Westminster
PLEASE ADJUST YOUR DRESS BEFORE LEAVING
IND THE GAP
9.99
NO SMOKING
City of Westminster
DRUG FREE ZONE
ADIES
PICCADILLY CIRCUS W1
CITY OF WESTMINSTER
GENTLEMEN

3.
GETTING THERE & GETTING AROUND

Getting to London from most countries is easy, as it's served by air from all the world's major cities, as well as by a direct rail connection with Brussels and Paris. London has no fewer than five international airports (City, Heathrow, Gatwick, Luton and Stansted, although the last three are a considerable distance from the capital). There are also regular ferry services to the south-east of the England from a number of European countries, although none have direct links to London itself. London is also the hub of domestic air, rail and road communications and therefore has excellent connections with the rest of the UK, and the centre of an extensive network of motorways and other major roads.

The city has a comprehensive public transport system encompassing suburban trains, underground (tube) trains, trams, buses and river ferries. Getting around London by tube, train and tram is quick and convenient, but travel by bus or car is slow due to the heavy traffic. It's also easy to get around central London by bicycle (although you'll need a smog mask and nerves of steel) or even on foot, particularly in the central area, which is surprisingly compact. (The best way to get to know – and enjoy – London is to wander the streets at random.)

☑ SURVIVAL TIP

However you plan to get around London, one of your first acts should be to buy a good street map, such as those produced by the Geographers A-Z Map Co. You can also find any street or postcode in London using the internet, e.g. Multimap (🖥 www.multimap. com) or Streetmap (🖥 www.streetmap.co.uk).

It isn't essential to own a car if you live in central London, where a car is a liability and parking is prohibitively expensive if you don't have a private garage or parking space. If you commute into London from one of the outer boroughs or surrounding counties, it will almost certainly be quicker by public transport, although you may need a car to get to your local railway or tube station (and for other purposes).

In common with most major cities, London is plagued by traffic congestion and many roads are permanently jammed with traffic, making travel by car slow and frustrating. Parking in central London is at best difficult (and expensive) and at worst impossible. During rush hours, from around 7 to 9.30am and 4.30 to 6.30pm, Mondays to Fridays, traffic flow is painfully slow, particularly in central London, where the average traffic speed is around 10mph (it takes as long to get around by car as it did 200 years ago in a horse and cart!).

In an effort to reduce traffic in central London, a 'congestion charge' was introduced in February 2003, which has proved successful (Transport for London claims that around

M25 Motorway

500,000 Londoners have abandoned their cars since the introduction of the congestion charge), although unpopular with those unable or unwilling to forsake their cars, who must pay £8 per day to enter the restricted area (see page 104).

However, although public transport, from a convenience and environmental point of view, is a better option than attempting to get around by car, services are often stretched to breaking point, particularly during peak hours and the summer tourist season.

The umbrella organisation for London transport is Transport for London (💻 www.tfl.gov.uk), and a wealth of information about public transport is also published by borough councils, local transport authorities and transport companies, many of which you'll find mentioned in this chapter.

☑ SURVIVAL TIP

What Londoners call the 'rush hour' actually extends to two to three hours both morning and evening. If you're fortunate enough not to be tied to the nine-to-five routine, you should avoid using London's transport system between 7.30 and 9.30am and from 4.30 to 6.30pm.

ARRIVING BY AIR

London is one of the busiest air transport hubs in the world and you can fly there from practically any country. Depending on whether you're travelling to London from Dublin, Denver or Delhi, you'll arrive at Heathrow, Gatwick, Stansted, Luton or City Airport (listed in order of size and passenger numbers below). With the exception of Heathrow and the small City Airport, all are some distance outside the city and entail a 30- to 60-minute journey into the centre (see the map of **Major Roads & Airports** opposite).

Heathrow Airport

Heathrow airport (☎ 0870-000 0123, 💻 www. heathrowairport.com) is 15mi (24km) south-west of the city centre and is one of the world's busiest airports, handling over 60m passengers a year. Over 90 airlines are based there, spread among its five sprawling terminals. Terminal 5 (British Airways) opened on 27th March 2008 and had a disastrous first couple of weeks, with hundreds of cancelled flights and tens of thousands of bags lost, described in the usual understated British way as 'a few teething troubles'. Demands from the airlines for a third runway (take-off and landing slots at Heathrow cost up to £10m) have been met with vociferous objections on the grounds of pollution, which would exceed EU limits.

Access

Train: The high-speed Heathrow Express rail service is by far the quickest and easiest way to get to or from central London – or at least as far as Paddington Station. The airport has two stations, operating direct trains to Paddington taking between 15 and 25 minutes (depending on which terminal you travel from). Trains run every 15 minutes between 5am and midnight and the single fare is £15 (£23 return). Alternatively, you

Major Roads & Airports

can take the cheaper and slower underground service: 50 to 60 minutes to Piccadilly Circus for £4 (adult single); trains operate between 5.30am and 11.30pm. Information is available from Travel Information Centres at Heathrow's tube stations, by phone (☎ 0845-600 1515) or via the internet (🖥 www.heathrowexpress.co.uk).

Bus: Bus services at Heathrow operate from the Central Bus Station above the underground station. The A2 service runs frequently between the five terminals and central London, but the journey takes over an hour and a half and an adult single ticket costs £6 (£10 for a return trip), therefore the tube is preferable. If you

arrive in the dead of night, you can catch the hourly night bus (N9) to Trafalgar Square – a leisurely trip of around 75 minutes and a bargain at just £2 single (90p with an Oyster Card – see page 90).

Taxi: The journey from Heathrow and the city centre by taxi costs between £50 and £70 and takes from 45 minutes to well over an hour, depending on traffic congestion.

Gatwick Airport

Gatwick airport (☎ 0870-000 2468, 🖥 www. gatwickairport.com) is 30mi (50km) south of London and is the UK's second-busiest airport – and the busiest single-runway airport in the world. It has two terminals (North and South) linked by a driver-less monorail system. International flights are handled by both terminals, while most domestic flights use the South terminal.

Access

Train: Gatwick Express (☎ 0845-850 1530, 🖳 www.gatwickexpress.com) operates a regular train service from 5.20am to 1.35am between the airport's South terminal and Victoria station (trains normally run every 15 minutes, but every hour before 6.50am and after 8.50pm). The journey takes 30 minutes and tickets, which you can buy on the train, cost £16.90 one way (£28.80 return). South Central's slower trains cover the same route for a slightly lower fare and run every 15 minutes during the day and every hour at night. There are also Thameslink trains running every 15 minutes from Gatwick to other London stations, including London Bridge, Blackfriars, City, Farringdon and King's Cross.

Bus: A cheaper but much slower option – the journey takes at least 80 minutes – is Shuttle bus 25, operated by National Express (☎ 0871-200 2233, 🖳 www.nationalexpress. com), which runs approximately every hour between 5.15am and 9.15pm to London's Victoria Coach Station (near the railway station). Single tickets cost £6.60 for adults (£12.20 return).

Taxi: A taxi from Gatwick to central London costs at least £70 and takes as long as the bus.

Stansted Airport

Stansted airport (☎ 0870-000 0303, 🖳 www. stanstedairport.com) is 34mi (60km) north-east of the capital. It's the newest of London's airports and the fourth-largest in the UK in terms of passenger numbers, serving over 60 destinations. It has two terminals and handles a range of flights within the UK and to most European countries.

Access

Train: The fastest way to get to central London from Stansted by public transport is using the Stansted Express (☎ 0845-600 7245, 🖳 www.stanstedexpress.com) to Liverpool Street station in the City of London, which

takes 45 minutes (single £15, return £24). Trains depart every 15 or 30 minutes between 8am and 8pm and hourly from 8pm to midnight and between 6 and 8am. Trains stop at Tottenham Hale on the Victoria underground line. A slower, stopping service is also available.

Bus: Three bus services link Stansted airport with London. The A6 to Victoria Coach Station (stopping at Golders Green and Finchley Road underground stations) operates 24 hours a day (every 20 minutes at peak times), and takes around an hour and 40 minutes (£10 single, £17 return). The Terravision Express Shuttle to Victoria Coach Station operates from 9am until 00.30am (every 45 minutes at peak times) and costs £8 single (£14 return), while the National Express A7 to Liverpool Street and Victoria stations is a night service operating every half hour between midnight and 4.30am (£10 single, £17 return);

Further information about bus services is available from National Express (☎ 0871-200 2233, 🖳 www.nationalexpress.com) and Terravision (☎ 01279-680028, 🖳 www. terravision.eu).

Taxi: A taxi to central London costs over £60 and the journey takes around an hour.

Luton Airport

Luton airport (☎ 01582-405100, 🖳 www. london-luton.co.uk), around 30mi (50km) north-west of central London, handles scheduled (around two-thirds of the total) and charter flights to a wide range of destinations in the UK and Europe. It opened the second of its two terminals in October 1999.

Access

Luton airport's promotional strapline is 'We're easier to get to than you think', which suggests (incorrectly) that transport links are poor.

Train: Trains operated by First Capital Connect (🖳 www.firstcapitalconnect.co.uk for information, 🖳 www.flybytrain.co.uk for bookings) from Luton Airport Parkway station offer a direct link (the 'Luton Express') with King's Cross station in Camden. Trains run every half hour or so, 24 hours a day, take between 25 and 50 minutes, depending on the number of stops, and cost £12 single. There are also trains to and from other London stations, including Hendon, Cricklewood, West Hampstead, Kentish Town, Farringdon, City, Blackfriars, London Bridge and East Croydon. A free shuttle bus runs between the airport and the station.

Bus: For a cheaper (£9 for an adult single) and slower (70 minutes) journey, you can take a Green Line 757 coach to the Green Line Coach station near Victoria Coach Station. Coaches run approximately every half an hour throughout the day and night.

Taxi: A taxi to central London from Luton isn't recommended, as it takes over an hour and costs at least £90.

City Airport

City airport (☎ 020-7646 0088, 🖥 www.londoncityairport.com) is the smallest of London's five airports and is just 9mi (14km) east of London's centre in Docklands. Only domestic and European flights operate from there (destinations include Amsterdam, Antwerp, Barcelona, Belfast, Bremen, Brussels, Cardiff, Cork, Dublin, Dundee, Edinburgh, Frankfurt, Geneva, Leipzig, Liverpool, Luxembourg, Manchester, Paris, Rotterdam, Swansea and Zurich) and the airport courts its largely business clientele by offering (allegedly) the fastest check-in and arrival times in Europe.

Access

Train: Silvertown & City Airport railway station (DLR – see page 98) is a ten-minute walk from the airport, and trains to the centre of London (linking with the tube system) run every 20 minutes.

Bus: Shuttle bus services operate every ten minutes between 7am and 9pm on weekdays, from 7.30am to 1pm on Saturdays and 11am to 9pm on Sundays between the airport and Canning Town (£4 adult single), Canary Wharf (£3) and Liverpool Street (£8) underground stations.

Taxi: Taxis to the City take up to 40 minutes (depending on the traffic) and cost around £25.

ARRIVING BY SEA

Regular car and passenger ferry services to the south-east of England operate from ports in Belgium, France and the Netherlands, but none dock in (or very near) London. Some services operate year round, while others run only during the summer (usually May to September), and the frequency of services varies from dozens a day on the busiest route (Calais/Dover) during the summer to a few a week on longer routes out of season.

Most ships have a restaurant, self-service cafeteria, children's play area and shops,

and some have 'executive' lounges, where for a few pounds extra you can enjoy superior facilities and a more relaxing atmosphere. Generally, the longer the route, the better and more comprehensive the facilities. Although Calais/Dover is the shortest (and cheapest) route and offers the most frequent crossings, ships on longer routes are generally less crowded and more relaxing.

On the longer routes (i.e. from France to Portsmouth and Poole, and Hook of Holland to Harwich), there are overnight services, which can 'save' you time.

Ferry Services

The following is a list of the services available in summer 2008, all of which employ conventional (i.e. slow) ferries unless otherwise stated:

Belgium

♦ Ostend/Dover: Norfolk Line;

France

♦ Boulogne/Dover: Speed Ferries – a fast ferry service;

♦ Caen/Portsmouth: Brittany Ferries;

♦ Calais/Dover: Norfolk Line, P&O Ferries and Sea France;

♦ Cherbourg/Poole: Brittany Ferries;

♦ Cherbourg/Portsmouth: P&O Ferries;

♦ Dieppe/Newhaven: Norfolk Line and Transmanche Ferries;

♦ Dunkirk/Dover: Norfolk Line;

♦ Le Havre/Portsmouth: P&O Ferries;

♦ Saint-Malo/Poole via Guernsey and Jersey: Condor Ferries.

♦ Saint-Malo/Portsmouth: Brittany Ferries;

Netherlands

♦ Hook of Holland/Harwich: Stena Line (🖳 www.stenaline.co.uk).

For more information about services, see the operator's website: Brittany Ferries (🖳 www.brittany-ferries.co.uk), Condor Ferries (🖳 www.condorferries.co.uk), Norfolk Line (🖳 www.norfolkline.com), P&O Ferries (🖳 www.poferries.com), Sea France (🖳 www.seafrance.com), Speed Ferries (🖳 www.speedferries.com), Stena Line (🖳 www.stenaline.co.uk) and Transmanche Ferries (🖳 www.transmancheferries.com);

Fares

Ferry companies offer a range of fares, including standard single and (unrestricted) return fares, and three- and five-day returns. Fares vary enormously, and you should check for offers, which are numerous and unpredictable. If you're able to book several months in advance, you can often pay up to 50 per cent less than the standard fare. It's worth shopping around for the best deal but, although a travel agency should be able to do this for you, they have no access to 'special' fares or 'privileged' information and you'll do as well (or better) to trawl the online ferry booking sites, which include the following:

🖳 www.channelcrossings.net;

🖳 www.ferrybooker.com;

🖳 www.ferrybookings.com;

🖳 www.ferry-tickets-online.co.uk;

🖳 www.ferry-tickets.uk.com;

🖳 www.intoferries.co.uk.

Note that it's difficult to compare ferry fares online, as you don't have access to the full range of fares and can only find prices by using the (time-consuming) booking form or quote facility.

ARRIVING BY RAIL

Since the opening of the Channel Tunnel in 1994, London has had a direct rail connection with continental Europe. There are two ways of travelling through the tunnel: by train (see **Eurostar**) and by car (see **Eurotunnel**).

Eurostar

Eurostar is an international train service linking London, Brussels, Lille and Paris. (There are also excursion trains to Disneyland Paris and, during the ski season, to La Plagne in the French Alps.) The high-speed rail link between Folkestone and London Waterloo was opened in October 2003, making it possible to reach London from Paris (Gare du Nord) and Brussels in less than three hours. On 14th November 2007 London's St Pancras station replaced Waterloo as the London Eurostar terminus, making journeys even faster (see box).

Journey Times

London to Paris – 2 hours 15 mins

London to Brussels – 1hr 51 mins

London to Lille – 1hr 20 mins

Fares vary considerably according to the class (there are three: standard, first and 'premium'), the date and time of travel, and the duration of the stay (in the case of return tickets). For example, it's possible to travel from Paris to London for as little as £42 return, but you can pay £309 for a premium class return. For details, timetables and bookings, contact Eurostar (☎ 08705-186186, 🖥 www. eurostar.com). Note that bookings made by telephone incur a £5 surcharge.

St. Pancras International is situated at the heart of central London with more underground connections than any other London station. There are three main Overground services from the station: East Midland trains, Eurostar and First Capital Connect. For more information, ☎ 020-7843 4250 or visit 🖥 www. stpancras.com.

Eurotunnel

If you want to travel to London through the Channel Tunnel by car, you must drive to Coquelles, near Calais and board a special train, which takes you to Folkestone near Dover (there's no road tunnel between France and the UK). This service is operated by Eurotunnel, whose trains run every 20 minutes and cross the Channel (running through the rock beneath the sea) in just 35 minutes. There are no services, other than toilets, on trains but you can stretch your legs inside the carriages.

Fares are higher than those for the Calais/ Dover ferry crossing (e.g. £127 one way for an average vehicle and up to four passengers), although off-peak, short break and 'frequent traveller' reductions are available. For details and bookings, contact Eurotunnel (☎ 08705-353535, 🖥 www.eurotunnel.com).

Trains carry all vehicles, including cycles, motorcycles, cars, trucks, buses, caravans and motorhomes. Fares are higher for vehicles exceeding around 6ft (1.83m) in height.

Note that a booking doesn't guarantee you a particular time, and you may have to wait for the next train at peak times. On the other hand, if you arrive early, you may be able to take an earlier train.

The travelling time to central London from the Folkestone terminal is normally around an hour, via the M20 motorway.

ARRIVING BY BUS

International bus services to and from the UK are provided principally by Eurolines, which operates through National Express (☎ 0871-200 2233, 🖥 www.nationalexpress. com), with regular services to around 200 destinations in Europe. Other operators provide services from Eastern European countries, such as Bulgaria, the Czech Republic, Latvia, Lithuania and Poland, including Capital Express, Ecolines, ETAP, Karolina, Kingscourt Express, Nordbecker and Orbis Transport. Most international services operate to and from Victoria Coach Station in Buckingham Palace Road near Victoria Station (☎ 020-7730 3466 for information or ☎ 020-7730 3499 for bookings, 🖥 www.tfl.gov.uk).

TRAVELLING TO LONDON BY ROAD

The web of motorways leading into London intersects with the M25, London's orbital motorway, and some continue towards the city centre before 'downgrading' to dual-carriageway and single-carriageway roads (see the map of **Major Roads & Airports** on page 83). The M25 (nicknamed 'the world's largest car park') was intended to consolidate the motorway system around the capital, drawing long-distance traffic away from the centre. However, it attracted a huge volume of local traffic, as a result of which long stretches have had extra lanes added, increasing the number of carriageways from three to four (mainly in the south-western section between the intersections with the M4 and M23) and further widening work is planned or in progress. There are also controversial plans to charge a toll for using it.

The major routes into London (starting in the north and working clockwise) are as follows:

♦ **M1** – The M1 pushes some way into London, ending at an intersection with the North Circular, the top half of the original (and now inner) London ring road. From here, follow the A41 for Regent's Park and the West End or, for Islington and the City, peel off the M1 one exit before it ends and join the A1.

♦ **A41** – One of the better roads leading into the city centre but, because it brings you into the heart of London's leisure and shopping areas. However, it can get clogged at unexpected times, for example, going into London in the early evening.

♦ **A10** – A good road from the north until it hits the North Circular, after which traffic speeds fall considerably.

♦ **M11 & A12** – The M11 enters London from the north-east, also terminating at the North Circular – at the same point as the A12, coming from Suffolk. However, there's no fast road on which to continue, leaving you to crawl along several miles of congested East End high streets before you reach the City.

♦ **M2 & M20** – South of the river, road access to the centre of London is frustratingly complicated. The best routes, the M2/A2 and M20/A20, both leave you with the choice between entering the Blackwall Tunnel under the river, from which you'll emerge still some way from the City and even further from the West End, and heading west up the Old Kent Road before crossing the river by bridge. Both options are likely to result in a lengthy crawl through congested urban streets.

♦ **M23** – The M23 arrives from the south and finishes soon after its intersection with the M25, becoming dual-carriageway for a few miles but soon degenerating into a crawl through a mass of crowded suburban high streets.

♦ **A3 & M3** – From the south-west, the A3 and M3 are completely separate roads, both of which continue as dual-carriageways some distance towards the centre of London after reaching the M25 (the M3 becomes the A316).

♦ **M4** – Entry to London from the west is via the M4, which runs to Chiswick in west London before becoming the A4 and merging with London's urban sprawl. The M4 is one of the UK's busiest motorways, carrying traffic from prosperous industrial towns such as Slough and Reading, tourist coaches bound for Windsor and the West Country, and swarms of taxis and buses to and from Heathrow airport. However, the M4 remains one of the fastest routes into central London outside rush hours.

♦ **M40** – The M40 from Birmingham to the north-west becomes the A40 inside the M25 and is dual-carriageway all the way to Regent's Park, although there are some bottlenecks along the way.

For information about driving in London, see page 102.

PUBLIC TRANSPORT IN LONDON

London has a comprehensive public transport system encompassing suburban trains, underground (tube) trains, trams, buses, river ferries and taxis. Most services are integrated and one ticket usually allows you to use the tube, buses and Overground trains. The network is divided into concentric pricing zones, where zone 1 is the central area and zone 6 the outlying areas (there are also a few tube and Overground stations in zones 7 to 9).

Getting around London by tube, train and tram (where it operates) is relatively fast and convenient, whereby travel by bus or car can be slow due to traffic congestion. However, although using public transport is usually a better option than attempting to get around by car, both from a convenience and environmental standpoint, services are often stretched to breaking point, particularly during peak hours and the summer tourist season. Tube users also have to put up with the never-ending 'engineering works', which often shut down lines and curb travel, particularly at weekends.

It's also relatively easy to get around central London by bicycle or moped/scooter (although you will need a smog mask) or even on foot,

particularly in the central area which is surprisingly compact. However, you will need a good street map, such as those published by the Geographers' A-Z Map Co.

The umbrella organisation for London transport is Transport for London (TfL), which has an excellent website (🖥 www.tfl.gov.uk) including a useful journey planner (🖥 www.journeyplanner.tfl.gov.uk). A wealth of information about public transport is also published by borough councils, local transport authorities and transport companies, many of which you will find mentioned in the relevant section in this chapter.

FARES

Despite more people using public transport in London than in any other European city – it has the world's largest rail and tube network – the city also has the most expensive public transport of any capital city in Europe, with basic (cash) fares two to four times higher than in most other major European cities. Public transport is, however, cheaper if you're able to take advantage of the wide range of discount, combination (e.g. rail, bus and underground), season and off-peak tickets available.

For the purposes of public transport, London is divided into six main concentric fare zones stretching 12mi (19km) from the centre (there are few stations in outlying areas, mainly on the Metropolitan tube line, designated as zones 7 to 9). The central area is designated zone 1, while the outer suburbs are in zone 6, and ticket prices depend on how many zones you travel through. You can buy a ticket for a single or day return trip, although a Travelcard provides better value if you're planning to use public transport extensively. Travecards offer unlimited travel for one day, seven days, one month or one year, and are valid on the underground (tube), the Docklands Light Railway (DLR), buses and many suburban trains.

If you're travelling into central London by rail, your ticket can include a Travelcard supplement so that you can use it for onward travel on the tube and buses. If you need a Travelcard for seven days or more (called a Seasonal Travelcard) or a child rate ticket for a child aged under 17, you'll need a free 'photocard', for which a passport-size photograph and proof of age is required for children.

Oyster Card

If you don't need a season ticket, one of the most convenient and cheapest ways to use London's public transport is with an Oyster card, which offers discounts of up to 50 per cent compared with single-journey tickets, e.g. a zone 1 tube journey costs £1.50 with an Oyster card, compared with £4 when you pay cash. Pre Pay Oyster cards don't need to be registered (you pay a refundable £3 deposit) but can be used like a debit card (you can store up to £90) on the underground, DLR, buses and Tramlink services. There's no queuing for tickets or hunting for change for machines and you simply touch your card on the card readers at tube and DLR stations, on buses and at tram stops. For more information see 🖥 www.tfl. gov.uk. You can also buy an Oyster card when abroad via the Visit Britain Direct website (🖥 www.viistbritaindirect.com).

If you're aged 60 or over or have an eligible disability and are a permanent London resident, you can apply for a Freedom Pass from your borough council. This entitles you to free travel on all London's public transport including buses, tube, trains, Docklands Light Railway and trams. Enquire at your borough council offices or visit the Freedom Pass website (🖥 www.freedompass.org).

It pays to have auto top-up for your Oyster card, which automatically tops up your card by £20 or £40 (you decide) when the credit balance falls below £5. This can be set up online at 🖥 www.tfl.gov.uk/oyster.

When using an Oyster card, always ensure that you card has registered the payment, e.g. when using buses – a beep indicates that you have insufficient funds on your card and you must pay the driver or get off at the next stop and buy a ticket. Inspectors frequently board buses to check tickets and card payments, and if your discovered not to have paid you must pay a penalty fare of £20 or face prosecution (the inspector decides).

UNDERGROUND RAIL (TUBE)

The London underground (tube) system is the oldest (parts of it have been around since the 1860s) and largest in the world, with some 500 trains and over 270 stations handling over 3m passenger journeys a day. Given the congestion above ground, London without its tube would be unthinkable and it's easily the fastest and most convenient way to get around the city and its suburbs (provided stations and lines aren't closed for engineering work – an increasing occurrence in recent years, particularly at weekends). Outside the central areas (and even within some of them) trains actually run above ground – something which, not surprisingly, many first-time visitors to the city find confusing.

In most European countries, an underground rail system is called a metro system, while in the US it's the subway. In London the underground vernacular is the 'tube' – a term derived from the tube-shaped tunnels through which the trains run under the city.

Although most Londoners like to criticise the tube service, it's nowhere near as bad as some people would have you believe. Despite hot, sticky and airless conditions in some older parts of the network (most trains aren't air-conditioned, although it's planned), there are other areas, such as the recently opened Jubilee Line extension to Greenwich, which are clean, efficient and air-conditioned. After years of neglect, the entire tube network is currently undergoing a transformation which involves rebuilding or updating, signals, tracks, stations and trains.

The East London Line was closed in December 2007 for a major extension of the line, which will become part of the Overground rail network. The northern extension will run from a new Shoreditch High Street station as far as Dalston Junction (2010) and on to Highbury & Islington (2011), via Hoxton, Haggerston, Dalston Junction and Canonbury. The southern extension (south of the river) will link with existing Overground lines to provide services to West Croydon (2010), with a further extension proposed from Surrey Quays via Peckham Rye to Clapham Junction. Further details of the scheme can be found at 🖳 www. ellp.co.uk or 🖳 www.tfl.gov.uk.

Tube Network

Free maps of the tube network are available at stations, Travel Information Centres and from Transport for London (☎ 020-7222 1234, 🖳 www.tfl.gov.uk/tube). The award-winning tube map (see opposite) is a model of clarity and the system is easy to understand. The network has 11 separate lines (strictly speaking the DLR – see above – is classed as part of the tube network), each of which is colour-coded on the tube map, e.g. yellow for the Circle Line, green for the District Line, red for the Central Line and so on. This makes it easy to follow your route and find your way to the correct platform (although you need to know whether you're travelling north, south, east or west in order not to catch a train going in the opposite direction). Some larger stations have electronic route planners where you input the name of your destination station and the shortest route is displayed.

Although the tube is most widely used in the centre of the city, where it provides a useful alternative to fighting your way through the London traffic, it also includes extensive coverage of the suburbs to the north, east and west of the city. There are fewer lines and stops south of the River Thames, where commuters tend to use the Overground rail network. The tube operates for some 20 hours a day, from around 5am until 00.30 or 01.00 – it varies with the day of the week, the station and the line (there are proposals to extend this so that the last trains leave the West End at 1am).

Smoking isn't permitted anywhere on the tube network (including stations) and drinking alcohol was banned on the tube (and all other forms of London public transport and stations) from 1st June 2008.

Stations & Tickets

A typical tube station has an entrance above ground, indicated by the Transport for London 'bull's eye' logo of a red circle with a horizontal line through the middle. Unlike on some other systems (such as New York) you don't have to worry about which direction you're travelling

Tube Train

when accessing a station, as all stations have access to trains travelling in all directions and to all connecting lines.

You can buy tickets from machines and from ticket windows at most stations. Most machines provide change and if a machine runs out of change it will display a message telling you to deposit the exact fare. It's advisable to carry some change when travelling on the tube, as queues at ticket windows in central London can be long (or preferably buy a multi-ride/season ticket or an Oyster card).

Like all London's public transport, the tube network is divided into fare zones. The city centre is designated zone 1, while the outer suburbs are mostly in zone 6 (a few on the Metropolitan line are in zones 7 to 9). A basic adult single cash fare starts at £3 (excluding zone 1) and increases depending on the number of zones and whether the journey includes zone 1; a single journey that includes zone 1 (up to zone 6) costs £4. A one-day Travelcard for zones 1 and 2 costs £6.80 during peak times (Monday to Friday from 7am and before 7pm) and £5.30 off-peak (all other times) and £15.00 for all 9 zones (£8.20 off-peak).

Three-day, seven-day, monthly and annual Travelcards are also available and offer better value if you're going to be using the system more extensively. You can limit a Travelcard to specific zones if your journey won't cover the whole network and it can also be used on the DLR, buses and many Overground trains (including National Rail).

Most central London stations have automatic ticket barriers that speed up the flow of passengers from the concourse to the platforms. Once you have your ticket, insert it into the slot on the front of the machine. It will pop out at the top and as you remove it the gates open to let you through. If you have an Oyster card (see page 90) just touch it on the sensor and the barrier will open. If you have problems, there's usually a member of staff nearby to help who also operate special wide gates for wheelchair users, those with children in pushchairs and bulky baggage.

Don't risk travelling without a ticket or without using an Oyster card, as prosecution for fare evasion will result in a large fine and possibly a criminal record.

Once through the barrier, access to platforms is via escalators (moving staircases) or lifts, although some stations have stairs only. Escalators can be tricky if you have young children with you, so fold pushchairs before you start and take extra care. Stand on the right – those in a hurry (half of London) like to stampede past you on the left – and hold the moving handrail at the side. If you have young children, you may need to help them to jump on and off at the right moment. One last fashion note – stiletto heels and long skirts can be a danger on escalators.

Once safely at the bottom of the lift or escalator, make sure that you're following the signs to the right line in the right direction, e.g. Northern Line south-bound or Piccadilly Line west-bound. There are electronic displays on platforms that indicate the time until the next train and its destination. Note that on many lines, trains can have more than one destination on the same line (i.e. a number of branches) and some trains terminate before the end of the line. Train doors usually open and shut automatically, although you may be required to press a button near the door to open them.

Travelling By Tube

The tube system can be very crowded, particularly during peak hours (around 8 to 9.30am and 5 to 6.30pm, Mondays to Fridays). It's advisable to avoid these times if you can. Standing in a train that's packed to the gills can be an uncomfortable and claustrophobic experience, and packed platforms and trains are a haven for pickpockets and gropers. Keep a tight hold on your valuables. The District Line is the busiest, although the shorter Victoria Line carries more passengers per mile, with Victoria and Oxford Circus the two busiest stations on the network.

At quiet times, tube travel can be moderately relaxing, provided you keep an eye on the frequent stops and don't miss your destination or interchange point. Each carriage has seats, although priority should be given to the elderly, pregnant, disabled or those laden with children or heavy bags. If you don't have a seat it's wise to hang on tight, as trains can hurtle through twisting tunnels at an alarming rate and it's easy to find yourself tumbling into the lap of a surprised stranger. There are plenty of rails to hold on to, as well as handles or 'straps' that dangle from the ceiling for support.

☑ SURVIVAL TIP

If you have small children with you, keep a firm grip on them, as it's easy to become separated in the crush on a train or platform. You should also stand well back from the platform edge.

If you stand too close to the edge of the platform, it's possible to fall or be pushed onto the live rail or under the wheels of an approaching train (the wind in the stations can be surprisingly strong as trains force pockets of air along the tunnels). New lines, such as the Jubilee line, have protective barriers between passengers and tracks, although there are no plans to upgrade stations on older lines. When you arrive at your destination, follow the directions to the exit. In central London you will probably have to negotiate more escalators or lifts and another set of automatic barriers. If your ticket has expired the machine will retain it.

Tube Information

Transport for London (TfL) centres provide extensive information about the tube network (plus bus services and the DLR). TfL centres are located throughout central London at Euston, King's Cross, Liverpool Street, Oxford Circus, Piccadilly Circus, Victoria, and St James's Park rail/tube stations and Hammersmith Bus Station (plus Heathrow Airport). Business hours vary, but there's also a 24-hour hotline (☎ 020-7222 1234) and a recorded information line (☎ 020-7222 1200).

Transport for London publishes a booklet about facilities for disabled passengers, called *Access to the Underground*, available free from ticket offices or from TfL's special Unit for Disabled Passengers (☎ 020-7941 4600, ✉ access&mobility@tfl.gov.uk). *Access in London: A Guide for People Who Have Difficulty Getting Around* by Gordon Couch, William Forrester and David McGaughay (Access Project), provides details of the most accessible tube stations and step-free routes for wheelchairs.

The internet positively pulsates with tube-related websites, both official (e.g. 🖳 www.tfl. gov.uk) and enthusiastically amateur – two of the best are Carter's Unofficial Guide to the London Underground (🖳 www.geocities.com/CollegePark/3812) and Going Underground (🖳 www.goingunderground.net), Annie Mole's cult blog.

BUSES

When you mention London buses, most people immediately conjure up the image of the old Routemaster buses: bright red double-deckers with a roving conductor or 'clippie' and a rear platform where you could hop on and off. Sadly for many, the last Routemaster buses were taken out of service on 9th December 2005 and were replaced with cheaper to operate, one-man buses. With conductor-less buses, you board at the front and pay the driver, so the new buses also tend to be slower – it's advisable to have the correct change ready,

which on some buses is mandatory. The new buses have step-free access, ramps, special areas for wheelchairs and space for unfolded pushchairs, making them the most accessible buses in the world.

Double-decker buses can be one of the most pleasurable and scenic ways to get around the capital (or out to the suburbs), provided you don't try to do it during the rush hour when progress can be painfully slow and it may be quicker to walk (seriously). Fares are reasonable, with a single cash fare costing £2 peak or £0.90 with an Oyster card (see page 90). Most bus routes accept Travelcards (see page 90) or you can buy a daily, weekly or monthly pass that's valid for any number of travel zones. A one-day adult pass costs £3.50 and allows travel on buses anywhere in London. Children aged under 16 travel free on buses and trams.

To catch a bus, first find a bus stop (a roadside poles with a red sign at the top) on the correct side of the road for the direction you want to travel. Many are request stops, which means you need to put your arm out to hail the bus as it approaches, otherwise it won't stop. There are many different routes serving the same stops, so check the front of the bus for its destination or study the bus routes by picking up a free bus map and timetable from a Travel Information Centre. Alternatively, you can buy a bus map; the Greater London Bus Map series (🖳 www.busmap.co.uk) are highly rated.

The regular red bus service operates from 6am until midnight, after which a restricted night bus service comes into operation. These buses have numbers prefixed with the letter 'N' (most routes radiate out from Trafalgar Square); they run approximately every hour and journeys cost the same as day buses: £2 cash or £0.90 with an Oyster Card. You can also use Travelcards (see above) on night buses. Night bus maps are available on the Transport for London website (🖳 www.tfl.gov.

uk/gettingaround/1110.aspx – click on night bus maps).

The outer suburbs of London within a 40mi (64km) radius are served by Green Line buses (☎ 0870-608 7261, 🖳 www.greenline.co.uk), most of which leave from Victoria Coach Station in Eccleston Street, SW1. Travelcards can be used on some Green Line bus services.

Further information about London's bus services can be obtained from Transport for London (☎ 020-7918 4300, 🖳 www.tfl.gov.uk/buses).

OVERGROUND RAIL NETWORK

The British railway system is the world's oldest, but has been the subject of controversy, scandal and tragedy in recent years. Privatised in 1996, the service went from boom (two years later) to bust when, in 2001, the operating company, Railtrack, went into liquidation with debts of £700m. It also suffered several fatal crashes as a result of poor maintenance and inept management. The new not-for-profit operator, Network Rail, has inherited something of a poisoned chalice, with unreliable services and an infrastructure badly in need of renovation. Network Rail owns the infrastructure but the trains are operated by a number of regional companies.

There's no a clear distinction between 'mainline' rail services between major cities and local services, and a train company may offer either or both services on its routes. Suburban or local trains stop at most stations along their route, while long distance trains are express services that stop only at major towns and often include first or 'executive' class carriages.

While it's usually possible to buy a meal on long-distance trains, either in a restaurant car or from a buffet, suburban trains usually offer just a snack trolley service or nothing at all. Toilets are provided on trains on all but the shortest services and smoking is banned on all British trains.

Travel during peak periods is best avoided, when packed trains (often standing room only) cause considerable discomfort for those commuting into central London from the suburbs and provinces.

Suburban Trains

London's suburban rail network is largely concentrated to the south of the city, where the underground service terminates, although there are also suburban services to the east, north and west of the city. Most lines are used by commuters in south-east England, living in what's known as the 'stockbroker belt' (from where hundreds of thousands of workers travel into London each working day).

The rail companies serving London stations (see map) are listed below:

Links to the websites of regional rail operators can be found on the Network Rail website (⌨ www.networkrail.co.uk), which contains timetables for all mainline services nationwide.

Cross-London Trains

London is the hub of most long-distance rail travel in the UK, although there are only a few cross-London Overground rail services; in most cases if you want to cross London by rail,

London Mainline Stations

Station	Region(s) Served	Train Operators	Information
Cannon St	south-east	South Eastern Trains	☎ 0871-200 4927
Charing Cross	south-east	South Eastern Trains	☎ 0871-200 4929
Euston	north-west, north Wales, Scotland	Silverlink, Virgin Trains	☎ 0871-200 4938
Kings Cross	Herts., Cambs., Luton airport, north and north-east, East Anglia, Scotland	Great North Eastern Railways (GNER), Wagn	☎ 0871-200 4959
Liverpool St	Stanstead airport, East Anglia	Anglia Railways, Wagn, First Great Eastern,	☎ 0871-200 4955
London Bridge	south-east	South Eastern Railway	☎ 0871-200 4952
Marylebone	the Chilterns	Chiltern Railways	☎ 0871-200 4969
Paddington	Heathrow airport, west, south-west, south Midlands, south Wales, Scotland	Arriva, First Great Western Heathrow Express, Thames Trains	☎ 0871-200 4972
St Pancras	east Midlands, south Yorkshire	Eurostar, Midland Mainline	☎ 0871-200 4977
Victoria	Gatwick airport, Channel Ferry ports, south, south-west	Gatwick Express, South Eastern Trains,	☎ 0871-200 4984
Waterloo	south, south-west, Wales	South Central Trains, South Eastern Trains South West Trains	☎ 0871-200 4992

Stations & Major Roads

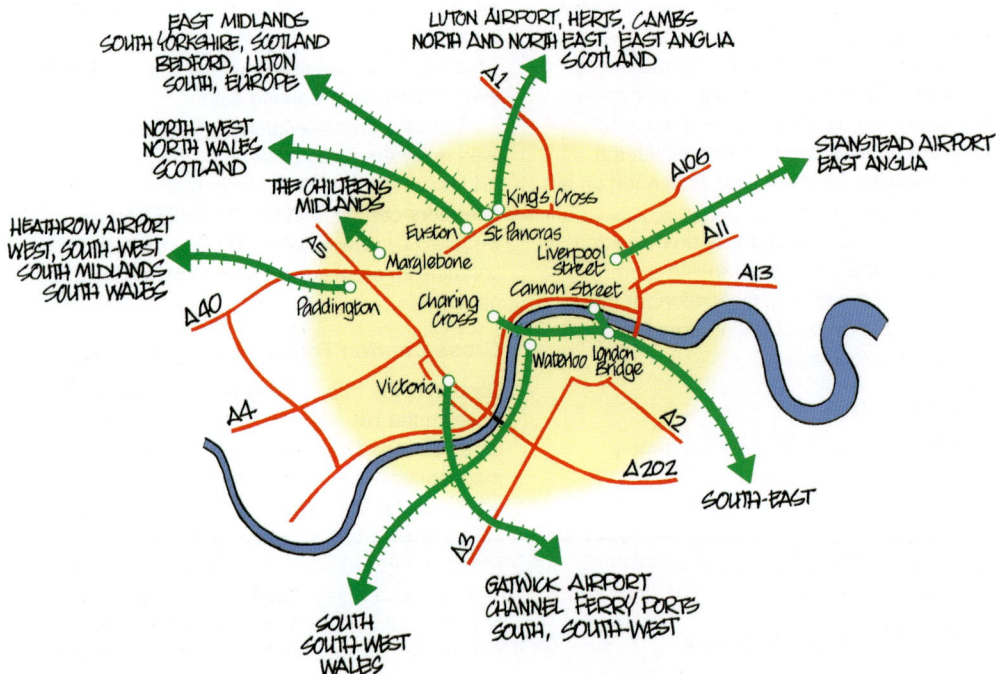

EAST MIDLANDS
SOUTH YORKSHIRE, SCOTLAND
BEDFORD, LUTON
SOUTH, EUROPE

LUTON AIRPORT, HERTS, CAMBS
NORTH AND NORTH EAST, EAST ANGLIA
SCOTLAND

A1

NORTH-WEST
NORTH WALES
SCOTLAND

A106

STANSTEAD AIRPORT
EAST ANGLIA

THE CHILTERNS
MIDLANDS

King's Cross

HEATHROW AIRPORT
WEST, SOUTH-WEST
SOUTH MIDLANDS
SOUTH WALES

A5

Euston St Pancras

A11

Marylebone

Liverpool
Street

A13

A40

Paddington

Cannon Street

Charing
Cross

Victoria

Waterloo London
Bridge

A4

A2

A202

SOUTH-EAST

A3

SOUTH
SOUTH-WEST
WALES

GATWICK AIRPORT
CHANNEL FERRY PORTS
SOUTH, SOUTH-WEST

you must make your way between stations by underground, bus or taxi. There are currently three cross-London train services connecting North and South London, which are listed below. A number of others are planned or have been proposed, including Crossrail (see below), City Tram and Cross River Transit and the East London Line Project .

London Overground Line: Formerly the North London line, the London Overground line operates in a semi-circle; routes include Richmond-upon-Thames to Stratford, Clapham Junction to Willesden Junction, Gospel Oak to Barking and Watford Junction to Euston (see ⌨ www.tfl.gov.uk/assets/downloads/London-Overground-Network-map.pdf for a map and ⌨ www.lorol.co.uk). It will be extended to the East London line in 2011.

South Central Line: One of South Central's lines runs from Watford in Hertfordshire just north of London to Brighton and other towns in the south-east via Harrow

& Wealdstone and Kensington north of the river, and Clapham Junction and Croydon south of the river.

Thameslink: This service, which dates from 1989 when the Snow Hill Tunnel under central London was re-opened, has two lines. One runs from Bedford in Bedfordshire to Brighton on the south coast via Luton and Gatwick airports and serves King's Cross, Farringdon, City, Blackfriars and London Bridge in central London, and East Croydon in the borough of Croydon. The other line runs from Luton and Luton Airport to Sutton, serving the same London stations listed above (except London Bridge) plus Mill Hill, Hendon, Cricklewood, West Hampstead and Kentish Town north of the river, and numerous stations south of the river including Elephant & Castle, Streatham, Wimbledon, South Merton, Morden, Sutton and Mitcham. For train information, see ⌨ www.firstcapitalconnect.co.uk.

A major (and severely delayed) upgrade to Thameslink, the north-south rail link through London, started in 2007 but isn't expected to be completed until 2015. Luton Airport Parkway station is being extended and will link with a new station at St Pancras (St Pancras Midland Road) and Eurostar services to Europe. The upgrade will benefit rail passengers across the south-east and will result in a doubling of capacity.

Crossrail: London's biggest project, Crossrail, is a new railway tunnel between Paddington & Whitechapel, enabling suburban trains to travel from Heathrow and Maidenhead in the west to Canary Wharf, Shenfield and Abbey Wood in the east. The scheme has a budget of £16bn and has been improved and is scheduled for completion in 2017 (but don't hold your breath). The core of the Crossrail scheme is the tunnel connecting the line into Paddington in the west to the lines out of Liverpool St in the east. Central London stations are proposed at Bond Street, Tottenham Court Road and Farringdon. The main beneficiaries from Crossrail include Abbey Wood, Hanwell, Hayes, Southall, Stratford and West Drayton. For more information, see 🖳 www.crossrail.co.uk.

Tickets

Although a number of companies may be involved, you can buy 'through' tickets to stations on a different company's network; the price shouldn't vary, irrespective of where you purchase your ticket, although individual train companies sometimes offer reduced fares on their own routes. Depending on the special offers available, you may obtain a better deal by purchasing separate tickets for different 'legs' of a long journey.

There's a bewildering array of discount tickets available, including child and youth discounts (up to 25-year-olds), family and group tickets, and discounts for the over 60s (known as 'seniors') and the disabled, as well as special holiday and advance purchase excursion (Apex) tickets.

Some tickets require the purchase of an annual 'railcard', which entitles you to discounts each time you buy a ticket. If you're a regular train traveller, you can buy a weekly, monthly or annual (point-to-point) season ticket, for which you need a passport-size photo.

Travelcards (see page 89) are valid on suburban trains and you can purchase a Network Railcard for £20 a year that provides discounts on most fares in the south-east of England. You may also be eligible for a Family, Senior or Young Person's Railcard (all £24 per year), which give a discount of 34 per cent off normal adult fares

Information about tickets is available from information and ticket offices at stations. To check timetables, book tickets and obtain other information, you can consult the Network Rail website (🖳 www.networkrail. co.uk) or go to 🖳 www.nationalrail.co.uk, 'the gateway to the UK's national rail network' operated by the Association of Train Operating Companies. Alternatively you can visit 🖳 www.thetrainline.com, run by the Trainline Rail Enquiry Service and Trainline. com – wholly owned subsidiaries of Trainline Holdings, which is owned by travel groups, Virgin Group Investments and Stagecoach Group.

If you're planning a long journey by train, bear in mind that buying a ticket doesn't guarantee you a seat on any particular train unless it's specifically reserved. If you know what time you plan to travel, it's advisable to reserve a seat, particularly during holiday periods and at weekends.

Station Facilities

Most main railway stations have restaurants, buffets and snack bars, although the quality of food generally leaves a lot to be desired and can be expensive. Smaller stations sometimes have vending machines for snacks, sweets and drinks. A majority of train stations have toilet facilities (sometimes for a fee – usually 20p) and many have baby changing facilities. All stations have payphones, most accepting credit/debit cards and coins, and most larger stations provide photo booths. Some larger stations have a First Class Lounge for passengers with first-class tickets, which usually have internet terminals, televisions, and lounge and shower facilities.

Car parking is provided at most country and suburban stations, although there's a high level of theft of (and from) cars parked at railway stations, so don't leave your belongings on the back seat.

Many stations and airports have luggage lockers or 'left luggage' offices and you can usually find a trolley to wheel your bags around; porters are rare these days and lifts aren't provided at many stations.

There are shops at most central London stations, and some termini have extensive shopping centres with banking facilities; Liverpool Street station is particularly well supplied with shops and other services, as is the new St Pancras International station.

Disabled Passengers

Wheelchairs are available at major railway stations and most trains have special facilities for their storage. Special arrangements can be made for disabled or mobility-impaired passengers when travelling by train, e.g. station staff can usually help passengers on and off trains, but cannot lift disabled passengers or heavy items such as mobility scooters.

☑ **SURVIVAL TIP**

When booking a journey, disabled passengers should provide as much information as possible regarding their needs.

On services with seat reservations, you can reserve a seat or wheelchair space without charge (ramps are provided at stations). Most trains can accommodate wheelchair users and new trains also have facilities to assist sensory impaired people, for example public information systems that are both visual and audible. Ramps for disabled access are provided at train stations, but you must ensure that your give staff sufficient time to help you.

Transport for London operate a Assisted Travel scheme – see their

website for information (🖥 www.tfl.gov.uk/modalpages/2669.aspx).

TRAMS & LIGHT RAIL SYSTEMS

The most recent development of London's transport system has been the introduction of 'light rail' systems, sometimes comprising trams, which are making a comeback in the UK after the original pre-war systems were abandoned in the 20th century. Familiar to Americans as 'transits' or 'streetcars', these systems are different from traditional railways. Short trains or 'trams' run as single or articulated units on tracks laid along streets, in cuttings or on elevated platforms. They usually stop more frequently than conventional trains, even where there's no driver. Fuel-efficient (they're electrically powered), quiet and non-polluting, they also help to reduce traffic congestion on London's busy roads.

London's two main light rail systems are the DLR, serving East London, and Tramlink, serving South London:

Docklands Light Railway (DLR): The DLR was one of the first success stories of the light rail revival. Treated as part of the underground network (see below) with regard to fares, the DLR covers the whole Docklands area and beyond, from Tower Gateway to Beckton, Stratford to the Isle of Dogs, Greenwich and Lewisham. It's also an excellent way to see some of the most interesting parts of London, where old meets new in a redeveloped and regenerated landscape. London's docks were once the busiest port in the world; now they're home to many of London's workers and to industries such as the UK's major newspapers, which moved from Fleet Street to the Canary Wharf development in the '80s.

The DLR has three lines: the Red line running north-south, the Green line running from east to west, and the Beckton line starting at Poplar station and running 5mi (8km) to the east. Unusually for light rail systems, the DLR uses modern station designs with high level platforms. The trains are driver-less and remotely operated from the permanently-staffed control centre situated at Poplar. Facilities for disabled passengers are excellent, with all stations

DLR train

having wheelchair access. Most stations are also unmanned, although they're equipped with closed-circuit TV for security purposes. Like underground stations, all DLR platforms are equipped with screens that display trains' destinations and their estimated arrival times.

The DLR network links with both the main Overground railway system and the tube, and a number of extensions are under construction or proposed. The Woolwich Arsenal extension will link Woolwich, on the south of the river, with DLR King George V station in North Woolwich, and is due to open in February 2009. A new Stratford International (a Eurostar station) DLR extension is set to open in 2010 with new stations at Star Lane, Abbey Road, Stratford High Street and Stratford International, in time for the 2012 Olympics. There is also a proposed extension to Dagenham Dock.

Information about the DLR is available from DLR Customer Service (☎ 020-7363 9700 and via the internet (🖥 www.tfl.gov. uk/dlr), where there's a map of the network. **Tramlink:** Tramlink (formerly called Croydon Tramlink) is a light rail system connecting New Addington and Addington Village (on one line) and Beckenham Junction, Birbeck and Elmers End (on another line) – situated in the east of the borough of Croydon – with Wimbledon in the borough of Merton (via East and West Croydon and Mitcham Junction). New stops and extensions are planned or under proposed, including Hattington Road to Crystal Palace (proposed completion date 2013); Sutton to Wimbledon; Sutton to Tooting; Streatham to Purley; and Crystal Palace to Beckenham Junction/ Croydon. Further details and a map of the system (now operated by Transport for London) can be found on 🖥 www.tramlink. net.

A number of other light rail systems are in the pipeline or have been proposed and are in various stages of planning, including the following:

City Tram – A proposed light rail system, running from Battersea to Hackney via Vauxhall, Elephant & Castle, Borough High Street, Bishopsgate and Shoreditch;

Cross River Tram – A proposed light rail system, expected to operate from King's Cross and Camden via Euston, Holborn and Waterloo to Peckham and Brixton; the scheme is still being planned but is expected to be completed by 2016.

Hounslow Tram Project – A proposed tram system aimed at relieving increased traffic congestion caused by Heathrow airport's

Terminal 5 , running from the airport to Hammersmith and possibly to Kingston;

For further information see the Light Rail Transit Association website (🖥 www.lrta.org), which provides everything you could ever want to know about light rail systems.

RIVER FERRIES

One method of getting around London that's often overlooked is river transport. If your daily route to and from work follows the line of the River Thames, It's a pleasant (but relatively expensive) way to travel, although most services don't operate in winter. However, in order to have broader appear and be a real alternative to other forms of public transport, the service needs to be more extensive, operate more frequently, be cheaper and operate all year round.

London River Transport Services

London River Services/LRS (☎ 020-7941 4500, 🖥 www.tfl.gov.uk/modalpages/2648.aspx) is a subsidiary of Transport for London, which aims to develop river passenger transport by providing new river piers and boat services. To this end, LRS has recently acquired seven piers: Bankside, Embankment, Greenwich, Temple, Tower, Waterloo (formerly Festival) and Westminster. It's also building a new pier at Blackfriars. Other piers on the river are in private or local government ownership. Its river taxi services include those listed below. Travelcard (see page ??) holders qualify for a one-third discount off most fares and Freedom Pass holders (see page ??) receive a 50 per cent discount.

For further details and to download timetables see 🖥 www.tfl.gov.uk/gettingaround/1131/aspx.

- ◆ **Embankment-Woolwich:** Daily service between mid-April and late October stopping at Canary Wharf, Bankside and Tower. An adult single ticket costs between £2.50 and £6.50.

- ◆ **Hilton Docklands-Canary Wharf direct service:** Daily service between early April and late September. An adult single ticket costs between £2.50 and £4.50.

- ◆ **Putney-Blackfriars:** Daily service all year round, stopping at Chelsea Harbour,

Thames Barrier

Cadogan and Embankment. An adult single ticket costs between £5.25 and £7.50.

♦ **Westminster-St Katharine's:** Daily service between early April and late October, stopping at Festival Pier, Embankment, Bankside and London Bridge. An adult single ticket costs between £3.00 and £6.40.

♦ **Westminster-Greenwich:** Daily service between late March and early November, stopping at Waterloo and Tower. An adult single ticket costs between £6.40 and £7.50.

♦ **Westminster-Barrier Gardens:** Daily service between early April and late October, stopping at St Katharine's and Greenwich. An adult single ticket costs between £5.40 and £7.50.

Other River Services

Other river taxi services operated by independent companies include those listed below. There are also a number of other services intended for tourists.

♦ **Putney-Blackfriars:** A Monday to Friday service between early April and late October. An adult return ticket for the whole route costs £13.50 and a single £7.50 (Putney-Chelsea costs £3.75 single and £6.00 return). For further details and bookings, contact Thames Executive Charters (☎ 01342-322440, 💻 www. thamesexecutivecharters.com).

♦ **Richmond-Hampton Court:** A daily service between mid-May and late September (Mondays only late July to late August), stopping at Kingston. An adult return ticket for the whole route costs £8.00 and a single £6.50. For further details and bookings, contact Turks Launches (☎ 020-8546 2434, 💻 www. turks.co.uk).

♦ **Woolwich Ferry:** Daily free ferry across the Thames operated by the borough of Greenwich (☎ 020-8921 5965) from Woolwich and North Woolwich, linking the north and south circular roads across the Thames.

TAXIS

London is famous for its purpose-built taxis or 'black cabs', although other taxi services are also provided (see **Minicabs** below).

They cover a vast area of around 610mi² (1,580km²) stretching well into the outer suburbs and are obliged to undertake journeys of up to 12m (19km) from anywhere in Greater London (or 20 mi/32km from Heathrow Airport).

Although most of London's purpose-built cabs are black, hence the name 'black cabs', they also come in other colours (usually thanks to advertisers), including *Financial Times* pink and *Evening Standard* 'newsprint' pattern. However, they all have a yellow 'For Hire' sign at the front and a white numbered license plate on the back. In addition to 'standard' cabs, there are also 'business-class' cabs with luxurious seats, soundproofing and a telephone (and higher fares than standard cabs). Cabs are licensed by the Metropolitan Police and bear a license number plate and the driver (known as a cabby) wears a badge bearing his driver number.

London's black cabs (which now come in around 12 colours!) are officially called Hackney Carriages, a term that has no connection with the name of the London borough but derives from an old French word *haquenée*, meaning a type of horse that could be hired.

Although they are an expensive mode of transport (unless three or four people share the fare), a licensed cab driver won't usually take anything but the shortest route between two points (unless he does so to avoid traffic congestion, when he may tell you). Before obtaining his licence, a cab driver must undergo a long training period and pass a stiff exam on what's known as 'The Knowledge' – an encyclopaedic test of London's geography. They almost always know where a landmark or street is without referring to a map. You can also be pretty sure that you won't be cheated by a London cabbie (unlike many other countries).

Taxis have a strictly regulated scale of fares and charges (see 💻 www.tfl.gov.uk/ gettingaround/taxisandminicabs/taxis/1140.

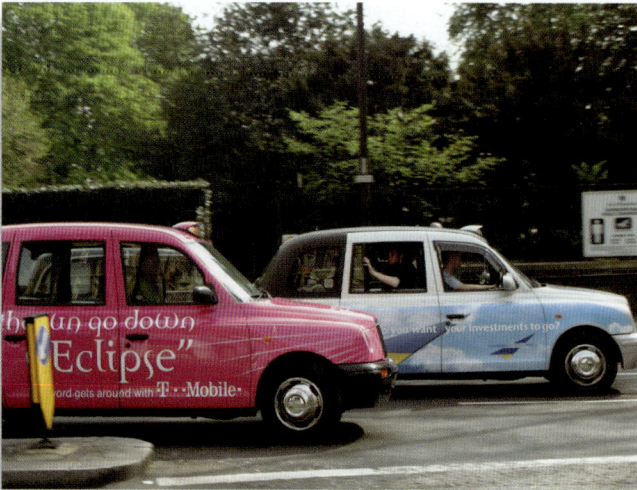

aol.com) or visit the London Black Taxis website (⌨ www.londonblacktaxis. net). Further information about London taxis is available from the Transport for London website (⌨ www. tfl.gov.uk/pco). If you have a complaint about a taxi driver, contact the Public Carriage Office (☎ 0800-300 7000, ✉ coms@pco.org.uk) with the cab's number and the driver's badge number.

Minicabs

As an alternative to a black cab, you can take a minicab, which, unlike a black cab,

aspx), to which it's customary to add a tip of around 10 per cent (although it isn't obligatory). Fares vary depending on the day and time, with a minimum charge of £2.20. Approximate fares are £4.40 to £8 for 1 mile (5 to 12 minutes), £6.80 to £10.60 for 2 miles (8 to 15 mins.), £11 to £18 for 4 miles (15 to 30 mins.) and £17 to £27 for 6 miles (20 to 40 mins.). The fare from London-Heathrow airport to central London costs between £40 and £70 and takes 30 to 60 mins. There are extra charges for journeys between 8-10pm Mondays to Fridays and at weekends, at night (between 10pm and 6am) and on public holidays.

The London boroughs and the Mayor of London finance a subsidised taxi service, called Taxicard, for Londoners with serious mobility impairments to whom public transport isn't usually accessible. The scheme varies slightly depending on the borough where you live, but generally members pay a flat fare of £1.50 per trip. For more information or an application form contact ☎ 020-7484 2929 or visit ⌨ www. taxicard.org.uk. Most drivers are pleased to help disabled passengers and wheelchairs can usually be stored inside the cab along with any luggage.

If you want to book a black cab, call Radio Taxicabs (☎ 020-7272 0272) or Dial-a-Cab (☎ 020-7253 5000), email the Licensed London Taxi Booking Service (✉ sttaxi@

cannot be hailed in the street and must be booked by phone. It's illegal for minicabs to ply for hire in the street like licensed taxis, although some do. Minicabs are cheaper than licensed taxis, but you have no guarantee that the driver will be reliable, honest or know his way around. There's no official training scheme for minicab drivers and there are dozens of companies available, so the best way to find a good one is to ask someone for a recommendation. The good news is that you may be able to negotiate the fee, which may be lower than for a black cab.

You must phone for a minicab in advance and agree the price to your destination before starting your journey, as they don't usually have meters. If you're female and worried about your safety late at night, you might wish to consider Ladycabs (☎ 020-7272 3300, ⌨ www.ladyminicabs. com), which employ women only.

In addition to taxi services, many taxi and minicab companies operate private hire (e.g. weddings or sightseeing), chauffeur and courier services, and provide contract and account services, e.g. to take children to and from school.

DRIVING IN LONDON

You need nerves of steel and the patience of Job to drive in central London – and it also helps to be a little crazy. Not only will it cost you dearly in terms of time, petrol (among the most expensive in Europe), insurance and headache pills, it's also virtually impossible to find affordable parking (see below) in central London. However, it isn't essential to own a car if you live in central London – in fact a car is a liability. If you commute into London from one of the outer boroughs, using public transport will almost certainly be faster than by car.

In common with most major cities, London is plagued by traffic congestion with many roads permanently jammed with traffic, making travel by car slow and frustrating. During rush hours, from around 7.30 to 9.30am and 4.30 to 6.30pm, Mondays to Fridays, traffic flow is painfully slow, particularly in central London, where the average traffic speed is around 10mph (it takes as long to cross London by car today as it did by horse and cart 200 years ago!).

⚠ Caution

An additional hazard of driving in London is having your car stolen. The number of cars stolen in London is among the highest (per capita) in Western Europe and if you live or work in central London and park your car there, there's a high risk of it being stolen or broken into.

Congestion on London's roads and the resulting air pollution has reached nightmare proportions in recent years. Getting anywhere by private car takes eons, and an accident at a busy intersection can cause long tailbacks or even gridlock for miles around. There has been a widespread debate about traffic congestion in recent years and various measures have been introduced to limit its effects, including the congestion charge (see below), special bus and cycle lanes, and punitive parking fees to discourage driving in the city.

There are a number of ways to reduce the cost of motoring, including car-sharing and short-term rentals via a car club. There are numerous such schemes in London

including Liftshare (🖳 www.liftshare.org) or Car Share (🖳 www.carshare.com), which has a directory of London car-share schemes. Another option is to join a car club, such as City Car Club (🖳 www.citycarclub.co.uk), Streetcar (🖳 www.streetcar.co.uk), Whizgo (🖳 www.whizgo.co.uk) or Zip Car (🖳 www.zipcar.com), where members can hire a car for an hour, day or as long as you like.

Speed Limits

UK speed limits are 30mph (48kph) in urban areas, 60mph (96kph) on unrestricted single-carriageway roads (outside towns), and 70mph (113kph) on motorways and dual-carriageways unless otherwise indicated.

Breakdown Assistance

If you break down anywhere in the UK, you can obtain roadside assistance, to keep the cost down (as locating and calling out a garage near to your breakdown can be hugely expensive!) it's advisable to be a member of a motoring organisation such as the Automobile Association/AA (☎ 0800-085 2721, 🖳 www.theaa.com), the Royal Automobile Club/RAC (☎ 08705-722 722, (🖳 www.rac.co.uk) and Green Flag National Breakdown (☎ 0845-246 1557, 🖳 www.greenflag.com). Membership costs between around £33 and £150 per year, depending on the level of cover required.

Congestion Charge

In an effort to reduce traffic and improve the traffic flow in central London, a 'congestion charge' was introduced in February 2003, which has proved successful, although unpopular with those unable or unwilling to forsake their cars, who must pay £8 per day to enter the restricted area. Transport for London claims that the congestion charge has reduced the number of cars entering central London by some 70,000 a day. Most vehicles (motorcycles, scooters and mopeds are exempt) must pay the fee to enter the Congestion Charge Zone between 7am and 6pm, Mondays to Fridays. There is no charge on weekends, local public holidays, designated non-charging days (e.g. between 25th December and January 1st) and between the hours of 6pm and 7am.

Congestion Charge Zone

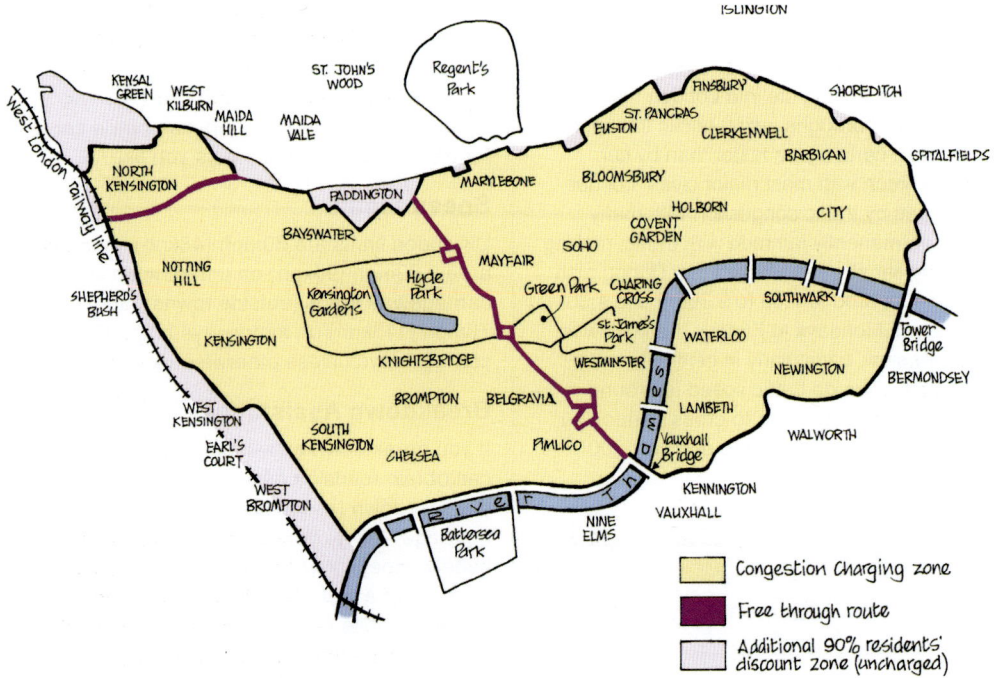

ISLINGTON

KENSAL GREEN, WEST KILBURN, MAIDA HILL, MAIDA VALE, ST. JOHN'S WOOD, Regent's Park, FINSBURY, SHOREDITCH, NORTH KENSINGTON, PADDINGTON, MARYLEBONE, BLOOMSBURY, ST. PANCRAS, EUSTON, CLERKENWELL, BARBICAN, SPITALFIELDS, West London railway line, BAYSWATER, HOLBORN, COVENT GARDEN, CITY, NOTTING HILL, Kensington Gardens, Hyde Park, MAYFAIR, SOHO, SHEPHERD'S BUSH, Green Park, CHARING CROSS, SOUTHWARK, KENSINGTON, Knightsbridge, St. James's Park, WATERLOO, Tower Bridge, WEST KENSINGTON, EARL'S COURT, BROMPTON, BELGRAVIA, WESTMINSTER, NEWINGTON, BERMONDSEY, SOUTH KENSINGTON, CHELSEA, PIMLICO, LAMBETH, WALWORTH, WEST BROMPTON, Vauxhall Bridge, River Thames, Battersea Park, NINE ELMS, VAUXHALL, KENNINGTON

Legend:
- Congestion Charging zone
- Free through route
- Additional 90% residents' discount zone (uncharged)

The charge zone (see map) is indicated by signs (signposts and road markings) showing a white C in a red circle. You can pay the charge by phone (☎ 0845-900 1234), text message (residents only), post (Congestion Charging, PO Box 2985, Coventry CV7 8ZR), online (💻 www.tfl.gov.uk/roadusers/congestioncharging/), at selected retail outlets and petrol stations, and at self-service machines.

You can pay up to 90 days in advance, for example you could pay for one day, three days, a week, two weeks, a month or a year. If you pay monthly or annually there are discounts available, and you can claim refunds in certain circumstances. You can pay the charge before or after the journey on the day of travel, but must pay by midnight. You can also pay the charge on the following day, but it increases to £10 and it can only be paid via the TfL website or call centre. If you travel on a Friday you have until midnight on the following Monday to pay.

⚠ Caution

If you fail to pay the charge by midnight on the following charging day you will be issued with a Penalty Charge Notice of £120, which is reduced to £60 is paid within 14 days but increases to £180 is not paid within 28 days.

CCTV cameras check whether your car remains in the charging area for longer than the period paid for, in which case you're liable to be fined. Certain vehicles and drivers are exempt from the congestion charge, including the disabled, vehicles using 'alternative' fuel (including electrically-powered vehicles and hybrid vehicles such as the Toyota Prius) and those with nine or more seats. Residents living within the congestion charging zone can register one private vehicle each and receive a 90 per cent discount, for which there's an annual £10 registration fee.

Plans to increase the congestion charge to £25 for vehicles with high emissions has been shelved following the election of a new mayor (Boris Johnston) in May 2008.

For more information, see 💻 www.tfl.gov.uk/roadusers/congestioncharging or 💻 www.tfl.gov.uk/assets/downloads/CC-brochure.pdf.

Parking

Parking in central London is at best difficult and expensive, and at worst impossible. Few central London properties have garages or off-road parking, although you may be fortunate to find a house or flat with a residents' parking scheme (see page ??). Very few employers provide workplace parking in central London and when they do it's usually for an elite few employees only. Parking meters are for temporary stays of up to two hours and private car parks (see below) are only for the seriously rich.

On-road parking (waiting) restrictions in the UK are indicated by yellow or red lines at the edge of roads, usually accompanied by a sign indicating when parking is prohibited, e.g. 'Mon-Sat 8am-6.30pm' or 'At any time'. If no days are indicated on the sign, restrictions are in force every day including public holidays and Sundays. Yellow signs indicate a continuous waiting prohibition and also detail times when parking is illegal, while blue signs indicate limited waiting periods. Loading restrictions for loading and unloading goods may be shown by one, two or three short yellow lines marked diagonally on the kerb and a sign.

Red lines along the side of a road indicate that it's a red route, which means that you aren't permitted to stop between the hours of 7am and 7pm (or as indicated by a sign) from Mondays to Fridays, except for loading or unloading. (Parking bays marked in red have similar restrictions.) A double red line indicates no stopping, loading or parking at any time. If you park illegally on a red route, your car will be towed away in the blink of an eye. For more information consult the *Highway Code*.

A summary of the road marking used to indicate parking and waiting restrictions in London and its suburbs is shown in the table below:

Road Marking Guide

Road Marking	Meaning
White zigzag line (e.g. by zebra crossing)	No parking or stopping at any time
Single red line*	No stopping between 7am and 7pm (or as indicated by a sign) from Mondays to Fridays, except for loading or unloading
Double red line*	No stopping, loading/unloading or parking at any time
Single yellow line	No parking between around 7am and 7pm on four or more days a week
Double yellow lines	No parking at most or all times (as indicated by signs)
Broken yellow line	Restricted parking (see sign for details)

* known as 'red routes'

In most towns there are public and private off-road car parks, indicated by a sign showing a white 'P' on a blue background. Parking in local authority (council) car parks usually costs from around 50p an hour. Parking in short-term (local authority) car parks may become progressively more expensive the longer you stay, although parking is generally cheaper (per hour) the longer you park, up to a maximum of around nine hours.

Information about parking regulations throughout London (including how to appeal against parking tickets) is available from the Parking Committee for London (New Zealand House, 80 Haymarket, SW1Y 4TE, ☎ 020-7747 4700, ✉ admin@pcfl.gov.uk).

Note that, unlike many other European countries, the UK doesn't have a cavalier attitude towards illegal parking and the authorities never turn a blind eye to it. In most parts of London you will get a parking ticket (or even have your car clamped or towed away) in a flash if you park illegally.

Car Parks

Parking in a private central London car park costs over £7 an hour or over £50 per day, although monthly and annual season tickets are usually available for commuters. National Car Parks (NCP), the UK's largest car park operator, has a number of 24-hour car parks in central London. A free map of NCP car parks can ordered by telephone (☎ 0870-606 7050) or an area can be searched using the Car Park Finder function on the NCP website (💻 www.ncp.co.uk).

In many areas there are short- and long-stay car parks. Fees may be reasonable for short stays of up to two or three hours, beyond which rates at short-stay car parks are much more expensive. Some car parks, such those operated by Westminster City Council, have introduced a scheme which links fees to demand, with fees starting as low as 20p an hour, although a six-hour stay can cost £25.

If you commute into London, it's cheaper to drive to a convenient railway station (where parking usually costs around £3 to £4 a day) and take a train into central London. Weekly, monthly and annual parking season tickets are usually available at rail and underground stations. Parking in car parks and at meters may be free on Sundays and public holidays, therefore check the notice before buying a ticket.

London's most expensive car park in 2008 was the NCP Pavilion Road multi-storey car park in Knightsbridge, where a six-hour stay costs £43.20!

Parking Meters

The maximum permitted parking period at meters varies from 30 minutes to two hours. Meter-feeding (i.e. returning to a meter to insert more money) is illegal, although many people do it. You're supposed to vacate a parking space when the meter time expires, even if it was under the maximum time allowed, and you shouldn't move to another meter in the same group. Meters usually accept a combination of coins and are usually in force from 7am until 7pm, Mondays to Fridays, and from 7am to 6pm on Saturdays (check the sign on a meter). Sundays are usually free, although meters at railway stations and airports may be in force 24-hours a day.

Don't park at meters that are suspended or out of service (as indicated), or your car can be clamped or towed away. If you remain at a meter beyond the excess charge period, you're liable for a fixed penalty (fine) handed out by a police officer or by London's infamous and much reviled traffic wardens. Parking meters are being phased out in many areas and replaced by pay-and-display parking areas.

Pay-And-Display

These are parking areas where you buy a ticket from a machine and display it behind your windscreen. It may have an adhesive backing which you can peel off and use to stick the ticket to the inside of your windscreen or a car window. Parking costs £4 an hour in most central London areas and machines usually accept only £1 coins. When you've inserted sufficient coins for the period required, press the button to receive your ticket. Pay-and-display parking areas usually operate from 7am until 7pm, excluding Sundays and public holidays.

Pay and display parking areas and tariffs for individual boroughs are shown on a map on borough websites (see www.london.gov.uk/london/links.jsp).

Parking Fines & Penalties

The fine for illegal parking depends on where you park. There's usually a fixed penalty ticket, e.g. £80 to £120 in the City of Westminster, for overstaying your parking period or parking illegally on a yellow line. Parking in a dangerous position or near a pedestrian crossing (i.e. on the zigzag lines or studded area) results in a higher fine, plus three penalty points on your driving licence. Penalties for non-payment or overstaying your time in a permitted parking area, e.g. at a parking meter or in a pay-and-display area, are set by the local authorities who issue parking tickets.

You shouldn't even think about parking illegally, e.g. in a residents' only area, on a double yellow line or at an expired meter. Illegal parking can result in your car being 'clamped', where a large metal device (a clamp) is fixed to one of its wheels, thus preventing you from driving it away. Thousands of cars are clamped each week in London and many more are towed away. If your car is towed and you don't collect it within a certain time, it can be sold at auction to pay

the fine and is likely to be sold for well below its market value – so don't park illegally before you go on a long holiday!

If your car is clamped, there will be a sticker on the windscreen – to prevent you inadvertently attempting to drive off and damaging your car and to instruct you how to get the clamp removed. You will need to pay a substantial fee (e.g. £70 to over £100, depending on whether it was clamped by the local authority or privately) before your car is released, plus the parking fine. If you've been clamped, you will have a lengthy wait even after you've paid the fine (some boroughs allow you to pay over the phone by credit card, while others insist that you pay in person). Companies say they will unclamp your car within four hours of receiving your payment, but they won't give you a precise time. If they do unclamp it and you don't remove the car quickly, e.g. within an hour, they're within their rights to clamp it again and the process starts all over again. If you don't arrange for release of the clamp within a certain period (e.g. four hours), it may be towed away.

If you find that your car is missing it has been either stolen or, more likely, towed away; call Trace Information (☎ 020-7747 4747) who will tell you whether it has been towed away and what to do to recover it. You must pay around £200 to get it released and a car pound won't release it until you've paid (in cash or by debit or credit card) and they charge a daily storage fee (e.g. £25-50) after the first 24 hours. You cannot be towed away from a pay-and-display area or a parking meter, unless the parking bay has been suspended.

If you believe that you've been treated unfairly there's a Parking Appeals Service (PO Box 1010, Sutton SM1 4SW, ☎ 020-7747 4700, 🖥 www. parkingandtrafficappeals.gov.uk). If you're in the habit of parking illegally, you can join the London Motoring Club (☎ 0845-601 8843, 🖥 www. londonmotoringclub.com), who will recover your car for you for an annual charge of £245 for up to two cars.

Note that the owners of private car parks or private land can clamp a car parked illegally and can set their own fees to remove clamps, which can run into hundreds of pounds.

It's inadvisable to park on private land, particularly where there's a 'clamping' sign, as private clamping is widespread throughout the UK. However, since May 2005 it has been a criminal offence to clamp a vehicle without a license from the Security Industry Authority (SIA), which has at least done away with some of the cowboys (now we have licensed cowboys).

Residents' Parking

Most central London residents – those whose postcode lies within a Controlled Parking Zone (CPZ) – can obtain a residents' parking permit which provides inexpensive local (on-street) parking in designated spaces. Any resident whose postcode lies within a CPZ can apply for a permit from his local council by providing proof of identity and residence (usually a Council Tax bill). Charges are set by local borough councils and vary considerably costing

from nothing (Hillingdon, first vehicle only) to up to £140 (Kensington & Chelsea, highest band) per year for the first car. The number of permits issued for a dwelling (usually up to three or four) also varies, as does the cost (a permit for a second car in Hammersmith & Fulham costs a whopping £450 per year). There are also special permits for disabled drivers who can park in reserved spaces, free at meters and in car parks, and ignore many on-road parking restrictions.

If you have a parking space, garage or even a plot of land, which isn't being used, you can rent it out on a daily, weekly or monthly basis. There are a number of websites that put space providers and users together, including 🖥 www.parkatmyhouse.com and 🖥 www.parklet.co.uk.

Car Hire

To hire (rent) a car you need at least a year's driving experience and must be aged at least 21 (or 25 with some hire companies). The major car hire (rental) companies in London include Avis (☎ 0844-581 0147, 🖥 www.avis.co.uk), Carrentals.com (☎ 0845-225 084539, 🖥 www.carrentals.co.uk), Europcar BCR (🖥 www.europcar.co.uk) and Hertz (🖥 www.hertz.co.uk). Shop around, as charges vary considerably – you may get a better deal from a small local company.

Disabled drivers can hire vehicles with hand controls from Hertz and other national car hire companies and specialist companies such as Wheelchair Travel (☎ 01483-233640, 🖥 www.wheelchair-travel.co.uk) based in Guildford (Surrey), 32mi (51km) south of London.

Breakdown Assistance

If you break down anywhere in the UK, you can obtain emergency roadside assistance from a garage or motoring organisation. However, to reduce the cost down it's advisable to a join a motoring organisation such as the Automobile Association/AA (☎ 0800-085 2721, 🖥 www.theaa.com), the Royal Automobile Club/RAC (☎ 08705-722 722, (🖥 www.rac.co.uk) or Green Flag National Breakdown (☎ 0845-246 1557, 🖥 www.greenflag.com). Membership costs between around £33 and £150 per year, depending on the level of cover required.

CYCLING

Short of walking, cycling is the cheapest way to get around central London and one of the fastest. It's also the most dangerous! If the traffic doesn't flatten you first, any positive effect on your physical fitness may be offset by the adverse effects of air pollution.

> ⚠ **Caution**
>
> When cycling in London, always wear a smog mask with a proper air filter as well as a safety helmet, and don't try it at all unless you and your children are capable and experienced cyclists.

Carrying children on the back of a bike in London's heavy traffic isn't advisable, but if you must do so, ensure that they're also fitted with a helmet and mask and are securely strapped into an approved child seat.

When you park your bicycle, make sure that you lock the frame to an immovable object or it's unlikely to be there when you return, although bicycles may be removed if you attach them to railings or street 'furniture'. There are a few cycle parking stands near Whitehall and Parliament Square and some multi-storey car parks in the City of London provide free cycle parking, which can potentially offer greater security than on-street parking. The London cycle guides (see below) list cycle parking facilities at stations.

All this is discouraging for cycling enthusiasts in London, who need to head out to the suburbs to enjoy cycling in relative safety. Unfortunately, many modes of public transport won't carry bicycles. Restrictions on suburban railways vary, so phone to check before attempting to take your bike on a train. The DLR has a blanket ban on bikes and only four tube lines (the District, Circle, Metropolitan and Hammersmith & City) allow them, and then only outside peak hours. Other tube lines allow them on Overground sections only, i.e. those in the outer suburbs.

However, things may be about to change. For over 25 years the London Cycling Campaign/LCC (2 Newhams Row, SE1 3UZ, ☎ 020-7234 9310, 🖳 www.lcc.org.uk) has been attempting to promote the rights of cyclists in London. The crisis in London's transport system is widely acknowledged and the London boroughs are setting up a network of 1,200mi (1,931km) of cycle routes throughout the capital, with the help of government funding. Routes (marked by blue signs showing a bicycle) bypass the major thoroughfares, usually taking fairly direct routes through residential areas that are unsuitable for heavy traffic. Companies are beginning to encourage employees to cycle to work and there are increased facilities for cycle parking at workplaces and elsewhere.

Annual membership of the LCC costs £32 (£14 for students, youths, the unemployed and senior citizens, £55 for families) and includes a subscription to the bi-monthly magazine, *London Cyclist*. The London Cycling Campaign publishes a number of information booklets, most of which can be downloaded from their website.

If you want to get a taste of what cycling in London is like, you can hire a bike for around £18 per day or £48 per week from a number of sites in central London (a deposit is necessary). Try the London Bicycle Tour Company on the South Bank (1a Gabriel's Wharf, 56 Upper Ground, London SE1 9PP, ☎ 020-7928 6838, 🖳 www.londonbicycle.com), which also organises cycle tours.

A series of 14 free cycle guides covering the whole of Greater London are produced by TfL using route information provided by the London Cycling Campaign. They are designed to assist Londoners to choose cycling as their mode of transport and are available from TfL (☎ 020-7222 1234, 🖳 www.tfl.gov.uk/modalpages/2663.aspx – and click on 'Cycle guides').

Lorry drivers in London are being given free safety mirrors (with Fresnel lenses) to help them spot cyclists in their 'blind spot', especially when turning left. Collisions with goods vehicles account for over half of all cycle deaths on London roads.

MOPEDS, SCOOTERS & MOTORCYCLES

You can also use a moped, scooter or motorbike to get around London, which are exempt from the congestion charge (see page ??) and certainly quicker than using a car and most public transport. However, unlike most other major European cities, mopeds and scooters aren't very popular with Londoners, even among those who are too young to obtain a car license. A proposal by the mayor in 2008 to allow motorcycles to use bus lanes was strongly opposed by cyclists, who believe it would put lives at risk.

There are designated motorcycle and bicycle parking bays throughout London, where parking bays may be marked 'Solo Motorcycles' with the area delimited by broken white lines. Motorcycle parking in council-owned, multi-storey car parks is often permitted free of charge, provided motorcycles are parked within the designated parking bays. You should, however, read the notice on the ticket machines to check whether payment is necessary.

The Motorcycle Parking website (🖳 www.motorcycleparking.com) provides comprehensive information about parking in London.

4.
SOMEWHERE TO LIVE

There are over 3m dwellings in London and some 20,000 new homes are built each year, which makes choosing where to live a difficult task, particularly as in most areas there's a wealth of accommodation to rent and buy, in every price range. However, prices in central London are astronomical and finding affordable property is difficult. Unless you're wealthy, you'll invariably have to compromise, for example, you'll probably need to pay more than you'd planned, buy or rent a smaller home than you'd like or live in a less desirable area. You may also need to live further from the centre and possibly further away from public transport and other amenities than you'd wish.

Before choosing somewhere to live it's recommended to check the present and planned public transport services, particularly if you'll be commuting to a job in central London or one of its suburbs. A planned improvement in local public transport – such as a new tube or rail extension – will not only make your journey easier or quicker but will also dramatically increase the value of your property.

Most Londoners don't live in central London but in the numerous suburbs, where life's still largely community-based. Many people who work in London commute into the city from the surrounding (home) counties, with thousands travelling from even further afield. Wherever you are in the suburbs, you're never far from a traditional 'parade' of shops selling the essentials of life, and all areas provide amenities such as schools, health and leisure facilities.

Four out of five people in the UK live in houses rather than flats (apartments) and most Britons aren't keen on apartment living or townhouses and want their own detached houses with a garden and garage. Nevertheless, the vast majority of Londoners live in flats. Much of London's suburbia is characterised by row upon row of brick terraced houses, mainly built in Victorian times to provide housing for the rapidly growing population, or tree-lined avenues of endless semi-detached properties dating from the '20s and '30s. The price of this kind of suburban home varies considerably with the area, although prices in London are generally much higher than in other parts of the UK. As in all large cities, there's a huge variation in the cost of housing in the various boroughs (see pages 325 & 326), as well as within boroughs.

Despite the astronomical cost of property, renting isn't as common in the UK as it is in many other European countries, and some 70 per cent of Britons own their own homes – one of the highest figures in Europe. The average age of first-time buyers is increasing and is now over 30, although it's still one of the lowest in the world. The 2007-08 credit crunch has made lenders more cautious about who they lend to and the amounts they lend and has caused them to ask for larger deposits, e.g. 15 or 20 per cent.

A number of books are published specifically for house hunters in London, including our sister publications *Buying, Selling & Letting Property* and *Where to Live in London* (Survival Books).

HOUSING MARKET

In summer 2008, the UK's housing market was described as being 'in crisis'. After over a decade of rapidly rising prices (in some areas, notably parts of central London, property tripled in value over this period), some commentators were predicting a slump, though others were talking in terms of an 'adjustment' in prices. Market analysts believe that prices are likely to fall by 10 per cent in 2008 and by up to a 30 per cent in the next few years, before recovering.

Such 'boom and bust cycles' are quite regular in the UK. For example, the boom years of the late '80s (when property values were doubling every few years in some areas) ended in a disastrous collapse during the recession of the early '90s, when mortgage interest rates soared to over 15 per cent and many people lost their homes or were left with negative equity (where the amount owed on their mortgage exceeded the value of their property). Negative equity was widespread in London and the south-east, where over 25 per cent of owners were affected in some areas.

The shock of falling home values hit the British particularly hard, as they traditionally view buying property as an investment rather than a home for life (as is normal in most of the rest of Europe). It took almost ten years for house prices to return to their late '80s level and there followed a strong recovery in property values in most regions.

In 2006, prices were still rising in all parts of London: the cost of buying in Kensington & Chelsea shot up by 16 per cent, for example. However, 2007 saw the 'sub-prime crisis' in the US, in which banks began to write off bad debts on home loans made to people with insufficient income to repay them ('sub-prime' candidates). Much of this debt was 'farmed out' to foreign banks, including those in the UK, thereby exporting the problem.

Housing Schemes

When London's population was growing at a rate of over 40,000 per year, the government planned to create four new 'cities' in the south-east of England: one near Milton Keynes to the north, one near Ashford to the south-east, one along the Thames Estuary (see **Thames Gateway** below) and one along the M11 corridor. Parts of these developments are already under way, principally (as far as Greater London is concerned) in the Royal Docks, which is within both the M11 and Thames Gateway areas, and at Stratford (see **Newham** on page 54).

Such schemes involve, and require, additions or extensions to London's transport network and, once these are in place (which is by no means a foregone conclusion), property prices tend to rise dramatically, as has happened in the case of the recent Jubilee Line and DLR extensions.

⚠ Caution

Like all plans, housing schemes are subject to change and even cancellation, so beware of buying a property on the assumption that a scheme will go ahead and cause local prices to rise.

Thames Gateway

The Thames Gateway is the name given to an ambitious East London regeneration and development programme – the largest such scheme in Europe – which aims to create between 60,000 and 200,000 (the government keeps changing its mind) 'affordable' homes and up to 150,000 jobs by 2015 along either side of the Thames between the Docklands and Thurrock (north of the river) and Dartford (south of the river). The scheme is being co-ordinated by the Thames Gateway London Partnership, an alliance of 13 local authorities, the Universities of East London and Greenwich, and the London Development Agency. An integral part of the project is the improvement of transport links in the area, including three new river crossings and stops on the new Channel Tunnel Rail Link to St Pancras (see page 87).

Property Prices

Property prices in London are the highest in the UK and among the highest in Europe and the world. For the price of a two-bedroom flat in London you can buy a substantial three- or four-bedroom detached house almost anywhere else in the country. Nevertheless, buyers have had to move fast in recent years, as good properties at realistic prices were being snapped up as soon as they came onto the market. Not surprisingly, first-time buyers are finding it hard to get their foot on the property ladder.

When property is advertised in the UK, the number of bedrooms and bathrooms is given and possibly other rooms such as a dining room, lounge (living/sitting room), study, breakfast room, drawing room, library, playroom, utility, pantry, cloakroom, cellar and conservatory. More expensive properties often simply list the number of reception rooms (e.g. lounge, dining room and study).

The total living area in square feet or square metres is almost never stated in advertisements, although knowing the size of a house (**and** the size you want) can save you time viewing houses that are too small – for many people the overall size is much more important than the number of bedrooms. The average size of new homes in inner London is: one-bedroom flat ($650ft^2$/$60m^2$), two-bedroom flat ($850ft^2$/$80m^2$), three-bedroom flat ($1,300ft^2$/$120m^2$), four-bedroom house ($2,000$-$2,500ft^2$/185-$230m^2$) and five-bedroom house ($3,000$-$3,500ft^2$/280-$325m^2$).

The table in **Appendix F** shows the average property prices in mid-2008 in 32 of the 33 London boroughs (the Land Registry has no figures for the City of London, where there are few dwellings). Note, however, that prices can vary by up to 400 per cent within some boroughs.

Apart from the cost, one of the most important criteria for many families when buying a home is the quality of local schools. Foxton, London's largest chain of real estate agents, has a useful facility on their website (💻 www.foxtons.co.uk/education/kensington-and-chelsea – click on the borough at the right of the screen) which shows the percentage of pupils attaining level 4 or above in the Key Stage 2 examination (English, Maths and Science) at primary schools and the percentage of pupils gaining five or more GCSEs with Grades A* to C at secondary schools, plus a list of sixth form colleges. You can then search for properties for sale and rent in the vicinity of a particular school.

LONDON HOMES

British homes are usually built to high structural standards and, whether you buy a new or an old home, it will usually be sturdy. There are stringent regulations in most areas regarding the style and design of new homes and the restoration of old (listed) buildings. The UK offers a vast choice of properties (few countries have such a variety of housing), including some of the most luxurious and expensive homes in the world. At the bottom end of the market properties are likely to be terraced or semi-detached houses, whereas more expensive homes are detached and are built on a half- or one-acre (2,000-4,000m²) plot.

In recent years Britons have taken to apartment living in London and other cities (often more out of necessity than choice), many of them more or less tasteful conversions of rambling old detached homes and even hospitals, schools, churches, mills, warehouses, offices and factories. 'Loft' conversions (e.g. of warehouses in the docks areas) are popular due to their high ceilings and general spaciousness. Barn conversions are also popular (and expensive), although rare due to the lack of barns (you can cheat and have a 'barn' home built from new).

The British usually prefer older homes with 'charm and character' to modern homes, although a common compromise is a new home with pseudo-period features such as wooden beams and open fireplaces. Although new properties may be lacking in character, they're usually well equipped with modern conveniences and services, which cannot be taken for granted in older properties. Standard fixtures and fittings in modern houses are more comprehensive and generally of better quality than those found in old houses. For example, central heating, double or triple glazing and efficient insulation are standard in new houses – and essential in the UK's climate.

Central heating may be gas-fired (the most common) or oil-fired, or a home may have electric night-storage heaters. Swimming pools are also rare and, if you buy a house with one,

you're unlikely to be able to use it for more than a few weeks a year unless you spend a fortune on heating or it's an indoor pool.

> Many houses don't have basements or utility rooms, so washing machines (usually provided) and dryers are located in the kitchen.

Some houses have lofts and garages that are often used for storage. An airing cupboard (linen closet) is common and usually contains the hot water boiler. Often shower attachments are run from a bath and don't have a separate power pump, which means that the water trickles out. Bathrooms occasionally contain a bidet, although they aren't common in the UK. In general, British plumbing is better than in many other countries, although Americans won't be impressed. Fitted wardrobes in bedrooms are rare in older homes and curtain rails aren't provided unless they're built-in.

Types of Home

The most common kinds of home in the UK are described below. Most of these can obviously be either 'old' or 'new' (see above).

♦ **Bungalow** – a single-storey detached or semi-detached house. Popular with the elderly, as they have no stairs;

♦ **Cottage** – traditionally a pretty little house in the country, perhaps with a thatched roof, but the term is often used nowadays to describe almost any small home except a flat. May be detached or terraced.

♦ **Detached house** – a house that stands alone, usually with its own garden (possibly front and rear) and garage;

♦ **Flat** – an apartment, usually on one floor, which may be in a block (apartment building), possibly high-rise, or in a large converted house (see below);

♦ **Houseboat** – available on various London waterways, including the Regent's Canal and the Thames, but moorings cost from around £2,000 per year;

● **Maisonette** – a cross between a flat and a semi-detached house, usually on two floors with its own outside entrance;

● **Mews house** – a house converted from stables or servants' lodgings (usually 17th to 19th century), usually on a quiet (often cobbled) side street, and the central London equivalent of a cottage. Quite common but expensive.

● **Mobile home** – a pre-fabricated timber-framed home that can be moved to a new site, although most are permanently located on a 'home park'. Available in some London suburbs.

● **Period property** – a property built before 1911 and named after the period in which it was built, e.g. Georgian;

In the UK, the term 'old', when applied to property, usually means pre-1940, while homes built before 1914 are generally referred to as 'period homes' and their age identified by reference to the monarch reigning at the time they were built, e.g. Georgian (1714-1830), William & Mary (1830-1837), Victorian (1837-1901) or Edwardian (1901-1910). In the case of Victorian properties, these are sometimes qualified as early, mid or late Victorian.

● **Semi-detached house** – a detached building comprising two separate homes joined by a common wall;

● **Stately home** – a grand country mansion or estate, usually a few centuries old and often reasonably priced, as the cost of maintenance is astronomical;

● **Terraced house** – one of several houses built in a row, usually two to five storeys high and often Victorian (and small). End-of-terrace houses are highly sought after.

● **Townhouse** – similar to a terraced house but more modern and usually with just two storeys, often with an integral garage.

Flats

New flats are invariably lavishly appointed, and the best are beautifully designed and fitted, as developers vie with each other to produce the most alluring interiors. These can include bespoke kitchens complete with top quality appliances; en suite bathrooms with separate showers; fitted carpets; built-in wardrobes; ceramic floors in kitchens and bathrooms; and telephone and TV points (including cable) in all rooms. Luxury flats often have a central control panel from where you can control the temperature, lighting, security, music system and TVs. Many luxury flats and houses also have air-conditioning, which may be called comfort cooling, air cooling or, more impressively, a climate-controlled refrigerated air system.

Modern apartment developments often have a leisure complex with a swimming pool, gymnasium, sauna and Jacuzzi, and tennis courts, plus secure parking and landscaped gardens. The price of luxury flats often includes a year's free membership of a health club.

> ### ▲ Caution
>
> Bear in mind, however, that amenities such as a health club or gymnasium don't come cheap and there are often high service charges.

Some developments, particularly retirement developments, also have an in-house medical centre, business centre, private meeting rooms for residents' exclusive use, a restaurant and a bar. Security is a key feature of many developments, which may have a 24-hour caretaker/concierge, CCTV surveillance and a security entry system with entry phones – some even have a camera/video entry system that takes a photo/video of callers who press your door button when you aren't at home!

Houses

The vast majority (over 80 per cent) of people in the UK live in houses rather than flats, although these are less common the nearer you are to the centre of London.

Most new homes are made of brick but some are made of pre-fabricated panels with foam insulation bolted together, which increases fuel efficiency and sound insulation. Although rare, stone (usually from a local source) is in vogue again as a building material for new homes.

In some areas, new homes must be styled to blend in with existing homes and many builders offer a number of 'mock' period styles, possibly using recycled materials (e.g. bricks, tiles, oak beams and fireplaces) from old properties, thus offering the best of both worlds for those who cannot decide between a period home and a maintenance-free new home. Some developers even create new houses in the style of barn conversions to keep up with demand. Homes with thatched roofs have always been popular and specialist builders offer thatched homes of almost any size – at a price!

New houses often contain a high level of 'luxury' features, depending on individual developments and (of course) the price. Some are part of purpose-built developments, which offer a range of sports facilities such as a golf course, swimming pool, tennis and squash courts, a gymnasium or fitness club, and even a bar and restaurant.

In the UK, the term 'old', when applied to property, usually means pre-1940, while homes built before 1911 are generally referred to as 'period homes' (see above). If you want a house with abundant charm and character (perhaps for renovation or conversion), outbuildings or a large plot, you must usually buy an old property. When buying a period building, you aren't just buying a home but a piece of history, part of the UK's cultural heritage, and a work of art that represents architects' and artisans' skills of a bygone age.

Further Information

Home and property magazines (see **Appendix B**) contain a wealth of information about new homes, including a list of developments throughout the country, and numerous advertisements from builders and developers. Daily newspapers are a good source of information about the property market in general, as well as specific areas and developments – particularly the quality Saturday and Sunday newspapers such as The Times and The Daily Telegraph (Saturday edition) and *The Sunday Times* and *The Sunday Telegraph*.

Many home and property exhibitions are held throughout the UK. The main London shows are the Ideal Home Show, staged in March/April at the Earls Court Exhibition Centre in Kensington & Chelsea, the 'House & Garden Fair' (June) at the Olympia Exhibition Centre (also in Kensington & Chelsea) and the Homebuyer Show (March) in Newham.

You can also find copious information and search for a new home, e.g. on the internet with Your New Home (💻 www.yournewhome.co.uk), new-homes.co.uk (💻 www.new-homes.co.uk), and Smart New Homes (💻 www.smartnewhomes.co.uk). See also **Appendix C**.

BUYING PROPERTY

Buying a house or flat in the UK has traditionally been an excellent long-term investment, depending, of course, on how long you're planning to stay in London. If you're staying for a short period only – say less than two years – you may be better off renting (see page 126). If you're planning to stay for longer than two years, have a secure job and can afford to buy, then you should probably do so, particularly as repaying a mortgage is generally no more expensive than renting and you could make a sizeable profit over the long term. For information about mortgages, see page 158.

Most houses in the UK, whether detached, semi-detached, terraced or townhouses, are owned freehold, i.e. there are no restrictions on the use of the property (other than those imposed by the law of the land). However, flats aren't usually owned outright under a system of co-ownership, as in many other countries, but are bought 'leasehold', with a lease of, for example, 99 to 999 years.

Flats

Flats (apartments) are common in central London, where houses are rare and prohibitively expensive. Most flats in London are sold leasehold and a property can change hands several times during the life of a lease, although when the lease expires, the property reverts to the original owner (the freeholder).

When buying a flat, the most important consideration is the length of the lease; if it has less than around 50 years to run, you'll have difficulty obtaining a mortgage. Most experts consider 75 years to be the minimum lease you should consider.

In an older development, you should check whether access to private grounds and a parking space are included in the lease. Garages and parking spaces may need to be purchased separately.

If you're buying a resale property, check the price paid for similar properties in the same area or development in recent months, but bear in mind that the price you pay may have more to do with the seller's circumstances than the price fetched by other properties. Find out how many properties are for sale in an old development; if there are many on offer you should investigate why, as there could be management or structural problems. If you're still keen to buy, you can use any negative aspects to drive a hard bargain.

Before buying a flat, it's wise to ask the current owners about the development or block. For example, do they like living there, what are the charges and restrictions, how noisy are other residents, are the recreational facilities easy to access, would they buy there again (why or why not?), and, most importantly, is the development well managed?

You may also wish to check on your prospective neighbours. A flat that has other flats above and below it is generally more noisy than a ground or top floor flat. If you're planning to buy a flat above the ground floor, you may wish to ensure that the building has a lift. Ground or garden level flats (and penthouses) are more susceptible to burglary and an insurance company may insist on extra security before they will insure a property. Note that upper floor flats are both colder in winter and warmer in summer, and may incur extra charges for the use of lifts. Flats under the roof may also have temperature control problems (hot in summer, cold in winter), although they enjoy better views.

Apartment prices in London, where many flats are purchased by investors, have risen considerably in recent years (see the table in **Appendix F**), although in mid-2008 prices were static or falling. In 2008, some areas had an over-supply of small, new-build flats which weren't selling, and many lenders were willing to lend a maximum of only 75 per cent or less on them. Nevertheless, London flats are generally a good long-term investment (provided, of course, you buy at a competitive price) and have good letting potential, always assuming that the rental market doesn't become saturated. Luxury flats and penthouses tend to sell like hot cakes, although few people can afford the astronomical prices (often millions of pounds).

Service Charges

Flat owners pay service charges for the upkeep of communal areas and for communal services. Charges are calculated according to each owner's share of the development. Ground floor owners don't usually pay for lifts and the amount that other owners pay depends on the floor (those on the top floors generally pay the most because they use the lifts most). Service charges cover such things as road and path cleaning; garden maintenance; cleaning, decoration and maintenance of buildings; a caretaker or concierge; communal lighting in buildings and grounds; water supply (e.g. for a swimming pool and gardens); insurance; administration; and fees for communal facilities such as a health club or gymnasium. Service charges may also include heating and hot water. Building insurance is provided by the freeholder, but you're usually required to have third party insurance for damage you may cause to other flats, e.g. through a flood or fire. Always check the level of service charges before buying a flat in a block or development.

If you're buying a flat from the previous owner, ask to see a copy of the service charges for previous years, as owners may be 'economical with the truth' when stating service charges, particularly if they're high. Charges vary considerably and can be high (many thousands of pounds a year) for luxury developments with a high level of amenities such as a health club and swimming pool. They may also increase annually. An apartment block with a resident caretaker will have higher charges than one without, although it's preferable to buy in a block with a caretaker. If a management company is employed to manage and maintain an apartment block, the service charges will be higher but the building will also usually be maintained better. High charges aren't necessarily a negative point (assuming you can afford them), provided you receive value and the development is well managed and maintained.

Provisional charges are usually billed monthly or bi-annually and adjusted at the end of the year when the actual expenditure is known and the annual accounts have been finalised – which can come as a nasty shock!

Disputes over service charges can be acrimonious, especially in old buildings. Under the 1996 Housing Act, leaseholders can take disputes over service charges or bad management to a Leasehold Valuation Tribunal (LVT), with a panel comprising a solicitor, a valuer and a third experienced person; such disputes are no longer decided by the courts. Many landlords have increased their service charges significantly in recent years, which often bear little or no relationship to actual costs, and many people have been hit by high charges for major repairs (see below). It's essential when buying a leasehold property to take legal advice and have the lease checked by a solicitor.

Maintenance & Repairs

Most developments have a sink or reserve fund to pay for major expenses, which is funded from general service charges, but it may be inadequate. You should check; otherwise, you may be charged an additional fee for 'exceptional' maintenance or repairs. You should check the condition of the common areas (including all amenities) in an old development and whether any major maintenance or capital expense is planned for which you could be assessed. Beware of 'bargain' flats in buildings requiring a lot of maintenance work or refurbishment. Many old buildings (e.g. Georgian) require a lot of upkeep, particularly roofs, although good preventive maintenance helps keep them in good condition.

Ground Rent

Ground rent is a nominal rent (e.g. £100 a year) for the land on which a flat or apartment block is built. The lease should indicate whether the ground rent is fixed or whether it can be reviewed after a certain period.

Covenants & Restrictions

Covenants are legally binding obligations on the freeholder and leaseholder to do or refrain from doing certain things, while restrictions are regulations governing how leaseholders are required to behave. Restrictions usually apply to such things as noise levels; the keeping of pets; sub-letting; exterior decoration and plants (e.g. the placement of shrubs); rubbish disposal; the use of health clubs and other recreational facilities; parking; business or professional use; and the hanging of laundry. Check the regulations and discuss any restrictions that you're unsure about with other residents. Permanent residents should avoid buying in a development with a high percentage of rental units, i.e. units that aren't owner-occupied, although you may have little choice in London.

Renewing & Buying

A lease may be renewable (this should be specified in the leasehold agreement). It's sometimes possible for lessees to buy the freehold of their flats and they may have a statutory right of first refusal if the landlord plans to sell.

The Leasehold Reform, Housing and Urban Development Act, 1993 gives certain lessees the right to acquire the freehold or a lease for a further 90 years. This right is available to tenants who have lived in a property for the preceding three years or three of the previous ten years, when the original lease was for 21 years or longer and the ground rent is above a certain amount. For information contact the Leasehold Advisory Service (LEASE), 31 Worship Street, London EC2A 2DX (☎ 020-7374 5380, 🖥 www. lease-advice.org), which provides free advice and maintains lists of valuers and solicitors specialising in leasehold properties.

Houses

The vast majority (over 80 per cent) of people in the UK live in houses rather than flats, although these are less common the nearer you are to the centre of London. Houses are also generally better value than flats and may be a better investment. If you decide to buy a house, your first decision will be whether to buy a new or an old home.

New Houses

The quality of new buildings in the UK is strictly regulated and they must conform to stringent building regulations and energy efficiency standards. Nevertheless, the quality of new houses is extremely variable and some developments in London suffer from poor quality, as they're built for the investment (letting) market and aren't suitable for owner-occupiers. They are usually smaller overall than old homes,

with much smaller rooms. Your best insurance when buying a new house is the reputation of the builder and it pays to buy from a long-established builder with a reputation for quality.

New houses often contain a high level of 'luxury' features, depending on individual developments and (of course) the price. You can also have a variety of 'custom' extras included at additional cost. An added advantage is that the cost of extras can be included in your mortgage, although it's important to check that they offer good value (many developers overcharge on extras, which is a common cause of complaints).

Some new houses built on private estates have a residents' association or management committee responsible for the upkeep of roads, gardens, trees, plants, lighting, etc., for which owners pay an annual fee. There are usually also a number of restrictive covenants

that owners must adhere to (see above). The cost of land is usually included when buying a detached house on its own plot, unless you agree a separate contract for the land and the house.

Warranty: Most new properties are covered by the Buildmark ten-year warranty of the National House Building Council (NHBC, ☎ 01494-735363, 🖳 www.nhbc.co.uk) or the Zurich Municipal Building Guarantee (☎ 01702-719 361, 🖳 www.zurich.co.uk/buildingguarantee). Most lenders will refuse to lend against a new house without a warranty. The NHBC warranty covers the owner for claims of up to £10,000 against the builder's failure to complete the house, for the loss of a deposit (up to 10 per cent of the agreed price) or any expenses incurred in completing building work.

Buying off Plan: When buying a new property in a development, you're usually obliged to buy it 'off plan', i.e. before it's built. In fact, if a development is finished and largely unsold, particularly in a popular area, you should beware as it usually means that there's something wrong with it that the locals know about! In recent years people have queued overnight to buy properties in new developments. In a rising market it's possible to make a good profit buying off plan; it isn't uncommon for a property to increase by 20-30 per cent between the time when you pay the deposit and when the property is completed a year or two later (when many people sell – termed 'flipping').

Some analysts advise buyers against buying off plan, which is undoubtedly risky. It may be better to wait until a property is almost complete before buying, or you could end up paying more than a property is worth or the developer could even go bust. You must put down at least 10 per cent of the price as a deposit and pay over £500 in legal fees to exchange contracts, which obliges you to go through with the purchase. If the developer goes bust, you may have to wait years for a property to be completed and there's no guarantee that it will be finished to the original specifications. Added to which you could lose your loan if bad publicity has an adverse effect on the market value of the property.

> **☑ SURVIVAL TIP**
>
> When buying off plan, choose a large developer or one who is selling different types of property in different areas, as he is better placed to weather a storm.

Old Houses

If you want a property with abundant charm and character, a building for renovation or conversion, outbuildings or a large plot, you must usually buy an old property. Old houses may also provide better value than new houses, although you must check their quality and condition carefully. As with most things in life, you generally get what you pay for and never buy a 'bargain' without fully investigating the renovation costs, which are invariably higher than you imagined or planned! Some old properties even lack basic services such as electricity, a reliable water supply and sanitation. If you're planning to buy a property that needs renovation, have a full structural survey and obtain an accurate estimate of the costs before buying it! While you may get more for your money when buying an old home, the downside is that they require much more maintenance and upkeep than new homes, and heating costs can be high.

For those who can afford them, at the top end of the scale there's a number of mansions available, even in central London, and the odd castle or stately home might come on the market in the outer reaches of the outer boroughs. But many large houses and mansions in and around London have been converted into luxury apartments and townhouses in recent years.

Council Tax

Council tax is a local tax on residents, levied by local councils to pay for such things as education, police, roads, waste disposal, libraries and community services. Each council fixes its own tax rate, based on the number of residents and how much money they need to finance their services, so charges vary considerably from borough to borough, although boroughs with a predominantly deal than private buyers (which, if true, could save you the cost of their fees). Some specialise in finding exceptional residences costing upwards of £1m.

Consultants can usually help and advise with all aspects of home purchase and may conduct negotiations on your behalf, organise finance (including bridging loans), arrange surveys and insurance, organise your removal to the UK and even arrange quarantine for your pets (see page 276). Most agents also provide a comprehensive information package for a chosen area, including details of employment prospects, health services (e.g. local hospitals), local schools (state and private), shopping facilities, public transport, sports and social facilities, communications, and amenities and services.

Relocation consultants charge a retainer of between £300 and £1,000, payable in advance, and, if they find you a suitable property, a fee of 1.25 to 2 per cent of the purchase price. The retainer is deducted from the fee when a property is purchased, but if no deal is done it's usually non-returnable. To find a consultant, contact the Association of Relocation Professionals (☎ 08700-737475, 🖳 www.arp.com) or look in the Yellow Pages under 'Relocation Agents'.

affluent population don't necessarily charge higher taxes than 'poor' boroughs; in fact, the opposite is often the case. In most boroughs you can expect to pay between £2,000 and £2,500 per year for a property worth over £320,000 – around £400 less for a property worth between £160,000 and £320,000. For exact council tax charges in each borough, see the table in **Appendix F**.

Relocation Consultants

If you know what sort of property you want, how much you wish to pay and where you want to buy or rent, but don't have the time to spend looking, e.g. you live abroad, you can engage a relocation consultant or property search company to find a home for you. This can save you considerable time, trouble and money, particularly if you have particular or unusual requirements. Many relocation consultants act as buying agents, particularly for overseas buyers, and claim they can negotiate a better

Estate Agents

Most property in the UK is bought and sold through estate agents (they aren't called real estate agents, realtors or brokers in the UK), who charge commission to vendors, although an increasing number of people are selling their own homes. Property sold by estate agents is said to be sold by 'private treaty' between the vendor and the buyer.

Although there are nationwide chains of estate agents in the UK, e.g. covering England and Wales, most agents are local. There's no multi-listing system, as there is, for example, in North America, and agents jealously guard their list of properties from competitors. If you wish to find an agent in a particular town or area, look under estate agents in the local Yellow Pages (available at main libraries in many countries) or check the internet (see below). Many estate agents also act as letting and management agents.

When instructing an agent to find you a property, make absolutely certain he knows exactly what you're looking for and what your price limit is (it pays to understate this by at least £20,000, as agents always send details of properties outside their clients' stated range).

Internet

You can search for an estate agent or a property on the internet, which is expected to dominate the market in future. It's particularly useful when you're looking for a property from abroad, as it allows you to peruse current property lists at your leisure. Some agents offer 'virtual viewing', whereby you can take a guided tour of a property from the comfort of your home.

A list real estate websites are listed in **Appendix C**, some of which offer properties for sale on behalf of one or more estate agents and allow you to search for homes and agents, e.g. by location and price. A directory of London agents' websites (there are hundreds of them) can be found on the Find a Property site (🖥 www.findaproperty.com).

Many estate agents produce free newspapers and magazines containing details of old and new houses, and colour prospectuses for new property developments.

☑ SURVIVAL TIP

Always choose an estate agent who's a member of a professional organisation, such as the National Association of Estate Agents (NAEA, ☎ 01926-496800, 🖥 www. naea.co.uk). You should also check whether an agent is a member of the Ombudsman Scheme for Estate Agents (☎ 01722-333306, 🖥 www.oea.co.uk), whose members must abide by a code of practice and to whom you can complain if you have a problem.

Contracts

When buying property in London (or anywhere else in England), prospective buyers make an offer subject to survey and contract. Either side can amend or withdraw from a sale at any time before the exchange of contracts (when a sale becomes legally binding). In a seller's market, gazumping, where a seller reneges on a 'deal' with one prospective buyer in order to sell to another for a higher price, is rampant and isn't illegal. There have been moves to speed up the home buying process (see below), which should reduce the risk of gazumping, although many people believe that the only way to stamp it out altogether is to follow the example of Scotland and many other countries, where the acceptance of an offer is legally binding. On the other hand, in a buyer's market a buyer may threaten to pull out at the last minute unless the seller reduces the price, known as 'gazundering'.

Home Information Pack

Controversial Home Information Packs (HIPS) were introduced on 14th December 2007 in England and Wales, ostensibly to improve and speed up the process of buying and selling a home and reduce the number of failed home sales. Prior to the introduction of HIPS, much of the information required by buyers was only available after the offer to purchase had been tendered, which meant that any problems regarding the condition of the property or its documentation wasn't revealed until costs had already been incurred. This often led to the need to renegotiate the terms of the sale, lengthy delays in the exchange of contracts and the failure of many transactions.

By far the most common reason so many sales fail, is that prospective buyers in the UK – unlike buyers in most other countries – aren't required to pay a deposit when they agree to buy a property. Therefore a 'buyer' can pull out of a deal anytime before the exchange of contracts without penalty.

HIPS have done nothing to reduce or eradicate gazumping (where the vendor agrees a price with a buyer and then sells to another buyer for a higher price) and gazundering (where the buyer drives down the agreed price by threatening to pull out of an agreed purchase at the last minute), both of which are rife in the UK.

For buyers, a HIP provides essential information about properties they are considering buying and reduces the chance of unwelcome surprises later on in the process, while for sellers it reduces the likelihood of any nasty surprises in the selling process that could delay the sale, as buyers will be able to make more informed decisions about purchasing their home.

A key component of the HIP is the Energy Performance Certificate (EPC), which rates a home's energy efficiency, using graphs like those on fridges and washing machines, and includes recommendations on how to cut fuel bills and reduce carbon emissions, encouraging people to make improvements to the energy efficiency of their homes (see also **Heating** on page 134).

A HIP must be provided by the vendor or the agent selling a property and should contain the following documents:

◆ an Energy Performance Certificate;

◆ an index of contents;

◆ terms of the sale;

◆ evidence of title – ownership details and title deeds;

◆ results of Land Registry, local council and utility searches;

◆ leasehold or commonhold documents (where appropriate).

If any documents are missing, it should be explained why, although until 31st December 2008 it's possible to market a property without all of the compulsory documents. However, if a property which falls within the scope of the scheme is first marketed from 1st January 2009, a HIP including the EPC should be available from the time it's first placed on the market.

The HIP can also include additional optional information that would be of interest to buyers such as a home condition report, other searches, guarantees and warranties on the property, details of any relevant planning or listed building regulations, and a legal summary. The regulations prohibit the inclusion of marketing or advertising material in the pack and sellers must ensure it includes only official material.

> A HIP must be commissioned by the seller or his agent (costing from around £200) and costs a buyer nothing.

The jury is still out on HIPS, but the general consensus is that they have done little or nothing to speed up sales – on the contrary they have actually slowed the sales procedure – and have deterred prospective sellers from putting their houses on the market.

For further information, see 🖥 www. homeinformationpacks.gov.uk.

Information

There are numerous books on the subject of buying a home in the UK, including **Buying, Selling & Letting Property** by David Hampshire (Survival Books). There are also many magazines published in the UK for homebuyers, including *What Mortgage*, *Mortgage Magazine*, *What House* and *House Buyer*, which contain the latest information about mortgages and house prices in London and throughout the UK. Most building societies and banks publish free booklets for homebuyers, most of which contain excellent (usually unbiased) advice.

RENTING

Renting accommodation is recommended for people who will be staying in London for one or two years only (when buying isn't usually practical) or those who don't want the trouble, expense and restrictions involved in buying a home. Unlike in most other European countries, there isn't a strong rental market in the UK (less than 10 per cent of private properties are rented in the UK, compared with around 20 per cent on the continent), where families traditionally prefer to buy rather than rent.

There's a chronic shortage of good rental properties in London, where one-bedroom properties in central London are in high demand and there's fierce competition; properties with three or more bedrooms in good areas are also in short supply. At the top end of the market rental accommodation can be prohibitively expensive, whereas cheaper properties often leave a lot to be desired. Some 95 per cent of rental properties in the UK are let furnished, although furniture and furnishings at the bottom end of the market can be poor.

The UK has one of the most unregulated letting markets in Western Europe and there's little consumer protection against unscrupulous agents and landlords.

One of the reasons for the unpopularity of renting in the UK is that it has traditionally been possible to obtain a 95 or even 100 per cent mortgage with repayments over 25 or 30 years, although mortgages over 80 or 85 per cent LTV were difficult to find in 2008. This means that it's usually been cheaper – or, at least, no more expensive – to buy a home in the UK than it is to rent. Buyers can also make a tax-free profit (or a tax-free loss!) in a relatively short period, as no capital gains tax is paid on any profit from the sale of your principal home.

Rental property can usually be found in two to four weeks in most areas, with the possible exception of large houses (four or more bedrooms), which are rare and very expensive. Family accommodation in particular is in short supply in London, with the possible exception of luxury homes with astronomical rents. Most people settle for something in the suburbs or country and commute to work.

Agents

Most rented property isn't let directly by landlords but through letting agencies or estate agencies, which charge a fee for 'administration', taking up references, drawing up tenancy agreements and making an inventory. You must usually pay one month's rent in advance, depending on the type of property and rental agreement, plus a deposit against damages equal to one to two months' rent.

When you agree to rent a property you're usually asked for a holding deposit of between £50 and £200 before an agreement is signed (this should go towards your rent but is often in effect an additional fee). Some agents charge a fee of around £100 to house hunters with the promise of finding them accommodation, in return for which they simply supply a list of 'vacant' properties, often just taken from newspapers. You shouldn't pay a letting agent an up-front fee to find you a property, which is, in any case, illegal.

If possible, you should deal only with a member of the Association of Residential Letting Agents (ARLA) or the National Association of Estate Agents (NAEA), both of which insist that members have a bonding scheme or professional indemnity cover to safeguard rental income and deposits (deposits must be protected in a government-authorised tenancy deposit scheme.

However, agents are totally unregulated in the UK and you may have no option but to deal with a 'cowboy'.

Agents usually have a number of properties available for immediate occupancy and lists are normally updated weekly. You should have no problem finding something suitable in most areas if you start looking at least four weeks before the date when you wish to take occupancy. Most letting agents require a reference from your employer (or previous employer if you've been less than one year with your current employer) and bank, and possibly a credit reference. Copies of audited accounts and status are required for company lets. Agents may ask to see a foreign resident's police registration certificate (see page 76).

Note that you must be over 18 to hold a tenancy agreement, and young people usually find it harder to find a rental property than older people, due to the usual prejudices that the young are unreliable, noisy, poor, itinerant, untidy and so on. If you're seeking cheap accommodation, you may find it more difficult in September, when the new university/ college term starts and students are looking for accommodation.

Local Housing Aid or Advice Centres offer advice on finding accommodation. Contact your local council for information. A Citizens' Advice Bureau can also offer advice regarding the legal aspects of letting and a tenant's rights. In some towns and cities there are council-run housing aid centres where you can obtain free advice on housing problems. There are also a number of useful books published detailing the legal rights and duties of both landlords and tenants, including the *Which? Guide to Renting and Letting* (Which? Books).

> ☑ **SURVIVAL TIP**
>
> Before taking on long-term accommodation, you may wish to check the council tax rate in the borough (see page 205).

Shared Accommodation

Finding accommodation in London that doesn't break the bank is a huge problem for young people and students (and anyone not earning a fortune). For many the solution is sharing with others, officially termed 'houses in multiple occupation' (HMOs). Sharing usually involves sharing a kitchen, bathroom, living room and dining room, and sometimes even a bedroom. Sharing also usually involves sharing all bills (in addition to the rent) including electricity, gas and telephone (though some landlords include electricity and gas, plus heating, in the rent) and may also include sharing food bills and cooking. You may also be sharing with the owner, which can be somewhat inhibiting. The cleaning and the general upkeep of a house or flat is also usually shared. As always when living with others, there are advantages and disadvantages, and success depends on the participants' ability to live together in harmony.

If you rent a property with the intention of sharing, you should ensure that it's permitted in your contract.

Shared accommodation in many areas is in old, run-down houses where even the living and dining rooms have been converted into bedrooms. In fact, at the bottom end of the market the UK has some of the worst rental accommodation in Western Europe, much of it featuring faulty plumbing, poor sanitation, decrepit furniture, insect and rodent infestations, dangerous wiring and unsafe gas appliances – although there's now legislation that gas appliances in rented properties must be checked annually and a safety certificate issued.

The cost of sharing a furnished flat varies considerably according to the size, location and amenities. Costs start from around £75 per week (single) or £100 per week (double) in an outer borough, up to £150 or £200 per week for a double room in central London.

Many newspapers and magazines contain advertisements for flat-sharers, such as the *Evening Standard, Loot* and *Time Out*. Capital FM (formerly Capital Radio) publishes a weekly flat-share list, available from the foyer of its offices at 30 Leicester Square, WC2 on Fridays after 6pm.

An alternative for those on a tight budget is to find lodgings (also called digs) in a private home, which is becoming increasingly common as many people are forced to take in lodgers to pay their mortgages. This is similar to bed and breakfast accommodation, except that you're usually treated as a member of the family and your rent normally includes half board (breakfast and an evening meal). In lodgings you have less freedom than in shared accommodation and are required to eat at fixed times. Lodgings are often arranged by English-language schools for foreign students.

A boarding house is similar to lodgings: the owner of a large property takes in a number of lodgers and may provide half board or cooking facilities. Lodgings or a room in a boarding house cost from around £125 per week in London, for a room with breakfast. With breakfast and an evening meal, the cost starts at around £175 per week.

Other options include hostels (including student and youth hostels), guesthouses, bed and breakfast, and cheap hotels, although these usually provide relatively expensive short-term accommodation only.

Studios & Bedsits

If you prefer to live on your own but don't want to pay a lot of rent (who does?), the solution may be a studio or bedsit (short for 'bedsitter', which is itself an abbreviation of 'bed-sitting room'). There's a fine line between a studio and bedsit, and in the UK a 'studio' is often just a posh name for a bedsit.

A bedsit usually consists of a furnished room, usually in an old house, where you live, eat, sleep and cook. It may have a separate bathroom or shower room and a small kitchenette or mini kitchen area, although in some properties you may have to share a communal bathroom and kitchen between one or more other bedsits.

A studio flat should always have its own bathroom and kitchen facilities, which may be a separate room or part of the main living area. There should be no shared facilities and you should have your own lockable front door. Studios are more spacious than bedsits and are more expensive. A single bedsit costs from around £100 per week (doubles start at around £150 per week), while studios start at around £150 per week, but can be much more expensive in central London or for large 'luxury' studios.

Rental Costs & Standards

Rental costs vary considerably, according to the size (number of bedrooms) and quality of a property, its age and the facilities provided. Not least, rents depend on the neighbourhood and are generally lower the further you are from the centre of London. Rents vary from around £400 per month for a tiny bedsit (studio flat) in a run-down area of London, to £5,000 per month (or much more) for a three- or four-bedroom detached house or luxury flat in a desirable area. (If you fancy renting a large house in Kensington, you'll need up to £40,000 to spare – per month!) It may be possible to find cheaper, older flats and houses for rent, but they're rare and generally small, and don't usually contain the conveniences that are standard in a modern home, e.g. central heating and double glazing (heating in old houses can be highly 'eccentric').

The table in **Appendix F** shows the range of monthly rents in mid-2008 in each London borough, listed in alphabetical order.

In addition to the rent, tenants must pay for utilities such as gas, electricity and phone, and also water if it's metered. If you like a property but think the rent is too high, you should try to negotiate a reduction or ask an agent to put an offer to the owner.

Kitchens normally contain an oven with a grill, a refrigerator (usually small) and fitted kitchen units, and occasionally also a dishwasher and a separate freezer. Most rental properties have baths (but not enough hot water to fill them!) and some have a separate shower or an en suite shower or bathroom. Unfurnished flats and houses usually have light fittings in all rooms, although there may be no bulbs or lampshades. Most houses, whether furnished or unfurnished, are fully or partly carpeted.

Many flats are part of old houses that have been converted into apartments. At the bottom end of the market, many properties have dreadful furnishings, e.g. flowery wallpaper which may 'match' the equally awful three-piece suite, with sickly green carpets and brown bathroom suites (or vice versa). Upmarket (i.e. expensive) property is, however, furnished to a high standard. It may be possible to 'throw out' the owner's or landlord's tatty furniture and replace it with your own (but you may have to pay to store it). In furnished accommodation you usually need to provide your own bedding and linen, although crockery, kitchen utensils and most household appliances are usually provided.

Rental Agreement

When you find a suitable house or flat to rent, you should insist on a written contract with the owner or agent, which is called a tenancy or rental agreement. According to the Housing Act, 1996 all new tenancies are automatically shorthold tenancies. An assured shorthold tenancy has a time limit, which may be just a few months or a number of years (there's no fixed period). You cannot terminate an

agreement (or be evicted) during the first six months; thereafter either you or your landlord must give two months' notice in writing.

If you don't have an agreement with your landlord, you're protected under the law and have the same rights as with an assured shorthold tenancy if your landlord doesn't live on the premises. Nevertheless, you should always try to obtain a tenancy agreement. If, after taking up residence, you're offered a holiday let, licence agreement or tenancy with board and service, you should refuse and contact a Citizens' Advice Bureau for advice. These agreements provide you with no security and few legal rights as a tenant.

Make sure that you also obtain a rent book, which is used to record all payments made. If you don't have a rent book, always pay by cheque and insist on a receipt. Your contract\may include details of when your rent will be reviewed or increased, if applicable. When you wish to leave rented accommodation, you must give at least one month's notice in writing, unless it's within the first six months of an assured shorthold tenancy, in which case you must pay the rent to the end of the period. If your landlord wants you to leave, the notice he must give you depends on your agreement with him and whether your tenancy is covered by the law. It's a criminal offence for your landlord to harass you in any way in an attempt to drive you out.

Don't sign an agreement unless you're sure you fully understand all the small print. Ask one of your colleagues or friends for help or obtain legal advice. English law usually prevents you from signing away your rights; nevertheless, it pays to be careful.

Most rental agreements forbid the keeping of pets (and smokers) – if they do, get in writing.

In order to avoid disputes, the agreement should spell out in detail who is responsible for maintenance, e.g. appliances, building, decoration and garden. If you have any questions regarding your rental agreement or problems with your landlord, you can ask a Citizens' Advice Bureau for advice. They will check your rental agreement and advise you of your rights under the law.

Information concerning rent allowances, rent rebates, 'fair rents' and housing benefits is contained in a series of free booklets published by the Department of the Environment and available from rent (registration) offices, local authorities, Citizens' Advice Bureaux and housing advice centres.

Flat-sharers

The law regarding flat-sharing is complicated, and it's simpler for one person to be the tenant and to sub-let to the others, although this must be permitted by the tenant's agreement. It is, however, possible for all sharers to be joint tenants with one tenancy agreement (in which case they're jointly and severally responsible) or individual tenants with individual tenancy agreements. Whatever the arrangement, you should have just one rent book and pay the rent in a lump sum. It's usually the occupants' responsibility to replace flatmates who leave during the tenancy.

Deposits

After signing an assured shorthold tenancy you must usually pay one month's rent in advance, depending on the type of property and the rental agreement, plus a deposit against damages equal to one to three months' rent. A deposit equal to one or two months' rent (the maximum permitted by law) must be paid when renting an unfurnished property and up to three months' rent for a furnished property.

Since 6th April 2007, all deposits (for rent up to £25,000 per annum) taken by landlords and agents for assured shorthold tenancies (AST) in England and Wales must be protected by an authorised Tenancy Deposit Scheme (TDS). However, although it's mandatory many landlords haven't signed up to it, despite the fact that if a landlord doesn't protect a tenant's deposit he must repay three times the amount received to the tenant.

The scheme is intended to implement a speedy and efficient settlement of deposit disputes and the rapid return of disputed deposit monies. It removes much of the mutual suspicion that builds up towards the end of a tenancy, which frequently leads to the last month's rent being withheld for fear of the landlord refusing to return a deposit. The TDS guarantees the return of tenants' deposits, less any legitimate expenses owed to the landlord, and removes the burden from letting agents of having to resolve irreconcilable differences of opinion between landlords and tenants.

For further information see 🖥 www.tenantdepositscheme.com or 🖥 www.tds.gb.com.

⚠ Caution

Since 1996, all rental properties with gas appliances must obtain a annual Gas Safety Certificate, which you should ask to see before signing a rental contract – if gas appliances are defective, they can be lethal.

Inventory

One of the most important tasks after moving into a new home is to make an inventory of the fixtures and fittings and, if applicable, the furniture and furnishings. When you've purchased a property, you should check that the previous owner hasn't absconded with any fixtures and fittings that were included in the price or anything which you specifically paid for, e.g. carpets, light fittings, curtains, furniture, kitchen cupboards and appliances, garden ornaments or plants. Note the reading on your utility meters (e.g. electricity, gas and water) and check that you aren't overcharged on your first bill. The meters should be read by utility companies before or soon after you move into a resale property, although you usually need to organise this yourself.

It's advisable to obtain written instructions from the owner or landlord concerning the operation of appliances and heating and air-conditioning systems; maintenance of grounds, gardens and lawns; care of delicate surfaces such as wooden or tiled floors; and the names of reliable local maintenance men who know the property and are familiar with its quirks. Check with your local town hall regarding local regulations about such things as rubbish collection, recycling and on-road parking.

GARAGES & PARKING

A lockable garage is important in London, where there's a high incidence of car theft and thefts from cars, and it's also useful to protect your car from climatic extremes such as ice, snow and heat.

A garage or private parking space isn't usually included in the price when you buy a flat in London, although private parking may be available at an additional cost, possibly in an underground garage. Modern townhouses, semi-detached and detached homes usually have a garage or car port. Smaller homes usually have a single garage, while larger homes often have integral double garages – often used as a play/storage/work area, with cars left permanently outside. Parking isn't usually a problem when buying an old home in an outer borough, although there may not be a purpose-built garage.

In a modern apartment or townhouse development, a garage or parking space may be available as an extra, although the price can be high, e.g. £20,000 to £30,000 for a space in an underground garage. The cost of an 'extra' garage or parking space isn't always recouped when selling, although it makes a property more attractive to buyers and may clinch a sale.

☑ SURVIVAL TIP

Bear in mind that in a large development, the nearest parking area may be some distance from your home. This may be an important factor, particularly if you aren't up to carrying heavy shopping hundreds of metres to your home and possibly up several flights of stairs.

Without a private garage or parking space, parking can be a nightmare, particularly in central London. In some areas of London it's necessary to obtain a resident's parking permit from the local borough council to park on public streets, although this doesn't guarantee that you'll be able to find a parking space. Free on-street parking is difficult or impossible to find in London and paid parking always has a time limit (and is very expensive).

UTILITIES

'Utilities' is the collective name given to electricity, gas and water supplies and sewerage services (it usually also includes telephone services – see page 280). All the UK's utility companies have been privatised in the last 15 or so years, and in most cases privatisation was quickly followed by increased prices and a deterioration in service. In the last five years, most people have been able to choose their electricity and gas supplier and the increased competition initially led to lower prices. However, bills have rocketed in recent years and many people are now paying up to twice as much as they were a few years ago.

Many companies now provide both electricity and gas, and offer contracts for the supply of both fuels, often called 'dual fuel', which may result in a discount (although you may be better off buying from separate companies). You can find a cost comparison of suppliers of electricity, gas and water on the internet (🖳 www.buy.co.uk), although which is the most economical for you may depend on your energy usage.

If you have a complaint about your electricity or gas bill or service and you don't receive satisfaction from your supplier within ten days, you can contact The Gas & Electricity Consumer Council, known as EnergyWatch (☎ 0845-906 0708, 🖳 www.energywatch.org.uk).

Electricity

The electricity supply in the UK is 240 volts AC, with a frequency of 50 Hertz (cycles). This is suitable for all electrical equipment with a rated power consumption of up to 3,000 watts. For equipment with a higher power consumption, a single 240V or 3-phase, 380 volts AC, 20 amp supply must be used (in the UK, these are usually installed only in houses with more than five bedrooms or industrial premises). Power cuts are rare in London, and electricity companies must pay compensation for a power cut lasting longer than 24 hours, although nothing is paid for cuts of less than 24 hours (which includes 99.9 per cent of cuts).

If you move into an old home in London, the electricity supply may have been disconnected by the previous electricity company and need reconnecting; in a new home you'll also need to have the electricity connected. You should allow at least two days for the supply to be (re)connected after signing a contract with an electricity company and there's usually a charge. If you're in London for a relatively short period, you may need to pay a security deposit or obtain a guarantor (e.g. your employer). You must contact your electricity company to get a final reading when you vacate a property.

Gas

Mains gas is available throughout London. But if you're looking for a rental property and want to cook by gas, you need to make sure it already has a gas supply (some houses have an unused gas service pipe). If you move into a brand new home you must have a meter installed in order to be connected to mains gas (there may be a charge for this, depending on the gas company). You're usually connected free if your home is within 25m of a gas main, otherwise a quotation is provided for the cost of the work involved.

If your new home already has a gas supply but you don't know who the supplier is, contact National Grid (formerly Transco), the gas supply watchdog (☎ 0845-605 6677, 🖥 www.nationalgrid.com). If you wish to use a different supplier, simply contact the company of your choice to have the gas supply reconnected or transferred to your name (there's a connection fee) and the meter read. You must contact your gas company to get a final meter reading when you vacate a property.

For further information and a wide range of gas brochures, contact your local gas company.

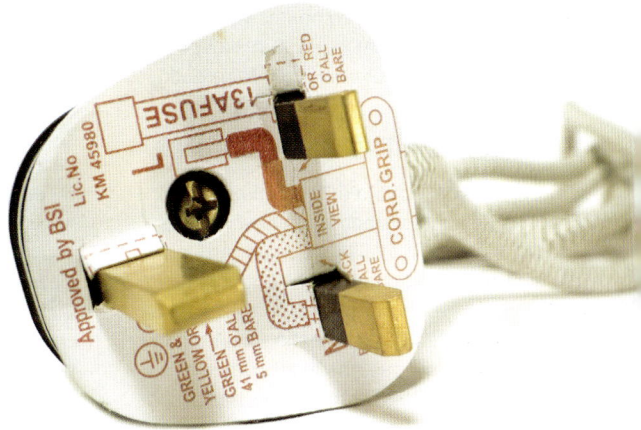

Water & Sewerage

The water industry in England and Wales was privatised in 1989, when ten regional water companies were created to provide water and sewerage services (there are also local water-only companies in some areas). You're unable to choose your water company (as you are your electricity and gas companies), which have a monopoly in their area – Thames and Southern cover different parts of Greater London. Less than 10 per cent of households in England and Wales have water meters, where you're billed for the amount of water you use (by the cubic metre). For all other households, water and sewerage rates are based on the 'rateable value' of a property (linked to its council tax value).

In addition to your consumption charge, you must pay an annual ('standing') charge of around £50 (for both water and sewerage), which is the same for all properties. Bills, which usually include sewerage, are sent out annually and can usually be paid in full, in two six-monthly payments or in ten instalments. In some cases, water and sewerage are handled by separate companies and homeowners receive bills from each company.

Since water privatisation in 1989, water bills have increased dramatically in real terms. The cost of water varies widely according to the local water authority, but the average unmetered annual water and sewerage bill was around £370 in 2008.

If you have a complaint that you cannot resolve with your water company, you should contact the Consumer Council for Water (☎ 0845-039 2837, 🖳 www.ccwater.org.uk).

HEATING & AIR-CONDITIONING

Central heating, double or triple glazing and good insulation are standard in new houses and are essential in the UK's climate. Around 80 per cent of British homes have central heating (including all new homes), most of which also provide hot water. Central heating systems may be powered by oil, gas (the most common), electricity (usually via night-storage heaters) or solid fuel (e.g. coal or wood). The huge increase in the cost of gas and electricity in the last few years has cause heating bills to rocket, which now average around £1,500.

Whatever form of heating you use, you should ensure that your home has good insulation including double glazing, cavity-wall insulation, external-wall insulation, floor insulation, draught-proofing, pipe lagging, and loft and hot water tank insulation, without which up to 60 per cent of heat goes straight through the walls and roof. Many companies advise on and carry out home insulation, including gas and electricity companies, who produce a range of leaflets designed to help you reduce your heating and other energy bills.

A key component of the Home Information Pack (see page 125) is the Energy Performance Certificate (EPC), which rates a home's energy efficiency using graphs like those seen on fridges and washing machines. It also includes recommendations on how to cut fuel bills and reduce carbon emissions, encouraging people to make improvements to the energy efficiency of their homes.

Energy Performance Certificates, tell you how energy efficient a home is on a scale of A to G. The most efficient homes – which should have the lowest fuel bills – are in band A. The Certificate also tells you what impact the home has on the environment (its carbon footprint), with higher-rated homes having less impact through carbon dioxide (CO_2) emissions. The average property in the UK is in bands D/E for both ratings. The Certificate includes recommendations on ways to improve a home's energy efficiency. For more information see 🖳 www.homeinformationpacks.gov.uk/consumer/17_energy_performance_certificate.html.

The cheapest method of central heating is gas (indicated in advertisements as GCH for 'gas central heating' or GFCH for 'gas-fired central heating'), which is estimated to be up to 50 per cent cheaper than other forms of central heating and hot water systems, particularly if you have a high-efficiency condensing boiler. However, many homes have storage heaters that store heat from electricity supplied at the cheaper off-peak rate overnight and release it to heat your home during the day. If an apartment block is heated from a central system, radiators may be individually metered so you pay only for the heating you use, or an averaged cost of heating (and hot water) may be included in your service charges.

If you wish to install heating in your home, you should use a company that's a member of the Heating and Ventilating Contractor's Association (HVCA), 34 Palace Court, London W2 4JG (☎ 020-7313 4900, 🖳 www.hvca.org.uk), which operates a guarantee scheme for domestic heating.

For information about saving energy and reducing your bills, contact your gas or electricity company (see above), EnergyWatch (☎ 0845-906 0708, 🖳 www.energywatch.org.uk) or the Energy Saving Trust (☎ 0800-512012, 🖳 www.energysavingtrust.org.uk). The National Energy Foundation (☎ 01908-665555, 🖳 www.natenergy.org.uk) will provide the names of energy surveyors in your area who will perform an energy survey for around £100.

Air-conditioning

Although London's summer temperatures can exceed 30°C (86°F – nearby north Kent experienced the UK's first recorded temperatures of over 100°F/38°C in August 2003), the capital's homes rarely have air-conditioning and aren't usually built to withstand extreme heat. However, in recent years many luxury flats and houses have been built with cooling systems. If you want to install air-conditioning you can choose between a huge variety of systems, including fixed or moveable units, indoor or outdoor installation, and high or low power. An air-conditioning system with a heat pump provides cooling in summer and economical heating in winter. Note, however, that there can be negative effects from air-conditioning if you suffer from asthma or respiratory problems.

HOME SECURITY

When moving into a new home it's often wise to replace the locks (or lock barrels) as soon as possible, as you have no idea how many keys are in circulation for the existing locks. This is true even for brand new homes, as builders often give keys to sub-contractors. It's wise to change the external locks or lock barrels periodically if you let a home.

If they aren't already fitted, it's recommended to fit high security (double cylinder or dead bolt) locks. Many modern developments have intercom systems, CCTV, alarms, security gates and 24-hour caretakers. In areas with a high risk of theft (i.e. many parts of London), your insurance company may insist on extra security measures and the policy may specify that all forms of protection must be employed when a property is unoccupied. If security precautions aren't adhered to, a claim can be reduced or even dismissed. It's usually necessary to have a safe for insured valuables, which must be approved by your insurance company.

You may wish to have a security alarm fitted, which is usually the best way to deter thieves and may also reduce your contents insurance (see page 168). It should include all external doors and windows, internal infra-red security beams (movement detectors), activate external and internal lights, and may also include a coded entry keypad (which can be frequently changed and is useful for clients if you let a home) and 24-hour monitoring – with some systems it's even possible to monitor properties remotely from another country via a computer. With a monitored system, when a sensor (e.g. smoke or forced entry) detects an emergency or a panic button is pushed, a signal is automatically sent to a 24-hour monitoring station. The duty monitor will telephone to check whether it's a genuine alarm (a password must be given) and if he cannot contact you, someone will be sent to investigate. Alarms should be approved by the National Security Inspectorate (NSI, ☎ 0845-006 3003, 🖥 www.nsi.org.uk).

You can deter thieves by ensuring that your home is well lit and not conspicuously unoccupied. External security 'motion detector' lights (that switch on automatically when someone approaches); random timed switches for internal lights, radios and televisions; dummy security cameras; and tapes that play barking

dogs (etc.) triggered by a light or heat detector may all help deter burglars.

It pays to look at your home through the eyes of a burglar and remedy any weak points. Bear in mind that prevention is better than cure, as stolen property is rarely recovered.

In remoter areas of the outer boroughs, it's common for owners to fit two or three locks on external doors, alarm systems, grills on doors and windows, window locks, security shutters and a safe for valuables. You can fit UPVC (toughened clear plastic) security windows and doors, which can survive an attack with a sledge-hammer, and external steel security blinds (which can be electrically operated), although these are expensive.

A dog can be useful to deter intruders, although it should be kept inside where it cannot be given poisoned food. Irrespective of whether you actually have a dog, a warning sign with a picture of a fierce dog may act as a deterrent.

If not already present, you should have the front door of a flat fitted with a spy-hole and chain so that you can check the identity of visitors before opening the door.

If you vacate your home for an extended period, it may be obligatory to notify your caretaker, landlord or insurance company, and to leave a key with the caretaker or landlord in case of emergencies. One way to avoid burglaries when you're away is to employ house sitters. Home insurance companies usually offer discounts for owners who employ house sitters – you should, in any case, tell your insurance company if you employ a sitter. There are a number of companies including Absentia (☎ 01279-777412, 🖥 www.home-and-pets. co.uk), Home and Pet Care (☎ 01697-478515, 🖥 www.homeandpetcare.co.uk) and Homesitters (☎ 01296-630730, 🖥 www. homesitters.co.uk). Check that house sitters are experienced and have been 'vetted' by the company. Companies charge a daily fee (e.g. £20 or £25) plus travelling expenses, a daily food allowance (e.g. £5 per day) – and extra for looking after pets. When closing up a property for an extended period, you should ensure that everything is switched off and that it's secure.

If you have a robbery, you should report it immediately to your local police station, where you must make a statement. You'll receive

a copy, which is required by your insurance company if you make a claim.

Another important aspect of home security is ensuring that you have early warning of a fire, which is easily accomplished by installing smoke detectors. Battery-operated smoke detectors can be purchased for around £5 or less (they should be tested periodically to ensure that the batteries aren't exhausted). You can also fit an electric-powered gas detector that activates an alarm when a gas leak is detected.

For information about home insurance, see **Building Insurance** on page 166 and **Home Contents Insurance** on page 168. See also **Crime** on page 270.

MOVING HOUSE

It usually takes just a few weeks to have your belongings shipped from within continental Europe. From anywhere else the period varies considerably, e.g. around four weeks from the east coast of America, six weeks from the US west coast and the Far East, and around eight weeks from Australasia.

Customs clearance is no longer necessary when shipping your household effects from one European Union (EU) country to another. However, when shipping your effects from a non-EU country to London, you should enquire about customs formalities in advance. If you're moving to London from a non-EU country, you must provide an inventory of the things you're planning to import. If you fail to follow the correct procedure you can encounter problems and delays and may be charged duty or even fined. The relevant forms to be completed by non-EU citizens depend on whether your London home will be your main residence or a second home. Removal companies usually take care of the paperwork and ensure that the correct documents are provided and properly completed (see **Customs** on page 74).

It's wise to use a major shipping company with a good reputation, e.g. a member of the British Association of Removers (BAR). For international moves, it's best to use a company that's a member of the International Federation of Furniture Removers (FIDI) or the Overseas Moving Network International (OMNI), with experience in the UK. Members of FIDI and OMNI usually subscribe to an advance payment

scheme that provide a guarantee. If a member company fails to fulfil its commitments to a client, the removal is completed at the agreed cost by another company or your money is refunded. Some non-UK removal companies have subsidiaries or affiliates in the UK, which may be useful if you encounter problems or need to make an insurance claim.

You should obtain at least three written quotations before choosing a company, as costs can vary considerably. Moving companies should send a representative to provide a detailed quotation. Most companies will pack your belongings and provide packing cases and special containers, although this is obviously more expensive than packing them yourself. Ask a company how they pack fragile and valuable items, and whether the cost of packing cases, materials and insurance (see below) are included in a quotation. If you plan to do your own packing, most shipping companies will provide packing crates and boxes. Shipments are charged by volume, e.g. the square metre in Europe and the square foot in the US. If you're flexible about the delivery date, shipping companies will quote a lower fee based on a 'part load', where the cost is shared with other deliveries. This can result in savings of 50 per cent or more compared with an individual delivery.

Make a list of everything to be shipped and give a copy to the removal company. Don't include anything illegal (e.g. guns, bombs, drugs or pornography), as customs checks can be rigorous and penalties severe. Provide the shipping company with detailed instructions how to find your London residence from the nearest motorway or main road and a telephone number where you can be contacted. If your London home has poor or impossible access for a large truck (which is common in central London) you must inform the shipping company. Note also that if furniture needs to be taken in through an upstairs window you'll usually need to pay extra.

☑ **SURVIVAL TIP**

Whether you have an individual or shared delivery, obtain a delivery date in writing, otherwise you may need to wait weeks or months for delivery!

Be sure fully to insure your belongings during removal with a well-established insurance company. It isn't wise to insure with a shipping company that carries its own insurance, as they will usually fight every penny of a claim. Insurance premiums are usually 1 to 2 per cent of the declared value of your goods, depending on the type of cover chosen. It's prudent to make a photographic or video record of valuables for insurance purposes. Most insurance policies cover for 'all risks' on a replacement value basis. Note that china, glass and other breakables can usually be included in an all-risks policy only when they're packed by the removal company. Insurance usually covers total loss or loss of a particular crate only, rather than individual items, unless they were packed by the shipping company. If there are any broken or damaged items, they should be noted and listed before you sign the delivery bill.

If you need to make a claim, be sure to read the small print, as some companies require clients to make a claim within a few days, although seven is usual. Send a claim by registered post. Some insurance companies apply an 'excess' of around 1 per cent of the total shipment value when assessing claims. This means that if your shipment is valued at £25,000, a claim must be for over £250.

If you're unable to ship your belongings directly to London, most shipping companies will put them into storage and some allow a limited free storage period prior to shipment, e.g. 14 days. If you need to put your household effects into storage, it's important to have them fully insured, as warehouses have been known to burn down!

After considering the costs, you may decide to ship only selected items of furniture and personal effects and buy new furniture in London. If you're importing household goods from another European country, it's possible to hire a self-drive van or truck, although you need to bear in mind that you usually need to return it to the country where it was hired. If you plan to transport your belongings to London personally, check the customs requirements in the countries you must pass through. Most people find it isn't wise to do their own move unless it's a simple job, e.g. a few items of furniture and personal effects only. It's no fun heaving beds and wardrobes up stairs and squeezing them into impossible spaces.

If you're taking pets with you, you may need to get your vet to tranquillise them as many pets are frightened (even more than people) by the chaos and stress of moving house.

Bear in mind when moving home that everything that can go wrong often does, so you should allow plenty of time and try not to arrange your move from your old home on the same day as the new owner is moving in. That's just asking for fate to intervene!

See also **Customs** on page 74 and the **Checklists** on page 78.

Guildhall, City of London

Lloyds of London building, City of London

5.
EARNING A LIVING

There are over 250,000 businesses in London, employing some 3.5m people (2m men and 1.5m women), the vast majority of which are small, almost 90 per cent employing fewer than 25 people and just 10 per cent with a turnover of over £1m. Compared with the UK as a whole, London has a high proportion of self-employed people, which has risen sharply in recent years; there are now almost 50 per cent more self-employed women in London than there were a decade ago. This trend looks set to continue, with large companies 'downsizing' and 'outsourcing', and an increasing number of small businesses being set up to provide services for them.

Despite a vast labour market and inflated salaries, London had the highest unemployment of any UK region 7.1 per cent in 2007; this varied considerably depending on the borough, from a high of 12.9 per cent in Tower Hamlets to just 3.4 per cent in Richmond. The percentage of people unemployed in each borough is shown in **Chapter 1**. As in most other countries, the majority of unemployed people are unskilled or young (or both) and newcomers tend to find that the job opportunities in London (and the UK in general) are far greater than those in their home countries.

> ⚠ **Caution**
>
> If you don't automatically qualify to live in the UK, for example as a national of a European Economic Area (EEA) country, obtaining a work permit will probably be more difficult than finding a job in London.

Average earnings in London have always been significantly higher than the UK average, although the cost of living is also higher (see page 163). Men in manual ('blue-collar') jobs earn around 12 per cent more than the UK average, while those in non-manual ('white-collar') occupations earn almost 30 per cent more (the figures for women are 15 and 27 per cent respectively). This is largely a reflection of the high earnings in the financial and business services sectors, the high salaries paid to managers and administrators generally, and the 'London weighting' applied to many salaries to compensate workers for the higher cost of living in the capital. The highest-paid workers in London earn over 35 per cent more than their counterparts elsewhere in the UK, and earnings in professional and technical occupations are 45 per cent higher than the UK average.

Over the past few decades there has also been a shift (throughout the UK, but more marked in the capital) away from manufacturing towards service industries. Today, London's job market is dominated by financial and business services (40 per cent) followed by other service industries such as education, social work and health (15 per cent), distribution, hotels and catering (15 per cent), transport, storage and communications (10 per cent), and public administration and defence (5 per cent).

The highest concentration of service industries is to be found in a 'corridor' across north and central London incorporating the boroughs of Barnet, Camden, City, Westminster, Kensington & Chelsea, Hammersmith & Fulham, and Wandsworth, where over 90 per cent of jobs are in the service sector. Certain areas concentrate on specific business sectors. The City of London, for example, is focused on finance and insurance, a sector which is also on the increase in neighbouring Tower Hamlets. Docklands (in Tower Hamlets), which is still being developed and will comprise over half a million square metres of office and retail space by the time building is completed (the workforce of Canary Wharf alone was around 100,000 in 2008 and is expected to double by 2028), is the home of the newspaper industry. On the other side of central London, Hammersmith & Fulham has recently become the focus of the entertainment industry, and Kensington & Chelsea has attracted the pharmaceutical and cosmetics industry, creative and media work, leisure and tourism. The cultural and media sectors are also significant in Lambeth.

Manufacturing now makes up just 10 per cent of London's GDP, most of it confined to the boroughs of Hackney and Barking & Dagenham, the latter being the only London borough to have a higher proportion (30 per cent) of employees in manufacturing than the UK average (18 per cent), thanks largely to the Ford plant at Dagenham. Other boroughs with a significant manufacturing industry include Brent (mainly food and drink), Haringey (footwear, printing and publishing, drink, food and tobacco, metal goods, motor vehicles, rubber and plastic products, timber and wooden goods), Tower Hamlets (mainly clothing and printing), Merton and Waltham Forest.

The UK is a nation of commuters (it's considered nothing for people to travel 100mi/160km or more to work and back each day), and nowhere is this more true than in and around London.

Teleworking is gaining momentum and has increased by an average of over 10 per cent a year for the past six years. Some 2.5m Britons now work from home on at least one day a week according to data from the Office for National Statistics or a total of around 7.5 per cent of the total workforce. Of these, 44 per cent do their main job at home. Expansion is expected to continue and some experts estimate that up to 25 per cent of workers will be involved in teleworking within the next decade.

QUALIFICATIONS

The most important qualification for working in London is the ability to speak fluent English. You should also ensure that your trade or professional qualifications and experience are recognised in the UK. If you aren't experienced, British employers usually expect studies to be in a relevant discipline and to have included work experience. Professional or trade qualifications are necessary to work in many fields in the UK, although these aren't as stringent as in many other European Union (EU) countries.

Theoretically, any qualifications recognised by professional and trade bodies in one EU country should be recognised in the UK. In practice, recognition varies from country to country, and in some cases foreign qualifications aren't recognised by British employers or professional and trade associations. All academic qualifications should also be recognised, although they may be 'less acceptable' than equivalent British qualifications, depending on the country and the educational establishment concerned. A ruling by the European Court declared that when examinations are of a similar standard and differences aren't extensive, individuals ought to be required to take additional examinations only in those subject areas which don't overlap in order for their qualifications to be acceptable.

All EU member states issue information sheets about occupations, each of which contains a common job description together with a table of qualifications which permit you to practise that occupation anywhere in the Union. They're intended to help someone with the relevant qualifications look for a job in another EU country and windows, and the first suitable applicant may be offered the job on the spot.

Your method of job hunting will also depend on your circumstances, qualifications and experience, but you should consider doing some or all of the following:

♦ Contacting the government employment service and visiting local Jobcentres (see below);

♦ Registering with private employment agencies and recruitment consultants (see page 124);

numerous trades and professions are covered. To obtain a comparison of British vocational qualifications and those recognised in other EU countries, contact the Department for Children, Schools and Families, Sanctuary Buildings, Great Smith Street, London SW1 3BT (☎ 0870-000 2288, 🖳 www.dfes.gov.uk). For a comparison of academic qualifications, contact UK NARIC, Oriel House, Oriel Road, Cheltenham, Gloucestershire, GL50 1XP (☎ 0871-330 7033, 🖳 www.naric.org.uk).

JOB HUNTING

When looking for a job in London, it's wise not to put all your eggs in one basket and to spread your net far and wide – the more job applications you make, the better your chance of finding the right job. Contact as many prospective employers as possible, either by emailing, telephoning, writing or calling on them.

It's important to tailor your approach to the type of job you're after. For example, the recruitment of executives and senior managers is handled almost exclusively by consultants, who advertise in the British quality national press (and also abroad) and interview all applicants before presenting clients with a shortlist. At the other end of the scale, manual or part-time jobs requiring no experience may be advertised at Jobcentres, in local newspapers and in shop

♦ Obtaining copies of British and London daily and weekly newspapers, most of which have 'positions vacant' sections on certain days;

♦ Surfing the internet, where there are literally hundreds of sites for jobseekers, including corporate websites, recruitment companies and newspaper job advertisements;

♦ Making applications direct to companies. You can obtain a list of companies operating in a particular field from trade directories, such as Kelly's (🖳 www.kompass.co.uk) copies of which are available at reference libraries in London and British Chambers of Commerce overseas. Most medium-size to large companies advertise job vacancies on the internet.

♦ 'Networking', which is basically getting together with like-minded people and is a popular way of making business and professional contacts in the UK. It can be particularly successful for those seeking an executive, managerial or professional job.

♦ Asking relatives, friends or acquaintances working in London whether they know of an employer looking for someone with your experience and qualifications.

If you're already in London, you can contact or join expatriate social clubs, churches, societies and professional organisations, or your country's chamber of commerce. Many good business contacts can also be made among expatriate groups.

Government Employment Service

Jobcentre Plus is the (latest) incongruous name of the government employment service, which is an executive agency of the Department for Work and Pensions. Its task is to provide help for the unemployed, but particularly those who have been jobless for over six months and those who are disabled or disadvantaged. It's responsible for paying them unemployment benefit (known as the 'Jobseeker's Allowance') through its network of offices, helping them obtain other benefits, and offering guidance and counselling so that they can find the best way to return to employment, e.g. through education or training. Jobcentre Plus offices advertise jobs and training courses, operate a number of programmes and training initiatives, and provide a wide range of publications about the help available.

The New Deal programme provides advice, support, training and direct work experience for young people aged between 18 and 24 and those aged 25 or over who have been claiming Jobseeker's Allowance for two years or more. It's also open to EU nationals. Information can be obtained from Jobcentre Plus offices or their website 🖥 www. jobcentreplus.gov.uk.

Jobcentre Plus offices aren't primarily geared towards finding jobs for foreigners; the vast majority of jobs advertised in Jobcentre Plus offices are manual or low paid and there are few managerial or professional positions (or jobs for 16- to 18-year-olds, which are advertised in careers centres). Jobs are displayed on boards under headings such as Building, Clerical, Domestic, Drivers, Engineering, Factory, Hairdressing, Hotel And Catering, Industrial, Motor Trade, Nursing, Office, Receptionists, Shops, Temporary and Latest Vacancies (where new vacancies are initially posted). If you see a job which is of interest, write down the reference number and take it to one of the staff, who will tell you more about the job and arrange an interview if appropriate.

You can register with a Jobcentre Plus office by completing a card and providing details of the kind of job you're looking for. If the office doesn't deal with your profession or industry, they should at least be able to tell you about other sources of information. When (or if) a job comes in that matches your requirements, you should be informed – but don't rely on it. Check the boards regularly, as new jobs are displayed each morning and good positions don't remain vacant for long. You can usually check on new vacancies by telephone.

Many cities and boroughs have their own employment centres or 'job shops' where jobs with the local council are advertised.

European Employment Service

Jobcentre Plus is also responsible for EURES operations in the UK. EURES is the EEA system for exchanging job applications and vacancies between member states, which participating employment services carry out on a monthly basis. Details are available in government employment service offices in each EEA country, as is advice on how to apply for jobs. Local offices have access to overseas vacancies held on the National Vacancy Computer System (NATVACS). Applicants are required to complete an application form, either in response to an advertised vacancy or to make a general application, which is valid for six months. For further information, see the EURES website (⌨ www.europa.eu.int/eures/home.jsp?lang=en).

Employment Agencies & Consultants

In London, private recruitment consultants and employment agencies outnumber even pubs – which is saying something. Most large companies are happy to engage consultants to recruit staff, but particularly if they're seeking executives and managers – in which case the consultancy or agency is often referred to as a 'headhunter'. Headhunters account for around two-thirds of all top level executive appointments in the UK.

Rather less grand agencies cover a wide range of occupations but most specialise in particular fields, e.g. computer or nursing personnel; accounting, sales, secretarial and office staff; engineering and technical specialists; catering, industrial and construction workers. Many more deal exclusively with temporary staff ('temps'): secretaries and clerical workers, baby-sitters, home carers, nannies and mothers' helps, housekeepers, cooks, gardeners, chauffeurs, hairdressers, security guards, cleaners, labourers and factory hands. Specialist nursing agencies, which are fairly common, also cover related occupations, such as physiotherapy, occupational and speech therapy, and dentistry. Many agencies also employ freelance staff on a contract basis, e.g. accountants, computer personnel, nurses, technical authors, draughtspersons and engineers (see **Contract Jobs** below).

Employment agencies make a lot of money from finding people jobs so, provided you have something to offer, they will be keen to help you (if you're a computer expert, you may get trampled in the rush to find you a job). If they cannot help you, they will usually tell you immediately and won't waste your (or their) time.

Agencies, which must be licensed by local councils, don't usually charge employees but receive a fee from employers equivalent to one to four months of the salary you'll be receiving, plus a fixed amount in many cases. Some agencies act as employers themselves, hiring workers and contracting them out to companies at a an hourly rate.

As a result of EU legislation, hourly rates paid should include an additional amount in lieu of holiday pay (after a qualifying period) if employees don't take a paid annual holiday. Agencies must (by law) deduct income tax and National Insurance contributions from payments.

The Recruitment and Employment Confederation (REC), 15 Wellbeck Street, London W1G 9XT (☎ 020-7009 2100, ⌨ www.rec.uk.com) is the trade association for recruitment agencies in the UK; a list of its members can be found on the website. To find agencies in your area, look both in the Yellow Pages under 'Employment Agencies' and in local newspapers, where their advertising is usually prominent. Agency jobs are also advertised on the internet.

If you're using agencies to look for work, check your rights, which you'll find outlined on the website above.

Publications

The national newspapers all have 'situations vacant' or 'appointments' sections, some of which are focused on particular fields or industries on certain days, e.g. Monday's *Guardian* for sales, marketing, PR and secretarial, Wednesday's *Times* for secretarial, and Thursday's *Daily Telegraph* for technical and managerial, sales and marketing positions. The Sunday broadsheet newspapers, such as the *Observer*, *Sunday Telegraph* and *Sunday Times*, have 'appointments' sections for management staff and professionals. The *Evening Standard*, which is London's only daily newspaper, has a job section in all weekday issues, each

The 'Gherkin', City of London

member of a recognised profession or trade, you can place an advertisement in a newspaper or magazine dedicated to your profession or industry.

There are numerous books written for those seeking a job, including *A-Z of Careers and Jobs* by Susan Hodgson (Kogan Page), *How to Get a Job You'll Love: A Practical Guide to Unlocking Your Talents and Finding Your Ideal Career* by John Lees (McGraw-Hill) and *What Color Is Your Parachute? A Practical Manual for Job-hunters and Career Changes* by Richard N. Bolles (Ten Speed Press).

Internet

The internet is fast becoming one of the most important resources for both job hunters and employers. In addition to consulting the sites listed below (and others), don't neglect newspaper websites (where jobs advertisements are usually posted) and company websites – many companies receive as many as half their job applications via advertisements placed on their websites. Listed below are some of the many websites for those seeking a job in London:

one featuring vacancies in a particular field. Details can be found on the *Standard*'s website (🖥 www.thisislondon.co.uk, which also has a link to its separate jobs site 🖥 www.londonjobs.co.uk). Most newspapers also list all jobs advertised on their websites, e.g. 🖥 www. jobs.guardian.co.uk (*Guardian*).

A number of free newspapers containing job advertisements are published in London from Monday to Friday, including *Metro* (☎ 020-7651 5200, 🖥 www.metro.co.uk), *The London Paper* (☎ 020-7782 7801, 🖥 www. thelondonpaper.com) and *London Lite* (☎ 020-7938 7421, 🖥 www.thelondonlite. co.uk). Most of these are available in central London at railway and tube stations as well as at newsagents' and pubs.

Placing an advertisement in the 'situations wanted' section of a local newspaper in London may prove fruitful and, if you're a

◆ www.badenochandclark.com – Badenoch and Clark, a recruitment consultant specialising in accountancy, banking/financial services, law and IT jobs;

◆ www.dotjobs.co.uk – Dotjobs, for jobs throughout the UK in the printing and packaging sectors;

◆ www.easynet.net – Easynet, a general job search site;

◆ www.hays.com – Hays (apparently 'a global leader in specialist recruitment') for office jobs;

◆ www.jobserve.com – Jobserve, offering jobs in all areas;

◆ www.jobsite.co.uk – Jobsite, listing vacancies in all sectors;

◆ www.monster.co.uk – Monster UK, a search engine for both job seekers and employers, which claims to be 'the world's leading career network';

◆ www.peoplebank.com – PeopleBank, a database of vacancies and CVs which matches jobseekers with employers;

◆ www.reed.co.uk – Reed Recruitment's site, on which you can post your CV and search for suitable jobs or careers.

Each London borough has its own website containing a wealth of information, including information about careers and jobs, which can be accessed via 🖳 www.london.gov.uk/london/links.jsp. The addresses of individual sites are www.[borough name].gov.uk (e.g. 🖳 www.brent.gov.uk or 🖳 www.barking-dagenham.gov.uk), with the exception of Hammersmith & Fulham (🖳 www.lbhf.gov.uk), Kensington & Chelsea (🖳 www.rbkc.gov.uk) and Waltham Forest (🖳 www.lbwf.gov.uk).

SELF-EMPLOYMENT & RUNNING A BUSINESS

British citizens, EEA nationals and permanent residents (those with indefinite leave to remain) can be self-employed or run a business in the UK, whether in a partnership or co-operative, as a franchise or private business, or on a commission-only basis. There have traditionally been few restrictions and little red tape for anyone wanting to start a business or become self-employed in the UK, although this has changed in recent years with a veritable tidal wave of employment legislation emanating from both the British government and the European Union. Many experts believe that red tape is strangling enterprise, so much so that many companies pay consultants a retainer just to be kept informed of new legislation!

> ⚠️ **Caution**
>
> You must be wary of employment legislation, especially as an employer; if you fire an employee and are subsequently sued for unfair dismissal, it can be very costly.

However, this doesn't deter most people and the UK is traditionally a country of enterprise and entrepreneurs – most of whom go bust within five years. The key to starting and running a successful business is exhaustive research, further research and yet more research. You need to select the area in which to establish your business even more carefully than you choose where to live. To give your business the best chance of success, make use of the many information and support services listed below, most of which are free.

Information & Support

Each borough, naturally, claims unique advantages, as they're keen to attract entrepreneurs who will stimulate the local economy and reduce the unemployment figures. Consequently there's no shortage of information and advice (most of it free) on all aspects of starting and developing a business, either in London as a whole or in a particular region or borough.

The organisations listed below provide general information about doing business in London (and in some cases other parts of the UK) and various support services.

◆ **Awards For All – London** (☎ 0845-600 2040, 🖳 www.awardsforall.org.uk) – provides Lottery-funded grants for projects enabling people to participate in community activities;

◆ **Business Link for London** (☎ 0845-600 0787, 🖳 www.businesslink.gov.uk) – part of the national Business Link network which provides independent advice, information and support services for small businesses, including benchmarking, market research, consultancy subsidies, seminars and training courses;

◆ **The Department for Business Enterprise and Regulatory Reform** (☎ 020-7215 5000, 🖳 www.berr.gov.uk) – provides a wealth of information and publications for budding entrepreneurs;

◆ **Greater London Enterprise** (☎ 020-7403 0300, 🖳 www.gle.co.uk) – provides support for small companies through loans, advice and training;

◆ **InBiz** (🖳 www.inbizonline.co.uk) – helps the long-term unemployed set up in business, through its 11 London offices.

♦ **The London Development Agency** (☎ 020-7593 8000, 🖳 www.lda.gov. uk) – has overall responsibility for the development of business in London;

♦ **PRIME** (☎ 020-8765 7833, 🖳 www. primeinitiative.org.uk) – a national organisation that helps those aged over 50 to set up in business;

♦ **Prince's Youth Business Trust** (☎ 020-7543 1234, 🖳 www.princes-trust.org.uk) – provides financial and other assistance to those aged 18 to 30 wanting to start a business;

♦ **Think London** (☎ 020-7718 5400, 🖳 www.lfc.co.uk) – the inward investment agency for London, providing a free and confidential service to companies considering London as a business location. It provides a general introduction to London and a complete relocation service, from assistance with company registration to identifying the best location and finding premises. It can also introduce companies to potential partners and investors.

♦ **TNG**, formerly The Training Network Group (☎ 020-8367 0647, 🖳 www.tng.uk.com) – is a national private training company, whose head office is in London.

Organisations that can help you once your business is established include the following:

♦ **Acas – London** (☎ 0845-747 4747, 🖳 www.acas.co.uk) – provides information, advice and training aimed at improving business performance and employment relations;

♦ **Business in the Community** (☎ 020-7566 8650, 🖳 bitc.org.uk) – provides advice and organises events for businesses;

♦ **London Chamber of Commerce and Industry** (☎ 020-7248 4444, 🖳 www. londonchamber.co.uk) – the largest business organisation in London, whose members range from small retailers to large 'blue chip' companies. It seeks to help businesses succeed by representing and promoting their interests, expanding their markets, providing them with information, co-ordinating trade missions, and organising training and networking events.

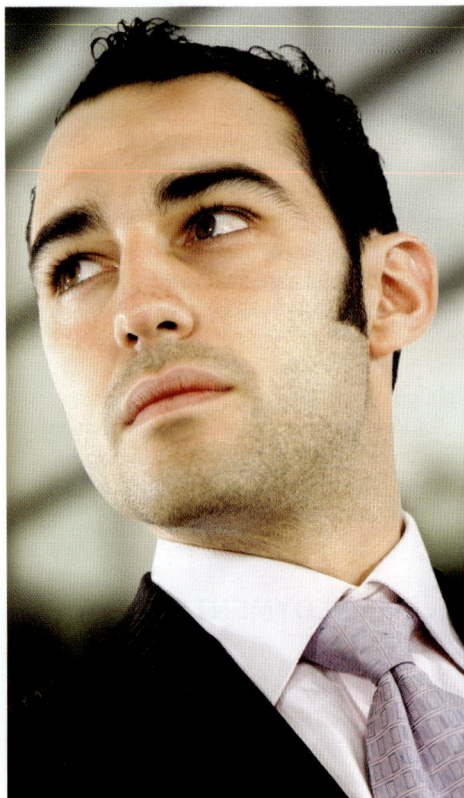

Area Organisations

Organisations that cover only a part of London include the following:

♦ **The Business Information Service** (☎ 020-8461 7897, 🖳 www.bromley.gov.uk/ business/intelligence) – serves Bromley and south-east London, providing information to help businesses with planning and marketing, although this isn't a free service;

♦ **The Other Media** (☎ 020-7089 5959, 🖳 www.othermedia.com) – provides impartial advice and help with all IT-related matters;

♦ **The Portobello Business Centre** (PBC, ☎ 020-7460 5050, 🖳 www.pbc.co.uk) in North Kensington – central London's leading enterprise agency, specialising in providing advice to new businesses in various sectors, including media, fashion, catering, design, building and craft manufacturing. The PBC also provides information about sources of funding and runs training programmes.

◆ **Prevista** (☎ 020-7609 4198, 🖥 www.prevista.co.uk) – a government-funded agency providing information and advice to those wishing to start a business in northern central London. Prevista works in partnership with Business Link for London (see above).

◆ **The South London Partnership** – fosters economic development in the boroughs of Croydon, Merton, Sutton and Wandsworth through training, courses, consultations and a recruitment service. For details, contact the council offices of the relevant borough (see **Chapter 1**).

◆ **West London Business** (☎ 020-8607 2500, 🖥 www.westlondon.com) – a Chamber of Commerce initiative aimed at maintaining the commercial competitiveness of west London (principally the borough of Hounslow), one of its goals being to attract businesses to the area.

Borough Organisations

London's boroughs compete vigorously for business investment and most have an Economic Development Unit (or something similar) that can provide local demographic and other statistical information, and an industrial profile of the borough, including local market information and wage rates. It can also provide a list of key local contacts and information about the local property market, house prices and availability; vacant office and industrial premises, development sites and managed workspaces; renting council premises; local suppliers; recruitment; business support services; grants, loans and funds for which you may be eligible; and the regulations concerning your business.

> Certain businesses require a licence, e.g. those selling food or alcohol, which are issued by borough councils.

Most councils have established Local Business Partnerships (e.g. with Chambers of Commerce and local businesses) to enable new businesses and local authorities to work together to streamline the various regulatory processes (e.g. consumer rights, health and safety, and standards). The aim is to make it easier for businesses to understand and comply with regulations, and consequently save money and become more competitive. Councils provide information about legal requirements and good business practice, explain how to apply for registration or approval, and co-ordinate with the relevant regulatory bodies to smooth your path. Councils may also have a Business Support Unit that will put you in touch with people and organisations who can provide the help and advice you need, and a Business Network providing links between businesses. Your local Chamber of Commerce may organise free, impartial business advice sessions, such as explaining the loans and grants available.

Local Organisations

There are also numerous local organisations offering help and information, some of which are listed below:

◆ **Brent** – Brent Business Venture (☎ 020-3110 2300, 🖥 www.bbv.co.uk) is a member of the Business Link for London partnership, and provides information and advice for people starting businesses in the borough.

◆ **Bromley** – Business Focus (☎ 0845-466 4700, 🖥 www.business-focus.co.uk) is run by Bromley's Chamber of Commerce and dedicated to support local businesses. The Bromley Business Help Line (🖥 www.bromley.gov.uk – click on 'Business') helps businesses wanting to move to the borough by providing details of vacant commercial property and relevant local support services.

◆ **Camden** – The Camden Enterprise Agency (CENTA) Business Services section (☎ 020-7278 5757, 🖥 www.centa.co.uk) provides a complete support service for people starting a business in the borough.

◆ **Enfield** – The Enfield Enterprise Agency (☎ 020-8443 5457, 🖥 www.enfieldenterpriseagency.co.uk) aims to help both new and established businesses.

◆ **Greenwich** – The Greenwich Business Support Service (☎ 020-8854 8888, 🖥 www.greenwich.gov.uk/Greenwich/Business/SupportAndAdvice) maintains a database of available commercial property, information on grants and other forms of financial assistance, and links to business support agencies in the borough.

♦ **Hackney** – HBV Enterprise (☎ 020-7254 9595, 🖥 www.hbv.org.uk) provides help, including loans, grants and training, to those wishing to become self-employed. Hackney Co-operative Developments (☎ 020-7254 4829, 🖥 www.hced.co.uk) is a non-profit organisation that helps women and people from ethnic minority groups to establish businesses and co-operatives. Social & Environmental Analysis (☎ 020-8983 9716, 🖥 www.wiseowls.co.uk) provides business start-up and self-employment training, including 'e-learning' courses, and information about sources of funding. Its parent organisation, Wise Owls Employment Agency, offers business support services for the over 45s and e-learning programmes for all, and its website (🖥 www.wiseowlslearn.org) includes a database of training providers in east and central London.

♦ **Hammersmith & Fulham** – Business Enterprise Centre (☎ 020-8746 0355, 🖥 www.bectek.co.uk) is a resource centre for small to medium-size companies. The Park Royal Partnership (☎ 020-3110 2300, 🖥 www.parkroyal.org) provides advice and assistance for businesses on the Park Royal estate.

♦ **Haringey** – The Haringey Business Development Agency (☎ 020-8376 6262, 🖥 www.hbda.org.uk) assists in the creation of new businesses and helps existing businesses to survive and expand. It also manages a loan fund. The Haringey Education Business Partnership (🖥 www.hebp.co.uk) provides work experience and training for young people in the borough.

♦ **Harrow** – Harrow In Business (☎ 020-8427 6188, 🖥 www.harrowinbusiness.com) provides advice, information and support for new and existing businesses.

♦ **Sutton** – The Sutton Business Federation (☎ 020-8642 9193), which is set to become the borough's Chamber of Commerce, provides support mainly for existing businesses.

♦ **Wandsworth** –The Economic Development Office (☎ 020-8871 7031) offers up to 25 per cent support towards the cost of refurbishing shop fronts and business interiors in the borough as part of its Town Centre Improvement Scheme. It also co-ordinates the Wandsworth Business Support Network, a bi-monthly forum for borough business matters.

Internet

The following websites are just a few of those providing help and advice to people planning to establish a business in London. See also **Appendix C**.

♦ 🖥 www.brint.com/interest.html – provides the text of business management and IT journals;

♦ 🖥 www.businesslink.gov.uk – the site of Business Link for London;

♦ 🖥 www.govgrants.com – the site of the private Enterprise Advisory Service for information on financial support available from the UK government and the EU;

♦ 🖥 www.tsnn.co.uk – provides information and help arranging an exhibition stand for your business;

♦ 🖥 www.netaccountants.com – the site of the Dyer Partnership, which provides accounting and tax information for small and medium-size businesses;

♦ 🖥 www.hmrc.gov.uk – HM Revenue and Customs' site, containing information on self-assessment, etc.;

♦ 🖥 www.reedbusiness.co.uk – the site of Reed Business Information, which provides publications and 'marketing solutions' for businesses.

REGENERATION

Many parts of London are either undergoing or are planned for regeneration, thanks to large injections of government, local council and/or private money. The most high-profile scheme is the transformation of London's former docks into the now thriving business area known as Docklands. Whether you're thinking of setting up your own business or looking for a job, there are many projects worth investigating, some of which are listed below. For the latest information, contact the relevant borough councils (see **Chapter 1**).

◆ **East Battersea** (Wandsworth) – there have been a number of proposals regarding the development of the old Battersea Power Station, none of which have borne fruit to date. For details see 🖳 www.batterseapowerstation.com.

◆ **Haringey** – has over 30 development sites, centred on Tottenham and Wood Green. Details can be found on the borough's website (🖳 www.haringey.gov.uk).

◆ **Leaside** (Tower Hamlets) – an area on the eastern edge of Tower Hamlets with the River Lea as its boundary. Its long-term regeneration scheme offers some of the best business opportunities in London; details can be obtained from the Leaside Regeneration Company (☎ 020-262 0846, 🖳 www.leasideregeneration.com). The Upper Lea Valley Partnership is one of the largest partnerships in the UK, investing £120m in the area over seven years; details can be obtained from the Learning and Skills Council (☎ 0870-900 6800, 🖳 www.lsc.gov.uk).

◆ **Olympic Park** (Newham) – the name of the main site in the Lower Lea Valley east London, which is the venue for the 2012 Olympic Games (🖳 www.london2012.com/plans/olympic-park). By the time of the opening ceremony, around 100,000 people will be working on the project, including 3,000 staff, and thousands of volunteers and contractors. Staff positions will be advertised at 🖳 www.london2012.com.

◆ **Park Royal** (Brent) – a huge industrial estate (home of Guinness, among 800 other companies), on which the Park Royal Partnership (☎ 020-3110 2300, 🖳 www.parkroyal.org) aims to create an additional 20,000 jobs;

◆ **Peckham** (Southwark) – the site of a recent £250m regeneration scheme. Other nearby areas due for redevelopment include the Aylesbury Estate, Elephant & Castle, Old Kent Road and Burgess Park. Details are available from Southwark council (☎ 020-7525 5000, 🖳 www.southwark.gov.uk).

◆ **Thames Gateway** – an ambitious scheme to develop east London and the largest urban regeneration project in Europe. Details are available from the Thames Gateway London Partnership (☎ 020-7673 4578, 🖳 www.thames-gateway.org.uk).

◆ **Wandsworth** – the site of a recent £20m regeneration programme co-ordinated by the Wandsworth Challenge Partnership (☎ 020-8871 6000, 🖳 www.wandsworth.gov.uk);

◆ **White City** (Lambeth) – this development scheme, which has been on the cards for 25 years, aims to develop a 40-acre site into a vast shopping and leisure centre. Details are available from Lambeth council (☎ 020-7926 1000, 🖳 www.lambeth.gov.uk).

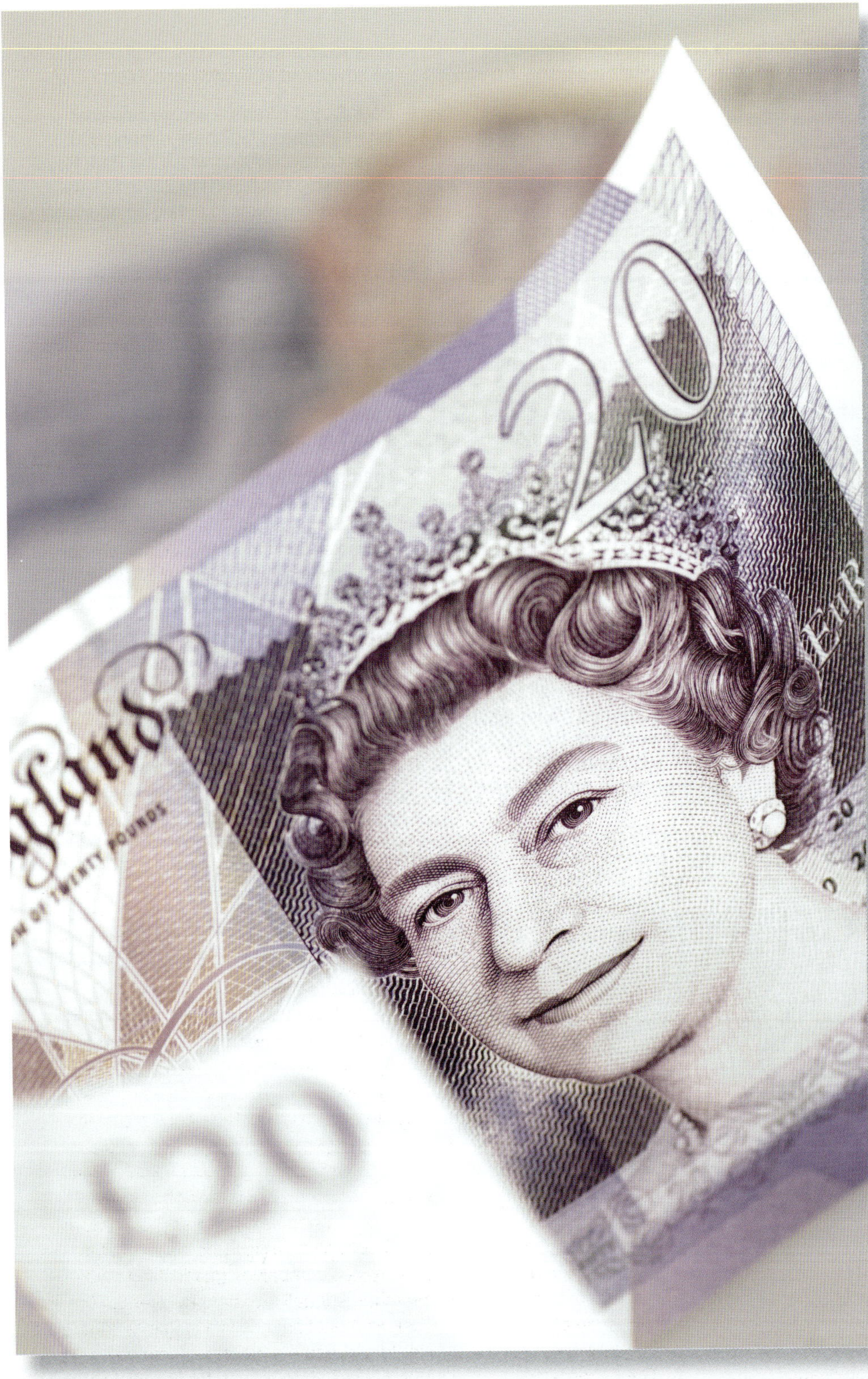
20
£20

6.

MONEY MATTERS & INSURANCE

Competition for your money is lively in the UK and, in addition to many British and foreign banks, financial services are provided by building societies, investment brokers, insurance companies, the post office and even large chain stores, supermarkets and service organisations. London is the most important financial market in Europe and one of the three most important in the world, with New York and Tokyo. In 2008, the City (London's financial centre) was hard hit by the credit squeeze caused by the US sub-prime loan scandal, which led to thousands of redundancies and the government bail-out of the Northern Rock bank.

The tax burden on individuals has increased in recent years, when direct and indirect taxes are taken into account, and deductions from gross salary, including income tax, social security and other benefit contributions, now total an average of over 30 per cent. However, taxes (particularly income tax) are still lower in the UK than in many other European countries. The cost of living has been steadily rising in recent years and the UK is now one of the most expensive countries in Europe, and London one of the most expensive cities in the world.

Among the many British eccentricities is the government's financial tax 'year', which runs from 6th April to 5th April the following year.

The UK is a credit-financed society (in recent years, debt has doubled, while savings have halved), although following recent problems and uncertainty in the financial markets, companies are more cautious about lending money and issuing credit. Credit cards have largely replaced 'real' money and are now used for over 75 per cent of all retail purchases. Britons owe over £60bn on credit cards and over 5 per cent of cardholders owe £5,000 or more. Paradoxically, however, your financial standing in the UK is usually determined by the number of cards you have and your ability to pay them off regularly, therefore remaining credit worthy. Cards include credit cards, cash cards, debit cards, cheque guarantee cards, charge cards, store cards and affinity cards. (There's no official credit rating system in the UK, as in some other countries.)

The UK has had one of the least regulated financial service industries in the developed world, in the sense that there are few controls over interest rates and charges, although recently created regulatory bodies should tighten things up. Anyone can set himself up as an 'investment consultant' and charge whatever fees he wishes. For this reason, the UK has been described as the financial rip-off centre of Europe and it's estimated that finance companies (particularly banks) overcharge small investors by over £500m per year. Personal finance is a jungle and there are plenty of predators waiting to pounce on your loot. Always shop around for financial services and never sign a contract unless you know exactly what the costs and implications are.

When you arrive in London to take up residence or employment, make sure you have sufficient cash, travellers' cheques, credit cards, luncheon vouchers, coffee machine tokens, silver dollars, gold bars and diamonds to last at least until your first pay day, which may be some time after your arrival. Don't, however, carry a lot of cash.

There are numerous books and magazines to help you manage your British finances, including *Be Your Own Financial Adviser* by Jonquil Lowe (Which?). Personal finance magazines include *Money Observer*, *What Investment*, *Moneywise* and *Which Money* (the latter is only available on subscription). Personal finance information (including the best loan and mortgage interest rates) is published in the financial pages of the Saturday and Sunday editions of national newspapers, and is also available via the internet, e.g. 🖥 www.moneywise.co.uk and 🖥 www. thisismoney.co.uk.

The figures and information contained in this chapter are based on current law and HM Revenue and Customs practice, which in the UK are subject to (frequent) change.

BANKS & BUILDING SOCIETIES

The major British banks with branches throughout London (termed 'high street' banks) include the Abbey (🖥 www.abbey. com), Barclays (🖥 www.barclays.co.uk), HSBC (🖥 www.hsbc.co.uk), Lloyds TSB (🖥 www. lloydstsb.com) and National Westminster (🖥 www.natwest.com). Other major banks with branches in London are the Co-operative Bank (🖥 www.co-operativebank.co.uk), the Bank of Scotland (part of HBOS Group, 🖥 www.bankofscotland.co.uk) and the Royal Bank of Scotland (🖥 www.rbs.co.uk) – the last two being completely separate organisations despite the similarity of their names.

There are also many private banks (mainly offering 'portfolio management' services for the wealthy), foreign banks (over 500 in the City of London alone) and internet banks such as Cahoot (🖥 www.cahoot.co.uk) and First Direct, 🖥 www.firstdirect.com), which don't have branches and are 'open' 24 hours per day. Most banks have websites and many offer online banking, a rapidly growing area.

> In recent years, banking services have been provided by an increasing number of institutions including internet banks (although usually aligned with or owned by one of the major High Street banks), supermarkets and stores such as Marks & Spencer.

British banks provide free banking for personal customers who remain in credit, pay (negligible) interest on account balances and offer a range of financial services (although they usually aren't the best place to buy insurance or pensions). If you do a lot of travelling abroad, you may find the comprehensive range of services offered by the high street banks advantageous. Many services provided by British banks are also provided by building societies (see below), which often offer better deals on financial 'products'.

The relationship between the major UK banks and their customers has deteriorated in the last decade. During the '90s recession, banks dramatically increased their charges to personal and business customers to recoup their losses on bad loans to developing countries. Few people in the UK have a good word to say about their banks, which are widely perceived to be profit-hungry and impersonal, and complaints have risen hugely in recent years. British banks made record profits (running into billions of pounds) in the last few decades, which served only further to annoy customers who think their banks are ripping them off; for example, it can take four days to transfer cash from one account to another via the internet, a transaction that should be instantaneous.

The global financial crisis of 2007 and 2008 saw British banks and buildings societies getting what some people see as their comeuppance, having to write off billions of pounds against bad debts and seeing their share prices plummet. A number of banks have had to raise additional funds from investors to shore up their assets.

To be fair, most banks have been trying to improve customer relations by introducing codes of conduct and payments for mistakes or poor service. In any case, you shouldn't allow considerations of 'loyalty' to prevent you from switching banks if it will save you money, as, when times are hard, your bank won't hesitate to withdraw your safety net (during recessions banks are directly responsible for the failure of hundreds of small businesses through arbitrarily withdrawing or refusing overdrafts and loans).

Building Societies

Building societies date back to 1775 and were originally established to cater for people saving to buy a home. Savers would deposit 5 or 10 per cent of the cost of a home with the building society, which then lent them the balance. A building society would rarely lend to anyone who wasn't a regular saver, although this changed many years ago. In 1987, the regulations governing institutions offering financial services were changed and, as a result, banks and building societies now compete head-on for customers. There has been a wave of mergers and take-overs in recent years, and the number of societies has fallen dramatically. Many building societies have converted to banks (called 'de-mutualisation') in recent years, offering account holders large cash incentives as an inducement to vote in favour of such moves. Many 'carpetbaggers' have increased their chance of such a pay-out by opening accounts at a number of building societies.

Nowadays, building societies offer practically all the services provided by banks, including current and savings accounts, cheque guarantee cards, cash cards, personal loans, credit cards, insurance and travel services. In an effort to woo customers away from banks, many building societies produce 'transfer packs' (even containing pre-printed transfer letters!). However, building societies don't always offer the same services, types of accounts or rates of interest (those offering the best interest rates are often the smaller ones).

If you're looking for a long-term investment, the number of branches may not be of importance, particularly if you do most of your banking via ATMs, as account holders at all major banks and building societies can use the ATMs of other banks (and building societies) free of charge via the LINK system.

Canary Wharf, Tower Hamlets

Deposit Protection

All banks and building societies, including branches and subsidiaries of foreign banks accepting sterling deposits in the UK, must be licensed by the Bank of England and contribute to the Deposit Protection Fund (DPF), which guarantees that deposits up to £35,000 (which covers over 95 per cent of savers) will be repaid if a bank goes bust. It was decided in 2008 to increase the guarantee to £50,000, although if you have more than this sum to invest, it's advisable to spread it around several banks and financial institutions.

Complaints

British banks are slow to rectify mistakes or to resolve disputes and rarely accept responsibility, even when clearly in the wrong. It has been estimated (based on proven cases) that banks routinely overcharge small business customers by hundreds of millions of pounds every year. If your bank makes a mess of your account and causes you to lose money and spend time resolving it, you're within your rights to claim financial compensation for your time and trouble in addition to any financial loss. However, banks typically stall complaints for years and use their financial muscle to wear down customers (some banks fight every case in the courts).

☑ SURVIVAL TIP

If you have a complaint against a British bank and have exhausted the bank's complaints procedure, you can apply for independent arbitration to the Financial Ombudsman Service, South Quay Plaza, 183 Marsh Wall, London E14 9SR (☎ 020-7964 0500, 🖳 www.financial-ombudsman.org.uk).

Business Hours

Normal bank (and building society) opening hours are from 9 or 9.30am until 3.30 or 4pm (some are open until 5.30pm) Mondays to Fridays, with no closure over the lunch period. Most branches are open late one day a week until 5.30 or 6pm and some open on Saturdays, e.g. from 9.30am until 12.30pm (some are open until 3.30pm). *Bureaux de change* have longer opening hours, including Saturdays and Sundays in tourist areas, but should be used in dire circumstances only, owing to their high commission and/or poor exchange rates. When banks are closed, you can change money at post offices, which are usually open from 9am to 5.30pm, Mondays to Fridays and from 9am to 12.30pm on Saturdays. All banks are closed on public holidays, which are generally called 'bank holidays'.

Most banks at major airports are open from 6.30 or 7am to 11 or 11.30pm, seven days per week, and some airports, e.g. London's Gatwick and Heathrow airports, have 24-hour banks. Some banks at London railway stations (e.g. Victoria) also have extended opening hours. Most banks, building societies and main post offices in the UK have 24-hour cash dispensers (officially called automatic teller machines/ATMs) at branches for cash withdrawals, deposits and account balance enquiries. Cash machines are also located in some supermarkets and other large shops.

Opening an Account

If you're planning to work in London and will be paid monthly, one of your first acts should be to open a current (or cheque) account with a bank or building society, like over 80 per cent of the British working population. Your salary will usually be paid directly into your account by your employer (many will insist that your salary is paid into an account) and your salary statement will either be sent to your home address or be given to you at work.

You may need to wait a month or more for your first pay cheque, therefore you should check with your employer, who may (if necessary) give you a salary advance. Employees who are paid weekly are often paid in cash, in which case it's up to you whether you open a bank or building society account (although it's difficult to survive without one).

Many people have at least two accounts, a current account for their out-of-pocket expenses and day-to-day transactions, and a savings account for long-term savings (or money put aside for a 'rainy day'). Many people have both bank and building society accounts.

Before opening an account, compare bank charges, interest rates (e.g. on credit cards) and other services offered by a number of banks.

If you're planning to buy a home with a mortgage, one of the best accounts is a a an all-in-one account or mortgage current account (see **Mortgages** on page 158).

To open an account, you simply go to the bank or building society of your choice and tell them you're living in London and wish to open an account. You will be asked for proof of identity, e.g. a passport or driving licence, plus proof of address in the form of a utility bill. Foreign residents may be required to provide a reference from their employer or a foreign bank. Many banks provide new account holders with a free cash card wallet, cheque book cover and statement file. After opening an account, don't forget to give the details to your employer – if you want to get paid.

Current Accounts

The facilities you should expect from a current account (equivalent to a US checking account) include a cheque book, a paying-in book, a cheque guarantee card (preferably £100 or £250) and a free cash/debit card, which often doubles as a cheque guarantee card. Other features usually include interest earned on credit balances, no charges or fees when in credit, monthly statements, an automatic authorised overdraft facility and the availability of credit cards. Other points that apply to current accounts include the following:

- A cheque book usually contains 30 cheques and some pre-printed paying-in slips (at the back), with which you can make payments into your account.

- Most people pay their bills from their current account, either by standing order or by cheque.

- Bank statements are usually issued monthly (optionally quarterly) but can usually be consulted at any time online.

- Interest may be paid on deposits (usually quarterly) and an overdraft facility may be provided. Some current accounts pay variable rates of interest according to the account balance. If you never overdraw your current account and aren't being paid interest, you're making a free loan to your bank (something they most certainly **won't** do for you).

- Most banks don't levy charges on a current account provided you stay in credit. However, if you overdraw your account without a prior arrangement with your bank, you may be billed for bank charges on all transactions for the accounting period

Some financial institutions allow free overseas cash withdrawals from a current or savings account, e.g. the Nationwide Building Society and the Post Office.

High-interest Cheque Accounts

Most banks and building societies offer high-interest cheque (i.e. current) accounts for customers who maintain a certain minimum balance, e.g. £1,000. These accounts offer a range of benefits, including a free or cheap overdraft facility, a £250 cheque guarantee card, monthly interest payments and (usually) no transaction or monthly fees. If you don't need instant access to large sums of cash, you're better off with a savings account (see below) than a high-interest cheque account.

Savings Accounts

All banks and building societies provide a range of savings accounts, also called deposit, term deposit or high-interest accounts, most of which are intended for short or medium-term savings rather than long-term investment. When opening an account, the most important considerations are how much money you wish to save, whether it's a lump sum or a monthly amount, how quickly you might need access to it and whether you're a taxpayer.

Before committing your money to a savings account, shop around – not just among banks and building societies but also among other financial institutions. Interest rates, conditions and fees vary, so take them into account. Banks and building societies often introduce new types of account paying increased rates of interest, but they don't usually notify existing customers of this (some even forbid staff to tell customers about accounts paying higher interest), so it's up to you to ask (regularly) about new options available to you.

The best savings interest rates are published in Saturday and Sunday newspapers such as *The Times* and *The Sunday Times*, and in financial magazines such as *Money Observer*, *Moneywise* and *What Investment*. *Which?* magazine (see **Appendix B**) also offers invaluable advice and surveys.

Savers 'lose' around £1billion a year in interest on obsolete savings accounts, compared with what they could be earning on high-interest accounts. Banks are under no obligation to transfer savings to a new account paying higher interest when an account becomes obsolete.

MORTGAGES

Mortgages are available from a large number of lenders, including building societies, high street and foreign banks (including offshore banks), finance houses and credit companies, insurance companies, developers, local authorities and even employers. The UK has a competitive mortgage business with around 150 lenders offering thousands of different mortgage products, although by mid-2008 mortgage providers had toughened their lending criteria following the economic 'slowdown' and the number of products had reduced some 50 per cent.

In mid-2008, mortgage rates were on the increase (at the same time as the Bank of England was reducing the base rate – an unusual development which underlined lenders' anxiety about the housing market), after a period which saw the lowest rates for half a century. There was a wide disparity in rates offered by different providers, as they tried to make sense of the confused economy and property market, making shopping around even more important than usual.

A voluntary Mortgage Code for lenders was introduced in the '90s, setting standards of good mortgage advisory practice and providing safeguards for clients. Details are contained in a booklet (published in large print, audio and Braille formats), available from lenders or from the Council of Mortgage Lenders, Bush House, Northwest Wing, Aldwych, London WC2B 4PJ (☎ 0845-373 6771, ⌨ www.cml.org.uk). However, the code has been criticised as too vague and is contravened by many lenders.

Four factors determine whether you can obtain a mortgage and its size: your income, your credit history, the size of the deposit you can make and the type and condition of the property itself (lenders won't lend on a ruin). If you're an employee in steady employment, you should have no problem obtaining a

mortgage – although whether it will be enough to buy the home you want is another matter entirely.

Lenders cannot require you to buy expensive building (or contents) insurance from them, but will insist that you **have** building insurance and will require evidence.

Income

You can usually borrow up to between 3 and 3.75 times your gross (pre-tax) salary or, if you're borrowing as a couple, 2.5 to 2.75 times your joint income. For example, if you earn £25,000 per year and your wife earns £30,000, you would qualify for a £151,250 mortgage (2.75 x £55,000) – just about enough for a Wendy house. A single person would need to be earning over £40,000 to obtain a similar mortgage. In 2008, lenders were less flexible on these multiples than in the recent past, even with people who have good career prospects (e.g. graduates). Until recently, some lenders would lend professionals up to five times their annual salary, although such deals are currently very thin on the ground. Up to four people can legally share the ownership of a property, although most lenders allow a maximum of three co-owners.

You can apply for a mortgage after an offer on a property is accepted, but it's much better to do so in advance. Most lenders will give you provisional mortgage approval over the phone and will provide a written 'mortgage promise' that you can show sellers to prove that you're a serious buyer and can obtain the required loan. If you're refused a mortgage, you can ask the Council of Mortgage Lenders (see above) for advice.

☑ SURVIVAL TIP

Use an independent broker to find the best mortgage deal and also save considerable time and trouble.

Self-certification Mortgages

The self-employed are entitled to take out a self-certification mortgage, i.e. on the basis of their own 'estimate' of their earnings rather than proof of income, of between 75 and 85 per cent of the value of a property. This may be a solution for those with an irregular income or who have been refused a conventional mortgage. However, the interest rates on self-certification mortgages are typically around 2 per cent above the standard rates, so you should only treat them as a last resort. Brokers may push self-certification mortgages to the self-employed, as they earn higher commission, but this doesn't mean that they're in your interest.

Percentage

The larger the deposit you can pay (as a percentage of the value of the property you're buying), the wider the choice of mortgages and deals available. In the past borrowers have been able to obtain 95 or 100 per cent mortgages, but 2008's credit crunch saw these evaporate like morning mist and in the current market a maximum of around 80 or 85 per cent is more common on old properties and only 70 or 75 per cent on new-build flats.

The size of a mortgage in relation to the price or value of a property is known as the 'loan-to-value' (LTV) ratio. For example, a £225,000 mortgage on a flat costing £300,000 represents an LTV ratio of 75 per cent.

Mortgage Indemnity Guarantee

If you borrow more than a certain percentage of a property's value, which varies according to the lender, you must usually have a mortgage indemnity guarantee (MIG) – also called a high lending fee, mortgage risk fee or maximum advance premium. This is to protect the lender in the event that you're unable to repay the loan and the lender is forced to repossess a property.

Where applicable, the difference between the LTV ratio and the lender's MIG threshold is the amount on which you must take out a MIG. The indemnity premium is typically 8 per cent of the amount of the loan being advanced above the lender's threshold. For example, if the lender's threshold is 75 per cent and you receive an 85 per cent mortgage on a £300,000 property, then the amount above the lender's threshold is £30,000 x 8 per cent = £2,400.

The MIG can be paid up-front or added to the mortgage and some lenders allow you to pay it over a few years without interest. If you add it to the mortgage, the MIG premium is likely to cost you three times as much over 25 years and if you pay off the mortgage early you don't receive a refund of a portion of the MIG.

The number of first-time buyers fell to an all-time low in mid-2008, when they were almost half of what they had been a year earlier.

Term

The usual home loan period in the UK is 25 years on a repayment mortgage and 40 years on an interest-only mortgage (see below). Overpaying on your mortgage in order to pay it off early can save tens of thousands of pounds in interest and is recommended when the interest paid on savings is low. For example, reducing the term from 25 to 20 years will save you £12,000 in interest on a £50,000 repayment mortgage. Most mortgages allow you to pay off lump sums at any time, which can also save you thousands of pounds in interest and reduce the term of your loan. For example, a lump sum payment of £5,000 results in a saving of £17,948 on a 20-year mortgage at 7.7 per cent and a payment of £10,000 a saving of £32,551. There are usually minimum lump sum payments, e.g. £500 or £1,000, and lenders may credit lump sum payments immediately, monthly

or annually. There are usually penalties with fixed rate loans.

Types of Mortgage

Once you've calculated how much you need to or can afford to borrow and the term of the loan, you must decide what kind of mortgage is best for you. The most common types of mortgage currently offered in the UK are described below.

Repayment Mortgage

Repayment mortgages account for some 80 per cent of mortgages in the UK. They're so called because you repay the original loan and interest over the period of the mortgage, as with most personal loans. Your monthly payment includes both interest and capital payments – mostly interest at the start and mostly capital towards the end of the term.

One advantage of a repayment mortgage is that the term of the loan can be extended if you have trouble meeting your monthly repayments. A disadvantage is that you must take out a form of life insurance called a 'mortgage protection policy' to ensure that your loan is paid off if you die. This policy isn't expensive, as it pays off the mortgage only if you die before the term of the loan is completed (and both the term and amount owed decrease over time).

For the majority of people, a repayment mortgage together with adequate life insurance is the best choice, as it's the only loan that guarantees to pay off your mortgage by the end of the term (provided you maintain regular payments).

Interest-only Mortgages

With an interest-only mortgage (these account for around one in five of mortgages), you pay interest as with a repayment mortgage. However, instead of also paying off the loan itself (capital), the loan simply stays in existence until you decide to repay it, which could be at any time from six months to 60 years after taking it out. It isn't necessary to have an insurance policy to repay the loan should you die, but it's recommended if others are dependent on your income.

Interest-only loans are good for single people with no dependants, those whose earnings fluctuate, people who expect to receive an inheritance and those whose salary is likely to rise substantially in the future. They are also popular among buy-to-let investors, as the mortgage repayments are much lower and should be covered by the rental.

The major disadvantage of interest-only mortgages is that most lenders will only lend up to 75 per cent of a property's value. For most people, it's essential to make provision for repaying the capital sum at the end of the original mortgage term, which can be done with an investment such as an Individual Savings Account/ISA, whose dividends are tax-free.

Endowment Mortgages

With an endowment mortgage you pay interest over the length of the loan at the same time as paying into an endowment policy, which should provide a large enough lump sum to pay off the mortgage at the end of the term, usually 25 years – 'should' being the operative word (see below). The policy also carries life insurance, which ensures that, if you die, the mortgage is paid off in full and any money left over is paid to your estate. The loan and endowment are separate and you can obtain them from different sources. You should obtain independent advice and try to find a lender with a low interest rate and an insurance company with a good track record.

If you're lucky, you'll be left with a tax-free sum at the end of the term after your loan has been paid off, although there are no guarantees. Investments depend on the stock market, which could performed badly. In the early 21st century, over 75 per cent of endowment policies were facing a shortfall amounting to thousands of pounds, which means that some 7.5m endowments could fail to repay mortgages. Some endowments

are worth less than the holders have paid in, even after ten years! **Consequently, in recent years mortgage advisers have advised most borrowers to avoid endowment mortgages like the plague!**

Interest Rates

Generally, you'll have a choice between a fixed-rate loan and a variable-rate loan. Fixed-rate loans, where the interest rate is fixed for a number of years (which may be as little as one year or as much as the whole mortgage term) no matter what happens to the base rate in the meantime, used to be rare in the UK and weren't popular with borrowers or lenders. Until recently (with falling rates) they were at a record low, but their popularity has recently risen. If interest rates go down, you may find yourself paying more than the current rate, but at least you'll know exactly what you must pay each month. Those on tight budgets who cannot afford an increase in their mortgage repayments are better off with a fixed-rate mortgage.

With a variable rate mortgage, the interest rate goes up and down in accordance with the base rate. Theoretically, when the base rate changes, the variable rate should rise or fall by the same percentage. However, when the base rate falls, many lenders don't pass on cuts (or the whole amount) to borrowers, ostensibly to protect savers, because when mortgage rates are cut the interest paid to savers must also be reduced. The Bank of England reduced interest rates in early 2008 in an effort to stave off recession, but rising inflation in mid-2008 led to fears that they would be increased again. In any case, lower interest rates hadn't resulted in lower mortgage rates for thousands of borrowers, as banks didn't pass on the cuts (they are under no obligation to do so). In fact, unsure about the strength of the UK property market and their ability to borrow money, banks actually increased their mortgage interest rates, while at the same time reducing the rates paid to savers!

To judge which type of mortgage is better for you, you must estimate in which direction interest rates are heading – a difficult feat that even the so-called experts cannot manage. The variable rate is usually around 1.5 per cent above the base rate (set by the Bank of England), although as mentioned above, this 'relationship' between the base rate and mortgage rates is no longer guaranteed. Building societies typically offer standard variable rate mortgages that are around half a percentage point below those of high street banks. If you have a fixed rate for a set period, after which the rate reverts to the standard variable rate (SVR), there are high penalties for switching lenders during this period.

An important (and often overlooked) aspect of a mortgage is how frequently interest is calculated, which may be daily, monthly or annually. Daily is the best method for borrowers as, when you make payments (or overpayments), they take effect immediately. With a repayment mortgage, payments include part interest and part capital repayments, and when interest is calculated annually the outstanding debt doesn't decrease daily or even monthly, but once per year. This results in your paying interest on money you've already repaid!

☑ SURVIVAL TIP

If you're unsure which way mortgage rates will go, you can take out a tracker mortgage, where the interest rate rises and falls in line with the base rate – and banks must pass on interest rate falls to borrowers.

Fees

There are various fees associated with mortgages. All lenders charge a fee for setting up a loan (variously called an arrangement, completion, booking or reservation fee), which is either a fixed amount or a percentage of the loan. Until recently, this was usually from £150 to £400 but in 2008 it was rising quickly and could be £2,000 or more. It must be paid when you apply for a loan or when you accept a mortgage. Set-up fees have been branded a rip-off by mortgage brokers and others in the loan business – particularly as some 20

per cent of purchases fall through and lenders keep the fee.

Some lenders charge an up-front application fee and a 'completion' fee when you accept the mortgage. Mortgage brokers don't usually levy a fee, as they are paid a fee or commission by lenders. In addition to mortgage fees, there's usually a valuation fee of around £200 and the lender's legal fees, although some lenders waive these.

Foreign Currency Mortgages

It's possible to obtain a foreign currency mortgage, e.g. in euros, Swiss francs, US dollars or Japanese yen. All these currencies have historically low interest rates and have provided huge savings for borrowers in recent decades. However, you should be cautious about taking out a foreign currency mortgage, as interest rate gains can be wiped out overnight by currency swings (e.g. in mid-2008 sterling was strong against the US dollar, but weak against the Euro). Most lenders advise against taking out a foreign currency loan unless you're paid in a foreign currency, and some lenders make this a condition of a loan. Euro loans are available for expatriates paid in Euros. These may offer lower interest rates than sterling but usually require a higher deposit (e.g. 30 or 40 per cent) and a high set-up fee.

The lending conditions for foreign currency home loans for UK residents are stricter than for sterling loans: they're generally granted only to those earning a minimum of £50,000 a year and may be for a minimum sum of £100,000 and a maximum of 60 per cent of a property's value.

If you take out a foreign currency loan with an offshore bank, switching between major currencies is usually permitted. When choosing between a sterling loan and a foreign currency loan, make sure that you take into account all charges, fees, interest rates and possible currency fluctuations.

Advice & Information

Whatever kind of mortgage you want, you should shop around and take time to investigate all the options available. One way to find the best deal is to contact an independent mortgage broker. Mortgage advice offered by lenders is often misleading and biased and not to be trusted (surveys have found that the mis-selling of mortgages is widespread among high street lenders). The best independent advice is found in surveys carried out by publications such as *Which? Money* magazine (see **Appendix B**), which accepts no advertisements, and daily newspapers (which do).

The best available mortgage rates are published in Sunday newspapers such as *The Sunday Times*, *The Sunday Telegraph*, *The Observer* and *The Independent on Sunday*, and in monthly mortgage magazines such as *What Mortgage* and *Mortgage Magazine*. You can also make comparisons on the internet (e.g. 🖥 www.hot-property.co.uk, 🖥 www.moneyextra.com and 🖥 www.moneynet.co.uk).

COST OF LIVING

No doubt you'd like to know how far your pounds will stretch and how much money (if any) you'll have left after paying your bills. The UK had one of the highest costs of living in the world according to figures from Employment Conditions Abroad (🖥 www.eca-international.com). High rates of duty on 'luxuries', including petrol, tobacco, alcohol to cars, make it one of the world's most expensive places to live – and London is one of the world's most expensive cities.

In a 2007 survey by Mercer Human Resources Consulting (🖥 www.mercer.com/costofliving), London was ranked the world's second most expensive city after Moscow.

British consumers pay more for food and the majority of consumer goods than people in most other developed countries, and while direct taxes are relatively low, indirect taxes are high. On the plus side, UK wages have soared in recent years and British workers take home a larger proportion of their pay after tax and social security than their counterparts in most other EU countries. The wealthy and upper middle classes have never been better off and the super-rich have so much spare cash they hardly know what to do with it. On the other hand, the gap between rich and poor in the UK is the largest since records began in 1886, and millions of state pensioners are unable to afford basic comforts such as a healthy diet, a car, heating and an annual holiday.

Your cost of living obviously depends on your circumstances and lifestyle. Your food bill will naturally depend on what you eat but is usually around 50 per cent higher in London than in the US and up to 25 per cent higher than in other western European countries. Approximately £300 should be sufficient to feed two adults for a month in most areas (excluding alcohol, fillet steak and caviar). Even in London, however, the cost of living needn't be astronomical. If you shop wisely, compare prices and services before buying and don't live too extravagantly, you may be pleasantly surprised at how little you can live on – with the exception of rent or mortgage payments. It's also possible to save a considerable sum by shopping for alcohol and other products in France, buying a car in Europe, and shopping via the internet for certain items.

The UK's inflation rate is based on the Retail Prices Index (RPI), which gives an indication of how prices rise (or fall) from year to year. The prices of around 600 'indicator' items are collected on a single day in the middle of each month (a total of around 130,000 prices are collected). On this basis, the UK's inflation rate in mid-2008 was around 3 per cent, although many analysts reckon that the real increase in the cost of living was around 10 per cent.

COUNCIL TAX

Council tax (until 1990 it was referred to as 'rates' and until 1993 as 'the poll tax') is levied by borough councils on local residents to pay for such things as further education, police, roads, waste disposal, libraries and community services, including the local police, fire and civil defence forces.

Each council fixes its own tax rates, based on the number of residents and how much money they need to finance their services. The amount payable depends on the value of your home, as 'rated' by your local council (not necessarily the market value). Properties in England are divided into the following bands:

Council Tax Bands

Band	Property Value
A	Up to £40,000
B	£40,001 to £52,000
C	£52,001 to £68,000
D	£68,001 to £88,000
E	£88,001 to £120,000
F	£120,001 to £160,000
G	£160,001 to £320,000
H	Over £320,000

Cynically, the government hasn't changed these bands since their introduction in 1993, so vast the majority of London properties now fall into Bands G and H and nothing except the smallest mobile home or garage into Bands

A-F. The 2008/09 rates for bands G and H for each borough are show in the table in **Appendix F**.

The full council tax assumes that two adults are living permanently in the dwelling. If only one adult lives in a dwelling (as their main home), the bill is reduced by 25 per cent. If a dwelling isn't a main home, e.g. it's unoccupied or is a second home, the bill is reduced by 50 per cent. Exempt dwellings include those that are unfurnished (exempt for up to six months) or undergoing structural alteration or major repair (exempt for up to six months after completion), and those that are left empty for certain reasons (e.g. the occupier is in hospital, a nursing home or prison, or is a student) or are occupied only by people under 18 years of age.

Certain people aren't counted when calculating the number of adults resident in a dwelling, e.g. full-time students and 18- and 19-year-olds who have just left school. If you or someone who lives with you has special needs arising from a disability, you may be entitled to a reduction in your council tax bill. Those receiving Income Support usually pay no council tax and others on low incomes have their bills reduced. You can appeal against the assessed value of your property and any errors due to exemption, benefits or discounts.

Council tax can usually be paid by direct debit from a bank or building society account, by post with a personal cheque, in person at council offices, by credit card, or at a bank or post office. Payment can be made in a lump sum (for which a reduction may be offered) or in ten instalments a year, from April to January.

All those who are liable for council tax must register with their local council when they take up residence in a new area and are liable to pay council tax from their first day of residence. A register is maintained by councils, containing the names and addresses of all people registered for council tax, which is open to public examination. If you don't want your name and address to appear on the register, you can apply for anonymous registration.

When moving to a new county or borough, you may be entitled to a refund of a portion of your council tax.

INSURANCE

In the UK you can insure practically anything, from losing your camera to your house falling down, and eventualities such as rain on your parade or village fête, having twins (or sextuplets) or missing a holiday. If your livelihood depends on a particular part of your anatomy, e.g. your voice, legs, teeth or posterior, you can insure it against damage or decline. For particularly unusual requests, you may be required to obtain a quote from Lloyd's of London, the last resort for unusual insurance needs (not only within the UK, but also internationally). Note, however, that if an insurance requirement is particularly unusual or risky, you may find the premiums prohibitively high and restrictions may be placed on what you can and cannot do.

The UK is renowned as a nation of gamblers, which is reflected in the relatively low cost of insurance, not only for such basic requirements as loss of income or car accidents, but also for homes and their contents. When it comes to health, many people tend to rely on state 'insurance' benefits, which come under the heading of 'social security'. These include sickness and unemployment pay, income support (for families on low incomes) and state pensions. Note, however, that social security usually provides for the most basic needs only and those who are reduced to relying on it often exist on or below the poverty line.

It isn't necessary to spend half your income insuring yourself against every eventuality from the common cold to a day off work, but it's important to be covered against any event which could precipitate a major financial disaster (such as telling your boss what you think of him when you've had a few too many drinks). There are just two cases in the UK when insurance for individuals is compulsory: building insurance if you have a mortgage (because your lender will insist on it) and third party car insurance, which is required by law. Voluntary insurance includes pensions, income protection, accident insurance (though you may need accident and third party insurance for high-risk sports), and health, home contents, personal liability, legal expenses, dental, travel, motor breakdown and life insurance.

As with everything to do with finance, it's important to shop around when buying insurance. Simply picking up a few brochures from insurance brokers or making a few phone calls can save you a lot of money (enough to pay for this book many times over).

If you're coming to London from abroad, you'd be wise to ensure that your family has full health insurance during the period between leaving your last country of residence and arriving in the UK. This is particularly important if you're covered by a company health insurance policy terminating on the day you leave your present employment. If possible, it's better to continue with your present health insurance policy, particularly if you have existing health problems that may not be covered by a new policy. If you aren't covered by the National Health Service, it's essential to have private health insurance.

If you want to make a claim against a third

party or a third party is claiming against you, you'd be wise to seek legal advice – unless it's a minor claim. Note that British law is likely to be different from that of your home country or your previous country of residence and you should never assume that it's the same.

Building Insurance

When buying a home, you're usually responsible for insuring it before you even move in. If you take out a mortgage to buy a property, your lender will usually insist that your home (including most permanent structures on your property) has building insurance from the time you exchange contracts and are legally the owner. Even when it isn't required by a lender, you'd be extremely unwise not to have building insurance, though if you buy the leasehold of an apartment, your building insurance will be arranged by the owner of the freehold.

Building insurance usually includes cover for loss or damage caused by fire, theft, riot or malicious acts; water leakage from pipes or tanks; oil leakage from central heating systems; floods, storms and lightning; explosions or aircraft impact; vehicles or animals; earthquakes, subsidence or landslides; and falling trees or aerials; as well as cover for temporary homelessness, e.g. up to £10,000. Some insurance companies also offer optional cover to include trees and shrubs damaged maliciously or by storms. There may be an excess (see below), which is intended to deter people from making small claims.

Building insurance should be renewed each year and insurance companies are continually updating their policies, so you must ensure that a policy still provides the cover required when you receive a renewal notice – and that there isn't a better option elsewhere.

Lenders fix the level of cover required when you apply for a mortgage and usually offer to arrange building insurance for you, but you're normally free to make your own arrangements. If you arrange your own building insurance, it must meet the specified level of cover. Most people take the easy option and arrange insurance through their mortgage

Docklands Marina

lender (premiums are usually added to your monthly mortgage payments and are therefore 'invisible'), although this is usually the most expensive option.

The amount for which your home must be insured isn't the current market value but the cost of rebuilding it, should it be destroyed. This varies according to the type of property and the area. Building insurance doesn't, however, cover structural faults that existed when you took out the policy, which is why it's important to have a full structural survey done before buying a property.

☑ SURVIVAL TIP

Many people pay far too much for their building insurance, as many insurance companies greatly over-estimate the cost of rebuilding. In many cases, building costs are calculated using the Royal Institute of Chartered Surveyors (RICS, 🖳 www.ricsfirms.com) Rebuilding Costs Index rather than the correct Tender Price Index (see 🖳 www.bcis.co.uk), which takes into account actual building prices.

Shop around, as many people can reduce their premiums by half – but don't believe the advertising blurb, as some companies that claim to save you money actually charge more than many of their competitors.

Most insurers provide index-linked building insurance. It is, however, your responsibility to ensure that your level of cover is adequate, particularly if you carry out improvements or extensions which substantially increase the value of your home. All lenders provide information and free advice. If your level of cover is too low, an insurance company is within its rights to reduce the amount it pays out when a claim is made, in which case you may find you cannot afford to have your house rebuilt or repaired, should disaster strike.

The cost of building insurance varies according to the insurer, the type of building and the area, and is calculated per £1,000 of insurance. In London, insurance rates are generally over £3 per £1,000. Therefore, insurance on a property costing £200,000 to rebuild usually costs from around £600 to £600 per year. In recent years, increased competition, particularly from direct insurers, has helped to moderate premium increases. Insurance for 'non-standard' homes, such as those with thatched roofs or timber construction, holiday homes, period properties and listed buildings, is usually much higher.

There may be different levels of cover, the highest usually covering damage to glass (windows and patio doors) and porcelain (baths, washbasins and WCs), although you may have to pay extra for accidental damage, e.g. when your son blasts a cricket ball through the bathroom window. Always ask your insurer what isn't covered and what it will cost to include it (if required).

Premiums can usually be paid monthly (although there may be an extra charge) or annually. Some home insurance policies charge an excess (deductible), e.g. £50 or £100, for each claim, while others have an excess for certain claims only, e.g. subsidence or landslide, which is usually £1,000 or £2,000. Owners of houses vulnerable to subsidence (e.g. those built on clay) and those living in areas susceptible to flooding (whose numbers are increasing, as more residential housing is built on flood plains and climate change increases the risk of flooding) are likely to pay much higher premiums. However, it's estimated that over a million people pay too much for their insurance cover, because their insurers have wrongly assumed that they're at risk from subsidence. Subsidence is a risk primarily in east and south England, exacerbated by a series of warm, dry years beginning in the '90s.

Should you need to make emergency repairs, e.g. to weather-proof a roof after a storm or other natural disaster, most insurance companies allow work up to a certain limit (e.g. £1,000) to be carried out without an estimate or approval from the insurance company, but check first. Most insurance companies provide emergency telephone numbers for policyholders requiring urgent advice. If you let your house (or part of it) or you intend leaving it unoccupied for a period of 30 days or longer, you may be required to inform your insurance company.

A booklet entitled *Buildings Insurance for Home Owners*, including a valuation table, is available from the Association of British Insurers (51 Gresham Street, London EC2V 7HQ, ☎ 020-7600 3333, 🖳 www.abi.org.uk).

Building insurance is often combined with home contents insurance (see below), when it may be termed household insurance, although it's sometimes cheaper to buy building and home contents insurance separately.

Contents Insurance

Contents insurance (also called home contents insurance) is recommended for anyone who doesn't live in an empty house. Domestic burglary is a major problem in parts of London; statistics for each of the London boroughs (except the City) are included in the table in **Appendix F**.

Although there's a lot you can do to prevent someone breaking into your home, it's often impossible or prohibitively expensive to make your home burglar-proof. However, you can ensure you have adequate contents insurance and that your most precious possessions are locked in a safe or safety deposit box.

Combining your home contents insurance with your building insurance (see above) may save you money, although it's sometimes cheaper to buy separate insurance. On the other hand, it can be advantageous to have your building and contents insured with the same company, as this avoids disputes over which company should pay for which item, which can arise if you have a fire or flood affecting both your home and its contents.

> ### ▲ Caution
>
> Take care that you don't under-insure your house contents and that you periodically reassess their value and adjust your premium accordingly, as half of all homeowners are thought to underestimate the value of their home contents.

Insured items should include everything that isn't a fixture or fitting, i.e. which you could take with you if you were moving house. If you under-insure your contents, your claim may be reduced by the percentage by which you're under-insured. It's wise to take photographs of your valuables and to keep a record of the make and serial numbers of valuable items.

Types of Policy

There are two kinds of contents insurance policy: 'sum-insured' (where you calculate the value of your contents and the insurer calculates the premium accordingly) and 'bedroom-rated' (where you pay a set premium based on the number of bedrooms in your home).

With a bedroom-rated policy, the insurance company cannot scale down a claim because of under-insurance; however, you're usually better off calculating the value of the contents to be insured. Some companies have standard and deluxe rates for contents valued, for example, at £50,000 and £100,000. You can also take out a special policy if you have high-value contents, although this usually requires a valuation and therefore may not be worthwhile.

A standard home contents policy (of either type) covers your belongings against the same sort of 'natural disasters' as building insurance (see page 166). It may cover locks, garden contents, heating oil and metered water, and may provide personal liability cover (up to £1m) and the cost of temporary accommodation. If not included, such 'risks' can usually be covered optionally. Some policies include legal expenses cover (e.g. up to £50,000) which covers disputes with neighbours, shops, suppliers, employers and anyone who provides you with a service (e.g. a plumber or builder).

A basic contents policy doesn't usually include such items as credit cards (and their fraudulent use), cash, musical instruments, jewellery (and other 'valuables'), antiques, paintings, sports equipment and bicycles, for which you normally need to take out extra cover. A basic policy doesn't usually include accidental damage caused by you or members of your family to your own property) or your home freezer contents (in the event of a breakdown or power failure), which are subject to an additional premium. Equipment used for business also isn't usually covered, or may be covered only for a prohibitive extra payment. If you have friends or lodgers in your home, their property won't usually be covered by your policy

You can usually insure your property for its second-hand value (known as 'indemnity' insurance) or its full replacement value ('new-for-old' insurance). The latter usually excludes clothes and linen, on which wear and tear is assessed. Replacement value is the most popular form of contents insurance in the UK. It's best to take out an index-linked policy, where the level of cover is automatically increased by a percentage or fixed amount each year.

Worldwide or extra cover is offered by most insurance companies as an extension to a home contents policy. With this type of policy, your possessions are covered against accidental loss or damage outside your home, anywhere in the world. Usually each item valued above a minimum sum, e.g. £250 to £1,000, must be declared in writing.

Premiums

Home insurance premiums depend largely on where you live (and the insurer). All insurance companies assess the risk by location based on your postcode. Check before buying a home, as the difference between low and high-risk areas can be hundreds of per cent (see 🖵 www.thisismoney.co.uk/codebreaker). The difference between premiums charged by different companies for the same property can also vary by as much as 250 per cent.

Annual premiums are usually calculated per £1,000 of cover and range from around £3 to £4 in a low-risk area to between £12 and £20 in a high-risk area, sometimes more – e.g. if you live in an area liable to flooding (see **Building Insurance** above). The cost of extra cover (see above) is between £15 and £35 per year for each £1,000 covered, depending on the insurer.

If you're already insured, you may find that you can save money by changing insurers, particularly if you're insured through a bank or building society, whose insurance is usually more expensive. However, watch out for penalties when switching insurers.

Those aged over 50 or 55 (and possibly first-time homeowners) are offered discounts or reduced rates by some companies (e.g. Saga, 🖵 www.saga.co.uk, which specialises in insurance for people over 50). Some companies also provide low-cost policies for students in college accommodation or lodgings (ask an insurance broker). Most insurers offer no-claims discounts or discounts for homes with burglar alarms, high security locks or smoke detectors, or in areas with neighbourhood watch schemes.

Beware of the small print in policies, particularly those regarding security, which insurers often use to avoid paying claims. In high-risk areas, good security is a condition of insurance. You'll forfeit all rights under your policy if you leave doors or windows open (or the keys under a mat or flower pot), particularly if you've claimed a discount due to your 'Fort Knox' security. If there are no signs of forced entry, e.g. a broken window, you may be unable to claim for a theft.

You should inform your insurer of any changes that may affect your policy, e.g. a loft conversion or extension. If you're going to leave your house empty for a long period, e.g. a month or longer, you should inform your insurer.

'THEY WANT YOUR PHONE!'

BEWARE
Street robbers are targeting persons using phones in this street!

7.
GETTING AN EDUCATION

Like all major capital cities, London is a social, economic and cultural potpourri, which is reflected in its education system. In few other places in the world can you find such a diversity of educational options at all levels, from pre-school to university postgraduate, nor such a variety of ethnic and linguistic backgrounds. (It's reckoned that over 200 different languages are spoken in London.) In some boroughs children from ethnic minority families account for over 90 per cent of school places. For example, in Tower Hamlets fewer than 15 per cent of primary school children are classed as white British, compared to almost two-thirds Bangladeshi Asian.

However, your range of choices may not be quite as wide as it appears at first glance. Some of the best establishments may be closed to you because they're too expensive, too exclusive or too popular, e.g. they cater for a religious group or nationality to which you don't belong, you cannot meet the entry criteria, you don't live within a particular catchment area or they're oversubscribed. Although London has some of the best schools in the country, within both the state and private (fee-paying) sectors, it also has some of the worst. These include a number of private schools and many state schools, some of which have failed official inspections and face closure if their standards don't improve.

The UK is currently suffering a chronic shortage of teachers, which means that average class sizes are increasing. A survey by the *Guardian* newspaper indicated that there were around 3,000 too few teachers in secondary schools.

Each London borough is also an education authority, which can provide information about its schools. Telephone numbers for each London borough are listed in **Chapter 1.**

Borough education authorities were formerly called Local Education Authorities (LEA) and, although officially obsolete (in favour of Borough Education Departments or something similar), the term is still widely used informally and is used in this chapter for convenience.

CHOOSING A SCHOOL

When choosing a school (or indeed somewhere to live on the basis of local schools), take care not to rely on out-of-date information: London is in a constant state of flux and an area that was firmly downmarket five years ago may have suddenly become fashionable, driving up house prices and demand for places at local schools. An inspired new head teacher or a glowing Ofsted report (Office for Standards in Education, a non-ministerial government department that regularly inspects schools, 🖥 www.ofsted.gov.uk) can have much the same effect.

Competition for places at the best and most popular London schools – whether fee-paying or state-funded – is fierce. Getting your children into a particular state school usually depend on where you live, therefore before buying or renting a home check the current position regarding school catchment areas directly with schools.

Obtain local authority information leaflets and visit and talk to the teachers to form your own impression of a school's atmosphere and the staff's attitude. How big are classes? How well qualified and experienced are the teaching staff? Are there regular parents' evenings and opportunities for consultation? Are there problems with maintaining discipline or with drugs? Is there a uniform? What extra-curricular activities are offered, such as sports and after-school clubs and societies? Talk to playgroup leaders, nursery teachers, school secretaries or parent governors, all of whom can pass on the kind of information the school may not care to reveal.

There are numerous books for parents faced with the task of choosing a suitable school for their children, one of the best being *The London Schools Guide* (Mitchell Beazley), which is updated annually. The weekly *Times Educational Supplement* (available from newsagents') contains news and opinion about education and schools in England, including management, governors, research and teaching posts. If you're seeking a state or private school that caters for a particular religion, see **Religious Schools** on page 178.

You can consult an independent advisory service such as Gabbitas Education (Carrington House, 126–130 Regent Street, London W1B 5EE (☎ 020-7734 0161, 💻 www.gabbitas. co.uk), which claims to be the UK's leading independent educational consultancy and can provide advice and information on any aspect of education in the UK. Information about full-time courses in Greater London is available from Floodlight (☎ 0800-100900, 💻 www.floodlight. co.uk) and from bookshops in London. The website features a 'course finder' service.

There are many other useful education-related websites, including Schoolsnet (💻 www.schoolsnet.com), 'the world's No.1 education website', and TSL Education (💻 www.tsleducation.com), which claims to be the UK's leading educational publisher. Learn Direct, part of the University for Industry (☎ 0800-150450, 💻 www.learndirect-advice. co.uk), is a government-funded charitable organisation providing free information and advice on courses and career paths.

The Advisory Centre for Education (ACE), 1C Aberdeen Studios, 22 Highbury Grove,

London N5 2DQ (☎ 020-7704 3370, 💻 www. ace-ed.org.uk), provides information on all matters related to state education and operates a telephone advice line from 10am to 5pm Mondays to Fridays (☎ 0808-800 5793).

An invaluable organisation for overseas students is the UK Council for International Student Affairs (UKCISA, 9–17 St Alban's Place, London N1 0NX, ☎ 020-7288 4330, 💻 www.ukcosa.org.uk), which is a registered charity established in 1968 to promote the interests and meet the needs of overseas students in the UK and those working with them as teachers, advisors or in other capacities.

The British Council (☎ 0161-957 7755, 💻 www.britishcouncil.org) provides foreign students with information concerning all aspects of education in the UK.

PRE-SCHOOL

Pre-school is for children aged two to five and takes place in nursery schools or nursery classes attached to a primary school. It may be private or state-maintained, but there's little state provision for pre-school education in London (or, indeed, in the UK as a whole). Workplace nurseries and crèches are often greatly over-subscribed, private nannies are expensive and places at private nurseries, pre-preps and prep schools in inner London are so rare that many people register their children at birth (or even before). Finding reliable and affordable childcare for the under-fours can be one of the biggest headaches for working parents. However, the government is now offering four-year-olds a free place in a private or community nursery school, playgroup, or special nursery class, and it has begun to extend the provision to three-year-olds.

There are too many nursery schools in London to list here, but there two organisations that can help you find those in your area. The British Association for Early Childhood Education (136 Cavell Street, London E1 2JA, ☎ 020-7539 5400, 💻 www.early-education.

whether a child will get better grades at a high-achieving school than at a low-achieving one.

Generally, schools in inner London achieve worse results than those in the outer boroughs, although there are notable exceptions. Pupils living in inner London boroughs such as Lambeth, Southwark, Hackney or Tower Hamlets frequently come from poorer families. There's also a much higher percentage of children who don't speak English as their first language. Because of the difficulties associated with teaching children in these areas, there's often a high turnover of teaching staff and a consequent lack of commitment and continuity.

Ofsted reports (see below) have spotlighted low teacher expectations in some inner London schools and poor teaching of basic literacy and numeracy skills at primary school level. The London borough of Hackney was the first education authority to be stripped of its powers and to have its education services put out to private tender. The government has implemented several measures to help improve standards in the worst inner London state schools, encouraging them to form 'Education Action Zones' (EAZs) run by partnerships of local authorities, private businesses and community groups.

Those who can afford to pay their way out of this situation do so, and the professional middle classes in inner London have largely deserted the state sector, most parents preferring to pay for private education, with the result that London now has the highest proportion of schoolchildren in private schools in the UK (around 10 per cent). Nevertheless, the Higher Education Funding Council for England has reported that state-school students achieve better degree results than private school students.

If you're going to be living in a London borough with poor schools – and you cannot afford private education – you may be able to get your child into a school in the neighbouring borough by living near a borough's border, as a school's catchment area often transcends a

org) is a voluntary organisation providing information about childcare and education facilities for under-eights. The Pre-School Learning Alliance (The Fitzpatrick Building, 188 York Way, London N7 9AD, ☎ 020-7697 2500, 🖥 www.pre-school.org.uk) was established in 1963 when parents, frustrated by the lack of nursery provision, decided to take matters into their own hands and created their own self-help nursery schools. Today it's a registered charity and the single largest provider of education and care for under-fives in England.

STATE SCHOOLS

In the UK, the term state schools refers to fee-free schools run by local education authorities; they aren't called 'public schools' – a term that confusingly refers to some private schools. Private schools are officially referred to as independent schools.

Standards

London state schools vary enormously in their facilities, the type and 'quality' of their pupils and the exam results those pupils achieve – which are perhaps the most important factors to take into account when choosing a school for your children. Of course, it's a moot point borough's border. For example, many families living in Hackney and Islington (which are among London's less successful education authorities) try to get their children into a Camden school, replacing the children who scramble over the border from Camden into Westminster!

You can obtain information about catchment areas for your borough by visiting their website and using their 'Education' services, for example, you can do a search for local state schools in Camden at 🖥 http://schoolsearch. camden.gov.uk/schools/schoolsearch.aspx.

The Department for Children, Schools and Families (DCSF) no longer publishes league tables of schools by Local Education Authority (LEA), which gave an unhelpful average picture of each area. Instead, it produces achievement and 'performance' tables for each school, which are assessed according to a variety of criteria, including absentee rates as well as exam results. These can be viewed on the DCSF website (🖥 www. dcsf.gov.uk/performancetables). The same reports can be viewed on the website of the Office for Standards in Education (Ofsted), a non-ministerial government department that regularly inspects schools (🖥 www.ofsted. gov.uk). See also **School Achievement & Attainment Tables** below.

Curriculum

The National Curriculum, introduced in 1989 and revised in 1993, is compulsory in all state schools in England and Wales, and affects pupils between the ages of 5 and 16. It's designed to ensure that all children have a broad and balanced education up to the age of 16, as well as standardising education in state schools throughout the country. So if you decide at a later date to move from London to Manchester or Bristol, the disruption to your child's education should be minimal. Bear in mind though, that Scotland operates an entirely different educational system.

The 'core' subjects of the National Curriculum are English, maths and science. So-called 'foundation' subjects include technology (incorporating design as well as computer-based information technology), history,

geography, music, art and physical education. Religious and sex education must also be provided, but parents have a right to withdraw children from these subjects if they wish.

A modern foreign language is no longer compulsory after the age of 14.

In 2002, the government added 'citizenship' to the curriculum, a subject that covers social and moral responsibility, community involvement and politics, and is compulsory between the ages of 11 and 16.

You can find further information about the curriculum on the National Curriculum website (🖥 www.nc.uk.net).

Types of School

In terms of funding, there are three kinds of state school in the UK: county schools, grant-maintained schools, and voluntary-aided or voluntary-controlled schools, which are described below. LEAs also provide schools for children with special educational needs (see **Specialist Schools** on page 178).

◆ **County schools** – owned by LEAs and wholly funded by them. They're non-denominational (not church-aided or supported) and provide both primary and secondary education.

◆ **Grant-maintained schools** – The 1988 Education Reform Act allowed primary and secondary state schools to opt out of LEA control and adopt grant-maintained status, provided that a majority of their governors and parents voted in favour. Grant-maintained schools receive funding directly from central government, based on the number of pupils. Schools must manage their own budgets and employ their own support staff, including caterers and cleaners. The last Conservative government heavily promoted grant-maintained schools and offered inducements, such as increased funding, to persuade schools to opt out.

◆ **Voluntary-aided & voluntary-controlled schools** – provide both primary and secondary education and are financially maintained by LEAs. A **voluntary-aided school** is a school where the governing body, as opposed to the LEA, employs the staff and decides the admission arrangements, but the school is funded by the state and cannot charge fees. In a **voluntary-controlled school** (almost always church schools), the land and buildings are often owned by a charitable foundation. However, the LEA employs the school's staff and has primary responsibility for admission arrangements. It's funded by the state and doesn't charge fees and pupils must follow the national curriculum.

There are various school structures in different boroughs of London, where state schools may be of the following types:

Type of School	Age Group
Nursery	Up to 5
Infants/First School	5 to 7 or 5 to 8
Primary	5 to 11
Junior or Middle	7 to 11 or 8 to 12/13
Secondary	11 to 18 or 12/13 to 18
Secondary Plus	11 to 16
Sixth Form College	16 to 19

Key Stages

To help parents keep track of their children's progress at school and what they're learning (or supposed to be learning) at various ages – schooling in the UK is divided into four 'key stages'. At the end of each key stage (when their children are 7, 11, 14 and 16) parents receive a report containing the results of Standard Assessment Tests (SATs). Note, however, that there are calls to abolish some or all SATs, as it's thought they put too much pressure on pupils and make education too target-oriented. The key stages are:

Key Stage	Age	Year Groups (Classes)
1	5 to 7	1 & 2
2	7 to 11	3 to 6
3	12 to 14	7 to 9
4	14 to 16	10 & 11

School Achievement & Attainment Tables

Each year the Department for Education and Skills publishes tables on the achievement and attainment of pupils in all schools, which provide a guide to how well a school is doing. They list key stage and GCSE test results for each school in England and show how they compare with other schools. The following four tables published annually:

◆ Key Stage 2 tables (Key Stage 2 test results for state primary schools in England)

◆ Key Stage 3 tables (Key Stage 3 test results for state secondary schools in England)

◆ Key Stage 4 tables (results for GCSEs and equivalent qualifications)

◆ post-16 tables (results in general and vocational AS and A levels, Key Skills at level 3, Advanced Extension Awards, other advanced vocational qualifications and intermediate vocational qualifications)

Test results don't provide a complete picture of how a school is performing, but will help you compare schools that you're considering.

Primary Schools

State primary schools are obliged to take local children from the term in which their fifth birthday falls, although some will accept younger children into nursery or reception classes. Many schools admit new pupils at just one point in the year (usually September), which means that they accept all children who will be five within the coming school year (September to August). Therefore, children born in the summer start school not long after their fourth birthdays, which is an advantage or a disadvantage depending on how you view it.

Primary schools usually consist of 'infant' departments, for children aged five to seven, and 'junior' departments, for those aged 7 to 11.

Primary schools tend to operate their admissions policies purely on catchment area, unless they're voluntary-aided and stipulate parental religious observance.

Secondary Schools

In the state sector, most children transfer from primary school to secondary school at the age of 11. Most secondary schools are 'comprehensives' (almost 90 per cent of English children attend them), which cater for children of all abilities, but there are still some selective or 'grammar' schools – mainly in the wealthier suburbs of south London – which are always vastly oversubscribed. These schools select pupils on the basis of academic attainment. The government has pledged that there will be no new grammar schools but will allow existing schools to continue, provided they have the support of local parents. Opinion polls have indicated that there's strong parental support for selection by ability, so their future – although by no means certain – seems fairly safe, at least in the short to medium term.

Most secondary (and primary) schools are mixed (co-educational), but single-sex schools are increasingly popular, particularly for girls. Many parents believe that girls do better without boys around to distract them and there are several good girls' schools in the capital.

Bear in mind that, if there are a lot of girls' schools in a particular area, local mixed schools may be male-dominated.

PRIVATE SCHOOLS

Parents seeking private education for their children will find many excellent schools in London (where there are over 400 in all), although the best schools are very expensive and have long waiting lists, so apply sooner rather than later (some people put a child's name down before he or she is born!). It's generally easier to find places at short notice in outer London than inner London private schools.

Private schools are sometimes called independent schools, referring to the fact that they're independent of the state system, although this is a misleading term, as not all independent schools are fee-paying.

Most private secondary schools are single-sex, at least until the sixth form, and most are day rather than boarding schools. Almost all of them are located in north, west and south London.

Fees for private schools vary from around £5,000 per annum (in the least expensive day schools) to £25,000 (for a top boarding school place). It's worth bearing in mind that, although you may be living and working in London, your children can be privately educated anywhere – even in your 'home' country.

Children pass through several stages within the private school system. Preparatory schools (known as 'prep' schools) take pupils from as young as two – if they have a nursery or pre-prep department, though more usually from six or seven – up to the age of 14. After prep school they progress to a senior school (sometimes confusingly called a 'public' school) where they take GCSE examinations at the age of around 16 and, if they stay on, A-levels two years later.

> ## ☑ SURVIVAL TIP
>
> Many private senior schools have associated junior, preparatory, pre-prep or even nursery schools. If you're likely to be staying in London for the majority of your children's education, this is a good way of ensuring continuity as they grow up.

Entry to some private schools involves a tough selection process, whereas others admit a wide ability range. Most day schools still use the '11 Plus' examination as an academic filter, while boarding schools tend to favour the Common Entrance Examination (CEE), usually taken two years later, at the age of 13. Details and past papers of both tests are available from the Independent Schools Examinations Board (☎ 01425-621111, 🖥 www.iseb.co.uk).

The internet is a valuable resource when researching private schools in London, and the website of publisher John Catt Educational (🖥 www.schoolsearch.co.uk) is an excellent starting point. It provides a free search facility via email, where you enter details about your child and your requirements and the publisher will suggest suitable schools. The site also offers links to schools' own websites. Most private (and many state) schools have websites, which should be examined in conjunction with their printed prospectuses.

John Catt publishes a number of annually updated books about private schools, including *Boarding Schools & Colleges*, *Education at 16*, *International Schools*, *Preparatory Schools* and *Which London School?*.

Other useful resources for those interested in private education include the following:

♦ **Independent Schools Council/ISC** (🖥 www.isc.co.uk) – the central body that co-ordinates and represents the interests of the various organisations concerned with private education in the UK, the most significant of which are listed below. Some 80 per cent of privately educated children in the UK attend ISC schools.

♦ **Girls' Day School Trust** (100 Rochester Row, London SW1P 1JP, ☎ 020-7393 6666, 🖥 www.2gdst.net) – founded in 1872 and the pioneer of 'quality' education for girls;

♦ **Girls' Schools Association/GSA** (130 Regent Road, Leicester LE1 7PG, ☎ 0116-254 1619, 🖥 www.gsa.uk.com) – represents around 220 independent girls' schools throughout the UK;

♦ **Headmasters' & Headmistresses' Conference/HMC** (12 The Point, Rockingham Road, Leicestershire, LE16 7QU, ☎ 01858-469059, 🖥 www.hmc. org.uk) – represents a membership of 250 heads of boys' and co-educational independent schools. The HMC is proud of the fact that its pupils come from a wide variety of backgrounds and that, although the assisted places scheme (whereby 'disadvantaged' pupils receive government grants) is now being phased out, many schools still provide bursaries and scholarships for over a third of their pupils. Over 90 per cent of pupils go on to higher education.

♦ **Independent Association of Preparatory Schools/IAPS** (☎ 01926-887833, 🖥 www.iaps.org.uk) – a professional body representing prep school heads throughout the UK and overseas. As well as completely independent prep schools, the association also represents schools affiliated to senior schools and offers day, boarding and, in some cases, flexible (e.g. weekday) boarding places. Schools range from rural to urban and single-sex to co-ed.

♦ **Society of Headmasters and Headmistresses of Independent Schools/ SHIS** (☎ 01858-433760, 🖳 www.shmis. org.uk) – represents a range of smaller independent schools, which include those catering for pupils with a specific religious orientation, pupils gifted in one of the performing arts and those with special needs. Most schools have no more than 300 pupils and are co-educational.

RELIGIOUS SCHOOLS

Schools linked to a particular church or religion include both state schools (e.g. many voluntary-aided schools) and private schools. The former often have wider catchment areas than other state schools, taking pupils from all over London who satisfy their entry requirements and whose families are devout.

State schools for particular religions in London include the Roman Catholic London Oratory School (favoured by former Prime Minister Tony Blair) and Sacred Heart High School (both in Hammersmith), the Anglican girls' comprehensive Lady Margaret in Parson's Green, and Hasmonean in Hendon, which serves the Jewish community.

Many private schools cater for particular religious beliefs. If you're looking for a fee-paying school with a particular religious affiliation, you should contact one of the organisations listed below:

♦ **Catholic Education Service** (☎ 020-7901 4880, 🖳 www.cesew.org.uk) – represents Catholic education interests in England and Wales with government and national agencies, advises teachers and supports the work of Catholic schools and colleges;

♦ **Methodist Education** (🖳 www. methodisteducation.co.uk) – takes administrative responsibility for Methodist colleges and schools, and provides advice to the church on the formulation of educational policy;

♦ **Muslim Educational Trust/MET** (☎ 020-7272 8502, 🖳 www.muslim-ed-trust.org.uk) – the UK's oldest national Muslim educational organisation, dealing with the concerns of Muslim parents and children. The MET arranges for teachers to give lessons in Islamic Studies in English to Muslim children in state schools and publishes a range of internationally orientated books and posters on Islam for use by pupils and teachers.

♦ **Sikh Education Council of the United Kingdom** (☎ 07870-138616, 🖳 www. thesikhway.com) – supports the religious and educational needs of Sikhs in the UK and assists parents, teachers and LEAs;

♦ **United Synagogue Agency for Jewish Education** (🖳 www.brijnet.org/aje) – provides training for teachers, runs an educational resource centre and acts as a liaison between secular institutions and the Anglo-Jewish community. It also acts as the examination board and internal inspectorate for Jewish educational institutions.

SPECIALIST SCHOOLS

Specialist schools include those that develop particular skills, e.g. in technology, languages, sports or the arts, as well as those that provide for children with unusual educational needs. There are almost 2,000 schools (both day and boarding) in the UK for pupils with such needs (sometimes known as special schools), some of which are contained within hospitals. The typical pupil-teacher ratio in special schools is around 6:1 compared to 20:1 in mainstream state schools. However, the government wishes to see more 'special needs' children entering mainstream schools.

State Specialist Schools

Specialist state schools in London include the following:

♦ **BRIT School For Performing Arts & Technology** (☎ 020-8665 5242, 🖳 www. brit.croydon.sch.uk) in Croydon, which is the UK's only free performing arts and technology school;

♦ **St Michael and All Angels Church of England Academy** (☎ 020-7701 4166,

🖥 www.stmichaelandallangelsacademy.org) in Southwark, a Church of England school specialising in health and science;

♦ **Bethnal Green Technology College** (☎ 020-7920 7900) in Tower Hamlets, specialising in IT;

♦ **Islington Arts & Media School** (☎ 020-7281 5511, 🖥 www.iamschool.co.uk) in Islington, specialising in arts, drama, multi-media and sports;

♦ **The London Nautical School** (☎ 020-7928 6801, 🖥 www.lns.org.uk) in Lambeth, which 'prepares its pupils to meet the requirements of society, either at sea or in any other occupation';

♦ **Loxford School of Science & Technology** (☎ 020-8514 4666, 🖥 www.loxford.net) in Redbridge, specialising in maths, science and information and other technologies.

Private Specialist Schools

Some private schools provide education wholly or mainly for children with unusual educational needs or learning difficulties such as dyslexia. They're required to meet similar standards as maintained special schools and their pupils should have access

to as much of the National Curriculum (see page 174) as possible. For example, the Dyslexia Institute, 2 Grosvenor Gardens, London SW1W 0DH is one of 27 UK centres under the auspices of the Dyslexia Institute (☎ 01784-222300, 🖥 www.dyslexiaaction. org.uk), a charitable body responsible for setting up a range of institutes providing instruction and support for pupils and teachers dealing with dyslexia.

Other private schools provide education for exceptionally gifted children and include the following:

♦ **Arts Educational Schools London** (☎ 020-8987 6666, 🖥 www.artsed. co.uk) in Chiswick, West London, which specialises in all the arts, including dance, music, drama and literature;

♦ **Belcanto London Academy** (☎ 020-8850 9888, 🖥 www.theatretraining.com) in Greenwich, a small school specialising in the performing arts generally;

♦ **Choir or Cathedral Schools** – parents of children blessed with an angelic voice are usually required to pay only a portion of the fees, and musical talent is generally deemed more important than religious beliefs. For further information contact the Choir Schools' Association (☎ 01962-890530, 🖥 www.choirschools. org.uk), which represents all cathedral and choir schools in England, of which three are in London: St Paul's Cathedral School, the Westminster Abbey Choir School and the Westminster Cathedral Choir School.

♦ **Italia Conti Academy of Theatre Arts** (☎ 020-7608 0047, 🖥 www.italiaconti. com) in Islington, Britain's first school of performing arts (founded in 1911 by the actress Italia Conti), specialising in dance, acting and singing;

♦ **The Royal Ballet School** (☎ 020-7845 7073, 🖥 www.royal-ballet-school.org. uk) in Richmond, with separate locations for the lower and upper schools; admits pupils on the basis of their ability to dance rather than academic standard;

♦ **Sylvia Young Theatre School** (☎ 020-7724 1949, 🖥 www. sylviayoungtheatreschool.co.uk) in

Westminster, specialising in music, dance and drama.

The world-famous Italian teaching system, Montessori, is popular in London, mainly in the pre-school age range. Information is available from the Maria Montessori Training Organisation (26 Lyndhurst Gardens, Hampstead, London NW3 5NW, ☎ 020-7435 3646, 🖳 www. mariamontessori.org).

Further Information

The Advisory Centre for Education (ACE, ☎ 020-7704 3370, 🖳 www.ace-ed.org. uk) can answer questions and give advice on specialist education. Contact your local LEA for information about specialist schools in your area or write to the Department for Education and Skills (Sanctuary Buildings, Great Smith Street, London, SW1P 3BT), which publishes numerous booklets about special education. There are several books available for parents of children with unusual needs, including *Which? School for Special Needs* by Derek Bingham (John Catt Education).

INTERNATIONAL & FOREIGN SCHOOLS

International schools teach foreign pupils in their home language but are also used by native Londoners who have family or working links with other countries or who want their children to be bilingual. London's international schools, as well as some of those teaching the curriculum of particular countries, are listed below.

◆ **American International Schools** – There's one ACS in London, in Hillingdon (☎ 01895-259771), and two just outside London, in Cobham (☎ 01932-867251) and Egham (☎ 01784-430800) in Surrey. Details of all three schools can be found on the ACS website (🖳 www.acs-england. co.uk).

◆ **American School in London** (☎ 020-7449 1200, 🖳 www.asl.org) in Westminster;

◆ **International Community School** (☎ 020-7935 1206, 🖳 www.ics.uk.net) in Westminster, part of the Skola Group of schools;

◆ **International School of London** (☎ 020-8992 5823, 🖳 www.islondon.com) in of Ealing, catering for all nationalities;

◆ **King Fahad Academy** (☎ 020-8743 0131, 🖳 www.thekfa.org.uk) in Ealing, which serves the Arab community;

◆ **Lycée Français Charles de Gaulle** (☎ 020-7584 6322, 🖳 www.lyceefrancais. org.uk) in Kensington & Chelsea;

◆ **Marymount International School** (☎ 020-8949 0571, 🖳 www.marymount london.com) in Kingston, which is part of a worldwide system of schools and colleges directed by the Sacred Heart of Mary, a Roman Catholic order;

◆ **Schiller International School** (🖳 www. schillerlondon.ac.uk) in Lambeth;

◆ **Southbank International School** (☎ 020-7243 3803, 🖳 www.southbank.org) in Kensington & Chelsea (it was originally on the south bank!), which accepts pupils from the age of three and teaches the IB curriculum;

◆ **Woodside Park International School** (☎ 020-8920 0634, 🖳 www.wpis.org) in Kingston.

For further information about schools teaching in a specific language contact your country's embassy in London (see **Appendix A**) or one of the organisations below.

◆ **Council of International Schools** (🖳 www. cois.org) – a non-profit association of schools and higher education establishments;

◆ **European Council of International Schools** (☎ 01730-268244, 🖳 www.ecis. org) – a non-profit organisation with 436 member schools, including three in London.

UNIVERSITIES & COLLEGES

London has the largest student population of any city in the world, totalling over 250,000, many of whom are from overseas. London's universities and colleges are listed below.

♦ **The American University in London** (🖳 www.aul.edu) in Islington;

♦ **American Intercontinental University London** (☎ 1888-567 5888, 🖳 www.aiulondon.ac.uk) in Westminster;

♦ **Brunel University** (☎ 01895-274000, 🖳 www.brunel.ac.uk) in Hillingdon;

♦ **City University** (☎ 020-7040 5060, 🖳 www.city.ac.uk) in Islington;

♦ **Huron University London** (☎ 020-7636 5667, 🖳 www.huron.ac.uk) in Kensington & Chelsea;

♦ **Guildhall School of Music & Drama** (☎ 020-7628 2571, 🖳 www.gsmd.ac.uk) in the City of London;

♦ **Kingston University** (☎ 020-8547 2000, 🖳 www.kingston.ac.uk) in Kingston;

♦ **London Metropolitan University**, 2 Goulston Street, E1 (university ☎ 020-7320 1000, students union ☎ 020-7423 0000, 🖳 www.londonmet.ac.uk);

♦ **London South Bank University** (☎ 020-7815 7815, 🖳 www.lsbu.ac.uk) in Southwark;

♦ **Middlesex University** (☎ 020-8411 5000, 🖳 www.mdx.ac.uk) on the borders between Barnet, Enfield and Haringey;

♦ **Richmond American International University In London** (☎ 020-8332 9000, 🖳 www.richmond.ac.uk) in Richmond;

♦ **Roehampton University** (☎ 020-8392 3000, 🖳 www.roehampton.ac.uk) in Wandsworth;

♦ **Royal Academy of Dramatic Art** (RADA, ☎ 020-7636 7076, 🖳 www.rada.org) in Camden;

♦ **Royal Academy of Music** (RAM, ☎ 020-7873 7373, 🖳 www.ram.ac.uk) in Westminster;

♦ **Royal College of Art** (RCA, ☎ 020-7590 4444, 🖳 www.rca.ac.uk) in Kensington & Chelsea;

♦ **Royal College of Music** (RCM, ☎ 020-7589 3643, 🖳 www.rcm.ac.uk) in Kensington & Chelsea;

♦ **The Slade School of Fine Art** (☎ 020-7679 2313, 🖳 www.ucl.ac.uk/slade). The Slade is a department of University College (part of the University of London – see below);

♦ **Thames Valley University** (☎ 0800-036 8888, 🖳 www.tvu.ac.uk), which has four campuses, in Brentford, Ealing, Reading and Slough.

♦ **University of East London** (☎ 020-8223 3000, 🖳 www.uel.ac.uk), which has a campus in Barking & Dagenham and three in Newham;

◆ **University of Greenwich** (☏ 020-8331 8000, 🖳 www.greenwich.ac.uk) in Greenwich;

◆ **University of London** (☏ 020-7862 8000, 🖳 www.lon.ac.uk), which has its heart in Bloomsbury but comprises around 30 colleges scattered across London: Birkbeck, Charing Cross, Goldsmiths, Heythrop, King's, Queen Mary, Royal Holloway (which is outside London, in Egham, Surrey), St Bartholomew's, University and Wye Colleges, plus the Westminster Medical School, Courtauld Institute of Art (see above), Eastman Dental Institute for Oral Health Care Sciences, Imperial College of Science, Technology and Medicine, the Institutes of Cancer Research, Child Health, Education and Psychiatry, the London Business School, London School of Economics & Political Science (LSE) and London School of Hygiene & Tropical Medicine, the Royal Free Hospital School of Medicine, Royal London Medical & Dental School, Royal Postgraduate Medical School and Royal Veterinary College, the School of Advanced Study, School of Oriental & African Studies and School of Pharmacy, St George's hospital Medical School, the United Medical & Dental Schools, and the University of London Computer Centre;

◆ **University of Westminster** (☏ 020-7911 5000, 🖳 www.wmin.ac.uk) in Westminster.

Entry Requirements

EEA nationals can freely enter the UK but if you're a non-EEA national it's important to check whether you need a student visa (see **Permits & Visas** on page 70). If you require a visa, you need to prove that you've been accepted for a full-time course of study, that you can meet the cost of your fees and maintenance (plus those of any dependants you bring with you) without recourse to public funds, and that you intend to leave the UK at the end of your course.

Note that universities insist that students possess a reasonable command of English, which may be tested, before they're enrolled on a course. If your mother tongue isn't English, you should check a college's prospectus or website for its requirements.

Applications & Information

All applications for full-time first degree (undergraduate) courses at British universities must be made to the Universities and Colleges Admissions Service (UCAS, PO Box 28, Cheltenham GL52 3LZ, ☏ 0871-468 0468, 🖳 www.ucas.co.uk). UCAS publishes a range of books of interest to students (see 🖳 www.ucasbooks.co.uk).

The National Union of Students/NUS's website (☏ 0871-221 8221, 🖳 www.nusonline.co.uk) is an invaluable source of information and advice on the courses available, your rights and what you can expect as a student in London. The free fortnightly newspaper, *London Student*, available in most student unions, is a mine of local information, and the weekly *Time Out* entertainment magazine contains a student section. Time Out (the publisher) also produces an annual *Student Guide*.

The Learning Skills Council (LSC, ☏ 0870-900 6800, 🖳 www.lsc.gov.uk) is responsible for funding and planning education and training for over 16-year-olds in England and is a useful source of general information.

An invaluable organisation for overseas students is the UK Council for International Student Affairs (☏ 020-7107 9922, 🖳 www.ukcosa.org.uk), which is a registered charity established in 1968 to promote the

interests and meet the needs of overseas students in the UK and those working with them as teachers, advisors or in other capacities. Another important organisation is the British Council (☎ 0161-957 7755, 🖳 www.britishcouncil.org), which has over 250 offices in some 110 countries and provides foreign students with information concerning all aspects of education in the UK.

For information about American universities in London, contact the Educational Advisory Service of The Fulbright Commission (☎ 020-7404 6994, 🖳 www.fulbright.co.uk).

Courses

The UK offers the widest choice of university courses in Europe. The main categories of course are as follows:

◆ Three- and four-year degree courses leading to qualifications such as Bachelor of Arts (BA) and Bachelor of Science (BSc). These tend to be taken by those who want a recognised academic qualification in a specific subject area, although there's scope to combine subjects in a modular degree (see below).

◆ Two-year Higher National Diploma (HND) or Diploma of Higher Education (DipHE) courses. These are generally related to particular career areas, such as agriculture, art and design, business studies, and hotel and catering. An **HND** is roughly equivalent to the second year of university and rated marginally below a bachelor's degree. It requires two years of full-time study or one year full-time following the successful completion of a Higher National Certificate (see below). A **DipHE** is a higher education qualification awarded after two years' full-time study at a university or other higher education institution.

◆ The Higher National Certificate (HNC), which is usually taken part time by those in employment. The attainment level is roughly equivalent to the first year of university.

As a general rule, you should allow at least five years for a part-time degree course. However, the distinction between part- and full-time study is becoming increasingly blurred and some institutions offer flexible arrangements to suit individual needs.

Many higher education establishments have adopted a modular structure for their courses, which allows students to build a personalised degree by choosing modules or units of study from a number of subject areas.

> ### ☑ SURVIVAL TIP
>
> To check whether a university course and qualifications are accredited and internationally recognised, visit 🖳 www.naric.org.uk or 🖳 www.britishcouncil.org.

Tuition Fees

Students ordinarily resident in the UK or another EU country qualify as 'home' students, as are non-EU students resident in the UK for at least three years immediately before the start of a course, except where residence was wholly or mainly for educational purposes. Other students are classed as 'overseas' students.

Home students enrolled on undergraduate courses must pay a tuition fee of up to £1,025 per year. The exact amount payable is means tested and dependent upon parental or individual income. Overseas undergraduate students should expect to pay up to £8,000 per year for an arts course, £8,500 for engineering, £9,000 for computing and £10,000 for optometry. Overseas postgraduates' fees range from £7,000 to £17,000. All fees are payable at the time of registration.

EU students are normally eligible to apply to the Department for Children, Schools and Families (DCSF, 🖳 www.dfes.gov.uk) for help with the payment of tuition fees. Further details can be obtained from the Education and Learning section of the government website 🖳 www.direct.gov.uk.

Living Expenses

In addition to tuition fees, students need sufficient funds to support themselves on a day-to-day basis, i.e. to cover accommodation, food, clothing, travel, books, equipment and entertainment. Under immigration regulations, you aren't usually permitted to work and study at the same time if you're from outside the EU. As a guide, you should therefore have funds of at least £10,000 per year if you're single and £15,000 per year if you're married. You should also bear in mind that you could incur 'extraordinary' expenses when you arrive in the UK, such as temporary hotel accommodation.

London can be expensive (see **Cost of Living** on page 163), although student concessions are available on public transport and entertainment tickets as well as at many shops and from other businesses, such as travel agencies and driving schools. In order to qualify for them you must obtain an NUS card or an International Student Identity Card (ISIC), available from student union offices. Information about the discounts obtainable in London can be found on 🖳 www. nuscard.com, and students' unions can provide information about the local discounts available.

Accommodation

General information about student accommodation is provided in university and college prospectuses. Many institutions have halls of residence, with or without catering facilities, some single-sex and some mixed, costs vary considerably but are usually from around £100 per week (actual costs can be obtained from individual colleges and universities). While a number of educational establishments guarantee accommodation for the first year, it's common for students in later years to rent accommodation off the campus. The staff at university accommodation offices can advise you about the costs and availability and may be able to help you find accommodation. See also **Renting** on page ??CH4.

If you're a mature student or will have a family living with you, you should check whether family accommodation is available within the university or college itself or elsewhere. An increasing number of universities and colleges make external housing provision for mature students and their families. You should make enquiries with accommodation offices well in advance, particularly if you require family accommodation.

The availability and cost of childcare facilities is also an important factor for families (see page ??ABOVE). If you're going to need support of this kind, you should contact the student services office of your chosen institution as far in advance as possible to check what childcare provision is available, what it costs and whether it will allow you sufficient time to study. Facilities and costs vary considerably from one institution to another, which may be a key factor in determining where you study.

⚠ Caution

Unless you're in a favourable financial position, you'll probably have to make sacrifices as a student and shouldn't expect your accommodation and general standard of living to match what you've been used to.

International Students House (ISH, 229 Great Portland Street, W1 5PN, ☎ 020-7631 8300, 🖳 www.ish.org.uk) is a useful meeting place for foreign students, where you can compare notes and share impressions of life and studying in London. It also has single, twin and dormitory rooms available for visiting students as well as sports facilities, a bar and restaurant. ISH also operates an excellent travel club with cheap rates for students.

Student Entertainment

London provides a wealth of entertainment (see **Chapter 9**), in addition to which most universities have student unions, which provide excellent entertainment including live music, often featuring world-class bands and are a valuable source of local information and support. Because student bars and entertainment are subsidised, most student unions admit only those with an NUS or ISIC card (see page 234). You aren't restricted to your own union and can visit any union – among the best student unions in London are the following:

◆ **Imperial College** (Beit Quad, Prince Consort Road, SW7 2A2, ☎ 020-7589 5111, 🖳 www3.imperial.ac.uk, South

Kensington tube) – big, basic and friendly, with cheap beer;

◆ **King's College** (Strand, WC2R 2LS, ☎ 020-7836 5454, 💻 www.kcl.ac.uk, Temple tube) – vies with the ULU (see below) as the best student union in town. It boasts a great venue for live music as well as a bar serving meals.

◆ **University of London** (Malet Street, WC1, ☎ 020-7862 8000, 💻 www.lon.ac.uk, Russell Square/Goodge Street tube) – affectionately known as ULU. With two bars, this is probably London's trendiest student union, frequently offering the hottest up-and-coming bands. See them here first!

◆ **University of Westminster** (35 Marylebone Road, W1, ☎ 020-7911 5000, 💻 www.wmin.ac.uk, Baker Street tube) – as you might expect given its location, the swankiest union in town.

VOCATIONAL COURSES

Vocational courses are career-specific and courses relate to a specific area of employment or industry sector. Courses tend to be practical and skills-focused, and many include work-related projects or work experience. If you want to learn more about a particular job or area of work, there are many vocational qualifications to choose from, ranging from general qualifications where you learn skills relevant to a variety of jobs, to specialist qualifications designed for a particular sector. Many have been designed in collaboration with industry so that they equip you with the skills and knowledge that employers require. Some of the most common are explained below:

BTECs & OCR Nationals: Among the most common are Business and Technical Education Council (BTEC) qualifications and OCR Nationals, which are particular types of work-related qualifications. BTECs and OCR Nationals are available in a wide range of subjects, including, art and design, business, health and social care, information technology, media, public services, science and sport. They are usually studied full-time at college, or sometimes at school (or in collaboration between a school and college). You can also take them part-time at college. For more information see 💻 www.direct.gov.uk/en/EducationAndLearning/QualificationsExplained/DG_10039020 or 💻 www.ocrnationals.com.

National Vocational Qualifications (NVQs): NVQs are work-related, competence-based qualifications that reflect the skills and knowledge needed to do a job effectively, and show that a candidate is competent in the area of work the NVQ represents. They are based on national occupational standards and cover all the main aspects of an occupation, including current best practice, the ability to adapt to future requirements and the knowledge and understanding that underpin competent performance.

NVQs don't need to be completed in a specified amount of time and can be taken by full-time employees or by school and college students with a work placement or part-time job that enables them to develop the appropriate skills. There are no age limits and no special entry requirements. For more information see 💻 www.dfes.gov.uk/nvq.

Modern Apprenticeships: These are a mixture of work-based training and education, of which there are two types: Foundation Modern Apprenticeship (FMAs), which last at least 1 year, and Advanced Modern Apprenticeships (AMAs) which last at least 2 years. For more information see 🖳 www.apprenticeships.org.uk.

The UK National Reference Point for Vocational Qualifications (UKNRP) provides a UK qualifications database (🖳 www.uknrp.org.uk). For more general information about vocational education and training in the UK, see the British Council website (🖳 www.britishcouncil.org/learning-vocationalpartnerships.htm). A useful publication is the *British Vocational Qualifications: A Directory of Vocational Qualifications Available in the UK* by Minerva Becker (Kogan Page).

FURTHER EDUCATION & DISTANCE LEARNING

Part-time day and evening classes in London cover a wide range of subjects, from hobbies such as flower-arranging and painting to academic and vocational courses (see above) leading to recognised qualifications in subjects such as information technology and accounting. Classes are usually provided by local education authorities.

The bible for part-time courses in London is *Floodlight Part-Time*. *Summertime Floodlight* is a guide to summer courses in Greater London. Both are published by Floodlight Publishing and available direct from them (🖳 www.floodlight.co.uk) and from book shops and newsagents in London.

Those who need (or prefer) to study at home or whose job frequently takes them away from home can enrol in a distance learning course. The Open University (OU), established in 1969, is the best known provider of such courses and offers everything from vocational qualifications to undergraduate and research degrees. Although course programmes are often broadcast on TV at crack of dawn, the widespread ownership of DVD and video recorders means that programmes can be viewed at a more 'civilised' hour. There are also courses that can be done via the internet. For information contact the Open University, PO

British Library Reading Room, British Museum

Box 197, Milton Keynes MK7 6BJ (☎ 0845-300 6090, 🖳 www.open.ac.uk).

The UK's largest provider of distance learning courses, the National Extension College (NEC), offers written home study courses and, depending on circumstances, the support of a local college. Qualifications offered primarily focus on GCSEs, A-levels and National Vocational Qualifications (NVQs). For information contact the National Extension College (☎ 01223-400200, 🖳 www.nec.ac.uk).

The London School of Journalism (126 Shirland Road, Maida Vale, London W9 2BT, ☎ 020-7289 7777, 🖳 www.lsj.org) is the longest-established writing school in Europe (founded in 1920) and runs summer schools for prospective journalists and writers as well as offering correspondence courses.

There are dozens of English-language schools in London for those who need to learn or improve their English. However, the cost and quality of teaching varies considerably and it's wise to enrol with a reputable school that's a member of the Association of Recognised English Language Services (ARELS), which has around 90 schools in the capital. For further details of these and other schools contact English UK, 219 St John Street, London EC1V 4LY (☎ 020-7608 7960 🖳 www.englishuk.com).

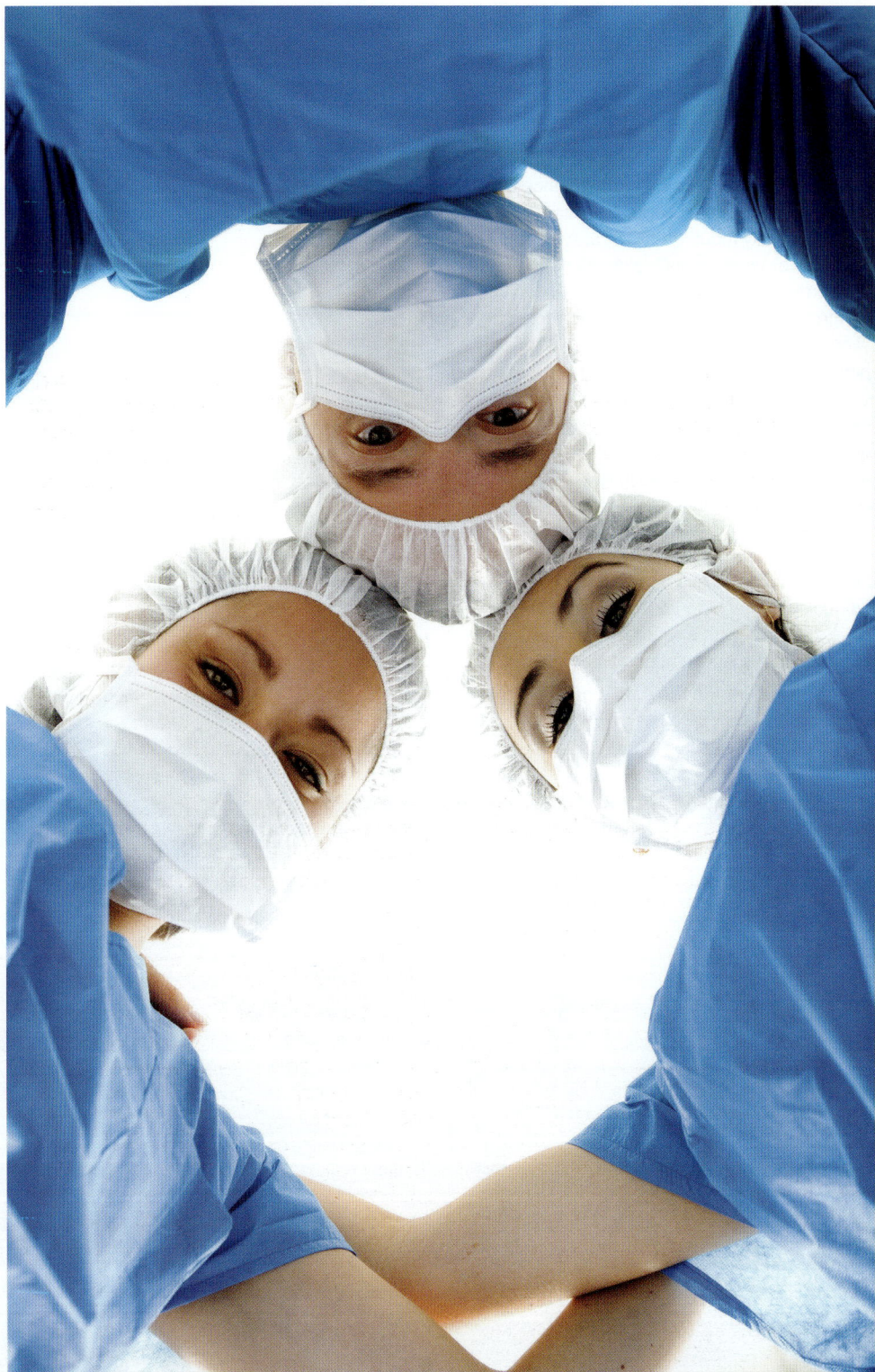

8.

STAYING HEALTHY

One of the most important aspects of living in London (or anywhere for that matter) is maintaining good health. The UK is famous for its National Health Service (NHS), which provides free or low-cost healthcare to all British citizens and most foreign residents. Many foreigners visit the UK for private medical treatment. The standard of training of British doctors and nursing staff is among the highest in the world, and British medical science is in the vanguard of medical technology and procedure (many pioneering operations are performed in the UK).

Harley Street in London is internationally recognised as having some of the world's pre-eminent (and most expensive) specialists, encompassing every conceivable ailment and treatment, from cardiac surgery to liposuction. It has the greatest concentration of medical expertise anywhere in the world, with over 1,400 specialist medical and dental consultants and practitioners in 'residence'. If money's no object and you're seeking the best treatment available, you should telephone The Harley Street Bureau (☏ 0171-580 9966), which is a non-profit organisation that provides a free advice service.

> ☑ **SURVIVAL TIP**
>
> If you don't qualify for healthcare under the public health service, it's essential to have private health insurance (in fact, you may not qualify for a residence permit without it). This is wise in any case if you can afford it, owing to the inadequacy of public health services in many areas and long waiting lists for specialist appointments and non-urgent operations. Visitors to the UK should have holiday health insurance if they aren't covered by a reciprocal arrangement.

If you're planning to take up residence in London, even for part of the year only, you may wish to have a health check before your arrival, particularly if you have a record of poor health or are elderly. There are no unusual health risks in the UK and no immunisations are required unless you arrive from an area infected with yellow fever. You can safely drink the water (unless there's a sign to the contrary), although it sometimes tastes awful, and many people prefer bottled water (when not drinking tea, wine or beer!).

EMERGENCIES

If you're unlucky enough to be involved in an accident or suffer a sudden serious illness in the UK, you'll be somewhat relieved to know that emergency transport by ambulance and treatment at a hospital Accident & Emergency (A&E) department is free to everyone. In a medical emergency, simply dial 999 from any telephone (calls are free) and ask for the ambulance service. State your name and location and describe your injuries or symptoms (or those of the patient) and an ambulance with paramedics will be despatched to take you to hospital (the time you must wait will depend on your location and how busy the ambulance service is at that time). Calls to 999 must be made in emergencies only and health authorities can levy a fee if an emergency ambulance is called unnecessarily. The UK doesn't have a national air ambulance service, although there are emergency helicopter services in London for critical cases.

In minor 'emergencies' or for medical advice, you should phone your family doctor if you have one. Failing this you can ring a directory enquiries service, such as ☎ 118 118 or 11 88 88, for the telephone number of a local doctor or hospital (or consult your phone book). Police stations keep a list of doctors' and chemists' private telephone numbers, in case of emergency. There are private 24-hour doctors' and dental services in London that make house calls, but check the cost before using them (see the Yellow Pages).

If you're able, you can go to the A&E department of an NHS general hospital, many of which provide a 24-hour service. Check in advance which local hospitals are equipped to deal with emergencies and the fastest route from your home. This information may be of vital importance in the event of an emergency, when a delay could mean the difference between life and death. Not all London hospitals have A&E departments and, of those that do, not all are open round the clock. Hospitals in inner London with 24-hour emergency facilities include the following:

◆ **Central** – St Mary's Hospital, Praed Street, W2 1NY (☎ 020-7886 6666, 🖥 www. st-marys.nhs.uk, Paddington tube) and University College Hospital, 235 Euston Road, NW1 2BU (☎ 020-7387 9300, 🖥 www.uclh.nhs.uk, Euston Square/Warren Street tube);

◆ **East** – Hackney & Homerton Hospital, Homerton Row, E9 6SR (☎ 020-8510 5555, 🖥 www.homerton.nhs.uk, Homerton rail) and Royal London Hospital, Whitechapel Road, E1 1BB (☎ 020-7377 7000, 🖥 www. bartsandthelondon.org.uk, Whitechapel tube/Liverpool Street rail);

◆ **North** – Royal Free Hospital, Pond Street, NW3 2QG (☎ 020-7794 0500, 🖥 www. royalfree.nhs.uk, Belsize Park tube) and Whittington Hospital, Magdala Avenue, N19 5NF (☎ 020-7272 3070, 🖥 www. whittington.nhs.uk, Archway tube);

◆ **South** – St Thomas's Hospital, Westminster Bridge Road, SE1 7EH (☎ 020-7188 7188, 🖥 www.guysandstthoms.nhs.uk, Waterloo/ Westminster tube), Guy's Hospital, Great Maze Pond, SE1 9RT (☎ 020-7188 7188, London Bridge tube) and St George's Hospital, Blackshaw Road, SW17 0QT (☎ 020-8672 1255, 🖥 www.st-georges.org. uk, Tooting Broadway tube);

◆ **West** – Charing Cross Hospital, Fulham Palace Road, London, W6 8RF (☎ 020-8846 1234, 🖥 www.hhnt.org, Barons Court/Hammersmith tube) and Chelsea & Westminster Hospital, 369 Fulham Road, SW10 9NH (☎ 020-8746 8000/8484, 🖥 www.chelwest.nhs.uk, bus Nos 14, 73, 211).

☑ SURVIVAL TIP

It's wise to keep a record of the telephone numbers of your doctor, local hospitals and clinics, ambulance service, first aid, poison control, dentist, and other emergency services next to your telephone.

Medic-Alert

If you have a rare blood group or a medical problem that cannot easily be detected, e.g. a heart condition, diabetes, epilepsy, haemophilia or a severe allergy, you should join Medic-Alert. Medic-Alert members wear a necklace or bracelet containing an internationally recognised symbol and engraved with their medical problem, membership number and a telephone number. When you're unable to speak for yourself, doctors, police or anyone providing aid can immediately obtain vital medical information by phoning a 24-hour emergency number.

Medic-Alert is a non-profit registered charity and life membership is included in the cost of the bracelet or necklace (costing from around £20). You must also pay an annual fee of around the same amount. For more information contact the Medic-Alert Foundation, 1 Bridge Wharf, 156 Caledonian Road, London N1 9UU (☎ 020-7833 3034, 🖥 www.medicalert.co.uk).

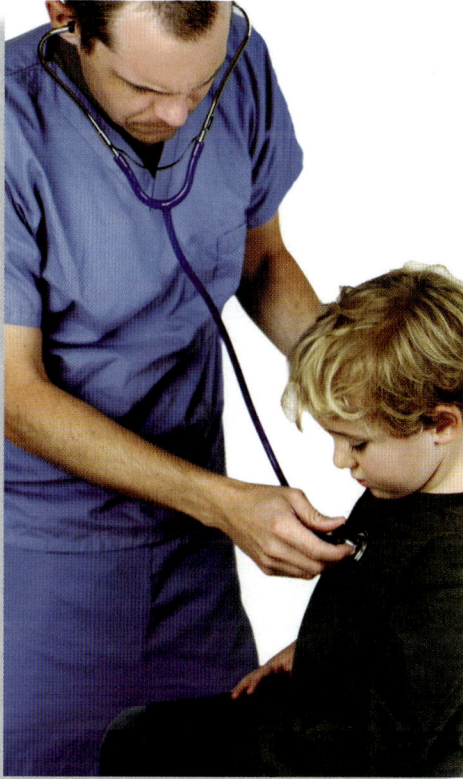

NATIONAL HEALTH SERVICE

The National Health Service (NHS) was established in 1948 to ensure that everyone had equal access to medical care. NHS services include family doctors, specialists, hospitals, dentists, chemists, opticians, community health services (e.g. the district nursing and health visitor services), the ambulance service, and maternity and child health care.

Originally, all NHS medical treatment was free, the service being funded entirely from general taxation and National Insurance contributions. However, as the cost of treatment and medicines has increased, part of the cost has been passed onto patients via supplementary charges. While hospital treatment, the ambulance service and consultations with doctors remain free, most patients must now pay fixed charges for prescriptions, dental treatment, sight tests and NHS glasses, although charges are usually well below the actual cost. Family doctors, called general practitioners (GPs), still make free house calls (but are reluctant to do so) and community health workers and district nurses visit people at home who are convalescent or bedridden or have newborn babies.

It's a sad fact that NHS health services aren't as 'universally available' as they once were. The quality of service you receive from the NHS depends very much on where you live, as waiting lists for specialist appointments and hospital beds vary from area to area, though you can be sure that the best GPs and dentists in London have waiting lists. In fact, even the type of treatment you can receive varies according to your local health authority, some of which don't provide certain expensive treatment (e.g. for cancer), as they simply cannot afford it.

The NHS provides free or subsidised medical treatment to all foreigners with the right of abode in the UK and to anyone who, at the time of treatment, has been a resident for the previous year. Exceptions to the one-year qualifying rule include European Union (EU) nationals with a European Health Insurance Card (which replaced the old form E111), refugees or those with 'exceptional leave to remain' in the UK, students on a course of over six months, foreign nationals coming to take up permanent residence in the UK, British pensioners living abroad, anyone with a permit to work in the UK, and the spouse and children of the above.

Nationals of countries with reciprocal health agreements with the UK also receive free or subsidised medical treatment, which include:

♦ Nationals of countries in the European Economic Area (EEA).

♦ Nationals of Armenia, Azerbaijan, Belarus, Bosnia and Herzegovina, Bulgaria, Croatia, Georgia, Kazakhstan, Kyrgyzstan, Macedonia, Moldova, Montenegro, New Zealand, Romania, Russia, Serbia, Tajikistan, Turkmenistan, Ukraine and Uzbekistan.

♦ Residents of Anguilla, Australia, Barbados, British Virgin Islands, Channel Islands, Falkland Islands, Gibraltar, Iceland, Isle of

Man, Montserrat, St Helena, and the Turks & Caicos Islands.

Exemption from charges for nationals of the above countries is generally limited to emergency or urgent treatment (e.g. for a communicable disease) required during a visit to the UK. For a comprehensive list of treatments available, based on your country of origin, visit 🖳 www.dh.gov.uk.

Anyone who doesn't qualify under one of the above categories must pay for all medical treatment received, although some medical and dental emergencies are treated free of charge, e.g. emergency treatment at a hospital outpatients department as a result of an accident or admission to hospital for no longer than one night.

NHS Reforms

The NHS has traditionally been a political football, with the ruling party making sweeping changes which seldom improve services and treatment. The Labour government, which came to power in 1997, brought in reforms which included self-governing hospitals, practice and prescribing budgets for GPs, funding and contracts for hospital services, and the creation of an NHS internal market. At the same time, £billions of extra funding was pumped into the NHS, but although waiting times for non-urgent operations have been reduced, there have been few other discernible improvements. This is due in no small part to the ever-increasing cost of staff, equipment and drugs, the increasing demands of an ageing population and the large influx of immigrants in recent years.

One of the most serious problems facing the NHS is a shortage of nurses (especially specialist-trained nurses), midwives and health visitors, who have been leaving the NHS in droves, mainly on account of low salaries (one in five nurses is forced to take a second job to survive), although poor working conditions,

long hours, a lack of resources and stress are also factors.

A shortfall in doctors has meant that many hospitals and deputising services are forced to recruit an increasing number of doctors from abroad. Foreign doctors have flooded into the UK in recent years. It's estimated that over a third of NHS doctors have qualified overseas; among junior doctors the proportion is over 40 per cent. One-fifth of all GPs practising in the UK are now from overseas, and some of them speak poor English or lack experience. The majority of supply doctors (also called locum doctors), who fill shortages when doctors are on holiday or sick, are also foreign. Not only does the UK not train enough doctors, it also loses many to other countries.

Staff shortages aren't the only problem, however. Although funding has been increasing (in real terms) for a number of years, demand is rising at an ever-faster rate. A shortfall in funds has resulted in hospital ward closures, causing long waiting lists for hospital beds (patients are sometimes left on trolleys in hospital corridors because no beds are available), cancelled operations, and long queues in hospital waiting rooms.

The upshot is that the most costly NHS health services are now 'rationed', i.e. allocated on the basis of a patient's chances of recovery or life expectancy. This means the elderly and obese, heavy smokers and alcoholics have little chance of receiving expensive life-saving operations such as heart surgery and transplants on the NHS. There are also long waiting lists for non-vital procedures such as hip replacements, varicose vein surgery, hernia operations and even sterilisation.

The present government has attempted to address the NHS's problems by injecting extra funds and resources, although it will take many years to resolve the problems of under-staffing and eradicate the waiting lists.

PRIVATE HEALTH INSURANCE

If you aren't covered by the NHS or a reciprocal agreement, you should take out private health insurance, as private medical treatment in the UK can be very expensive (see **Private Treatment** below), the cost of an operation and hospitalisation running into thousands of pounds.

Long-stay visitors should have long-stay health insurance or an international health policy, which covers you when you when travelling and in most foreign countries. A health insurance policy should cover you for essential healthcare required as a result of an accident and injuries (e.g. a sporting injury), whether they occur in your home, at your place of work or when travelling. Don't take anything for granted, but check in advance that you're covered.

When deciding on the type and extent of health insurance, make sure that it covers **all** your family's present and future health requirements in the UK **before** you receive a large bill.

Even if you're eligible for NHS treatment, you may wish to consider taking out supplementary private health insurance, the main advantage of which is the reduced waiting time for non-emergency operations. One in five operations in the UK is performed privately.

The number of people with private health insurance in the UK increased from around 1.5m in 1966 to some 7.5m in 2007, half of whose premiums are paid by their employers. If you're taking up a job in the UK, check whether your employer pays for private health insurance – some 'share' the premiums with their employers.

Most people with private health insurance are insured with provident associations such as BUPA and PPP, which pay for specialist and hospital treatment only and don't include routine visits to doctors and dentists (which are covered by the NHS). Private policies don't usually include a comprehensive health check-up or screening, which can be performed at private clinics throughout the UK for around £400 to £600. But private patients are free to choose their own specialists and hospitals.

Most health insurance policies fall into one of two main categories: those providing immediate private specialist or hospital treatment (e.g. BUPA, PPP and WPA) and so-called 'budget' or 'waiting-list' policies, where you're treated as a private patient only when waiting lists exceed a certain period. Under waiting-list policies, if you cannot obtain an appointment with an NHS specialist or an NHS

hospital admission within a certain period (e.g. six weeks), you can do so as a private patient.

The cost of private health insurance depends on your age and the state of your health. There are maximum age limits for taking out health insurance with some insurers, e.g. 65 for BUPA, although age limits may be higher if you're willing to accept some restrictions. Some companies have (expensive) policies for those aged over 50 or 55. Once you have a policy, there are generally no restrictions on continuing membership, irrespective of age.

Treatment of any medical condition for which you've already received medical attention or were aware existed up to five years before the start date of the policy may not be covered. However, existing health problems (often referred to as 'pre-existing' conditions) are usually covered after two years' membership, provided that no further medical attention has been necessary during this period. Some group

policies do, however, include cover for existing or previous health problems. Other exclusions are listed in the policy rules.

Standard policies may offer three scales (usually designated A, B and C) of hospital treatment, which may include London NHS teaching hospitals (A, high scale), provincial NHS teaching hospitals (B, medium scale) and provincial non-teaching hospitals (C, low scale). Accommodation is usually in a private room, but in some hospitals it may be in a twin or four-bedded ward.

Premiums range from a few pounds a week for a budget plan offering limited benefits at C-scale hospitals up to £50 a month for a single person and from around £140 for a family for a comprehensive policy with A-scale treatment; some companies offer lower premiums but have a compulsory annual excess of £500 or £1,000.

If you need treatment, you may be required to pay in advance and reclaim the cost from your insurance company later, although some insurers will pay bills directly. If you must pay up front, you'll need to ensure that you have sufficient funds and that you understand how to make claims.

Private Treatment

Private hospital care in the UK is provided in entirely private clinics and hospitals, and in private wings or wards of large NHS hospitals. Many NHS consultants also treat patients privately. Private treatment includes health checks and screening, complementary medicine and cosmetic surgery (see below), none of which are available on the NHS.

If you need to see a GP or specialist privately, you (or your insurance company) must pay the fee, This is at the doctor's 'discretion', but you should expect to pay at least £50 for a routine visit to a GP.

Always make sure that a medical practitioner is qualified to provide the treatment you require, as (surprisingly) anyone can call himself a doctor in the UK.

The quality of private treatment isn't necessarily superior to that provided by the NHS and you shouldn't assume that because a doctor (or any other medical practitioner) is in private practice he is more competent than his NHS counterpart. In fact, often you'll see the same specialist or be treated by the same surgeon on the NHS and privately. If you see a private doctor, his offices will be plush and welcoming, you'll be greeted courteously by his receptionist, he will have more time to spend on you (NHS GPs can be abrupt and even downright rude!) and his bedside manner will be impeccable. However, he won't necessarily be a better doctor than the one in the high street community clinic.

When selecting a private specialist or clinic, you should be extremely cautious and only choose someone who has been recommended by a doctor or organisation that you can trust. It's sometimes wise to obtain a second opinion, particularly if you're diagnosed as having a serious illness or requiring a major operation. According to some reports, unnecessary operations are becoming increasingly common in the UK – though not under the NHS! Private patients don't have the same protection as NHS patients, although complaints about treatment paid for by a private health insurance policy may be taken up by your insurance company. As a last resort, you can complain to the General Medical Council, provided a medical practitioner is a qualified doctor.

Medicentres

An innovation in recent years has been the introduction of private 'Medicentres' (☎ 08456-808999, 🖳 www.medicentre. co.uk), where doctors and nurses are on hand for consultations and to perform tests, screening, health checks, vaccinations and minor treatment. A Medicentre offers a walk-in service – there's no need to be registered and you don't require an appointment. Patients pay around £65 for a 30 minute appointment with a doctor, £39 for a nurse consultation and £20 for repeat prescriptions. A full list of treatments and fees are on the Medicentre website).

Medicentres are located in the 'high street', main railway stations and shopping centres. Centres in London include: Victoria Station, Waterloo Station, Euston Station, Bank (City), Fenchurch Street (City), the Plaza Shopping Centre (Oxford Street), Paddington Station, Eldon Street (City) and Lower Marsh Road (near Waterloo Station).

COMPLEMENTARY MEDICINE

Growing fears about the side-effects of medicines and general disillusionment with the NHS have led to a huge growth in complementary (or alternative) medicine in the last decade, although the UK is still way behind many other EU countries, particularly France and Germany. Complementary treatments are chosen by some 5m British patients a year, although most aren't covered by the NHS or private health insurance in the UK.

Practitioners can be found using the following resources:

♦ **Acupuncture** – To find a doctor practising acupuncture, contact the British Acupuncture Council, 63 Jeddo Road, London W12 9HQ (☎ 020-8735 0400, 🖳 www.acupuncture.org.uk).

♦ **Chiropractic** – If you're seeking a chiropractor, contact the British Chiropractic Association, 59 Castle Street, Reading RG1 7SN (☎ 0118-950 5950, 🖳 www. chiropractic-uk.co.uk).

♦ **Holistic medicine** – For a holistic practitioner contact the British Holistic Medical Association, PO Box 371,

Bridgwater, Somerset TA6 9BG (☎ 01278-722000, 🖳 www.bhma.org).

♦ **Homeopathy** – To find a homeopath or homeopathic chemist in your area, contact the British Homeopathic Association, Hahnemann House, 29 Park Street West, Luton LU1 (☎ 0870-444 3950, 🖳 www. trusthomeopathy.org).

London is the base for Europe's largest provider of complementary medicine, the Royal London Homeopathic Hospital NHS Trust, which is the only independent public sector hospital in Europe dedicated to complementary medicine.

♦ **Reflexology** – Contact the Association of Reflexologists, 5 Fore Street, Taunton, Somerset TA1 1HX (☎ 01823-351010, 🖳 www.aor.org.uk) to find a therapist in your area.

A list of professional bodies governing complementary medical practitioners is contained in the *Time Out Guide to Shopping & Services in London*.

DOCTORS

There are excellent family doctors, usually referred to as GPs (short for general practitioners), in all areas of the UK. The best way to find a doctor, whether as an NHS or a private patient, is to ask colleagues, friends or neighbours – especially healthy ones – if they can recommend someone. Alternatively you can consult a list of GPs in your Community Health Council (CHC) office or published by your local Family Health Services Authority (FHSA). FHSAs publish lists of doctors, dentists, chemists and opticians in their areas. These are available at libraries, post offices, tourist information offices, police stations and citizens' advice bureaux. You can also look up doctors in the Medical Directory, available in public reference libraries. GPs are listed under Doctors (Medical Practitioners) in Yellow Pages.

Some universities and colleges have a health centre, where you should register. Otherwise, doctors' offices are known in the UK as surgeries.

Surgery hours vary but are typically from 8 or 8.30am to 6 or 7pm, Mondays to Fridays, with early closing one day a week, e.g. 5 or 5.30pm on Fridays (evening surgeries may also be held on one or two days a week). Emergency surgeries may be held on Saturday mornings, e.g. from 8.30 or 9am to 11.30am or noon. Some practices have no surgeries during lunch hour, e.g. from noon to 1pm. Most doctors' surgeries have answering machines outside surgery hours, when a recorded message informs you of the name of the doctor on call (or deputising service) and his telephone number.

NHS Doctors

NHS doctors are contracted by their local FHSA to look after a number of patients (around 2,000 on average) in their 'catchment' area. Doctors can refuse to register you as a patient if they have no vacancies – or for any other reason – and can 'strike you off' their list for any reason. GPs often drop patients who ask 'too many' questions, and almost 100,000 patients are removed from GP lists each year. Most GPs don't like detailed medical questions or patients who refuse treatment or ask for a second opinion – you're simply supposed to do as you're told!

If you have trouble getting onto an NHS doctor's list, contact your local FHSA, which has a duty to find you a doctor. If you're living in a district for less than three months or have no permanent home, you can apply to any doctor in the district as a temporary resident. After three months, you must register with a doctor as a permanent patient. An NHS doctor must give 'immediate necessary treatment' for up to 14 days to anyone without a doctor in his area, until the patient has been accepted by a doctor on a permanent basis. It's wise to meet a prospective doctor before deciding whether to register with him.

All NHS GPs must produce practice guides for patients, containing the names of the doctors, times of surgeries and any special services provided, such as ante-natal, family planning and 'well woman' or diabetic clinics.

An NHS medical card is issued when you first register with a GP, which contains your NHS number and other information such as your name, address, date of birth, and details of your registered practice or individual doctor. When you register with a new GP, you will be asked for your NHS medical card. If you don't have one the receptionist will give you a form (GMS1) to complete. If your already have a medical cards and are registering with a new doctor, your medical records will be transferred to your new GP. Your NHS medical card – which is sent to you by mail – includes your unique NHS number, which is used as the common identifier for patients across different NHS organisations.

Your doctor is able to give advice or provide information on any aspect of health or medical after-care, including preventive medicine, blood donations, home medical equipment and special counselling. He should also be able to advise you about the range of medical benefits provided under the NHS, including maternity care, contraceptive help and psychiatric treatment. NHS patients must always be referred by a GP to a specialist, e.g. an eye specialist, gynaecologist or orthopaedic surgeon.

If you'd like a second opinion on any health matter, you may ask to see a specialist, although, unless it's a serious matter, your doctor will probably refuse to refer you. If your doctor refuses, you won't be able to obtain a second opinion from another NHS doctor unless you change doctors. The only other possibility is to consult another doctor or specialist as a private patient. Patients who have a foreign (i.e. not British) private health insurance policy may be free to make appointments directly with specialists.

> ### ⚠ Caution
>
> In many cases where a second opinion is sought, the second doctor doesn't confirm the first doctor's diagnosis.

Group Practices

Around 80 per cent of GPs work in a partnership or group practice, around 25 per cent of them in health centres, which provide a house bound or too ill to visit their surgery. In fact, a doctor is responsible for his patients 24 hours a day and, when he's unavailable, must make alternative arrangements, whether through his partners in a group practice, by means of a voluntary rota between individual doctors or via a deputising service. Note, however, that when you call your GP outside normal hours, he's unlikely to attend you personally at home; most GPs use deputising services (using locum doctors), which exist

range of medical and nursing services. Health centres may have facilities for immunisation, cervical smears, health education (known as a 'well person clinics'), family planning, speech therapy, chiropody, hearing tests and physiotherapy and other remedial treatment. Many also offer dental, ophthalmic, hospital outpatient and social work services. Most health centres and group practices have district nurses, health visitors, midwives and clinical psychologists in attendance at certain times.

If your doctor is part of a partnership or group practice and is absent, you'll automatically be treated by a partner or another doctor (unless you wish to wait until your doctor returns).

Appointments & House Calls

Most doctors operate an appointment system. You cannot just turn up during surgery hours and expect to be seen; if you're an urgent case (but not an emergency), your doctor will usually see you immediately, but you should still phone in advance. Standard appointment times are short and patients often overrun, so you may have to wait well past your appointed time to see a doctor. If you need to have an in-depth discussion of your symptoms or have more than one health problem, ask the receptionist for a double appointment.

NHS doctors make free house calls and emergency visits outside surgery hours (at their discretion) in cases when patients are

to provide house calls and an 'after hours' service.

Changing Doctors

It's easy to change doctors and you don't need to inform your old doctor; you can simply visit a new doctor's surgery and ask to be registered. If, out of courtesy, you wish to inform your existing doctor that you intend to change, take care what reason you give as some doctors may be wary of accepting a patient who has had a 'disagreement' with a colleague. One 'safe' reason for changing doctors is that you wish to be treated by a doctor of the opposite sex to your present one. Your new doctor will require details of your previous GP in order to obtain your medical records.

Complaints

If you have a complaint against an NHS GP, you should first contact your local FHSA, usually within eight weeks of the event. If you need help to make a complaint, you can ask your Community Health Council or a citizens' advice bureau. In the event of serious professional misconduct, your complaint will be passed to the General Medical Council, although it exists to represent its members, doctors, so you'll have a hard time obtaining redress without recourse to a court of law.

Information booklets outlining your rights and complaints procedures are published by the British Medical Association (BMA) and are available from doctors' surgeries, clinics and chemists or direct from the BMA.

DENTISTS

Britons' annual consumption of over 750,000 tonnes of sweets (over 13kg per person) ensures that dentists (and sweet manufacturers) remain financially healthy. Despite the efforts of dentists to promote preventive dentistry, millions of Britons never go near a dentist (mostly out of fear) unless they're 'dying' from toothache. Fortunately, when you need help there are excellent dentists in all areas, although the number of dentists offering treatment on the NHS has dwindled in recent years (see **NHS Treatment** below).

The best way to find a good dentist, whether as an NHS or a private patient, is to ask colleagues, friends or neighbours (particularly those with perfect teeth) if they can recommend someone. Dentists are listed under Dental Surgeons in the Yellow Pages and are permitted to advertise any special services they provide, such as an emergency or 24-hour answering service, dental hygienist, and evening or weekend surgeries. The British Dental Association (64 Wimpole Street, London W1G 8YS, ☎ 020-7935 0875, 🖥 www.bda.org) can also provide a list of dentists in your area.

In some areas, community clinics or health centres provide a dental service for children, expectant and nursing mothers, and disabled adults. Some hospitals provide a free emergency service, e.g. on Sundays and public holidays. Dental hospitals in London provide a free emergency service on most days. Around 50 per cent of dentists hold an evening surgery one day a week or open on Saturday mornings.

Many family dentists in the UK are qualified to perform specialised treatment, e.g. periodontal work, although you must usually see a specialist. In the UK, false teeth (dentures) are made (and repaired) by a dental technician and prescribed and fitted by a dentist.

Fees vary considerably according to the area and the dentist. The cost of dental treatment has risen considerably in recent years and you can pay at least £35 for a private check-up – recommended every six months in the UK.

NHS Treatment

In theory, dental care is covered by the NHS, although it's only completely free to those under the age of 18 (19 if in full-time education), pregnant women, mothers with a baby under one year of age and those who are receiving certain state benefits (Income Support, Jobseeker's Allowance, Family Credit or Disability Working Allowance). In theory, other patients must pay a proportion of their treatment costs, which is currently around £5 for a check-up, plus the cost of any work carried out.

Patients who don't qualify for free treatment must pay 80 per cent of the set NHS fees for 'normal' dental treatment, e.g. fillings, extractions, hygiene work, and standard bridges and dentures, according to a fixed scale of fees, as shown below.

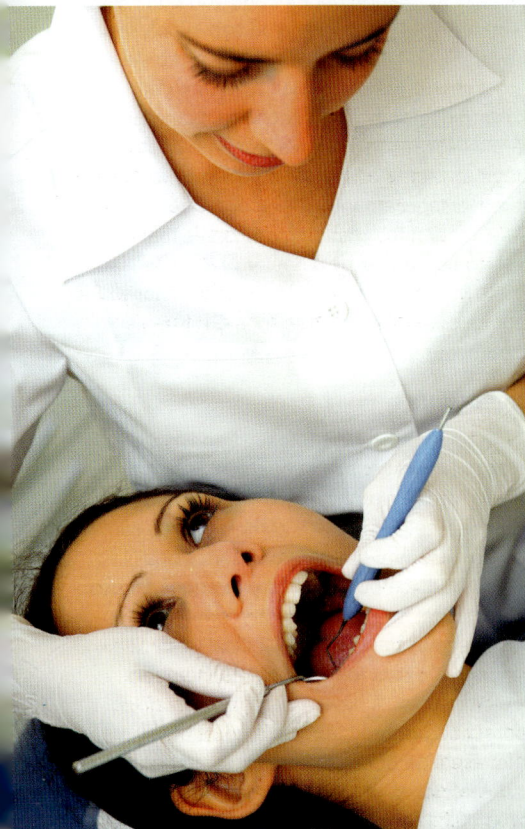

NHS Dental Charges

♦ **£16.20** This charge includes an examination, diagnosis and preventive care. If necessary, this includes X-rays, scale and polish, and planning for further treatment. Urgent and out-of-hours care also costs £16.20.

♦ **£44.60** This charge includes all necessary treatment covered by the £16.20 charge plus additional treatment such as fillings, root canal treatment or extractions.

♦ **£198** This charge includes all necessary treatment covered by the £16.20 and £44.60 charges plus more complex procedures such as crowns, dentures or bridges.

Note that you can still be charged more than the above figure under certain circumstances, particularly for crowns, dentures or bridges. In practice, dentists are over-stretched in London (as elsewhere in the UK) and many are unwilling to accept new NHS patients if their quotas are already full (which they usually are). If you're fortunate enough to find an NHS dentist, and to avoid misunderstandings, you should ensure that the dentist knows that you expect NHS treatment when you register and that you remain entitled to NHS-subsidised treatment by attending regular check-ups – otherwise you may find yourself dropped from the dentist's NHS list.

> You should take your NHS medical card (see **NHS Doctors** above) to the dentist when you have your initial examination and each time you visit the dentist you should re-confirm that you'll be treated as an NHS patient.

NHS dental patients aren't required to live within a certain catchment area and can change dentists whenever they like. Once you're registered as an NHS patient, a dentist cannot refuse to treat you and essential work is always completed under the NHS when clinically necessary.

If you're unable to obtain NHS treatment (which is likely), you have no option but to pay for private treatment. Private dentistry usually involves less waiting, and treatment may be of a better quality (e.g. you can decide the quality of fillings, etc.), but it's much more expensive. Dentists may ask for payment in advance.

Dentists aren't obliged to treat you if you aren't a registered patient, even in an emergency. If you miss a dental appointment without giving 24 hours' notice, your dentist may charge you a standard fee.

Many dentists operate an emergency service and in some areas an emergency dental service is operated by the local health authority. If you're suffering from agonising toothache and you cannot find a dentist who will see you, you can try Guy's Hospital Dental School, Guy's Hospital, Great Maze Pond, SE1 9RT (☎ 020-7188 7188, London Bridge tube), which provides a free emergency dental service from 9.30am to 4pm Mondays to Fridays, as does the Eastman Dental Hospital, 256 Gray's Inn Road, WC1X 8LD (☎ 020-7915 1000, 🖳 www.eastman.ucl.ac.uk, Chancery Lane/King's Cross tube), from 8.30am until 5.30pm weekdays.

Complaints

If you have a complaint about dental treatment received under the NHS, you should write to your local FHSA within six months of the end of the course of treatment. For complaints about private treatment, you must contact the General Dental Council, 37 Wimpole Street, London W1G 8DQ (☎ 020-7887 3800, 🖳 www.gdc-uk.org). The British Dental Association doesn't handle complaints.

OPTICIANS

Opticians are listed under 'Opticians-dispensing' or 'Opticians-ophthalmic (optometrists)' in the Yellow Pages and may advertise their services, such as contact lenses or an emergency repair service. Opticians (like spectacles) come in many types. Your sight can be tested only by a registered ophthalmic optician (or optometrist) or an ophthalmic medical practitioner, who tests eyesight, prescribes glasses and diagnoses eye diseases. Most 'high street' opticians are both ophthalmic opticians and dispensing opticians, who make up spectacles. An ophthalmologist is a senior specialist or eye surgeon; an orthoptist is an ophthalmologist who treats children's eye problems. If you need to see an ophthalmologist or orthoptist, you must usually be referred by your GP. The Eye Care Trust (☎ 0845-129 5001, 🖥 www.eye-care.org. uk) can provide advice and direct you to an appropriate eye specialist.

The 'eye business' is competitive in the UK and, unless someone is highly recommended, you should shop around for the best deal. Recent years have seen a flood of 'chain store' opticians such as Dollond & Aitchison, Specsavers and Vision Express opening in high streets and shopping centres; these may offer better prices than independent opticians.

Prices for both spectacles and contact lenses vary considerably, so it's wise to compare costs (although make sure you're comparing like with like) before committing yourself to a large bill, particularly for contact lenses. The prices charged for most services (spectacle frames, lenses, hard and soft contact lenses) are often lower in the UK than elsewhere in Europe, although higher than North America.

Help the Aged, Pentonville Road, London N1 9UZ, (☎ 020-7278 1114, 🖥 www.helptheaged. org.uk) collects unwanted spectacles, which they distribute to the elderly in Africa and Asia.

Sight Tests

Certain people receive free sight tests under the NHS, including children under 16, full-time students under 19, the registered blind and partially sighted, diagnosed diabetics and glaucoma sufferers, and people receiving state benefits. NHS leaflet G11, *NHS Sight Tests and Vouchers For Glasses*, explains in detail who is entitled to free sight tests and NHS vouchers for glasses; it's available from social security offices, NHS family doctors and opticians.

If you aren't entitled to a free sight test under the NHS, you must pay between £15 and £20. Some opticians offer a lower price (or even a free test) to pensioners. Sight tests are valid for two years, although you should be aware that

your eyesight can change considerably during this time.

You don't need to buy your spectacles (lenses or frames) or contact lenses from the optician who tests your sight, irrespective of whether you're an NHS or private patient, and you have the right to a copy of any prescription resulting from an NHS or private sight test.

Complaints

If you have a complaint about an optician which you're unable to resolve, you should write to the Association of Optometrists, Consumer Complaints Service, 61 Southwark Street, London SE1 0HL (☎ 020-7261 9661, 🖥 www. assoc-optometrists.org) or, for dispensing opticians, the Association of British Dispensing Opticians, 199 Gloucester Terrace, London W2 6LD (☎ 020-7298 5100, 🖥 www.abdo.org.uk).

CHEMISTS & MEDICINES

Medicines ('drugs' in British English normally refers to illegal drugs or narcotics, though the word 'medication' is sometimes used instead of medicine) are obtained from a chemist (pharmacy), most of which provide free advice regarding minor ailments and suggest appropriate medicines.

There are three categories of medicine in the UK:

◆ medicines that can be prescribed only by a doctor (via an official form called a prescription) and purchased from a chemist (see **Prescriptions** below);

◆ medicines that can be sold only with the approval of a chemist (e.g. travel sickness pills);

◆ medicines (such as aspirin and paracetamol) that can be sold 'over the counter' in chemists and are available from other retail outlets, such as petrol stations and supermarkets, although you may be restricted as to how much you can buy at a time.

If you're taking regular medication, you should bear in mind that the brand names of medicines vary from country to country, and should ask your doctor for the generic name. If you wish to match medication prescribed medicines prescribed or sold to them.

If you need medicines after normal hours, there are a number of chemists' that regularly open late in central London including Bliss (5/6 Marble Arch, W1H 7AP, ☎ 020-7723 6116), which is open from 9am until midnight daily, and Boots (75 Queensway, W2 4QH, 🖳 www.boots.com), open from 9am to 10pm Mondays to Saturdays and from 2pm to 10pm on Sundays. If you require medicine urgently when all chemists' are closed, you should contact your GP or local police station.

Most chemists also sell toiletries, cosmetics, health foods and cleaning supplies. Some, such as Boots, may have departments selling everything from CDs and books to electrical and photographic equipment (in addition to those items mentioned above).

A health food shop sells anti-allergy and diet foods, homeopathic medicines and eternal-life-virility-youth pills and elixirs, which are quite popular in the UK (even though their claims are usually in the realms of fantasy).

Prescriptions

To obtain medicines prescribed by a doctor, simply take your prescription form to any chemist's. Your prescription may be filled immediately if it's available off the shelf or you may be asked to wait or come back later. NHS prescriptions for medicines are charged at a fixed rate of £7.10 per item, although certain people qualify for free medicines (see below). Those who need to pay for more than three prescription items in three months or 14 items in 12 months, can save money by buying a prepayment certificate (PPC), which costs £27.85 for three months and £102.50 for 12 months. You can buy a PPC from some chemists, by phone (☎ 0845-850 0030) or online (🖳 www.ppa.org.uk).

Many people qualify for free prescriptions, including hospital outpatients and day patients; children aged under 16 and full-time students under 19; pensioners (men over 65, women over 60, although the State Pension age for

abroad, you'll need a prescription with the medication's trade name, the manufacturer's name, the chemical name and the dosage. Most medicines have an equivalent in other countries, although particular brands may be difficult or impossible to obtain in the UK. It's also recommended to take some of your favourite non-prescription medicines (e.g. aspirins, cold and flu remedies and lotions), as they may be difficult to find or much more expensive. If applicable, you should also take spare spectacles, contact lenses, dentures or hearing aids.

Some medicines requiring a doctor's prescription in the UK are sold freely in other countries, although other medicines that are controlled elsewhere are freely available in the UK. Increasing numbers of previously restricted medicines are now available over the counter. Some medicines aren't recognised (i.e. reimbursed) by the NHS, in which case your doctor will usually inform you and may offer to prescribe an alternative. If you insist on having an unrecognised medicine, you must usually pay for it yourself. Requests for repeat prescriptions may be accepted by your doctor by post, telephone or online. Most chemists use a computer to store information about the health problems of regular customers and the women will rise gradually from age 60 to 65 from 2010 to 2020); expectant mothers and those who have had a baby in the last year; those with certain medical conditions (e.g. diabetes or epilepsy) or a permanent disability which prevents them getting around without help; and people on low incomes receiving state benefits.

With the exception of children under 16 and pensioners, all those entitled to free prescriptions (as listed above) must apply for an exemption certificate or a refund (forms are available from local social security offices, hospitals, dentists and opticians). When you're exempt, you must also complete and sign the declaration on the back of the prescription form.

Leaflet HC12, *NHS Prescriptions*, contains information about NHS charges, and Leaflet HC11 tells you whether you're exempt from payments. Both leaflets are available from social security offices and can be downloaded from the Department of Health website (🖳 www.doh.gov.uk).

☑ SURVIVAL TIP

Some medicines prescribed by a doctor (e.g. certain painkillers) can be replaced by substitute medicines that can be purchased over the counter for less than the prescription charge. Boots, the UK's largest chain of chemists' with over 1,300 stores, and supermarkets are often the cheapest place to buy non-prescription medicines (many sell 'own brand' products).

HOSPITALS & CLINICS

All London boroughs have one or more NHS hospitals or clinics, indicated by the international hospital sign of a red 'H' on a white background. There are many kinds of hospital in London, including community hospitals, district hospitals, teaching hospitals and (unlikely as it may seem) cottage hospitals – small, localised institutions. A list of London hospitals can be found on 🖳 www.medinet. co.uk/phlonhos.htm.

Major hospitals are called general hospitals and provide treatment and diagnosis for inpatients, day patients and outpatients. Most have a maternity department, infectious diseases unit, psychiatric and geriatric facilities, and rehabilitation and convalescence units, and cater for all forms of specialised treatment. Some general hospitals are designated teaching hospitals, which combine treatment with medical training and research.

In addition to general hospitals, there are specialist hospitals – for children, the mentally ill and disabled, the elderly and infirm, and for the treatment of specific complaints or illnesses. There are also dental hospitals.

Only major hospitals have an Accident & Emergency (A&E) department. Some NHS hospitals have sports injury clinics, although you must usually be referred by your GP, and some have minor injuries units. In many areas there are NHS 'well woman' clinics, where women can obtain medical check-ups and cervical smear tests, and NHS family planning clinics. You can be referred to these clinics by your GP or can refer yourself. You can also refer yourself to an NHS sexually transmitted diseases (STD) clinic for an examination.

Since 2003 hospitals have been 'star graded' and the 'best' hospitals given Foundation status, which means that they receive extra funding and enjoy greater autonomy from the NHS; this has been criticised as being a step towards the privatisation of the health service and, perhaps towards hospitals choosing their patients on the basis of how their treatment will affect the hospital's grading rather than on the basis of need.

Choosing a Hospital

Except for emergencies, you may be admitted or referred to an NHS hospital or clinic for treatment only after consultation with a GP or a consultant (or from an NHS clinic such as a family planning or well woman clinic). Patients with private health insurance may be treated at the hospital of their choice, depending on their insurance cover. NHS patients can ask to be treated at a particular hospital or to be referred to a particular consultant, but have no right to have their request met. In an emergency you'll be treated at the nearest hospital.

NHS Hospitals

NHS hospital accommodation is in wards of various sizes, e.g. 12 beds, some of which are mixed. Many NHS hospitals have private rooms (known as 'pay beds') and they're permitted to charge for extras such as single accommodation, a telephone or TV or a wider choice of meals. In most NHS hospitals, you choose your meals the day before and provision is made for vegetarian and other diets. Some wards have dining rooms for those who are sufficiently mobile and most have day rooms for patients.

The service, facilities and standards of NHS hospitals vary considerably with the area, and the best compare favourably with private hospitals (apart from a possible lack of 'luxury' faculties). On the other hand, some NHS hospitals are dingy and depressing – hardly the place you'd wish to be when you're ill. However, there's one consolation to being in an NHS general ward: just think how lonely and bored those poor private patients must be, ensconced in their luxury rooms with nobody to talk to all day!

Private Hospitals & Clinics

There are around 50 private hospitals and clinics in London, of which some of the largest and more famous are listed below:

♦ **The Clementine Churchill Hospital**, Sudbury Hill, Harrow, HA1 3RX (☎ 020-7872 3872, 💻 www.bmihealth.co.uk, Harrow-on-the Hill tube or rail) – provides sophisticated diagnostic and screening services;

♦ **The Cromwell Hospital**, Cromwell Road, SW5 0TU (☎ 020-7460 2000, 💻 www.cromwell-hospital.co.uk, Earls Court/Gloucester Road/High St Kensington tube) – one of the major private hospitals in the capital. It specialises in cancer treatment, treatment liver disease, pancreas and kidney transplants, neurosurgery, spinal surgery, heart surgery, gamma knife surgery (radio surgery) and IVF.

♦ **The Devonshire Hospital**, 29–31 Devonshire Street, W1G 6PU (☎ 020-7486 7131, Baker Street tube) – specialises in the rehabilitation of those suffering from neurological conditions such as head and spinal cord injuries and strokes;

♦ **The Harley Street Clinic**, 35 Weymouth Street, W1G 8BJ (☎ 020-7935 7700, 💻 www.theharleystreetclinic.com, Regent's Park tube) – an acute care hospital specialising in cardiology and cancer treatment;

♦ **The Lister Hospital**, Chelsea Bridge Road, SW1W 8RH (☎ 020-7730 7733, 💻 www.thelisterhospital.com, Sloane Square/Victoria tube) – has a wide range of specialities, including assisted conception and skin lasers;

♦ **The London Bridge Hospital**, 27 Tooley Street, SE1 2PR (☎ 020-7407 3100, 💻 www.londonbridgehospital.com, London Bridge tube) – specialises in wide range of medical, interventional and diagnostic services and specialties, including cardiology, gynaecology, neurology and sports rehabilitation;

♦ **The London Clinic**, 20 Devonshire Place, W1G 6BW (☎ 020-7935 4444, 💻 www.thelondonclinic.co.uk, Regent's Park tube) – an independent, non-profit hospital

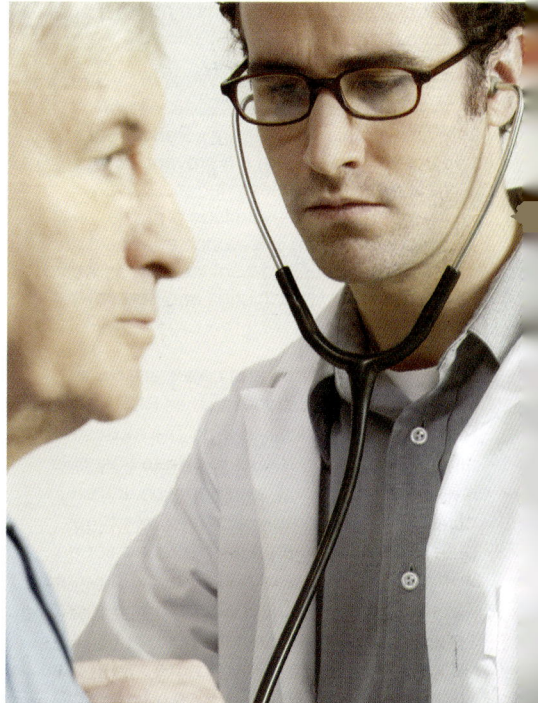

situated in the heart of London's medical community in Harley Street, the London Clinic is internationally renowned and the largest single private hospital in the UK. It provides a wide range of diagnostic services and treatment options.

♦ **The Portland Hospital for Women and Children**, 205–209 Great Portland Street, W1W 5AH (☎ 020-7580 4400, 🖳 www. theportlandhospital.com, Great Portland St/ Regent's Park tube) – the only private London hospital entirely dedicated to caring for women and children. Not surprisingly, it specialises in obstetrics, gynaecology and paediatrics.

♦ **The Princess Grace Hospital**, 47 Nottingham Place, W1U 5NY (☎ 020-7486 1234, 🖳 www.theprincessgracehospital. com, Baker St/Regent's Park tube) – another acute unit specialising in many disciplines. It also has a sleep apnoea clinic and is a major centre for the diagnosis and treatment of all forms of hepatitis.

♦ **The Wellington Hospital**, Wellington Place, St Johns Wood Road, NW8 9LE (☎ 020-7483 5148, 🖳 www.thewellingtonhospital. com, St John's Wood tube) – one of the largest, purpose-built private hospitals in the UK, offering all the resources of a first-class general hospital. It also has a major sport injuries clinic.

♦ **The Wellman Clinic**, 32 Weymouth Street, W1G 7BU (☎ 020-7637 2018, 🖳 www. wellmanclinic.org, Regent's Park/Great Portland Street tube) – a preventative healthcare centre designed exclusively for men. Specialities include prostate cancer treatment, impotence treatment and testosterone replacement therapy, as well as treatment for sport injuries and general health screening.

Many private hospitals and clinics are owned by provident associations such as BUPA and PPP and other health insurers. The most striking difference between NHS and private hospitals is in the standard of accommodation. Instead of being housed in a public ward with other patients, you have a private room equipped with all the comforts of home, including a radio, TV, telephone, en suite bathroom and room service (a visitor can usually enjoy a meal with a patient in the privacy of his room). The corridors are carpeted, the food edible and

there are frills and extras galore – which may even include interpreters and foreign cuisine for overseas patients – and the nurses and other staff will wait on you hand and foot.

If you don't have health insurance or are a visitor to the UK, you may be asked to pay a (large) deposit in advance, particularly if there's any doubt that you'll survive the ordeal. Private hospitals usually accept credit cards, and some offer interest-free loans to pay hospital bills (e.g. a 10 per cent deposit with the rest payable over 12 months). This is one solution for those who cannot afford health insurance and don't want to wait for an operation. However, make sure that you aren't being overcharged, as you can often have an operation cheaper elsewhere in the UK or even abroad (e.g. in France) and possibly save thousands of pounds. Many private hospitals provide fixed-price surgery, subject to an examination by a consultant surgeon.

According to Action for Victims of Medical Accidents (AVMA), there are higher surgical health risks in private hospitals than in NHS hospitals, and there may be less emergency equipment and fewer experienced staff. On the other hand, your chances of acquiring a 'superbug' infection – the bane of NHS hospitals – is negligible in a private hospital.

☑ **SURVIVAL TIP**

You have almost no protection under the law when you're treated at a private clinic or hospital compared with your rights as an NHS hospital patient, and when things go wrong (as they occasionally do) you're usually better off in an NHS hospital.

Many experts believe that the best solution is a private ward in an NHS teaching hospital, where, if anything goes wrong and your life is on the line, you're far better off than you are in a small private clinic.

Cosmetic Surgery

A glance through the advertisements in many women's, and increasingly men's magazines will give you some indication of just how big (and lucrative) a business cosmetic surgery has become in London. If your nose, ears or derrière are too big, or you'd love to fill a full C cup, just pop down to your local plastic surgeon, who will remove unwanted bits or make others more prominent as fast as you can say £3,000. If you're contemplating cosmetic surgery, you'd be well advised to contact one of the following for advice before parting with any money:

◆ The British Association of Plastic, Reconstructive and Aesthetic Surgeons (BAPRAS), c/o The Royal College of Surgeons of England, 35–43 Lincoln's Inn Fields, London WC2A 3PE (☎ 020-7831-5161/2, 🖳 www.bapras.org.uk);

◆ The Breast Implant Information Society (BIIS), Highway Farm, Horsley Road, Cobham, Surrey KT11 3JZ (☎ 07041-471225, 🖳 www.biis.org) – an independent advisory body.

They above websites have search facilities for finding surgeons in a particular speciality, and the BAPRAS site also contains a handy glossary of esoteric medical terms.

A few of the best-known clinics specialising in plastic surgery in and around London are the Pountney Clinic (☎ 0800-028 2114, 🖳 www. pountneyclinic.co.uk) near Heathrow Airport, which performs the whole range of cosmetic surgery for face and body; the Cosmetic Surgery Clinic, 100 Harley Street, W1 (☎ 020-7486 5111, 🖳 www.100harleystreet.com), which specialises in breast enhancement; and Guy's Nuffield House (☎ 020-7188 7188), which is attached to Guy's Hospital and emphasises extensive consultation and counselling before surgery.

CHILDBIRTH

Childbirth in the UK normally takes place in a hospital, where a stay of a few days is usual. If you wish to have a child at home, you must find a doctor or midwife (see below) who is willing to attend you, although it's generally impossible for the birth of a first child. Some doctors are opposed to home births, particularly where there's a higher than average risk of

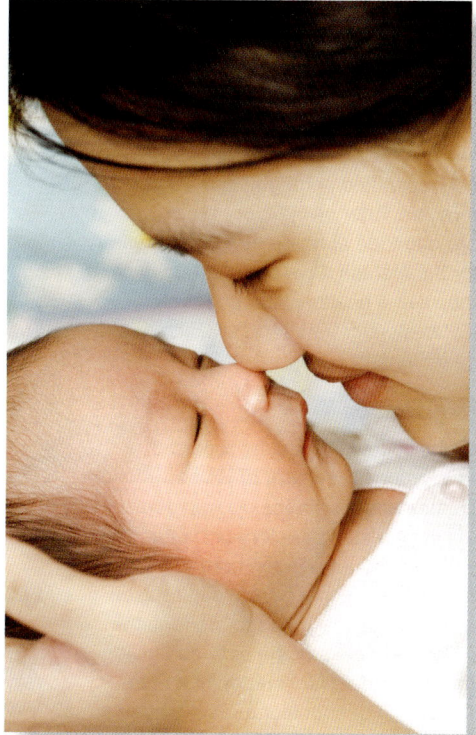

complications and when specialists or special facilities (e.g. incubators) may be required.

For hospital births, you can usually choose (with the help of your GP or midwife) the hospital where you wish to have your baby. You aren't required to use the hospital suggested by your GP but should book a hospital bed as early as possible. Your GP will also refer you to an obstetrician. Find out as much as possible about local hospital methods and policies on childbirth, either directly or from friends or neighbours, before booking a bed.

The policy regarding a father's attendance at a birth varies with the hospital. A father doesn't have a legal right to be present during labour or childbirth (which is at the consultant's discretion), although some doctors expect fathers to attend.

If the presence of the father is important to you, you should check that it's permitted at the hospital where you plan to have your baby and any other rules that may be in force.

In the UK, midwives are responsible for educating and supporting women and their families during the childbearing period.

Midwives can advise women before they become pregnant, in addition to providing moral, physical and emotional support throughout a pregnancy and after the birth. Your midwife may also advise on parent education and antenatal classes for mothers. After giving birth, mothers are attended at home by their midwife for the first ten days or so, after which they see a health visitor and their GP to monitor their child's health and development.

Registration

Births in the UK must be reported to your local Registrar of Births, Deaths and Marriages (look in your local telephone directory or on the website of your London borough – see **Chapter 1**). Either parent can register a birth by simply going to the registrar within six weeks of the birth and giving the child's details. You don't have to take proof of birth along – although it's useful to bring the mother's hospital discharge summary if you have one. The health authority or hospital where the child was born will also notify the registrar of the birth.

Both parents must report to the registrar if they aren't married and they both want their details to be included on the birth certificate; if only the mother registers the birth, only her details are listed. A birth is usually registered in the area where the baby was born but can be registered with another office. Births of foreigners in the UK may also need to be reported to a consulate or embassy – for example, to obtain a national birth certificate and passport for a child.

FAMILY PLANNING SERVICES

Family planning services, including the provision of contraceptives (including the morning-after pill) and, if necessary, abortions, are free to foreign nationals living and working in the UK. For information visit your doctor or a family planning clinic. To find your nearest clinic contact the FPA (formerly the Family Planning Association), 50 Featherstone Street,

EC1Y 8QU (☎ 020-7608 5240, 💻 www.fpa. org.uk). The International Planned Parenthood Federation, 4 Newhams Row, SE1 3UZ (☎ 020-7939 8200, 💻 www.ippf.org) provides general information on contraception, condoms and abortion, while the National Childbirth Trust (☎ 0870-444 8707, 💻 www.nct.org. uk) provides information and support to women during pregnancy, childbirth and early parenthood. Information about contraception, pregnancy and abortion is available from a number of organisations, including the British Pregnancy Advisory Service (☎ 0845-365 5050, 💻 www.bpas.org.uk), the Brook Advisory Centre, 421 Highgate Studios, 53–79 Highgate Road, NW5 1TL (☎ 020-7284 6040, 💻 www.brook. org.uk) and Marie Stopes International, 153–157 Cleveland Street, W1T 6QW (☎ 0845-300 8090, 💻 www.mariestopes.org.uk).

Abortions can legally be performed under certain conditions, when continuing with the pregnancy involves a greater risk to the physical or mental health of the woman, or her existing children, than having a termination. Under British law, abortions can only be performed within the first 24 weeks of pregnancy (confirmed by Parliament in 2008) and must be agreed by two doctors (or one in an emergency) and carried out by a doctor in a government-approved hospital or clinic.

For the two sides of the abortion argument – which isn't nearly as controversial in the UK as, for example, it is in the USA, see Abortion Rights (☎ 020-7923 9792, 🖳 www.abortionrights.org.uk) and Life (☎ 0800-915 4600, 🖳 www.lifecharity.org.uk).

SEXUALLY TRANSMITTED DISEASE

The UK has more than its share of sexually transmitted diseases (STDs) – second only to Portugal in Europe – and at the end of 2007 an estimated 93,000 people were living with the deadly acquired immune deficiency syndrome (AIDS), from which some 20,000 people have died to date. London accounts for over 40 per cent of new AIDS cases in the UK. The spread of AIDS (and other STDs) in the UK is accelerated by prostitutes, many of whom are also drug addicts. But as prostitution is illegal in the UK, it's almost impossible for the government to effect any control over the spread of sexually transmitted diseases by prostitutes. For this reason, if no other, you should avoid prostitutes – literally – like the plague. Gonorrhoea is on the increase (there are over 20,000 cases per year) and the antibiotic ciprofloxacin is losing its effectiveness, while Chlamydia (which can cause infertility) is thought to affect one in ten sexually active British women and it also affects men.

Many hospitals have clinics for sexually transmitted diseases or you can go to a sexually transmitted diseases or venereal disease (VD) clinic. Both provide free tests, treatment and advice. You can also obtain free confidential advice, diagnosis and treatment at the Centre for Sexual Health, Genito-Urinary Clinic, Jefferiss Wing, St Mary's Hospital, Praed Street, W2 (☎ 020-7886 6666), which will also help with non-sexually transmitted genital diseases such as cystitis and thrush.

If you'd like to talk to someone in confidence about AIDS, there are many organisations and self-help groups providing information, advice and help. These include the National AIDS Trust (☎ 020-7814 6767, 🖳 www.nat.org.uk). Those who have been diagnosed with AIDS can obtain help and advice from the Terrence Higgins Trust (☎ 020-7812 1600, 🖳 www.tht.org.uk). All cases of AIDS and HIV-positive blood tests in the UK must be reported to the local health authorities (patients' names aren't published) so that statistics can be kept up to date.

☑ SURVIVAL TIP

Condoms are available free from family planning clinics and can be bought from chemists', some supermarkets, men's hairdressers', and machines in public toilets in pubs and other places.

INFORMATION & HELP

There are many health 'helplines' in London covering a broad range of medical and related problems, many operated by volunteers. Some helplines provide a 24-hour service, although most have limited 'business' hours, so if you there's no reply, try again later. Some of the most useful helplines are listed below.

◆ **Alcoholics Anonymous** (☎ 0845-769 7555, 24 hours a day) – to discuss an alcohol-related problem. Alcoholics Anonymous organises meetings where alcoholics support each other in their efforts to kick the habit and will even send someone to accompany you to your first meeting.

◆ **Childline** (☎ 0800-1111) – a free, confidential, 24-hour national helpline for children and young people in danger or trouble;

◆ **Medical Advisory Service** (☎ 020-8995 8503, 5 to 10pm Mondays to Fridays) – can offer help with almost any health-related problem;

◆ **Narcotics Anonymous** (☎ 020-7251 4007, 10am to 10pm daily) – provides the same sort of services for drug addicts as Alcoholics Anonymous does for those with an alcohol problem;

♦ **NHS Direct** (☎ 0845-4647) – a 24-hour health advice and information service staffed by NHS nurses, who can advise on particular symptoms or health conditions and refer you to local healthcare services such as doctors, dentists, late night chemists' and self-help and support organisations;

♦ **Samaritans** (☎ 0845-790 9090, 24 hours) – will help you talk through any emotional problem and isn't, as many believe, purely for those contemplating suicide.

Useful websites on UK health issues include:

♦ **BBC Health News** (🖥 www.bbc.co.uk/health) – part of the encyclopaedic BBC site;

♦ **NHS Choices** (🖥 www.nhs.uk) – the official NHS site;

♦ **NHS Direct** (🖥 www.nhsdirect.nhs.uk) – has information on particular health conditions and local healthcare services;

♦ **Surgery Door** (🖥 www.surgerydoor.co.uk) – has information on a wide range of family health topics, from pregnancy to immunisation.

The National Institute for Health and Clinical Excellence (71 High Holborn, London WC1V 6NA, ☎ 0845-003 7780, 🖥 www.nice.org.uk) publishes information on a wide range of health topics (a catalogue is available), much of which is available free from chemists, clinics and doctors' surgeries.

⚠ Caution

Note that information obtained from recorded telephone helplines, websites and books, although usually recorded, written or approved by medical experts, must be viewed with caution and shouldn't be used as a substitute for consulting your family doctor.

DEATH

Like births (see above), deaths in the UK must be reported to your local Registrar of Births, Deaths and Marriages (look in your local telephone directory or on the website of your London borough – see **Chapter 1**).

When someone dies, a medical certificate must be completed by a doctor and taken to the registrar within five days. If someone dies suddenly, accidentally, during an operation or in unusual circumstances, or if the cause of death is unknown, the doctor will notify the police and/or a coroner, who will decide whether a post-mortem is necessary to determine the cause of death.

In any case, the registrar will need certain information about the deceased, including his date and place of birth and death, details of a marriage (if applicable), and whether he was receiving a state pension or any welfare benefits. The registrar then issues a death certificate and a 'notification of disposal', which authorises a funeral to take place. The death certificate must be given to a funeral director (also known as an undertaker) to arrange the burial or cremation or for the body to be shipped to another country. If you wish to remove a body from London, permission must be obtained from a coroner at least four days before shipment.

You may wish to announce a death in a local or national newspaper, giving the date, time and place of the funeral, and your wishes regarding flowers or contributions to a charity or research.

In the UK, the traditional dress for a Christian funeral is black or dark clothing.

Cost

Funerals are expensive in the UK, where the increase in the cost of dying in the last few decades has exceeded the increase in the cost of living. The average London funeral costs around £3,000; you can save money by having a body cremated rather than buried, although the cost is still high at around £2,000.

You can pay in advance for your funeral through a variety of pay-now-die-later schemes, with price and service guaranteed, although there are no legal safeguards and the prepaid funeral trade is ripe for fraud, mismanagement and over-selling (a number of companies offering funeral plans have gone bust in recent years, making a lot of living people wish they were dead). Pre-paid funeral schemes cost between £1,000 and £3,000 and have been taken out by some 250,000 people (this is expected to increase tenfold in the next few years).

Information

The Pension Service (⌨ www.thepension service.gov.uk), which is a government agency, gives advice about procedures to be followed in the event of a death. HM Revenue & Customs has a telephone helpline for inheritance information (☎ 0845-302 0900) and publishes a leaflet *What Happens When Someone Dies* (IR45). Help the Aged (⌨ www.helptheaged.org.uk) publishes a free booklet entitled *Bereavement*. Other useful books include *What to Do When Someone Dies* by Paul Harris (Which? Books) and *Through Grief* by Elizabeth Collick (Darton, Longman and Todd). Cruse Bereavement Care (PO Box 900, Richmond, Surrey TW9 1RG, ☎ 0844-477 9400, ⌨ www.crusebereavementcare.org.uk) can also provide comprehensive help and advice.

Westminster Abbey

Notting Hill Carnival

9.

TIME OFF

Whether your idea of a good time is a quiet stroll around an art gallery or a deafening dance at a thumping nightspot, London is one of the best places in the world to enjoy yourself. It doesn't matter whether you're 19 or 90, a drinker or a thinker, gay or straight, single or a mother of four, there's something for you. The variety of leisure opportunities in London is enormous and it provides more cultural activities than any other city in the world, including over 1,500 events per week – sufficient to entertain over 400,000 people. There are even stately homes, zoos and theme parks in – or very near – the capital.

TOURIST INFORMATION

This chapter provides just a taste of what London has to offer and doesn't include details of famous sights such as Big Ben, the Tower of London and the London Eye (a giant wheel opposite the Houses of Parliament offering superb views of the city). Information about these and other tourist attractions is available from a multitude of guides, newspapers (many of which publish free weekly entertainment guides) and magazines, including London's weekly *Time Out* guide. Time Out (the publisher) also produces a number of excellent annual guides for visitors and residents alike, including the essential *London Visitors' Guide*. The latest tourist information is available from Visit London (🖥 www.visitlondon.com) and there are many other excellent websites including 🖥 www. bbc.co.uk/London, 🖥 www.thisislondon.co.uk (*Evening Standard*), and 🖥 www.timeout.com. For a comprehensive list see **Appendix C**.

Disabled Help

Most London museums and galleries have special access for the disabled or provide wheelchairs – for information see their websites. There are numerous organisations in London working for the disabled, many of which provide information about access to arts and entertainment in London; one of the most useful is Artsline (🖥 www.artsline.org.uk) and a number of others are listed on the *Time Out* website (🖥 www.timeout.com).

ART GALLERIES

London has an international reputation for the number and quality of its art galleries, boasting some of the world's finest collections of fine art and antiquities. Many galleries don't charge for admission and you can wander in and out as you please (subject to the obligatory security searches), making a visit worthwhile even if you have only an hour or two to spare. However, opening hours vary, so you should check before making a special journey.

National Gallery & Portrait Gallery

London's flagship art gallery is the **National Gallery** (☎ 020-7747 2885, 🖥 www. nationalgallery.org.uk, Leicester Square or Charing Cross tube) in Trafalgar Square, where you can see over 2,000 priceless paintings dating from the 13th to 20th centuries, including masterpieces such as Constable's *The Hay Wain* and Van Gogh's *Sunflowers*. Admission is free, an audio guide can be rented at the entrance and you can lounge on leather sofas when you get tired or want to soak up a particular painting. Don't miss a visit to the Micro Gallery, where you can display any of the gallery's paintings on a screen and print a reproduction.

The **National Portrait Gallery** (☎ 020-7306 0055, 🖳 www.npg.org.uk, Leicester Square or Charing Cross tube) is next door to the National Gallery in St Martin's Place and, as the name suggests, it specialises in portraits of famous people through the ages. Here you can look into the eyes of William Shakespeare or Princess Diana, plus a host of kings, queens and political figures from the past. Admission is free and the gallery also stages regular themed exhibitions.

Tate Britain & Modern

The **Tate Britain** (☎ 020-7887 8888, 🖳 www.tate.org.uk, Pimlico tube) at Millbank – formerly the Tate Gallery – supplements and complements the National Gallery. It houses an impressive collection of British art from the 16th century to the present day, including masterpieces by Hogarth, Constable, Reynolds and Turner, as well as showcasing contemporary artists such as Lucian Freud and David Hockney. Admission is free.

A 'Tate to Tate' boat service links Tate Britain to its highly successful younger sister, the Tate Modern, and runs every 20 minutes, stopping at the London Eye on the way. Tickets are available from desks at both museums, on board boats (for information ☎ 020-7887 8888) and online at 🖳 www.tate.org.uk.

Housed in the old Bankside Power Station, the cavernous **Tate Modern**, Bankside, SE1 9TJ (☎ 020-7887 8888, 🖳 www.tate.org. uk, Blackfriars tube) is as awe-inspiring as the displays, which, as the name suggests, are exclusively – and often shockingly – contemporary.

Other central London Galleries

The **Courtauld Institute** at Somerset House, Strand (☎ 020-7872 0220, 🖳 www.courtauld. ac.uk, Covent Garden tube) usually charges £5 (£4 concessions) for admission, although it provides free admission from 10am to

2pm on Mondays. Recently restored, the building houses some wonderful paintings by Impressionist and Post-impressionist artists such as Degas, Cézanne, Monet, Renoir, Gauguin and Toulouse-Lautrec, as well as works by Botticelli, Brueghel and Rubens.

The **Hayward Gallery** (☎ 0871-663 2501, 🖳 www.southbankcentre.co.uk, Embankment or Waterloo tube) is part of the South Bank Centre by the river, which also houses the National Theatre and Royal Festival Hall complexes. It has no permanent collection but is one of the best venues in London to see temporary exhibitions, although admission charges can be high (usually around £10 to £12).

The **Royal Academy of Arts**, Piccadilly (☎ 0870-848 8484, 🖳 www.royalacademy. org.uk, Piccadilly Circus or Green Park tube) is famous for its annual Summer Exhibition, as well as for a range of themed arts events.

The **Institute of Contemporary Arts**, The Mall (☎ 020-7930 3647, 🖳 www.ica.org.uk, Piccadilly Circus or Charing Cross tube) is celebrated for its exhibitions of challenging avant-garde work.

Outer London Galleries

There are two notable galleries outside central London.

The **Dulwich Picture Gallery** (☎ 020-8693 5254, 🖳 www.dulwichpicturegallery.org.uk, North Dulwich or West Dulwich railway station) houses a magnificent collection of old masters, including Canaletto, Gainsborough, Poussin, Rembrandt, Rubens and Watteau. The critically acclaimed loan exhibitions and the Gallery's setting in the beautiful 18th-century village of Dulwich make it a must for all art lovers. The Gallery has recently undergone extensive refurbishment and now has impressive new facilities, including a café.

The **Queen's Gallery** (☎ 020-7766 7300, 🖳 www.royal.gov.uk, St James's Park or Victoria tube) at Buckingham Palace provides a year-round showcase for displays from the Royal Collection – as well as the only opportunity to see inside the famous 'Buck House'.

MUSEUMS

London has some 300 museums, containing world-renowned collections and covering a wide range of subjects. The greatest concentration of museums is in South

Kensington, where you can spend several days exploring the delights of the Natural History Museum, the Science Museum and the Victoria & Albert Museum (see below).

Although some national museums have introduced entrance fees in the last 15 years (thanks to government funding cuts), most are still free. Like private art galleries, private museums charge an admission fee, although students, the unemployed, the disabled, carers and pensioners often receive a reduction (or 'concession') on production of an identity card, and are sometimes admitted free. Many museums allow everyone free entrance for the last hour or two of the day, and some offer annual family season tickets.

The London Pass (🖥 www.londonpass. com) could save you money if you want to visit a number of more expensive venues in a single day. The pass costs from £38 for adult (child £24) and allows you 'free' access to over 50 sights and attractions.

The Victorian method of displaying artefacts in dusty wooden cabinets within silent, cavernous halls is largely a thing of the past in London. Many of the capital's museums have replaced static exhibits with bright new interactive models and multimedia displays designed to appeal to everyone – not just scholars and enthusiasts (though their appeal to scholars and enthusiasts may be limited).

Some of London most famous and popular museums are listed below. For a comprehensive list of London's museums (and links to their websites) see Wikipedia (🖥 http:// en.wikipedia.org/wiki/List_of_museums_in_ London).

British Museum

Probably the best place to start a London museum tour is the **British Museum**, Bloomsbury (☎ 020-7323 8000, 🖥 www. britishmuseum.org, Holborn, Russell Square or Tottenham Court Road tube) is the capital's leading tourist attraction, with over 6m visitors a year – it's also free! It takes days to see the whole museum (and many more treasures are hidden out of sight), but must-sees include the eerie Clocks Room, the unrivalled collection of Egyptology, the Sutton Hoo ship burial artefacts and the famous Elgin Marbles (the subject of a long-standing and vociferous ownership wrangle between the UK and Greece).

Natural History Museum

The **Natural History Museum**, Cromwell Road (☎ 020-7942 5000, 🖥 www.nhm.ac.uk, South Kensington tube) has changed out of all recognition in the past decade, although

Victoria & Albert Museum, South Kensington

Flight Lab you can take the controls inside a full-size aeroplane cockpit and kids can experiment with a range of interactive machines at the Launch Pad. There's a hands-on area for three- to six-year-olds in the basement, called 'The Garden', and another for 7- to 11-year-olds called simply 'Things'. There's also the ultra-modern 'Wellcome Wing', heralded as the 'world's leading centre for the presentation of contemporary science and technology.'

Victoria & Albert

The **Victoria & Albert Museum**, Cromwell Road (☎ 020-7942 2000, 🖥 www.vam.ac.uk, South Kensington tube) – familiarly known as the V&A – houses unrivalled collections of sculptures, historical costumes, jewellery and musical instruments, outstanding examples of the applied and decorative arts (from Korean ceramics and Lalique glassware to Raphael cartoons) and a whole gallery devoted to Frank Lloyd Wright, one of Britain's foremost architects. In recent years the museum has tried to foster a 'trendier' image, housing retrospectives on such fashion luminaries as Giorgio Armani, Coco Chanel and Gianni Versace.

Imperial War Museum

The **Imperial War Museum**, Lambeth Road (☎ 020-7416 5320, 🖥 www.iwm.org.uk, Lambeth North or Waterloo tube) is situated south of the river. Nearly 200 years ago the building housed the infamous 'Bedlam' lunatic asylum, but it's now a grim reminder of the heroism and horror of warfare. In addition to static exhibits of the machinery of war, including a Spitfire and V2 rocket, it features multimedia 'experiences' which bring to life the First World War trenches and London's Blitz during the Second.

National Maritime Museum

The **National Maritime Museum**, Greenwich (☎ 020-8858 4422, 🖥 www.nmm.ac.uk, Greenwich or Maze Hill railway station or Island Gardens on the DLR) is where you can

the famous dinosaur skeletons remain (and have been joined by a robotic T Rex), and it's worth visiting for the extraordinary Victorian architecture alone. But the fusty displays, reluctantly peered at by generations of British schoolchildren, have given way to interactive 'Life Galleries' – a nightmarish collection of 'creepy crawlies', including a giant animatronic scorpion – and 'Earth Galleries', which replaced the old Geological Museum and where you can ride a vast escalator through the centre of a rotating globe, experience an earthquake and marvel at (real) moon rocks.

Science Museum

The **Science Museum**, Exhibition Road (☎ 0870-870 4868, 🖥 www.sciencemuseum.org.uk, South Kensington tube) contains a wealth of technological wonders, from Stephenson's Rocket (the first locomotive) to the command module of Apollo 10. In the appreciate the importance of Britain's maritime heritage – and the central role seafaring has had in its history. There's an interactive gallery called 'All Hands' where you can send a signal in Morse Code or display it in flags, as well as more traditional – and poignant – displays such as the uniform in which Admiral Nelson died at the Battle of Trafalgar.

Madame Tussauds & Dungeon

Madame Tussauds, Marylebone Road (☎ 0870-999 0046, 🖥 www.madame-tussauds.co.uk, Baker Street tube) – which should, of course, be Madame Tussaud's, after Marie Tussaud, who founded it in 1835 – is a traditional waxworks museum that (somewhat bafflingly) continues to draw the crowds. Admittedly, it has recently made some attempt to move with the times in becoming more interactive – visitors can now sing to a waxwork of *Pop Idol* judge Simon Cowell and receive a torrent of abuse for their trouble – but queues are interminable, access is ludicrously poor and most of the models (of historical and modern-day figures, from kings and queens to Hollywood stars and footballers) are about as lifelike as, well, waxworks. The highlight of a visit to Madame Tussauds for many people is the Chamber of Horrors with its roster of serial killers and assorted other infamous criminals.

London Dungeon

If you enjoy the Chamber of Horrors (see Madame Tussauds), you might like to visit the even grislier London Dungeon, Tooley Street (🖥 www.thedungeons.com, London Bridge tube). It isn't for young children (or squeamish adults), who might be terrified by the graphic scenes of torture and death or by the costumed actors who 'enliven' the experience.

Museum of London

The **Museum of London**, (☎ 0870-444 3852, 🖥 www.museumoflondon.org.uk, Barbican/Moorgate or St Paul's tube) on London Wall near the Barbican Centre, presents the capital's history, from prehistoric times to the present day. Don't miss the Roman London gallery, which uses thousands of Roman artefacts, including recent archaeological discoveries, to recreate life in Londinium.

CINEMAS

Film-lovers are spoilt for choice in London, where there's not only mainstream cinema – centred on Leicester Square and including suburban 'multiplexes' with several screens showing different current movies – but also a thriving 'fringe' or 'arthouse' cinema scene, in which low-budget, cult and B movies are screened, as well as numerous foreign films, usually with subtitles.

Films on general release are classified by the British Board of Film Censors (BBFC, 🖥 www.bbfc.co.uk) according to their suitability (or unsuitability) for young people, as shown below:

Film Classification

♦ **U** – suitable for children aged four and over but usually aimed at a general or 'family' audience;

♦ **Uc** – particularly suitable for pre-school age children (parents must suffer in silence);

♦ **PG** – stands for 'parental guidance', which, according to the BBFC, means that it shouldn't upset children of eight or more but may be watched by children of any age, unaccompanied (would you allow your seven-year-old to go to the cinema alone?);

♦ **12A** – No one under 12 may watch unless accompanied by an adult (the classification 12 applies to DVDs, which may not be bought or rented by anyone under 12).

♦ **15** – No one under 15 admitted.

♦ **18** – No one under 18 admitted.

In practice, most U and PG films are targeted at families with young children, while 12-, 15- and 18-rated movies have increasingly adult content – either 'bad' language or scenes of a violent or sexual nature, though the last is often considered to be more potentially 'damaging' even than extreme violence.

If you want to be among the first to see a major new releases, you must usually go to the Odeon Leicester Square or the Empire, which face each other across Leicester Square, both of which have huge screens and excellent sound systems. Many areas have a local a local cinema – most multi-screen – owned by chains such the Cineworld, Empire, Odeon and Vue chains, which offer 'passes' that are good value for film buffs.

Notable independent cinemas in London include the Everyman Cinema in Hollybush Vale, NW3 6TX (☎ 0870-066 4777, 🖳 www.everymancinema.com, Hampstead tube), the Lux Cinema (☎ 020-7684 0200, Old Street tube) in Hoxton Square and the National Film Theatre (🖳 www.bfi.org.uk, Embankment or Waterloo tube/rail) on the South Bank. You can see French films at the Institut Français, 17 Queensberry Place (☎ 020-7073 1350, 🖳 www.institut-francais.org.uk) and German films at the Goethe Institut, 50 Princes Gate (☎ 020-7596 4000, 🖳 www.goethe.de/ins/gb/lon), both in South Kensington.

You can read film reviews and details about films old and new, plus details of where they're currently showing, in newspapers and magazines, including the *Evening Standard* and *Time Out* magazine (which also publishes an annual *Film Guide*).

THEATRES, OPERA & BALLET

London is renowned for the quality, quantity and variety of its theatre, which are respectively among the highest, greatest and widest in the world. There are over 150 theatres in London (50 in the West End), producing up to 25 new productions every week, ranging from modern drama to classical plays; comedies; modern and traditional musicals; revue and variety shows; and pantomime and other children's entertainment. There's also, of course, a wide variety of opera and operetta, ballet and contemporary dance.

The theatre is widely patronised and is one of the delights of living in London. Fringe theatre is lively and extensive, and provides an excellent training ground for new playwrights and companies. Many London and provincial theatres support youth theatres (e.g. 14 to 21) and people of all ages who see themselves as budding stage stars can audition for local amateur dramatic societies.

> The cost of tickets for most major London musicals and plays ranges from around £20 to over £100.

Opera: The main opera venues in London are the Royal Opera House, Bow Street, Covent Garden, WC2 (☎ 020-7304 4000, 🖳 www.royalopera.org, Covent Garden tube) and the London Coliseum, St. Martin's Lane, Trafalgar Square, WC2 (☎ 020-7632 8300, 🖳 www.eno.org, Charing Cross, Leicester Square, Embankment, Covent Garden tube stations).

Ballet: The country's premier ballet company is the Royal Ballet, which performs at the Royal Opera House (see above), while the English National Ballet (🖳 www.ballet.org.uk) performs at the Royal Festival Hall, the London Coliseum (see above) and various venues throughout the UK.

Contemporary Dance: There are a number of excellent comtemporary dance companies and venues in London including Sadler's Wells, Rosebery Avenue, EC1 (☎ 0844-412 4300, 🖳 www.sadlerswells.com, Angel tube), which styles itself London's dance house, with a dynamic contemporary programme showcasing the best of international and UK dance. The Place, 17 Duke's Road, WC1H (☎ 020-7121 1100, 🖳 www.theplace.org.uk, Euston and Russel Square tube stations) is also a leading centre for contemporary dance, and home of the London Contemporary Dance School. See also 🖳 www.londondance.com for information about all forms of dance in London.

Theatre listings are provided in newspapers and magazines, including London's weekly *Time Out*, and information is also available (and booking can also be made) on the internet (🖳 www.officiallondontheatre.co.uk and 🖳 www.whatsonstage.com).

MUSIC

London is one of the world's great musical centres and you can hear every type of music imaginable somewhere in the capital.

Classical

As far as classical music goes, London is one of the two or three leading 'venues' in the world. It has no fewer than five major orchestras: the London Symphony Orchestra or LSO (🖥 http://lso.co.uk), the London Philharmonic Orchestra or LPO (🖥 www.lpo.co.uk), the Royal Philharmonic Orchestra or RPO (🖥 www.rpo.co.uk), the Philharmonia Orchestra (🖥 www.philharmonia.co.uk) and the BBC Symphony Orchestra (🖥 www.bbc.co.uk/orchestras/so), plus many excellent smaller ensembles such as the English Chamber Orchestra and the Academy of St Martin-in-the-Fields.

London also has a wealth of classical venues, including:

◆ **The Barbican Centre**, Silk Street, EC2 (☎ 020-7638 4141, 🖥 www.barbican.org.uk, Barbican or Moorgate tube) is Europe's largest multi-arts and conference venue, comprising theatres, libraries, galleries and the Guildhall School of Music as well as a large concert hall;

◆ **Blackheath Concert Halls**, Lee Road, SE3 (☎ 020-8318 9758, 🖥 www.blackheathhalls.com, Blackheath rail) is, along with Croydon's Fairfield Halls, the largest concert venue outside central London;

◆ **Fairfield Halls**, Park Lane, Croydon CR1 (☎ 020-8688 9291, 🖥 www.fairfield.co.uk, East Croydon rail/Tramlink) lays claim to be 'south London's premier arts, entertainment and conference centre';

◆ **The South Bank Centre,** Waterloo (☎ 0871-663 2501, 🖥 www.southbankcentre.co.uk, Waterloo tube) is London's premier classical music venue, incorporating the recently refurbished Royal Festival Hall, the smaller Queen Elizabeth Hall and the intimate chamber music venue, the Purcell Room;

◆ **St John's Smith Square**, Smith Square, SW1 (☎ 020-7222 1061, 🖥 www.sjss.org.uk, Westminster tube) is a deconsecrated church regarded as one of the masterpieces of English Baroque and one of London's finest concert venues;

◆ **Wigmore Hall**, Wigmore Street, W1 (☎ 020-7395 2142, 🖥 www.wigmore-hall.org.uk, Bond Street tube) is a 'cult' venue for solo and chamber music recitals.

As well as the above secular venues, many central London churches provide live music, particularly free lunchtime recitals, which are popular with workers. Drop in at St Bride's, Fleet Street, EC4 (☎ 020-7427 0133, 🖥 www.stbrides.com, Blackfriars tube), St James's, Piccadilly, W1 (☎ 020-7734 4511, 🖥 www.st-james-piccadilly.org, Piccadilly Circus tube) or, best of all, St Martin-in-the-Fields, Trafalgar Square, WC2 (☎ 020-7766 1100, 🖥 www2.stmartin-in-the-fields.org, Charing Cross tube), which also stages (not free) concerts in the evenings featuring its own top-class classical ensemble. Free lunchtime concerts are also given

by students of the Royal Academy of Music, Marylebone Road, NW1 (☏ 020-7873 7373, 🖳 www.ram.ac.uk, Regent's Park or Baker Street tube) and the Royal College of Music, Prince Consort Road, Kensington, SW7 (☏ 020-7589 3643, 🖳 www.rcm.ac.uk, South Kensington tube).

Festivals

One of the great joys of London is its summer music festivals. The biggest and best known – and one of the most famous classical music festivals anywhere in the world – is the BBC Sir Henry Wood Promenade Concerts, known as the Proms. It takes place between July and September at the Royal Albert Hall, Kensington, SW7 (☏ 020-7589 8212, 🖳 www.royalalberthall.com, South Kensington tube) and combines musical favourites with contemporary works (including many world premieres). If you're prepared to queue for hours, you can get standing tickets for just £6, but tickets for the celebrated 'Last Night' concert are allocated by ballot.

Often derided as jaded, jingoistic and juvenile, the Last Night of the Proms is broadcast live on TV and radio (and not only in the UK) and inevitably culminates in raucous renditions of *Jerusalem*, *Rule Britannia* and *Land of Hope and Glory*, accompanied by flag waving, cheering and other 'good-natured fun'.

Details of all concerts are available from the annual *Proms* guide, published in May in book form and on the internet (🖳 www.bbc.co.uk/proms).

Other festivals include the City of London Festival (🖳 www.colf.org), held at the Barbican Centre, EC2 (🖳 www.barbican.ork.uk) and other city venues during June and July; Meltdown at the South Bank Arts Centre, SE1 (🖳 www.southbankcentre.co.uk) in June/July featuring avant-garde music; and the Kenwood Lakeside Concerts, outdoor events featuring classical favourites (and often fireworks displays and rain) held on Saturday evenings from June to September outside Kenwood House, Hampstead, NW3 (🖳 www.picnicconcerts.com, East Finchley or Golders Green tube, then courtesy shuttle bus).

Pop

The main venues for rock and pop concerts are divided between the mega-stadiums and the smaller concert halls and clubs. Stadium

Royal Albert Hall, South Kensington

gigs can be spectacular, but what you gain on the lasers and inflatables you often lose on the human scale – the performers are likely to be dots in the distance or blown-up images on a huge screen above the stage. Unless you're down the front, you're often better off buying the tour DVD. Nevertheless, you can see the big bands at the soulless Earls Court exhibition hall (☎ 020-7385 1200, 🖳 www.eco.co.uk, Earls Court tube), the cavernous London Arena in the Isle of Dogs (🖳 www.londonarena.co.uk, Isle of Dogs DLR) and the recently reopened former Olympic swimming pool, Wembley Arena (🖳 www.wembleyticket.com, Wembley Park or Wembley Central tube).

Concert hall venues include the following:

♦ **Astoria**, Charing Cross Road, WC2 (☎ 020-7434 0403, Tottenham Court Road tube) – a converted theatre that welcomes bands during the week and hosts club nights at weekends;

♦ **Carling Brixton Academy**, Stockwell Road, SW9 (☎ 020-7771 3000, 🖳 www.brixton-academy.co.uk, Brixton tube) – a converted Victorian hall that welcomes medium-league bands rather than the really big names.

♦ **The Forum**, Highgate Road, NW5 (🖳 www.meanfiddler.com, Kentish Town tube) – once called the Town and Country Club and possibly the best place to see live bands in London.

♦ **Hammersmith Apollo**, Queen Caroline Street, W6 (☎ 08448-444748, 🖳 www.hammersmithapollo.net, Hammersmith tube) – a former cinema and the largest such venue;

♦ **London Palladium**, Argyll Street, W1 (🖳 www.london-palladium.co.uk, Oxford Circus tube) – a former music hall which stages all kinds of music and theatre, occasionally featuring something of interest to rock or pop fans.

Obscure bands, some playing their first gig, can be seen at the Rock Garden, Covent Garden, WC2 (🖳 www.rockgarden.co.uk, Covent Garden tube), the Bull & Gate, Kentish Town Road, NW5 (☎ 020-7093 4820, Kentish Town tube) and the Hope & Anchor, Upper Street, N1 (☎ 020-7354 1312, Angel/Highbury & Islington tube).

Bottom of the pop pecking order are the clubs – the places where all bands serve their apprenticeships. Like dance clubs, these come and go, but some of the longest established and best are The Borderline, Orange Yard, W1 (🖳 www.meanfiddler.com, Tottenham Court Road tube), which sometimes features 'secret' gigs by top bands playing under pseudonyms, the Dublin Castle, Parkway, NW1 (🖳 www.thedublincastle.com, an unofficial website, Camden Town tube) and the Half Moon, Lower Richmond Road, SW15 (☎ 020-8780 9383, 🖳 www.halfmoon.co.uk, Putney Bridge tube) – the last two being pub venues.

Jazz

The most famous jazz club in London is the poky (and formerly smoky) Ronnie Scott's, Frith Street, W1 (☎ 020-7439 0747, 🖳 www.ronniescotts.co.uk, Leicester Square tube), where you can sit at a table or stand at the back to see and hear the big jazz names. The 100 Club, Oxford Street, W1 (☎ 020-7636 0933, 🖳 www.the100club.co.uk, Tottenham Court Road tube) is one of London's most popular music venues where you can enjoy jazz, blues, indie and comedy nights. Other central London jazz venues worth visiting are Chelsea's 606 Club, Lots Road, SW10 (☎ 020-7352 5953, 🖳 www.606club.co.uk, Earls Court or Fulham Broadway tube) and the Jazz Café, Parkway, NW1 (☎ 020-485 6834, 🖳 www.jazzcafe.co.uk, Camden Town tube), which has a broad definition of the term 'jazz'.

Out of town there's the excellent Vortex, Stoke Newington Church Street, N16 (☎ 020-7254 4097, 🖳 www.vortexjazz.co.uk, Stoke Newington rail) or the Bull's Head, 373 Lonsdale Road, Barnes Bridge, SW13 (☎ 020-8876 5241, 🖳 www.thebullshead.com, Hammersmith tube, then the no.9 bus, or Barnes rail), which attracts some big British names.

Nightlife

When the sun goes down in London (if it has bothered to make an appearance that day), the city really comes alive and the sheer diversity of entertainment on offer can bewilder even the most dedicated night owls, who must choose between techno, hard house, hardcore, deep house, garage, drum 'n' bass, jungle and speed garage, as well as the older hybrids acid-jazz and swing/hip-hop and, who knows, the latest as yet unknown music style.

During the last decade or so, the accent has shifted from pubs and discos to clubs and club bars, some of which are exclusive and for members only, although most aren't members-only clubs but charge entry fees. The secret of the club scene's success is its mutability – no other European city offers such a variety of constantly changing venues. It's in a constant state of flux, reacting swiftly to the latest developments in style and dance music. It would be impossible to list every club in London and such information would, in any case, go out of date even before publication, so the list below is confined to some of the more established venues.

◆ **The Complex**, Parkfield Street, N1 (☎ 020-7288 1986, Angel tube) – a fashionable club that plays a wide variety of radical sounds. It has four floors, including the self-explanatory Love Lounge. Catch its Camouflage night on Saturdays for excellent funk, swing and US garage.

◆ **The End**, 18 West Central Street, WC1A 1JJ (🖳 www.endclub.com, Covent Garden, Holborn or Tottenham Court Road tube) – owned by Mr. C of The Shamen, who you'll have heard of if you're up on dance music history. It's a spacious, minimalist chrome club but plays a wide range of music.

◆ **The Fridge**, Brixton Hill, SW2 (🖳 www. fridgerocks.com, Brixton tube/rail) – south London's biggest rock club, whose musical policy runs the gamut from funk to techno and garage;

◆ **Hanover Grand**, Hanover Street, W1 (☎ 020-7499 7977, Tottenham Court Road tube) – a super-cool club catering to London's glitterati, with a balconied dance floor upstairs, an incredible light show and some serious 'style police' on the door at weekends. Midweek, it's home to Fresh 'n' Funky playing R&B and hip-hop.

◆ **Heaven**, Villiers Street, WC2 (☎ 020-7930 2020, 🖳 www.heaven-london.com, Embankment or Charing Cross tube) – probably the most famous gay club in the capital. Packed to the rafters on a Saturday night, it plays mostly commercial house.

◆ **Neighbourhood**, 12 Acklam Road, W10 (☎ 0871-223 1282, Ladbroke Grove tube) attracts a trendy west London crowd and is hugely popular.

◆ **The Ministry of Sound**, 103 Gaunt Street, SE1 (☎ 0870-060 0010, 🖳 www. ministryofsound.com, Elephant & Castle tube) – London's most famous dance club and still trendy, despite its downmarket setting in one of the poorest parts of town. It has an exceptional sound system and attracts some of the biggest name DJs from the US as well as home-grown talent.

◆ **Turnmills,** Clerkenwell Road, EC1 (☎ 020-7250 3409, 🖳 www.turnmills.com, Farringdon tube) – hosts three popular one-nighters: The Gallery house party on Fridays and Heavenly Jukebox on Saturdays, which morphs into gay marathon Trade (🖳 www. dircon.co.uk/trade) from 4am until Sunday afternoon;

A fairly recent development in club culture is the club/pub hybrid called, unsurprisingly, the club bar. These are bars that stay open later than the traditional pub closing time of 11pm (although they charge for admission after a certain time) and have in-house DJs playing club-style music. Although drinks tend to be expensive, food is usually on offer and you can sit around and hold conversations more easily than in a club, while still enjoying the music.

Now becoming popular with the in-crowd, club bars fill the void between traditional London pubs and full-scale nightclubs, and can be great places for a late night out.

Listed below are some of the top club bars around the capital:

◆ **A.K.A.**, West Central Street, WC1 (☎ 020-7836 0110, 🖳 www.akalondon.com, Tottenham Court Road tube) – a chrome-infested minimalist bar next door to The End (see above), where the focus is on quality underground electronic music.

◆ **Alphabet**, 61-63 Beak Street, W1 (☎ 020-7439 2190, 🖳 www.alphabetbar.

com) in the heart of the West End at (Oxford Circus tube) – serves gorgeous food. Try the upstairs lounge with its luxurious leather sofas.

♦ **Dogstar**, 389 Coldharbour Lane, SW9 (☎ 0871-223 1790, Brixton tube) – a converted pub (with a restaurant), which turns into a music 'club' at weekends, playing techno, house and disco.

♦ **The Embassy Bar**, 119 Essex Road, Islington, N1 (☎ 020-7226 7901, Angel tube) – a retro-styled, suave joint with a sweeping chrome bar and a fashionable, diverse music policy;

♦ **Village Soho**, 81 Wardour Street, W1 (☎ 020-7434 2124, Piccadilly Circus tube) – a gay club bar with separate entrances leading to its café and very busy bar.

If all this is a little cutting-edge for you and all you want is a good old-fashioned nightclub or disco, there's still plenty of choice. Many places cater for the more mature, conservative crowd, who think 'garage' is a place where cars are parked. Here are some alternatives to the fashionable club scene, ranging from smart and exclusive nightclubs to mass-market discos:

♦ **Browns**, 4 Great Queen Street, WC2 (☎ 020-7832 0802, Holborn tube) – Lots of celebrity parties are held in this ultra-chic two-floor nightspot.

♦ **Café de Paris**, 3 Coventry Street, W1 (☎ 020-7395 5806, 🖥 www.cafedeparis.com, Leicester Square or Piccadilly Circus tube) – another chic nightspot housed in a classic '20s ballroom beautifully restored to its original elegance, with a balcony from where you can watch the dancing, and an excellent restaurant;

♦ **The Emporium**, 62 Kingly Street, W1 (☎ 020-7734 3190, Oxford Circus tube) – a busy club popular with the rich and famous;

♦ **The Equinox**, Leicester Square, WC2 (☎ 020-8215 6003, Leicester Square tube) – a typically cavernous West End disco with lots of lights and lasers where you can dance to mainstream 'commercial' music;

♦ **Stringfellows,** Long Acre, WC2 (☎ 020-7240 5534, 🖥 www.stringfellows.co.uk, Covent Garden or Leicester Square tube) – a cross between disco and strip joint run by and named after the ageing 'king of clubs', Peter Stringfellow, it attracts primarily be-suited businessmen in pursuit of pleasure, featuring table-dancing from Mondays to Thursdays, though at weekends it brings in a more straight-ahead disco crowd. It also has a restaurant.

London, particularly Soho, positively pulsates with seedier places to spend your leisure time, from strip bars and lap-dancing joints to so-called 'gentlemen's clubs'.

Before making plans to visit a club, phone or check the website, or obtain up-to-date information from a weekly listings magazine such as *Time Out* (🖥 www.timeout.com), which will also tell you the best times to arrive and a club's current 'door policy' – i.e. the appropriate

clothes to wear if you want the 'bouncers' (doormen) to let you in.

Most clubs open at between 10pm and midnight and don't close until after dawn. The majority open every night, others at weekends only, while some are strictly 'one-nighters', hosted by an umbrella venue that features a different attraction each night of the week.

Tickets

When buying tickets for any event, whether at the theatre, cinema, opera or concert hall, it's wise to purchase directly from the venue. Theatre box offices are usually open from around 10am daily on performance days. Tickets can also be purchased from most box offices by post, simply by writing and requesting tickets for a particular performance (give alternatives if possible), by phone or via the internet.

It's possible – and sometimes more convenient – to buy tickets from agencies, but these charge a booking fee of between 15 and 25 per cent of the value of the ticket. Before buying, you should therefore check the official box office price so that you know exactly how much commission you're being asked to pay. Most ticket agencies have an allocation of tickets on sale or return by a certain date. If you desperately want to see a show and cannot wait, you may be able to buy a ticket from a tout, although you may be asked for two to three times a ticket's face value, and there's no guarantee that it will be genuine.

PARKS

Few cities in the world are better endowed with public parks and open spaces – almost 30 per cent of London is 'green'. Although surrounded by some of the busiest roads in the world, London's parks are surprisingly peaceful, even when packed with mobile-phone-toting office workers, MP3-playing schoolchildren and camera-clicking tourists.

Hyde Park, Kensington Gardens, Green Park and St James's Park form an extensive, almost continuous green swathe across central London, although bisected by the hurly-burly of Hyde Park Corner and the grandeur of Buckingham Palace, the main London residence of the British royal family. Right in front of the Palace, St James's Park could almost be the Queen's front garden (you can rest assured that she has ample private grounds to the rear) and is perhaps the capital's prettiest park, with a variety of waterbirds in its tree-fringed lake.

In Hyde Park you can see Rotten Row, where the fashionable members of society used to parade on horseback. Near Long Water in Kensington Gardens keep an eye out for two beautiful Edwardian statues, George Frampton's 'Peter Pan' and George Frederick Watt's 'Physical Energy', before marvelling at that Victorian monument to 'bad taste', the Albert Memorial, which stands opposite the Royal Albert Hall.

In neighbouring Kensington Gardens is Kensington Palace, another royal residence and the former home of Diana, Princess of Wales.

Further north is Regent's Park (containing London Zoo) and the kite-flyers' Mecca, Primrose Hill, not forgetting the 900-acre dog-walkers' paradise of Hampstead Heath. Further from the centre, you might consider a visit to Victoria Park in the east, Finsbury Park in the north, Battersea Park in the south, and Richmond Park and Kew Gardens (London's celebrated botanical gardens) in the west.

London's parks aren't just lawns and lakes. There's plenty to see, too: palaces, villas, gardens, statuary and water features fill the parks, and are there to be enjoyed by all – mostly free of charge. Regent's Park has a boating lake fed by an underground river, a bandstand, a ravishing rose garden and a magical open-air theatre where Shakespearean productions are performed on summer evenings – provided it doesn't rain! Non-Muslims are sometimes allowed to visit the London Central Mosque at the park's western edge to learn more about Muslim faith (see 🖳 www.iccservices.org.uk, St John's Wood tube).

In Hyde Park you can swim at the Serpentine's open-air Lido (☎ 020-7706 3422, 🖳 www.serpentinelido.com, High Street Kensington tube) during the summer.

PUBS & BARS

Leaving aside the recent 'club bar' hybrids described above (see **Nightlife**), most London pubs (short for public houses) – and there are literally hundreds – are an institution. (It's hardly surprising that one in 25 Londoners has a drink problem and over 250,000 consume harmful quantities of alcohol.) Many pubs began life as coaching inns long before the age of motor travel and served as the focal point for local communities in much the same way as a church or village hall. The best traditional pubs serve good, unpretentious food, as well as a range of 'real ales' (made by traditional methods and hand pumped rather than mass-produced and filled with gas – it's also perishable, so go somewhere with a high turnover) and have a buzzy, convivial atmosphere. On the other hand, may London pubs serve poor 'fast' food in dingy and decrepit surroundings.

A few London pubs cling to the old division between 'public' and 'saloon' (or lounge) bars, the former being a 'rough-and-ready' room where men in working clothes can unwind after their labours, while the latter is a more comfortable place for the better dressed, where women won't feel like aliens. You tend to find the snooker and pool tables, dartboards, jukeboxes and gambling machines in the public bar, and food in the saloon – where drinks are more expensive.

Most London pubs, however, have shed such outdated class-consciousness and consist of just one huge 'lounge' bar. Many welcome anyone and everyone to all areas, though some have specific areas for families with children or gardens where youngsters can play. Children aren't supposed to sit in a bar until they're 14 and cannot drink alcohol until they're 18, but children of any age are allowed into a restaurant area, family room or outdoor area. All British bars and restaurants (and many other places) are now non-smoking.

Although the UK is supposed to have gone metric, you'll be hard-pressed to find a pub that sells beer by the litre – you can have a pint or half-pint. If you visit a 'free house', i.e. a pub that isn't tied to a specific brewery for its supplies, you can sample a range of real ales from around the UK, from companies such as Greene King, Flower's or smaller independents.

London has two long-established breweries, which produce fine real ale: Fuller's (🖳 www.fullers.co.uk) and Young's (🖳 www.youngs. co.uk).

There's also a wide range of bottled beers available from good brewers throughout the UK and further afield, many of which are excellent. If you want to learn more about good British ale, buy a copy of the CAMRA (Campaign for Real Ale) *Good Beer Guide* edited by Jeff Evans. *The Good Pub Guide* (Ebury Press) edited by Alisdair Aird is also worth a read.

Spirits such as whisky, vodka, gin and rum are sold in measures of 24ml, a 'double' (or 'large') being 48ml. Mixers and soft drinks are where publicans make most of their money, so don't expect a non-alcoholic option to be cheaper than the hard stuff (which is a sore point among teetotallers). Wine is simply sold by the glass (size unspecified, but often 'regular' or 'large' – the latter often being equivalent to almost half a bottle),

offer late food or entertainment. However, relatively few establishments open 24 hours, although many pubs now remain open all day, rather than closing in the afternoon The new laws are controversial and have been blamed (along with cheap supermarket booze) for binge drinking and alcohol-fuelled violence.

Drink-driving laws are strictly enforced by London's police, but the densely-populated city is a great place for a 'pub crawl' on foot or by tube or taxi. Just make sure you don't get too drunk to find your way home!

If pubs aren't your scene, you might like to try a hotel bar. All the larger, ritzier hotels (mostly in the Mayfair area) open their bars to non-residents, although drinks (particularly those extravagant cocktails) are **very** expensive and the dress code is usually a jacket and tie for men.

Some hotel bars are unofficial pick-up joints, where high-class prostitutes hang out – so don't expct that 'chance encounter' to lean to romance!

The pick of London's hotel bars has to be Claridge's, Brook Street, W1 (☎ 020-7629 8860, 🖥 www.claridges.co.uk, Bond Street tube), which serves marvellous cocktails at stratospheric prices, is furnished in Art Deco style and staffed by waiters who look as though they've stepped straight from a P.G. Wodehouse novel. Other upmarket hotel bars include:

♦ **The Dorchester** (☎ 020-7629 8888, 🖥 www.dorchesterhotel.com, Hyde Park Corner tube) in Park Lane – owned by the Sultan of Brunei and refurbished in fantastic style to his specifications;

♦ **Langham Hotel**, Portland Place, W1 (☎ 020-7636 1000, 🖥 http://london. langhamhotels.co.uk, Oxford Circus tube) – frequented by BBC staff from Broadcasting House over the road and serves a ridiculous number of different vodkas in its Tsar Bar;

♦ **Waldorf Hilton Hotel**, Aldwych, WC2 (☎ 020-7836 2400, Covent Garden tube) – has a wonderfully relaxed Palm Court bar, where you don't need to wear a tie and a pianist entertains you in the evening.

wine sold in traditional pubs is of poor quality (although the general standard is improving) and you may get a choice of 'red' or 'white' only (it saves having to remember all those fancy names). Go to a wine bar if you want a selection of good wines, although wine bars were rather an '80s fashion and aren't as common now.

Many pubs feature entertainment such as live music or stand-up comedy, while others have karaoke or single-sex nights, the latter featuring male or female strippers. Some are gay or lesbian haunts and some attract ethnic minorities of one kind or another – for example, Irish pubs in predominantly Irish areas such as Kilburn.

The UK's standard licensing laws allow pubs to open from 11am until 11pm, Mondays to Saturdays, and from noon until 10.30pm on Sundays, with pubs closing in the afternoon, e.g. from 2.30pm to 6pm. However, since late 2005, drinking establishments can apply for licences to stay open and serve alcohol for 24 hours or vary their licences to either extend their opening times by an hour or two, or to

For more information consult the *Evening Standard London Pub and Bar Guide* by Edward Sullivan (Simon & Schuster) or the *Time Out Eating and Drinking Guide*.

RESTAURANTS

Many foreigners (and most French people) fondly nurture an image of a London full of 'greasy spoon' establishments specialising in fried food, burnt meat and overcooked vegetables, washed down with milky tea or warm beer. However, those who think that a period spent in London means bringing your own food supply or facing starvation or death by food poisoning are in for a pleasant surprise. There has been a revolution in London restaurants over the last few decades and the capital now boasts a wealth of excellent eateries offering culinary delights to rival those of Paris – and an infinitely wider variety of cuisines. You need only open the pages of the latest restaurant guide to realise that British food doesn't always live up (or down) to its dreadful reputation, and London is now at the cutting edge of food fashion. On the negative side, prices for good food (and, especially, wine) are often astronomical and even modest restaurants can be costly.

It's another cliché that England has no recognisable 'national' cuisine, but although traditional English cooking has undergone something of a renaissance in recent years, you're unlikely to come across much English food in London's restaurants – unless you count the UK's favourite dish: curry! On the other hand, London has a huge variety of ethnic restaurants (representing some 70 countries) and some of the best Chinese and Indian restaurants outside Asia (it's said that the British founded an Empire so they could get some decent food!), and numerous establishments serving admirable French, Italian and other foods.

The best bet for those wishing to eat well and cheaply is ethnic restaurants, where the standard of food is invariably high and a filling meal can be had for around £15 per head (sometimes including a drink). A good example is the restaurant chain Wagamama (💻 www.wagamama.com), which currently has 23 establishments in central London and another six in Greater London. It's modelled on the ramen shops popular in Japan, ramen being Chinese-style thread noodles, served in soups with toppings or griddle-cooked with a selection of meat and/or fish and/or vegetables.

Always phone ahead to check opening hours and ask whether you need to book a table. Most restaurants stop serving between 10.30 and 11.30pm, so it's usually best to eat before going to a show or club. There are, however, a number of notable exceptions, mainly in the traditionally nocturnal Soho area. Chinese restaurant Mr Kong (☎ 0871-332 7465, Leicester Square or Piccadilly Circus tube) remains open until around 2am and the 24-hour Old Compton Cafe in Old Compton Street (☎ 020-7439 3309) is an energetic round-the-clock eatery, mostly frequented by gays.

Most restaurants accept all major credit cards and are licensed to serve alcohol. Tipping is discretionary, but check whether a service charge is added to your bill before leaving a tip, as there's no need to pay twice.

Below is an area-by-area guide to some of London's most popular restaurant districts.

⚠ Caution

Americans should note that appetites aren't as large in London as on the other side of the pond and you may be disappointed by portion sizes until your stomach acclimatises!

Soho

Many of London's best restaurants are concentrated around Soho, where the capital's 'Chinatown' district is to be found – south of Shaftesbury Avenue. For Cantonese cuisine try Chuen Cheng Fu (☎ 020-7437 1398, Leicester Square tube) at 17 Wardour Street. It's an enormous and wholly authentic Hong Kong-style restaurant serving real dim sum and a huge range of other dishes. If sushi's more to your taste, go to Kulu Kulu (☎ 0871-426 0088, Piccadilly Circus tube) at 76 Brewer Street, which is a friendly and compact

restaurant with the accent on excellent food rather than expensive decor. One of London's best Pan-Asian (Japan, China and Thailand) restaurants is Cocoon, 65 Regent Street, Corner of Air St (☎ 020-7494 7600, 🖥 www.cocoon-restaurants.co.uk, Piccadilly Circus tube), a cool bar/restaurant with a series of six gloriously glamorous spherical dining rooms, sushi bars and luxurious lounge. For European food try Andrew Edmunds (☎ 0871-223 8022, Oxford Circus/Piccadilly Circus tube) at 46 Lexington Street, which is a tiny but very popular bistro.

Covent Garden

Covent Garden is another hotspot for restaurants, although there are some terrible tourist traps serving overpriced burgers and other 'fast' foods. For superb French food at an affordable price look no further than Mon Plaisir, 21 Monmouth Street (☎ 020-7836 7243, 🖥 www.monplaisir.co.uk, Covent Garden or Leicester Square tube). If you're starving, Café Pacifico, 5 Langley Street (☎ 020-7379 7728, Covent Garden tube) serves enormous portions of superior Mexican food. Stephen Bull, 12 Upper St Martin's Lane (☎ 020-7379 7811, Leicester Square tube) is one of those new wave of restaurants serving 'modern British food'; its fish and puddings are highly recommended and good value.

Bloomsbury & Fitzrovia

Bloomsbury and Fitzrovia traditionally make up London's intellectual quarter, although judging by the number of good restaurants there one could be forgiven for thinking that its inhabitants are keener on feeding their stomachs than their minds. The Diwana Bhel Poori House, Drummond Street (☎ 0871-332 8344, Euston tube), in the oriental quarter, serves vegetarian southern Indian food and is a great place for a weekday lunch. At 67a Tottenham Court Road you'll find Ikkyu (☎ 020-7436 6169, Goodge Street tube), which serves authentic Japanese cuisine.

St James's & Mayfair

St James's and Mayfair are home to the 'poshest' of haute cuisine restaurants with formal dress codes (e.g. jacket and tie for men) – try the elegant but not too expensive Mirabelle, Curzon Street (☎ 0871-971 3314, Green Park tube). Quaglino's, 16 Bury Street (☎ 020-7930 6767, 🖥 www.quaglinos.co.uk, Green Park tube) was one of the most fashionable places in London a few years ago, but now the beautiful people have largely moved on to be replaced by tourists who gawp at its splendid converted ballroom ambience (if only the food was as good).

If you want to be informal, try the trendy Momo, Heddon Street (☎ 0871-971 6457, Piccadilly Circus tube), where the Moroccan food is so good you need to book weeks in advance. Nobu, Metropolitan Hotel, 19 Old Park Lane (☎ 020-7447 4747, 🖥 www.noburestaurants.com, Hyde Park Corner tube) is another celebrity favourite and features the famous black cod with miso. Gordon Ramsay at Claridge's, Brook Street (☎ 020-7499 0099, 🖥 www.gordonramsay.com, Bond Street tube) is one of London's top restaurants – with prices to match!

Kensington & Chelsea

Stylish European restaurants abound in Kensington and Chelsea. Try ultra-smart Polish restaurant Wodka, 12 St Albans Grove, W8 (☎ 020-7937 6513, Gloucester Road or High St Kensington tube), named after its extensive range of flavoured iced vodkas, or the noisy and popular Portuguese eatery O Fado, Beauchamp Place (☎ 020-7589 3002, Knightsbridge tube). For exceptional Italian fare try Zafferano, 15 Lowndes Street (☎ 020-7235 5800, Knightsbridge tube), or for gamey Scottish haute cuisine head to Boisdale, 15 Ecclestone Street (☎ 020-7730 6922, Victoria tube), owned by a latter-day clan chief.

City

London's business and financial quarter isn't packed with fine restaurants but you could do worse than Singapura, Limeburner Lane off Ludgate Hill (☎ 020-7329 1133, St Paul's or Blackfriars tube), which serves a strange but delicious hybrid of Chinese and Malay food from Singapore. Rampant carnivores might like to brave the portals of St John, 26 St John Street (☎ 020-7251 0848, Farringdon tube) near Smithfield meat market, a vegetarian's nightmare specialising in offal dishes, including 'treats' made from brains and bones.

East End

The East End boasts some fine Asian restaurants such as Cafe Spice Namaste, 16 Prescott Street (☎ 020-7488 9242, Tower Hill tube), serving Kashmiri and Goan delicacies, or the cheap but authentic Pakistani restaurant Lahore Kebab House, 2 Umberton Street (☎ 020-7488 2551, Aldgate East tube), which has stewed sheep's feet on the menu along with more mainstream fare. There's a good Vietnamese restaurant, the Viet Hoa, at 70-72

Kingland Street, Shoreditch, E2 (☎ 020-7729 8293, catch a no.67, 149 or 242 bus or hail a taxi).

Camden & Hampstead

In arty, middle-class Hampstead and Camden is a cheerful African eatery Wazobia, 257 Royal College Street (☎ 020-7284 1059, Camden Town tube), which serves Nigerian and West African dishes, or, if you fancy Russian cuisine, try Trojka, Regent's Park Road, Primrose Hill (☎ 020-7483 3765, Chalk Farm tube). Solly's, Golders Green Road (☎ 020-8455 2121, Golders Green tube) is a popular kosher restaurant, and excellent Greek food can be found at the popular Lemonia, Regent's Park Road (☎ 020-7586 7454, Chalk Farm tube).

Bayswater, Marylebone & Notting Hill

In the Marylebone/Bayswater/Notting Hill area, try the classy Sudanese restaurant, The Mandola, 139 Westbourne Grove (☎ 020-7229 4734, Notting Hill Gate/Queensway tube) – the spiced coffee comes highly recommended – while nearby at 21–23 Westbourne Grove is The Standard (☎ 020-7727 4818), serving some of the most delicious (and best value) Indian food in London. In the same road, Brazilian restaurant Rodrizio Rico (☎ 020-7792 4035) specialises in grilled meats; and if you want good English fish and chips there are few better places than Sea Shell, Lisson Grove (☎ 020-7224 9000, Marylebone tube).

South London

South of the river, try Brixton's 'global' eatery Helter Skelter, 50 Atlantic Road (☎ 020-7274 8600, Brixton tube), the welcoming Gujerati restaurant and takeaway Hot Stuff, 19 Wilcox Road (☎ 020-7720 1480, Vauxhall tube), or Fina Estampa, 150 Tooley Street (☎ 020-7403 1342, London Bridge tube), London's only Peruvian restaurant, specialising in seafood and serving a selection of South American wines.

Restaurant Guides

If you want to check out these or any other restaurants further before paying them a visit, get yourself a copy of a good restaurant guide such as the *Time Out Eating and Drinking Guide*, listing over 1,300 restaurants, cafés and bars, the *Evening Standard London Restaurant Guide* by Nick Foulkes (Simon & Schuster) or *London Restaurants: The Rough Guide* by Charles Campion (Rough Guides). If you prefer internet reviews, try the *Evening Standard* website (🖥 www.thisislondon.com), which contains reviews of restaurants, or 🖥 www.london-eating.co.uk.

☑ SURVIVAL TIP

If you love eating out but cannot afford (or refuse to pay exorbitant prices for) the wine, obtain a copy of *Capital BYOs: A Guide to London's Bring Your Own Wine Restaurants* by Victoria Alers (Hankey VBAH).

CAFES

London doesn't have a café culture like most other major European cites – drinking coffee in the rain doesn't have the same appeal as it does on a sunny sidewalk in Paris or Rome – but nevertheless, London has plenty of places where you can enjoy a coffee (or what passes for coffee in the UK – tea is safer) and croissant and watch the world go by.

There has been a burst of café openings in recent years, with large chains such as Starbucks (🖥 www.starbucks.co.uk), Costa Coffee (🖥 www.costa.co.uk) and Caffé Nero (🖥 www.cafenero.com) having outlets on almost every street corner. Smaller backstreet cafes provide a more cosmopolitan environment to relax, usually with pavement seating. Many family-owned cafes offer home made food (rather than the plastic fare dished up by the chains), although it can be hit and miss – but once you have found your preferred local café it's likely to become a regular haunt.

Although discerning coffee (and tea) lovers may not be spoilt, there are a wealth of places to choose from, particularly in the Soho area, a number of which are mentioned below:

Bar Italia, 22 Frith Street, W1D (☎ 020-7437 4520, 🖥 www.baritaliasoho.com) has been an all night Soho favourite since 1923; packed to the rafters whenever there's a televised Italian football match, it's noted for its great atmosphere.

Café in the Crypt, Covent Garden, WC2N (☎ 020-7783 9434), with reasonably priced 'easy' food and a unique underground location.

Napket, 342 King's Road, Chelsea, SW3 (☎ 020-7352 9832) is a boutique café-delicatessen offering a chic environment for respite and refreshment. Murano glass chandeliers and dark wood flooring reclaimed from a church provide an ideal backdrop for Napket's 20 varieties of speciality pound cakes.

Cake Boy, Juniper Drive, SW18 (☎ 020-7978 5555) has a 'glam' setting with champagne afternoons, weekly baking classes, a range of organic foods and fair-trade coffee.

Coffee, Cake and Kink, 61 Endell Street, Covent Garden, WC2 (☎ 020-7419 2996) is a stylish café, gallery and shop, specialising in handmade cakes, toys, books, prints and all things kinky.

Internet Cafés

Internet (or cyber) cafés have proliferated in London in recent years in order to meet the demand for internet access from those who aren't online at home and don't have access at their workplace or college – or who simply like to socialise while surfing. Most London internet cafés serve drinks and food, and a few offer limited free surfing – one is Room Service @ the Vibe Bar, Truman Brewery, Brick Lane (☎ 020-7426 0491, 🖥 www.vibe-bar.co.uk, Aldgate East tube) – although most charge around £2 to £5 an hour.

The bright orange frontage of the easyInternet cafes makes them easy to spot and there are branches dotted across London, including outlets at Baker Street, Camden, Kensington High Street and Trafalgar Square (🖥 www.easyeverything.com). Café Internet (☎ 020-7233 5786) at Victoria tube/rail has around 20 terminals, while the Buzz Bar, Portobello Road (☎ 020-7460 4910, 🖥 www.portobellogold.com, Notting Hill Gate or Ladbroke Grove tube) is one of the friendliest places to surf the web in London.

You can find internet cafes in London and other hotspots via a number of websites including Londonist (⌨ http://londonist. com/2007/05/free_wifi_in_lo.php) and My Hotspots (⌨ www.myhotspots.co.uk/results. aspx?Town=LONDON). MacDonalds also provide free wifi in many of their restaurants.

RIVER TRIPS

For an alternative view of the capital, you can take one of several river trips, which include the following:

◆ **Greenwich to Gravesend/Tilbury** – Wednesdays and Saturdays during the summer. Operated by the Lower Thames & Medway Passenger Boat Company (☏ 01732–353448).

◆ **MV Balmoral & Paddle Steamer 'Waverley' from Tower Pier** – trips to Tilbury and Southend and up the River Medway aboard these historic vessels during June, July, September and October. Operated by Waverley Excursions (☏ 0845-130 4647, ⌨ www. waverleyexcursions.co.uk).

◆ **From Embankment Pier** – trips including lunch or dinner with entertainment passing Westminster and the Tower of London daily. Operated by Bateaux London (☏ 020-7695 1800, ⌨ www.bateauxlondon.com).

◆ **From Festival Pier** – circular trip passing Westminster, the Tower of London and the Globe Theatre after a ride on the London Eye, daily from mid-April until the end of October and at weekends the rest of the year (☏ 0870-500 0600, ⌨ www.ba-londoneye.com);

◆ **From Greenwich Pier** – circular trip passing the Tower of London and Westminster on Sundays from early May until the end of September. Operated by various firms for the London Borough of Greenwich (☏ 020-7930 4097).

◆ **From Westminster Pier** – trips including dinner and entertainment, passing Westminster and the Tower of London daily. Operated by City Cruises (☏ 020-7740 0400, ⌨ www.citycruises.com).

Boat Piers

A wealth of London landmarks are situated close to boat piers, including those listed

below. (For further information contact London River Services/LRS, ☏ 020-7222 1234, ⌨ www.tfl.gov.uk/gettingaround).

◆ **Bankside** – Clink Museum, Globe Theatre, Tate Modern and Vinopolis City of Wine;

◆ **Blackfriars** – City of London and St Paul's Cathedral;

◆ **Canary Wharf** – Canary Wharf Tower, Isle of Dogs and London Arena;

◆ **Embankment** – Cleopatra's Needle, Covent Garden, London Transport Museum and Trafalgar Square;

◆ **Festival** (in front of the South Bank complex) – Imax Cinema and Royal Festival Hall and South Bank complex;

◆ **Greenwich** – Cutty Sark, Greenwich Market, Greenwich Park, National Maritime Museum, Royal Naval College and Royal Observatory;

◆ **Hampton Court** – Hampton Court Palace;

- **Kew** – Kew Bridge Steam Museum and Kew Gardens;

- **London Bridge** – Britain at War Museum, City Hall, Clink Museum, Hay's Galleria, HMS Belfast, London Dungeon, Old Operating Theatre Museum and Southwark Cathedral;

- **Millbank** – Tate Modern Museum;

- **Richmond** – Richmond Town and Richmond Park;

- **St Katharine's** – St Katharine's Dock and Tower Bridge;

- **Tower** – St Katharine's Dock, Tower Bridge and Tower of London;

- **Waterloo** – FA Premier League Hall of Fame, Imax Cinema, London Aquarium, London Eye, Royal Festival Hall and South Bank complex;

- **Westminster** – Houses of Parliament and Westminster Abbey.

EXCURSIONS

If you want a change from the big city, there are many interesting places and attractions to visit within a few hours of London. Many historic cities and towns are within easy reach of the capital by train or road (see below), plus many fine cathedrals, castles and stately homes.

If you're looking for historic sites, the National Trust (NT) should be your first point of reference. It's a privately funded charity that looks after historic buildings, gardens and parks throughout the UK. Membership gives you free access to all NT properties and you receive a *Family Handbook* packed with ideas for family day trips. Contact the National Trust (⌨ www.nationaltrust.org.uk) or go to any NT property for membership information.

You can also join English Heritage, which entitles you to 'free' admission to over 350 properties and numerous events. For information contact English Heritage (Membership Department, Freepost WD214, PO Box 570, Swindon SN2 2UR, ☎ 0870-333 1182, ⌨ www. english-heritage.org).

If you're keen on gardens, you may wish to join the Royal Horticultural Society (80 Vincent Square, London SW1P 2PE, ☎ 0845-062 1111, ⌨ www.rhs.org.uk), in return for which you receive free entry to beautiful gardens throughout the country.

Cambridge

The ancient university city of Cambridge is just 50 minutes from King's Cross or you can drive

River Thames panorama

there on the M11 (exit at junction 11 or 12). The oldest college buildings (at Peterhouse in Trumpington Street) date from the 13th century, and Corpus Christi in the same street was built in the 14th century. Most famous of all is the Gothic King's College Chapel, home to the world-famous boys' choir that sings at evensong each afternoon during term time. Check the university's main website (💻 www.cam.ac.uk), which has links to the colleges and their attractions.

You can picnic on the grassy area called the Backs behind the main parade of colleges or hire a punt on the river Cam and lie back lazily as you drift along, propelled by one of the professional boatmen – or you can try your hand at punting yourself: take a change of clothing!

While you're in the city don't miss the marvellous Fitzwilliam Museum in Trumpington Street, which has a collection as grand as many London museums and galleries. There are also excellent second-hand bookshops and a bustling open-air market in the central square. For further information, consult Visit Cambridge (☎ 01223-457577, 💻 www.visitcambridge.org).

Oxford

Oxford, the UK's other world-famous university city, is an hour from London by train from Paddington or by road via the M40 (junction 8) and the A40. It's even older than Cambridge,

the oldest buildings being at University College (13th century), but the finest architecture is to be seen at Christ Church with its wonderful chapel and Magdalen with its unparalleled grounds. Information is available on the university website (💻 www.ox.ac.uk). As in Cambridge, you can punt on the river (though from the opposite end of the craft) – either on the Isis, a tributary of the River Thames, or on the Cherwell. Oxford also has a fine art gallery (Modern Art Oxford, ☎ 01865-722733, 💻 www.modernartoxford.org), and the Pitt Rivers Museum of Archaeology and Anthropology (☎ 01865-270927, 💻 www.prm.ox.ac.uk) has an amazing collection of ethnic art. There's a covered market dating from 1774 and a huge range of antique shops in Park End Street. The Tourist Information Centre (☎ 01865-252200, 💻 www.visitoxford.org) is at 15-16 Broad Street, Oxford OX1 3AS.

Windsor

Windsor Castle (☎ 020-7766 7300, 💻 www.royal.gov.uk), standing on a steep chalk bluff overlooking the River Thames, is the world's largest inhabited castle. It's one of the UK's premier tourist attractions and has been a home to British royalty continuously for over 900 years, having been originally built by William the Conqueror in 1070 (the family, originally German, took its name from the place). The castle is open to the public from 10am to 5.30pm from mid-March to the end

of October and from 10am to 4.30pm the rest of the year. Highlights include the State Apartments (badly damaged by fire in 1992 but now restored to their former glory), St George's Chapel and Queen Mary's Dolls' House.

If you have any energy left, you may wish to take a stroll in Windsor Great Park, from where there are marvellous views of the castle. Nearby Eton College (☎ 01753-671000, 💻 www.etoncollege.com), which is open to the public from 2 to 4.30pm during term time and from 10.30am to 4.30pm during Easter and summer holidays, dates from the 15th century and is the UK's most exclusive public school (where the royal princes William and Harry were educated).

Windsor is just 20m (32km) from central London, taking 50 minutes by train from Waterloo (direct) to Windsor & Eaton Riverside station or 35 minutes from Paddington to Windsor & Eton Central station (change at Slough), or around the same time by car (via the M4).

Brighton

Brighton, 50 minutes from London (Victoria) by train, is in many ways an outpost of London by the sea. It's bright, breezy and incorrigibly trendy, with a liberal, slightly eccentric atmosphere, due in part to its large student population and thriving gay community. It also has much that has survived from the forgotten age of British seaside towns – including a delightfully camp charm. Don't fail to visit the gaudy Brighton Pier – where fish and chip shops and candy-floss vendors rub shoulders with slot machines and a summer funfair. The outrageous Royal Pavilion (☎ 0127-290900, 💻 www.royalpavilion.org.uk), which bears an uncanny resemblance to the Kremlin, was built by John Nash in 1823 for the Prince Regent.

Children love the Sea Life Centre (☎ 01273-604234, 💻 www.sealife.co.uk), and you can spend your life savings shopping for antiques and knickknacks in The Lanes, a maze of specialist shops, pubs and cafés.

Unless you have to get back to the city, it's worth staying late to sample nightspots such as the Pussycat Club (☎ 07803-905038) and Honey (☎ 07000-446639).

There's also a good 'arthouse' cinema (☎ 0871-704 2056) in Preston Circus. Brighton's tourist information centre is at 10 Bartholomew Square (☎ 07906-711 2255, 💻 www.visitbrighton.com).

Stratford-upon-Avon

Stratford-upon-Avon is, of course, Shakespeare's native town, and not surprisingly one of the UK's most visited places. It's rather a long haul from London, taking 2 hours 10 minutes from Paddington by train or you can drive via the M40 (junction 15) and the A46. The literary tourist trail takes in Shakespeare's birthplace (☎ 01789-204016, which is also the number for the next two sites), his wife Anne Hathaway's cottage and his mother Mary Arden's childhood home. If you can afford it, round off your day with a trip to the Royal Shakespeare Theatre (💻 www.rsc.org.uk – be sure to book well in advance), home of the world-famous Royal Shakespeare Company (RSC) – though London's Globe theatre, a recreation of the original theatre, is more fun. When you've had your fill of Shakespeare, you can admire the brightly-painted narrowboats on the River Avon and Stratford Canal.

LONDON FOR CHILDREN

London can sometimes be an unfriendly place to bring up a family, mainly due to the lingering English attitude that children should be seen and not heard. Kids aren't made welcome in many pubs or restaurants – except the kind that serve plastic burgers, chips and chicken nuggets and have a multicoloured play centre in the corner.

However, in addition to the parks (see page 222) and the largely child-friendly museums (see page 212), there are a number of attractions specifically aimed at children, including those detailed below.

There are a number of books dedicated to entertaining children in London, including *Children's London* (Nicholson) and *Evening*

Standard Children's London by Linda Conway (Prentice Hall). See also **Excursions** above.

Zoos & Aquariums

London Zoo (☎ 020-7722 3333, 🖥 www.zsl. org/zsl-london-zoo) is situated in the north-eastern corner of Regent's Park (Camden Town or Baker Street tube). It's great fun for kids (there's even a 'petting' area where they can touch and handle animals), although older animal-lovers may find it depressing. The zoo does its best to make the enclosures 'humane', but London's climate is hopelessly inappropriate for many of the animals locked up there. Nevertheless, along with its out-of-town partner at Whipsnade in Bedfordshire, the zoo carries out valuable work in saving endangered species. Don't miss the '30s spiral penguin pool or the Lord Snowdon-designed aviary resembling a huge aluminium tent.

Children also adore the London Aquarium, County Hall, Westminster Bridge Road (☎ 020-7967 8000 or for tours ☎ 020-7967 8007, 🖥 www.londonaquarium.co.uk, Westminster or Waterloo tube/rail). It contains a wonderful display of aquatic life on three levels, with sharks and rays which you can touch.

Battersea Park, Albert Bridge Road, SW11 (🖥 www.batterseapark.org, Battersea Park rail or Queenstown tube) has a small children's zoo and a free adventure playground. You can also visit the Buddhist Peace Pagoda in the park. In August the park hosts a huge 'Teddy Bears' Picnic'.

London is also home to many 'city farms' where children can get a feel for rural life without crossing the M25. One of the best – and, at 35 acres (14ha), London's largest – is Mudchute City Farm, Pier Street, Isle of Dogs, E14 (☎ 020-7515 5901, Crossharbour, Mudchute or Island Gardens DLR). As well as farmyard animals, it has llamas, a pets' corner, a riding school, a Young Farmers' club and a study centre. College Farm, Fitzalan Road, Finchley (☎ 020-8349 0690, Finchley Central tube) is a former dairy farm where you can see horses, donkeys, pigs, highland cattle and rabbits.

To the south of the city, Crystal Palace Farm (☎ 020-8778 4487, Crystal Palace rail) is also well worth a visit and boasts some rare farm animals and birds. Finally, right in the centre of town in Guildford Street, WC1 lie Coram's Fields (☎ 020-7837 6138, Russell Square tube) on the site of the old Foundling Hospital, where illegitimate and abandoned children were once cared for. The grounds, which are now home to farmyard animals, are closed to adults unless accompanied by a child and there's a large free playground, huge sandpits, a basketball court and football pitches.

Indoor Activities

If the weather is bad (as it so often is, even in summer), London has some indoor play centres for children of all ages. At Ladbroke Grove there's Bramley's Big Adventure, Bramley Road (☎ 020-8960 1515, Ladbroke Grove or Latimer Road tube), with a wide range of activities for all

ages and an adult crèche where kids can park their parents to read in peace! There's also a wealth of shows and events, particularly during the school holidays.

Many small London cinemas hold Saturday morning or afternoon shows especially for kids. One of the best events in the centre of the city is the Barbican Family Film Club (☎ 0845-120 7528, 🖳 www.barbican.org.uk, Barbican or Moorgate tube) on a Saturday afternoon at the cavernous Barbican Centre.

London boasts several dedicated children's theatres. The Unicorn Theatre, Tooley Street (☎ 020-7645 0560, 🖳 www.unicorntheatre.com, London Bridge tube) is the oldest professional children's theatre in London and stages plays, mimes and puppet shows at weekends and during school holidays. Islington's Little Angel Theatre, Dagmar Passage, N1 (☎ 020-7226 1787, 🖳 www.littleangeltheatre.com, Angel or Highbury & Islington tube) is a permanent puppet theatre and has shows for three to six-year-olds on weekend mornings and for older children in the afternoons. The Bull Theatre, High Street, Barnet (☎ 020-8449 0048, High Barnet tube) to the north of the city has also gained a reputation for good shows in recent years. Many of London's smaller, independent theatres cater for children with special shows at weekends, including the Lyric Theatre, Hammersmith (☎ 0871-221 1729, Hammersmith tube) and the impressive, glass-fronted Tricycle Theatre, Kilburn High Road (☎ 020-7328 1000, Kilburn tube), which also runs courses and workshops for budding junior actors.

Theme Parks

If your children won't be amused by anything but a full-scale theme park, the most accessible is Chessington World of Adventures (☎ 0870-999 0045, 🖳 www.chessington.com) in Surrey, just 30 minutes by train from Waterloo to Chessington South or, by car, just off junction 9 of the infamous M25 (more a car park than a theme park). It's expensive and just a little tacky, but kids love the terrifying white-knuckle rides – don't miss Rameses' Revenge and the Samurai ride. There's also a zoo, so arrive early!

Thorpe Park (☎ 0870-444 4466, 🖳 www.thorpepark.co.uk) is a larger, more modern theme park 45 minutes from Victoria by train (change at Clapham Junction for Staines, then catch a shuttle bus), or by car (junction 11 or 13 of the M25). It's a 500-acre park with all the usual Disneyland-style rides and shows as well as a real working farm.

Legoland (☎ 0871-222 20001, 🖳 www.legoland.co.uk), just outside Windsor (train as above for Windsor or by car via junction 13 of the M25). As its name suggests, it promotes the perennial building toy, Lego (invented in Denmark in the 1930s), and it includes not only incredibly elaborate miniature copies of cities from around the world, but inventive and original theme park rides for all ages, including some gentle ones for tiny tots and grannies, and a chance to pan for 'gold' (children get a medal when they've found a certain amount) in the Wild Woods. The accent is on originality and good design rather than thrills and nausea, food and drink is expensive and the park is so popular that you can spend more time queuing for the main attractions than actually having fun.

If your kids prefer animals to rides, take a trip to Whipsnade Wild Animal Park in Dunstable (☎ 01582-872171, 🖳 www.zsl.org/zsl-london-zoo/whipsnade), set in 600 acres of parkland. It's around 30 minutes from King's Cross by train (to Luton followed by a bus ride) or from central London by car on the M1 (to junction 9), A5 and B4540. As well as doing valuable work in the conservation of endangered species – you'll see elephants, hippos, wallabies and Chinese water deer – it features a children's farm, miniature railway and a great play area.

Not far from Whipsnade is Woburn Abbey (☎ 01525-290333, 🖳 www.woburnabbey.co.uk), which is 30 minutes by train (from Euston to Bletchley) or by car on the M1 (junction 13) and the A4012. This 18th-century stately home was built on the foundations of a 12th-century monastery, but children love it less for its architecture than for the Safari Park, 🖳 www.woburnsafari.co.uk) in the grounds where you can see lions, tigers and bears. There are also five adventure playgrounds, including one for under-fives.

London Marathon

10.

SPORT & FITNESS

Sports facilities are generally excellent in London and whether you're a novice or an experienced competitor there's plenty of opportunity to be active and get fit. Among the most popular sports are football (soccer), rugby (union and league), cricket, athletics, fishing, snooker, horse racing, golf, walking, cycling, squash, badminton, tennis, swimming and skiing, an inordinate number of which were British inventions (but which almost everybody is better at than the British nowadays). A useful general website for further information about many of these activities in the UK is 💻 www. 24hoursport.co.uk.

The sports industry in the UK is big business and new sports facilities and complexes, including golf clubs, indoor tennis courts, dry slope ski centres and health and fitness clubs are opening all the time. Many sports owe their popularity (and their top sports stars' their fortunes) to television (TV) and the increased coverage (and competition for TV rights) generated by the proliferation of cable and satellite stations – with the attendant increase in sponsorship and advertising.

Despite the excellent sports facilities in the UK and the estimate that over 25m people over the age of 13 regularly participate in sport and exercise, around half the population takes part in none at all (apart from strolling to the local pub and staggering back).

Facilities for spectators have also improved greatly over recent years. Most football stadia have now abandoned the traditional 'terraces', where the majority of spectators were expected to stand, with no protection from the cold and rain. Following a number of terrible accidents, football clubs were obliged (for safety reasons) to convert to all-seat stadia, many of which are among Europe's best.

London's flagship stadium is Wembley, HA9 (☎ 0844-980 8001, 💻 www.wembleystadium. com, Wembley Park tube or Wembley Stadium rail), which was rebuilt after the original building was demolished in 2002 and re-opened in March 2007 (over a year late); it has a capacity of 90,000. Other major stadia in London are the nearby Wembley Arena and Conference Centre, Engineers Way, Wembley, HA9 (☎ 020-8795 8000, 💻 www.wembley.co.uk, Wembley Park tube) and the Crystal Palace National Sports Centre, Ledrington Road, Crystal Palace, SE19 (☎ 020-8778 0131, Crystal Palace rail), which hosts Grand Prix athletics competitions in summer and other activities and events throughout the year.

Most areas of London have a community sports or leisure centre (also called recreation centres), usually run and financed by the local Borough Council. A huge range of sports and activities is catered for, including badminton, basketball, netball, swimming and diving, indoor football (five-a-side), roller-skating, BMX biking, gymnastics, yoga, weight training, table tennis, tennis, squash and racketball, aerobics, cricket, climbing, canoeing (in the swimming pool), archery, bowls, hockey, martial arts and snooker. Councils publish a wealth of information about local sports and leisure centres on their websites. London has facilities to suit every pocket – far too many to list here – you can obtain details from your London Business phone book or call Sportsline (☎ 020-7222 8000) for information.

For information about sports facilities in the UK, contact Sport England, Third Floor, Victoria House, Bloomsbury Square, London WC1B 4SE (☎ 020-7273 1551, 🖥 www.sportengland.org). The names and addresses of sports associations and federations can be obtained from either Sport England or the Central Council of Physical Recreation (CCPR), Francis House, Francis Street, London SW1P 1DE (☎ 020-7976 3900, 🖥 www.ccpr.org.uk), the national association of governing bodies of sport and recreation in the UK.

Sports results are given on the television, numerous internet sites (such as 🖥 http://news.bbc.co.uk/sport and 🖥 www.skysports.com) and are published widely in daily newspapers. The Sunday broadsheet newspapers provide comprehensive coverage and a nationwide results service – particularly for cricket (in the summer) football and rugby (the rest of the year), often in a separate sports supplement. Numerous magazines are published for all sports, from angling to yachting, most of which are available (or can be ordered) from any newsagent.

Some of the sports and activities most widely practised in London are detailed below (in alphabetical order).

CRICKET

Perhaps the archetypal English game, cricket is played throughout London – at both local and international level. The season runs from April to September, though matches are, not surprisingly, often 'rained off'. Although the English invented cricket, they're regularly beaten nowadays by their former colonies, including Australia, India, New Zealand, Pakistan, South Africa and the West Indies. The big events of the London season are five-day test matches, played at Lord's, St John's Wood Road, St John's Wood, NW8 (☎ 020-7616 8500, 🖥 www.lords.org, St John's Wood

tube – tickets £20–£60) and The Oval, Kennington, SE11 (☎ 0871-246 1100, 🖥 www.surreycricket.com, Oval tube – tickets £5–£50), where there are also one-day internationals and regular inter-county matches, Lord's being the home of the 'Middlesex' team and the Oval of Surrey.

The Marylebone Cricket Club/MCC (☎ 020-7616 8500, 🖥 www.lords.org/mcc) is the body that's responsible for the administration and laws, and their website contains a wealth of information about every aspect of the game. For information about how to find a local cricket team, see 🖥 www.play-cricket.com.

CYCLING

Cycling isn't as popular in the UK as on the continent and only some 3 per cent of journeys are made by bicycle in the UK compared to 18 per cent in Denmark and 27 per cent in Holland. Over 1.5m bikes are sold each year (over a third bought to replace stolen machines!), which adds up to an awful lot of (potential) cyclists. But most people in the UK buy bikes for shopping or getting around towns, rather than for pleasure, exercise or sport (e.g. touring or racing).

If you want to cycle for pleasure (rather than to get form A to B), there are cycle paths in or alongside all of London's royal parks –

Kensington Gardens, Hyde Park, Green Park and St James's Park – which form a continuous green corridor running from West to East across the West End. These parks allow you to travel from Notting Hill to Trafalgar Square and Parliament Square completely car free (with the exception of road crossings). Other royal parks such as Richmond, Bushy and Greenwich are also excellent places to cycle, and can be reached via the Thames' towpaths.

If you'd rather burn round a track than risk your life trying to commute across town by pedal power, you can go to the Lee Valley Cycle Circuit, Temple Mills Lane, E15 (☎ 020-8534 6085, Leyton tube), where you can take part in BMX racing, time-trialling, road racing and cyclo-cross (bikes are for hire). Alternatively, try the oldest cycle circuit in the world at the Herne Hill Velodrome, Burbage Road, Herne Hill, SE24 (🖳 www.hernehillvelodrome.org.uk, Herne Hill rail).

An interesting book for Londoners is *On Your Bike*, published by the London Cycling Campaign, 2 Newhams Row, London SE1 3UZ (☎ 020-7234 9310, 🖳 www.lcc.org.uk). Other useful books include *Richard's New Bicycle Book* by Richard Ballantine (Pan), which is a guide to choosing and using a bicycle, and the *Complete Bike Book* by Chris Sidwells (Penguin). A number of magazines are published for cyclists in the UK, including *Cycling Plus*, *Cycling Weekly*, *Cycle Sport*, *Mountain Bike Rider* and *Procycling*. See also **Cycling** on page 109.

FOOTBALL

Football (the British rarely use the word soccer) is the UK's national spectator and participation sport. The league season in England officially runs from August to May (although professional football seems to be expanding continually in one way or another to fill the rest of the year, with internationals and qualifying rounds for the UEFA Cup in the summer). There's no mid-season winter break, as in many other European countries, although many clubs would like one. Most matches are still played on Saturdays, although some clubs play regularly on Friday evenings and there are increasing numbers of Tuesday, Wednesday, Sunday afternoon and Monday evening

Premiership and Football League matches, many of which are televised live on Sky TV and Setanta.

> The Football Association (FA) runs the world's oldest cup competition, the FA Cup (instituted in 1888), while England's top 20 clubs play league football in the Premiership, which was formed in the 1992/93 season.

There are three lower divisions, with 24 teams in each: the Championship, Division One (though, of course, it's really Division Three) and Division Two (Four).

London's current Premiership clubs are:

◆ **Arsenal** (Emirates Stadium, 75 Drayton Park, N5, ☎ 020-7704 4000, 🖳 www.arsenal.com, Holloway Road tube) – known as the 'Gunners';

◆ **Chelsea** (Stamford Bridge, Fulham Road, Chelsea, SW6, ☎ 0871-984 1955, 🖳 www.chelseafc.co.uk, Fulham Broadway tube) – know as the 'Blues';

◆ **Fulham** (Craven Cottage, Stevenage Road, SW6, ☎ 0870-442 1222, 🖳 www.fulhamfc.com, Putney Bridge tube) – know as the 'Cottagers';

◆ **Tottenham Hotspur** (White Hart Lane Stadium, 748 High Road, Tottenham, N17, ☎ 0844-499 5000, 🖳 www.tottenhamhotspur.com, White Hart Lane rail) – known as 'Spurs';

◆ **West Ham United** (Boleyn Ground, Green Street, Upton Park, E13, ☎ 020-8548 2748, 🖳 www.whufc.com, Upton Park tube) – know as the 'Hammers';

You can obtain information about these clubs and their fixtures from the Premiership's official website (🖳 www.premierleague.com).

London's current Championship clubs are Charlton Athletic (south-east), Crystal Palace (south) and Queens Park Rangers (west); the current Division One clubs are Leyton Orient (east) and Millwall (south-east); and the current Division Two clubs Barnet (north) and Brentford (west). Below these four professional leagues are the three leagues of the Football Conference, which bridge the gap between the professional and amateur leagues, the latter confusingly known as 'non-league football' even though most clubs compete in league competitions.

The cost of tickets to football matches has risen at well over double the rate of inflation in recent years to fund expensive new all-seat stadia and now averages around £60 for Premiership games. Annual 'season' tickets vary greatly in price between clubs (even in the same division) and can cost well over £1,000, although the average for a Premiership club is around £600. One of most expensive London clubs to watch is Arsenal, which charges an average of £1,355 for a season ticket.

However, the high cost of tickets doesn't seem to deter supporters and many Premiership clubs sell out for every home game (although bottom-of-the-league clubs often struggle to fill their grounds), and tickets for big matches are difficult to obtain. It isn't necessary to buy a ticket in advance for most matches in the lower leagues, although local derbies (matches between neighbouring clubs) and cup matches are usually 'all-ticket', meaning that tickets must be purchased in advance.

For information about football coaching and local clubs at all levels, contact the London Football Association (☏ 0870-774 3010, 🖥 www.londonfa.com). To find a local football club, see the Football Associations's website (🖥 www.thefa.com/grassrootsnew/player/postings/2000/03/findaclub).

⚠ **Caution**

British football fans have a long-standing (and well deserved) reputation for drunkenness and violence and, although it's generally safe for women and children to attend major matches, the language heard in and around stadia often leaves a lot to be desired and the experience certainly isn't what you could call 'refined'.

GOLF

Surprising as it may seem, you can play golf in London, though not of course in the city centre. There are 18-hole public courses and many exclusive private clubs – most of which are very expensive and have long waiting lists (although you may be lucky enough to play as a quest) – throughout the suburbs, although none are on the tube network.

Among the many public courses are two in Richmond Park (🖥 www.richmondparkgolfclub.org.uk), Chingford Golf Course at Bury Road, E4 (☏ 020-8529 5708, 🖥 www.chingfordgolfclub.com), Dulwich and Sydenham Hill, Grange Lane, College Road, Dulwich, SE21 (🖥 www.dulwichgolf.co.uk) and the Hainault Forest Golf Complex, Romford Road, Chigwell, Essex IG7 (☏ 020-8500 2131, 🖥 www.hainaultforestgolf.co.uk).

At a public course, it isn't necessary to have your own clubs, as they can be hired for around £10. Second-hand clubs can be bought for as little as £50, while new sets start at around £250. Green fees (the term used for the cost of a round) are reasonable at most public golf clubs, averaging around £10 to £15 for 18 holes, whereas fees at top private courses are £100 or more (and you must be accompanied by a member). Fees are usually around 20 to 25 per cent lower on weekdays, and nine-hole courses charge less, and many public courses offer under 18s a discount. Fees may be reduced in winter.

If you don't have the time to play a round of golf, you can keep your swing and putting in trim – or hopefully improve it – at a golf/health club or a driving range, of which there are a number in London.

The English Golf Union (☏ 01526-354500, 🖥 www.englishgolfunion.org) provides information about clubs, coaching and many other aspects of the game, and also has a directory of courses in the London area. Numerous golf books are published, including the *AA Golf Course Guide* (AA Publishing), containing details of 2,500 courses in Britain and Ireland. Useful websites include 🖥 www.golfuk.co.uk and 🖥 www.golfingguides.net

GREYHOUND RACING

The poor man's horse racing, greyhound racing (the 'dog track') is especially popular in

London. For an authentic East End experience and the chance to win some 'bread and honey' (money), try Walthamstow Stadium, Chingford Road, Walthamstow, E4 (☎ 020-8498 3300, 🖳 www.wsgreyhound.co.uk, Walthamstow Central tube/rail, then the no.97 or 215 bus). Races are at 2pm Mondays, 11.30am Fridays and 7.30pm Tuesdays, Thursdays and Saturdays. Admission costs £1–6. A south London alternative is Wimbledon Stadium, Plough Lane, Wimbledon, SW17 0BL (☎ 0870-840 8905, Tooting Broadway tube, Wimbledon tube/rail or Haydons Road rail). Races are at 7.30pm on Tuesdays, Fridays and Saturdays, and admission is £5.50.

GYMNASIA & HEALTH CLUBS

Working out is popular in London, where many companies have their own health and leisure centres or pay for corporate membership of a local centre as a staff benefit (the idea being that fit workers take less time off sick …). London has a huge range of private gyms and health clubs, where the cost of membership is around £40 to £80 per month; the most popular chains with 'branches' in the capital are listed below:

◆ **Cannons Health Fitness Club** (☎ 020-8336 2288, 🖳 www.cannons.co.uk) – branches in Battersea, Bloomsbury, Brondesbury Park, City, Covent Garden, Fulham, Norbury, Paddington, Richmond, Twickenham, Wandsworth, West End and Wimbledon. Membership rates vary from club to club. Most Cannons clubs are well equipped, with top-notch fitness rooms and at least one aerobics studio. Many also have pools, a spa, steam room and sauna, beauty suites and women-only areas.

◆ **David Lloyd Leisure** (🖳 www.davidlloyd. co.uk) – branches in Ealing, Enfield, Finchley, Fulham, Hounslow-Heston, Kensington, Kingston and Raynes Park. David Lloyd Leisure clubs have hi-tech gymnasiums and aerobic and dance studios, indoor and outdoor tennis courts, squash courts and non-slip badminton courts, plus the usual sauna, spa, steam-room and relaxation areas.

◆ **Esporta Health Fitness Club** (☎ 0118-912 3576, 🖳 www.esporta.com) – clubs in

Chigwell, Chislehurst, Chiswick, Croydon, Enfield, Friern Barnet, Ilford, Islington, Kingston, Northwood, Romford, Swiss Cottage, Wandsworth and Wimbledon. Firmly at the top (i.e. priciest) end of the market, Esporta clubs have the latest machines, swimming pools, and squash and tennis facilities, plus the ubiquitous health suites with saunas, steam rooms, spa, whirlpools and solarium. Some also offer physiotherapy and sports injury treatment.

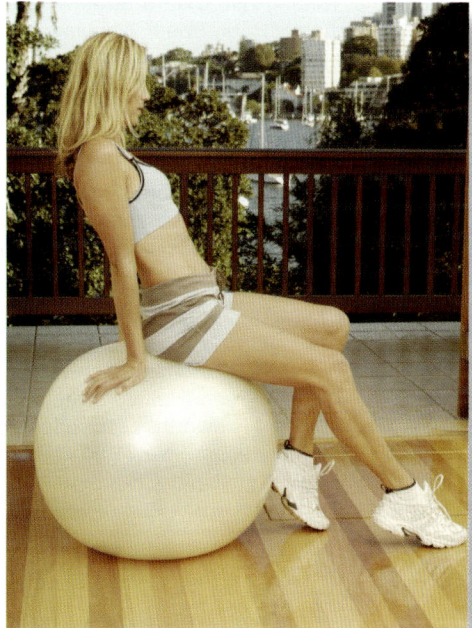

◆ **Fitness First** (☎ 01202-845000, 🖳 www. fitnessfirst.co.uk) – currently the largest health club operator in Europe, with branches in Acton, Alperton, Balham, Bow Wharf, Brixton, Camden, central London (America Square, Berkeley Square, Bloomsbury, Chancery Lane, Covent Garden, Embankment, Fetter Lane, Gracehurst Street, Great Marlborough Street, High Holborn, Kingly Street, Liverpool Street, London Bridge, Old Street, Palace Street, Regent's Park and Victoria), Clapham, Croydon, North Finchley, Hammersmith, Harrow, Holloway, Islington, Kilburn, Kingsbury, Lewisham, Leyton Mills, Pinner, Shepherd's Bush, South Kensington, Teddington, Uxbridge,

Walworth Road and Woolwich. Fitness First clubs have large gym and fitness rooms, as well as aerobics studios with a wide range of classes. Most clubs also have health suites.

♦ **Holmes Place** (☎ 0845-130 4747, 🖳 www.virginactive.co.uk) – clubs in Barbican, Bromley, Brook Green, Canary Riverside, Chelsea, Chigwell, Clapham, Crouch End, Croydon, Ealing, Fulham Pools, Hendon, Holloway Road, Kensington, Kingston, Marylebone, Moorgate, Notting Hill, Oxford Street, Putney, Regent's Park, South Wimbledon, Strand and Streatham. Holmes Place (part of Virgin Active) caters for the premium end of the market, offering luxurious health and fitness facilities, including a swimming pool, sauna, steam room, gym and studios. A range of memberships is available and prices vary between the clubs; the most expensive are in central London.

♦ **LA Fitness** (☎ 01302-892310, 🖳 www. lafitness.co.uk) – clubs in Bayswater, Croydon, New Barnet, Bromley, Edgware, Finchley, Golders Green, Hallam Street, Highgate, Holborn, Isleworth, Leadenhall, London Wall, Marylebone, New Barnet, Piccadilly, South Kensington, Southgate, St Paul's, Sydenham, Victoria, Waldorf

and West India Quay. Some clubs have a women-only workout area and all have spas, saunas and steam rooms.

In addition to the above private clubs – where you normally pay a joining fee and then a monthly subscription – there are fitness rooms at most public sports and leisure centres, where you pay per session. Some of the best public facilities are listed below:

♦ **Jubilee Hall Leisure Centre** (☎ 020-7836 4835, Covent Garden tube) in the Covent Garden piazza– enormous, well equipped and provides a vast selection of free weights in its cavernous gym, plus aerobics, step and martial arts classes;

♦ **Kentish Town Sports Centre**, Prince of Wales Road, London NW5 (☎ 020-7267 9341, Kentish Town tube) – has two swimming pools, a teaching pool, exercise studios and a gymnasium, with belly dancing, body conditioning and Tai Chi Yoga classes on offer;

♦ **Michael Sobell Leisure Centre**, Hornsey Road, N7 (☎ 020-7609 2166, Finsbury Park or Holloway Road tube) – another enormous centre, boasting a climbing wall, trampolines and a gym;

♦ **Putney Leisure Centre**, Dryburgh Road, London SW15 (☎ 020-8785 0388, 🖳 www. dcleisure.co.uk, East Putney tube) – has an air-conditioned gym, precision cycling studio, air-conditioned dance studio, cafeteria and purpose-built crèche;

♦ **Queen Mother Sports Centre**, Vauxhall Bridge Road, SW1 (☎ 020-7630 5522, Victoria tube) – has a gym, two dance studios, a sauna and steam room, and a swimming pool. Martial arts and aerobics classes are offered.

♦ **The Sanctuary**, Floral Street, WC2 (☎ 0870-770 3350, 🖳 www.thesanctuary. co.uk, Covent Garden tube) – for women only and expensive, at over £65 per visit, but worth it to luxuriate in the tropical-plant-filled interior or swim naked in the wonderful pool. The admission fee includes unlimited use of a sauna, Jacuzzi and steam room, and there's a range of beauty treatments if you have money to spare.

♦ **Seymour Leisure Centre**, Seymour Place, W1 (☎ 020-7723 8019, Edgware Road or Marble Arch tube) – centrally located, with a sports hall and cardiovascular suite, as well as the usual steam room, sauna and Jacuzzi. It offers classes in aerobics, step and body conditioning.

♦ **YMCA Sport & Fitness Centres** (🖥 www.ymca.org.co.uk) in Barbican, City, Great Russell Street and Kingston & Wimbledon. The YMCA's HQ in London is Central YMCA, **112 Great Russell Street, WC1 (☎ 020-7343 1700, 🖥 www. ymcaclub.co.uk, Tottenham Court Road tube), which has** 4,000 members and boasts a superb gym, a huge exercise to music programme and a 25-metre pool. Membership of Central YMCA also entitles you to use gyms, classes and swimming pools in 85 other public centres across London that comprise the London Fitness Network (🖥 www.londonfitnessnetwork. org).

A good gym or health club should carry out a physical assessment, including a blood pressure test, fat distribution measurements and heart rate checks, and tailor your exercise programme to your condition.

⚠ **Caution**

Middle-aged 'fatties' shouldn't attempt to get fit in five minutes (after all it took years of dedicated sloth and over-eating to put on all that weight), as overexertion can result in serious sports injuries. In your pursuit of the body beautiful it pays to take the long route and give the intensive care unit (or mortuary) a wide berth.

HORSE RIDING

There are various opportunities to ride horses in London. Hyde Park Stables, Bathurst Mews, W2 (☎ 020-7723 2813, 🖥 www. hydeparkstables.com, Lancaster Gate tube) is one of the most pleasant, where a group riding session for an hour costs around £50 during the week, £55 at weekends. Hourly private tuition fees are £70 during the week and £85 at weekends.

Further out, there's Belmont Riding Centre, Ridgeway, NW7 (☎ 020-8906 1255, Mill Hill East tube), which has a large indoor school and a cross-country course on 160 acres (65ha), and provides tuition for all ages and levels, from beginner to advanced. Wimbledon Village Stables, High Street, Wimbledon, SW19 (☎ 020-8946 8579, 🖥 www.wvstables.com, Wimbledon tube) is a smaller operation, offering a range of classes and riding in Richmond Park or on Wimbledon Common (watch out for the Wombles!).

ICE SKATING

There are a number of skating rinks in London, including:

♦ **Broadgate Ice Rink**, Broadgate Circus, EC2 (🖥 www.broadgateinfo.net, Liverpool Street tube) – a friendly outdoor rink famous for a bizarre game called 'broomball', played on Monday to Wednesday evenings;

♦ **Lee Valley Ice Centre**, Lea Bridge Road, E10 (☎ 01992-717711, 🖥 www. leevalleypark.org.uk, Blackhorse Road tube);

♦ **Leisurebox**, Queensway, W2 (☎ 020-7229 0172, Bayswater or Queensway tube) – runs general and family sessions, and trains young skaters after school. Friday and Saturday nights are ice-disco nights.

♦ **Streatham Ice Arena**, Streatham High Road, SW16 (☎ 020-8769 7771, 🖥 www. streathamicearena.com, Streatham rail).

MOTORSPORTS

Motor racing has a large following in the UK and embraces a plethora of 'disciplines', including Formulas One, Two and Three; Formula 3000; sports car and Formula Ford; rallying; hill-climbing; historic sports car racing; competitions among specific makes of car (such as TVR, Renault 5, Maxda MX-5, Honda CRX and Mini, to name but a few); autocross;

speedway; stock car racing; drag(ster) racing; motorcycle racing (including grand prix racing at 125cc, 250cc, 350cc, 500cc levels and 'superbike'– over 1,000cc); and go-karting and bantam racing for kids.

The most famous British motor racing venues include Brands Hatch, Swanley, Kent, DA3 (☎ 0870-950 9000, 🖥 www.motorsportvision.co.uk), Donington Park, Derby, DE74 2RP (☎ 01332-810048, 🖥 www.donington-park.co.uk) and Silverstone, Northamptonshire, NN12 (☎ 08704-588200, 🖥 www.silverstone.co.uk), host of the British Grand Prix (which well be held at Donington Park from 2010).

> The British Grand Prix is one of the UK's most expensive events (of any kind), an 'average' ticket for the 2007 race costing around £200.

A number of magazines are dedicated to motorsports in the UK, such as *Motorsport* (🖥 www.motorsportmagazine.co.uk), and many websites, including 🖥 www.autosport.com, 🖥 www.fia.com, 🖥 www.motorsport.org.uk, 🖥 www.motorsport.co.uk and 🖥 www.f1-racing.org.

RACKET SPORTS

There are facilities in London – both public and private – for playing badminton, squash, racketball, table tennis and tennis, as detailed below. To find clubs and facilities in your area look in the Yellow Pages, enquire at your local library or contact the appropriate national association (see below).

Charges for all racket sports at public centres are usually lower before 5pm on weekdays and after 5pm at weekends, although lunch-time periods may be charged at peak rates for some sports, e.g. squash. Courts in public sports and leisure centres can be booked up to two weeks in advance, while private clubs may allow bookings to be made further in advance. Rackets, shoes and towels can usually be hired (or purchased) from both public sports centres and private clubs. Most centres and clubs organise internal leagues, ladders and knockout competitions, and also participate in local and national league and cup competitions. Leagues and competitions are also organised by many companies and schools, and some of the latter have their own courts.

Badminton

Badminton has an estimated 2.5m players in the UK, making it more popular than tennis. The cost of hiring a badminton court in a sports centre is around £8 per hour at peak times, £5 at off-peak times. Badminton England is the sports governing body (National Badminton Centre, Bradwell Road, Milton Keynes MK8, ☎ 01908-268400, 🖥 www.badmintonengland.co.uk).

Squash

Squash has been declining in popularity since its heyday in the '80s but is still widely played (England has more players and courts than any other country in the world), with an abundance of courts in sports centres and private squash clubs (although the number is falling) in all areas of London. Private clubs usually cater exclusively for squash, and clubs combining squash and tennis (or some other sport) are rare. Many private squash clubs have a resident coach, providing both individual and group lessons.

The cost of hiring a court in a sports centre is from around £8 for a 40- or 45-minute session or £10 for an hour. Off-peak (before 5pm) fees may be around £5 for 45 minutes and students and the unemployed are entitled to use council facilities for half price during off-peak hours in some areas. Annual membership of a private squash club varies from around £100 to £400 per year; off-peak, family and junior membership may also be available. Court fees may be included in the annual fee or extra.

England Squash (Rowsley Street, Manchester, M11, ☎ 0161-231 4499, 🖥 www.englandsquash.com) is the governing body for squash and racketball in England and is responsible for the organisation and promotion of both sports. It comprises 38 County Associations, approximately 1,000

Clubs and 50,000 individual members aged from 8 to 80.

Racketball

Racketball is an 'easy' version of squash, played on squash courts in the UK, with shorter rackets and a bigger, bouncier ball; rackets and balls can be hired at most squash clubs and centres.

Table Tennis

Table tennis is popular in the UK and is played both as a serious competitive sport and as a pastime in social and youth clubs. Most sports centres have a number of table tennis tables for hire for as little as £5 an hour and bats can be hired for a small fee. If you want to play seriously there are clubs in many parts of London. Costs vary, but it's an inexpensive sport with little equipment necessary. More information can be found at 🖥 www. englishtabletennis.org.uk

Tennis

Tennis isn't much fun in the cold and rain that often afflicts London, and indoor tennis courts are relatively scarce (although as number of

gyms and health centres have indoor courts – see page 241). Many of London's parks have tennis courts, which you can hire by the hour for a modest fee, but you must usually book. Courts are available at Hyde Park (☎ 020-7262 3474), Regent's Park (☎ 020-7486 4216), Victoria Park (☎ 020-8986 5182), Hampstead Heath (☎ 020-7284 3648) and Battersea Park (☎ 020-8871 7542). Alternatively, there's the fashionable (and more expensive) Islington Tennis Centre, Market Road, N7 (☎ 020-7700 1370, Caledonian Road tube), which has three floodlit outdoor, three indoor courts and provides coaching. You don't need to be a member to use the facilities.

If you're a serious tennis player you may be interested in joining a private club. Costs vary but can be high, e.g. a £200 enrolment fee plus a £500 annual subscription for single membership of an exclusive tennis club with both indoor and outdoor courts. Many private clubs also have gymnasia and swimming pools that can be used by members, sometimes for an extra fee. Reduced rates are usually available for couples and families. Private clubs (and public sports centres) usually have coaches available for both private and group lessons.

If you're a tennis fan, you might be keen to go to Wimbledon, where the Grand Slam championship is played in the last week of June and the first week of July on the hallowed lawns of the All England Lawn Tennis and Croquet Club, Church Road, Wimbledon (☎ 020-8944 1066, 🖥 www.wimbledon.org, Southfields or Wimbledon Park tube and a long walk or, during the tournament, a courtesy bus).

If you want a ticket for one of the 'show' courts and aren't a member of a tennis club (who are eligible to be entered into the annual ticket ballot), you have two options: to queue at the club from early morning (or even the night before) in the hope of getting one of the few hundred tickets sold 'at

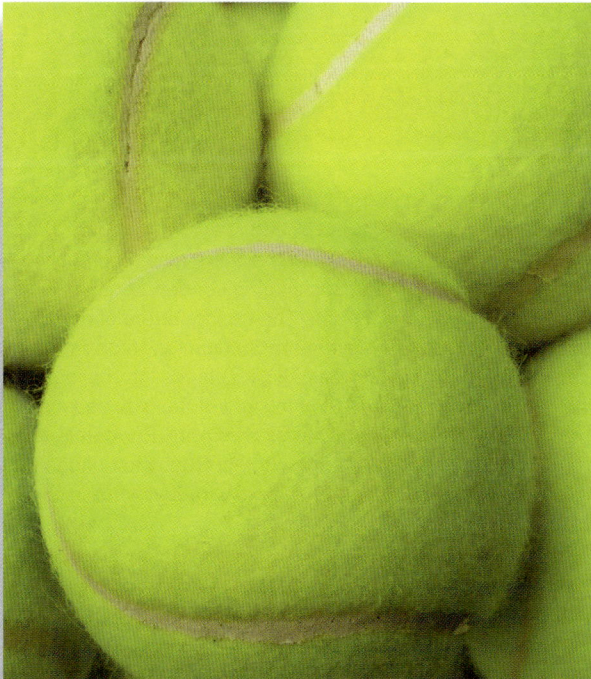

the door' each day; or to obtain an application form and submit it between 1st September and 31st December of the previous year, enclosing a stamped addressed envelope. Your name will go into the ballot and you'll be informed later whether you've been successful.

Even to gain access to the 'outside' courts at Wimbledon, you normally have to queue for hours, and need to arrive before 9am for a realistic chance of getting in by the time play starts (usually at 1pm).

You can also watch top-class men's tennis at Queen's Club, Palliser Road, W14 (☎ 020-7385 3421, 🖥 www.queensclub.co.uk, Baron's Court tube), where the June tournament is the 'curtain-raiser' to Wimbledon. Once again, applications must be made the previous year by 30th September to go into a ballot for tickets, although returns are for sale on match days.

Further information about playing and watching tennis in London is available from the Lawn Tennis Association (National Tennis Centre, 100 Priory Lane, Roehampton, London SW15 5JQ, ☎ 020-8487 7000, 🖥 www.lta.org. uk), which publishes a leaflet, *Where to Play Tennis in London*.

RUGBY

Two kinds of rugby (properly known as rugby football) are played in the UK: 15-a-side rugby union, the code more common in London, and 13-a-side rugby league, which is played mainly in the north of England. London has two top rugby union teams: Harlequins (☎ 020-8410 6000, 🖥 www.quins.co.uk), based at the Stoop Memorial Ground in Twickenham (☎ 020-8979 2427, 🖥 www. twickenhamrugby.com, Twickenham rail) and Wasps (☎ 0870-414 1515, 🖥 www.wasps. co.uk, Ealing Common tube), based at Twyford

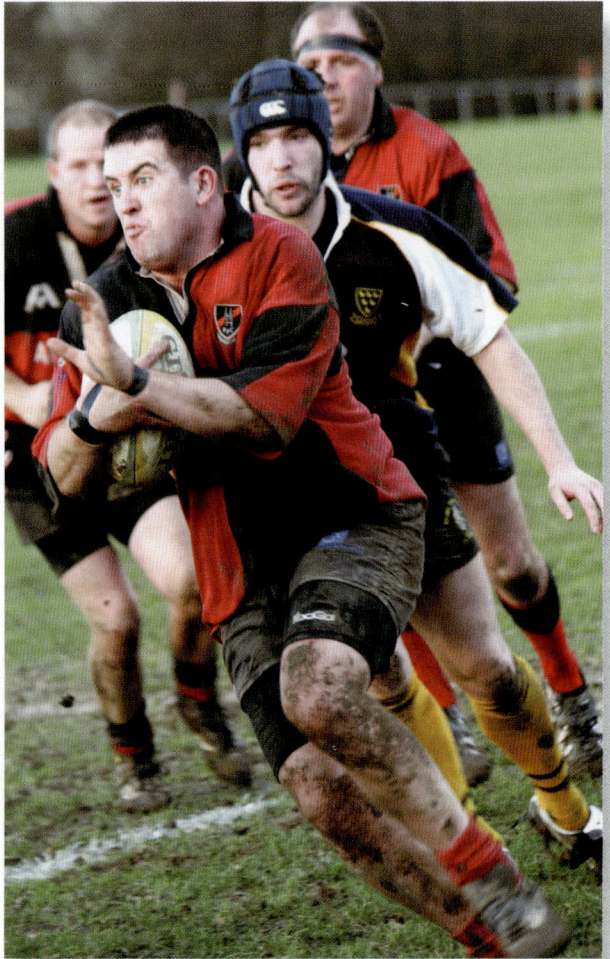

Avenue Sports Ground, Twyford Avenue, W3 9QA in Ealing. There are also a number of other teams, including London Scottish and London Irish. The headquarters of rugby union is Twickenham Stadium, Whitton Road (Twickenham rail), which stages international matches and the highlight of the club season, the Pilkington Cup Final in April. For details of clubs in your area, contact Rugby in London (☎ 020-8963 400, 🖥 www.rugbyinlondon.com)

SKIING

Skiing is a popular sport with the British, who have made up for their lack of snow (and mountains) with dry-slope skiing. As well as being an excellent training ground for the 'real thing', dry-slope skiing has become a popular sport in its own right. Most centres have a ski racing team, and dry-slope competitions are held regularly throughout the year. Learning to ski on a dry slope can save you time and money, and also helps skiers find their ski-legs before arriving in a winter resort.

A dry slope consists of around 21,000ft² (2,000m²) of matting, usually with separate areas for beginners and advanced skiers. The maximum descent of 'pistes' is around 1,00ft (500m), although most are 650 to 1,000ft (200m to 300m). Button ski tows are usually provided and floodlights allow you to ski in the evenings.

⚠ Caution

You can use your own ski boots on a dry slope but don't use good skis, as they don't take kindly to the artificial surface. Wear old clothes, as the matting can damage ski suits (and you'll look a wally in one) and gloves (which are usually compulsory). The most common injury on a dry slope is to thumbs, bent backwards by the matting.

Equipment hire is usually included in the hourly rate, which varies considerably. Many centres offer weekly and season tickets. Centres can get extremely crowded at weekends, particularly towards Christmas, when 'everyone' is keen to get in a bit of practice before heading off to the Alps. Tuition is provided at all levels for both adults and children; a three-hour course costs from around £60, depending on the centre.

There are a number of dry ski centres in and around London, including Bromley Ski Centre, Sandy Lane, St Paul's Cray, Orpington, Kent BR5 3HY (☎ 01689-876812, 🖥 www.c-v-s. co.uk/bromleyski), which boasts a 120m main slope served by two lifts, a mogul run for accomplished skiers and a nursery slope for beginners. The centre is open all year and has

a licensed bar, so you can also practice your après-ski (although *glühwein* may not be on the menu). Warley Ski Centre, Holdens Wood, Warley Gap, Brentwood, Essex, CM13 3DP (☎ 01277-211994), offers ski and snowboard tuition. For information and a map showing all the UK's dry ski centres, see 🖥 www.skiclub. co.uk

Skiing can also be practised indoors on a new type of artificial snow, which feels just like the real thing. The only centre currently offering this within range of London is the Snowzone, 602 Marlborough Gate, Milton Keynes, MK9 3XS (☎ 0871-222 5670, 🖥 www. snozonemiltonkeynes.com). The Snowzone gets really cold – the temperature is never above -3°C (27°F) – so wrap up well.

If you're looking for a book about learning or improving your skiing, *Inner Skiing* by W. Timothy Gallwey (Random House) and *All-Mountain Skier: The Way to Expert Skiing* by T Mark Elling (McGraw-Hill) are among the best. A number of ski magazines are published in the UK, including *Snow* and *Ski and Board*. The *Daily Mail* International Ski Show is staged at Earls Court in November, with the latest equipment and clothing on show.

SWIMMING POOLS

There are dozens of swimming pools in London, both indoor and – perhaps surprisingly, given the English weather – outdoor. Two of the best indoor pools are the Ironmonger Row Baths, Finsbury (☎ 020-7253 4011, 🖥 www.aquaterra.org, Old Street tube) and, more centrally, the Oasis Sports Centre, Covent Garden (☎ 020-7831 1804, Holborn tube). For details of other indoor pools, visit individual London Borough Council websites (see **Chapter 1**).

London has a fine selection of lidos (outdoor swimming pools) for those all too infrequent hot summer days, including:

♦ **Brockwell Lido**, Dulwich Road, SE24 (☎ 020-7274 3088, 🖥 www.brockwell-lido. co.uk, Herne Hill Rail) – with its 1930s Art Deco café, this south London pool is something of a local landmark.

♦ **Charlton Lido**, Charlton Park Lane, Charlton, SE7 (☎ 020-8856 7180, Charlton rail) – open only during the school summer holidays. Facilities include a 50m pool and toddlers' splash pool.

◆ **Finchley Lido**, Great North Leisure Park, High Road, Finchley, N12 (☎ 020-8343 9830, East Finchley or Finchley Central tube) – a good option for north Londoners.

◆ **Parliament Hill Lido**, Parliament Hill Fields, Gordon House Road, NW5 (☎ 020-7485 5757, Gospel Oak rail or C11 bus) – has a 60m pool and the early morning swimming session is free – if you're brave enough;

◆ **Serpentine Lido**, Hyde Park, W2 (☎ 020-7706 3422, 🖳 www.serpentinelido.com, Knightsbridge or South Kensington tube) – open to the public in the summer and the perfect place to cool off if you work in central London;

◆ **Tooting Bec Lido**, Tooting Bec Common, SW16 (☎ 020-8871 7198, Tooting Bec tube or Streatham rail) – open to the public from late May until the end of September. It has a 90m pool and a children's paddling pool.

WATERSPORTS & SAILING

Not surprisingly, as an island nation, the UK is one of the world's leading countries when it comes to watersports, particularly rowing and sailing. Among the capital's leading rowing clubs is the London Rowing Club, Embankment, Putney, SW5, one of the oldest rowing clubs in London (☎ 020-8788 0000, 🖳 www.londonrc. org.uk). The capital is also home to many sailing clubs, including the Royal Thames Yacht Club (🖳 www.royalthames.co.uk), the oldest sailing club in the UK (est. 1775), and the London Corinthian Sailing Club (🖳 www.lcsc.org.uk), established in 1984.

Since being abandoned by commercial ships, London's docklands have become a Mecca for watersports enthusiasts and boast three watersports clubs:

◆ Docklands Sailing and Watersports Club at Millwall Dock, E14 (☎ 020-7537 7774, 🖳 www.dswc.org) – which provides a variety of courses; Membership costs from £10 (day membership) to £200 (annual, family membership). Facilities for the disabled are available, including dinghies and mini-yachts.

◆ Docklands Watersports Club at King George V Dock (☎ 020-7511 7000, Gallions Reach DLR or North Woolwich rail) – where you can learn to jet-ski;

◆ Royal Docks Waterski Club (☎ 020-7511 2000, 🖳 www.waterskilondon.com), close to London City Airport.

For further information about watersports' clubs in London, see 🖳 www.londononline.co.uk/local/Sports_and_Recreation/Watersports.

OTHER SPORTS & ACTIVITIES

The following is a selection of other popular sports and activities that can be enjoyed in (or near) London. For addresses and telephone numbers of national sports associations, contact Sport England (☎ 020-7273 1551, 🖳 www.sportengland.org) or the Central Council of Physical Recreation (☎ 020-7976 3900, 🖳 www.ccpr.org.uk).

Many foreign sports and pastimes have a group of expatriate fanatics in the UK, including American football, baseball, *boccia*, *boules* (and *pétanque*), Gaelic sports (hurling, Gaelic football), handball and softball. For information enquire at council offices, libraries, tourist offices, expatriate social clubs, embassies and consulates.

Archery

Still a popular sport in the UK, many years after the British army was issued with more lethal weapons, but the UK is still searching for a modern Robin Hood who can win an elusive Olympic gold medal. Crossbow shooting is also practised in some clubs.

Basketball

Basketball is increasingly popular with the British (there are over 1,000 clubs in the UK). It doesn't have a strong following as a professional sport, although the top teams participate in the European Clubs Championship.

Boxing

Legalised punch-ups are popular as a spectator 'sport' (many people enjoy watching a good fight, as long as they're out of harm's way). There are many boxing clubs in London, particularly in the East End, and the UK has produced a stream of world champions over the years.

Bungee Jumping

If you fancy a thrill, try a bungee jump with the UK Bungee Club, which meets in London at The Horseshoe Inn, 26 Mellor Street, SE1 and charges around £50 per jump. Those who like being tied upside down to the end of a rubber band can find further information on 💻 www.viewlondon.co.uk/experiences/london-bungee-jump.

Darts

Not actually a sport, but an excuse to get drunk. Around 5m people play darts regularly in the UK (which boasts some of the world's leading competitors), usually in pubs, most of which have teams playing in local leagues.

Fencing

A sport which has lost a lot of its popularity since the invention of the gun, although a hard core of enthusiast swordsmen are holding out in a small number of clubs.

Frisbee

Believe it or not, throwing plastic discs around has actually developed into a competitive 'sport', with national and local league and cup competitions.

Hockey

Hockey is a very old sport and has gained wider appeal in the UK since the British team won the Olympic gold medal in Seoul in 1988, although it still faces an uphill battle to woo youngsters away from football, rugby and cricket. It's equally popular among both sexes.

Lawn Bowls

Lawn bowls is a quintessentially English sport and there are many bowling clubs in London. For information, contact Bowls England

(🖳 www.bowlsengland.com) or the English Bowling Federation (🖳 www.fedbowls.co.uk).

> King Henry VIII once banned lawn bowling for all but the wealthiest, as people were allegedly spending so much time at it that they were neglecting their jobs. The ban wasn't lifted until 1845, some 300 years after his death in 1547.

Martial Arts

Unarmed combat techniques such as Aikido, Judo, Karate, Kung Fu, Kushido, Taekwon-Do and T'ai Chi Ch'uan are taught and practised in many leisure centres and clubs. Judo is the most popular martial art in the UK and a sport at which the UK has enjoyed considerable international success.

Rollerskating & Skateboarding

Rollerskating/rollerblading/skateboarding/BMX bike rinks are found in some of London's leisure centres, and there are unofficial 'centres' throughout London (e.g. under the South Bank Centre). The cost of using purpose-built facilities is around £5 (including the hire of a bike) or just a couple of pounds if you provide your own bike.

Rounders

The forerunner to baseball, rounders is popular in schools and is primarily a female sport in the UK.

Tenpin Bowling

After a decline in the '70s, tenpin bowling made a comeback at the end of the 20th century. There are a number of venues in the capital – for a list see 🖳 www.accessentertainment.co.uk/tenpin/london.htm.

Head of the River Race

Burlington Arcade, Piccadilly

11.
SPEND, SPEND, SPEND

London is one of the world's great shopping cities, catering for all tastes and pockets. It has an abundance of smart department stores and unique boutiques – the equal of any European or American city, although the prices aren't always as keen – as well as an ever increasing number (and decreasing range) of ubiquitous chain stores. London shops are also increasingly under threat from vast out-of-town shopping centres such as Bluewater in Kent and Thurrock in Essex. However, London is fighting back, with the vast Westfield shopping centre (Europe's largest) in Shepherds Bush, which opened in 2008.

It's often said that London isn't so much a city as a collection of villages (from which it grew) and nowhere is this more evident than when shopping. The cheap tourist 'trinkets' on sale in the eastern half of Oxford Street have little in common with the exotic wares of Covent Garden or the exclusive goods to be found in Old Bond Street, yet these areas are little more than a mile apart.

On the other hand, in every suburb of the metropolis you'll find branches of supermarkets and chain stores that have spread throughout the UK, which makes one shopping street seem much like any other. Chains include the mid-range fashion stores French Connection, Gap, Laura Ashley, Monsoon, Next, Oasis and Warehouse; cheap-and-cheerful budget fashion stores BHS, H&M, Miss Selfridge, New Look and Top Shop/ Top Man; toiletries giants The Body Shop, Boots and Superdrug; record stores HMV and Zaavi (formerly Virgin); book chains Sussex Stationers, Waterstones and WH Smith; and supermarkets Asda, Co-op, Marks & Spencer, Morrisons, Sainsbury's, Tesco and Waitrose – not to mention the all-purpose store for the budget-conscious, Woolworths.

To make the most of shopping in London you need to know where the interesting independent shops are: where you can buy a unique pair of shoes or an organic vegetarian sausage, and how to find ex-army fatigues or a left-handed potato peeler. Below – after some general information on London shops –

is a region by region 'tour' of London's principal shopping districts, highlighting the best (and some of the worst) retailers the capital has to offer.

While it's true that London's most exclusive shops are ruinously expensive, there's also much to offer the budget shopper, including a wealth of discount stores, charity shops and street markets.

If you aren't a citizen of a European Union country, you can apply for reimbursement of British value added tax (17.5 per cent) on purchases. Shops will give you a form to complete, which you must have stamped by customs when you leave the country with the goods.

For further information, obtain a copy of the annual *Time Out Guide to Shopping & Services in London*, listing over 2,000 shops and *Frommer's Born to Shop London* by Suzy Gershman (both John Wiley & Sons). If markets are more your style, try *The Markets of* London by Alec Forshaw & Theo Bergström (Penguin) or *The London Market Guide* by Andrew Richard Kershman & Ally Ireson (Metro).

If you're looking for second-hand bargains, try the periodicals *Exchange & Mart* or *Loot* or any local newspaper.

General Information

The following information applies to most shops in London (and in the rest of England).

Delivery

Many large shops make free home delivery within a certain radius and many despatch items by post to anywhere in the country (and abroad). Shopping from home took a giant leap forward with the advent of the internet (see page 285), and most major supermarket chains now offer home shopping via the internet if you live within a certain distance of a participating store. Although little more than a pilot scheme a mere few years ago, this service has now spread throughout London – try Sainsbury's (💻 www.sainsburys.com), Tesco (💻 www.tesco.com) or Waitrose (💻 www.waitrose.com). Those with Sky digital television (see page 289) can use its interactive shopping service, Open, to order goods from a growing number of stores, including groceries from Somerfield, CDs from Woolworths and books from WH Smith (but check to see whether your area qualifies for home delivery).

Disabled Access & Help

Although central London's crowded streets can present difficulties for wheelchair users, some shops and malls operate shop mobility (see below)

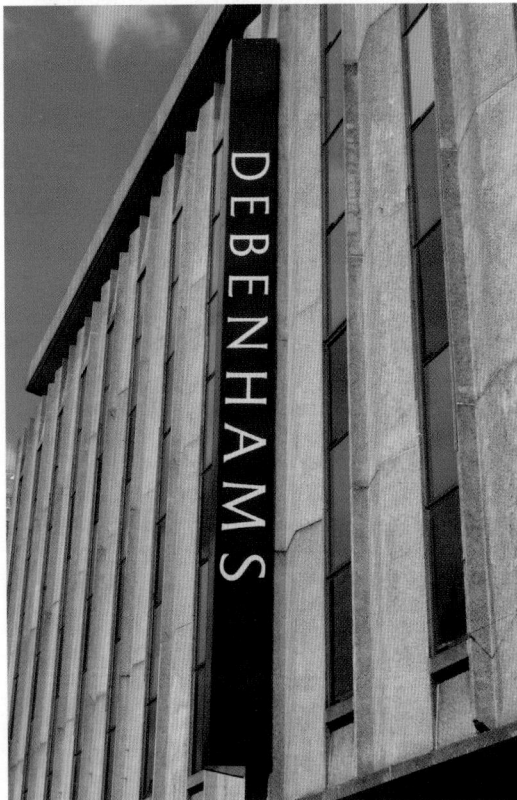

schemes and access to shops and services in London has improved significantly in recent years. Under the Disability Discrimination Act (DDA), service providers have to make reasonable adjustments for disabled people, such as providing extra help and removing physical barriers. Most large stores provide assistance for disabled people. For example, someone who is blind can get help reading labels and choosing items and anyone with a mobility impairment can get help reaching items and carrying them to the check-out. Disabled people can also use personal shoppers for personalised service.

Shopmobility (💻 www.shopmobilityuk.org) is a scheme which lends manual wheelchairs, powered wheelchairs and powered scooters to members of the public with limited mobility to shop and to visit leisure and commercial facilities. Shopmobility is for anyone, young or old, whether a disability is temporary or permanent.

Access to London's shops for disabled people is detailed on a useful website (💻 www.visitlondon.com/maps/accessibility) and in a book called *Access in London: A Guide for People Who Have Difficulty Getting Around* by Gordon Couch, William Forrester and David McGaughay (Access Project).

Measurements

The UK officially 'went metric' on 1st October 1995 and all retailers must now price goods in kilograms, litres and metres, despite the fact that many Britons haven't got a clue whether a pound (454 grams) weighs more or less than a kilogram (1,000 grams) nor how many centimetres there are in an inch (2.54) or a foot (30.48). However, British measures such as pounds, pints and feet can be (and invariably are) used alongside metrication and many stores display conversion tables. For those who aren't used to buying goods with British measures and sizes, a list of comparative weights and measures is provided in **Appendix D**.

Opening Hours

Opening hours for shops in central London are usually from between 9 and 10am until 5.30 or 6pm, Mondays to Saturdays. Shops don't shut for lunch and some stay open until between 7 and 8pm at least one day a week (usually Wednesday or Thursday) and daily in the run-up to Christmas. Shops are permitted to open on Sundays between the hours of 10am and 6pm, and many major stores open from noon until 6pm, although you should check in advance if you're planning to visit a particular store.

Payment & Refunds

In most shops you have a choice of payment methods: cash, cheque (with a guarantee card), debit card or credit card, although some British supermarkets have stopped accepting cheques and more retailers are expected to follow their example. Most of the larger department stores and chains issue their own 'store cards' (credit cards with, usually, high rates of interest) and some (e.g. Marks & Spencer) won't accept any other cards. Travellers' cheques and foreign currency are rarely accepted.

British law allows you to return goods that prove to be faulty for a full refund or a replacement, but make sure you keep your receipt as proof of purchase. If you simply change your mind about something you've bought or (in the case of clothing) discover it doesn't fit, a shop isn't obliged to change it for another item or refund your money. However, some stores will make cash refunds for any reason and most will give you a credit note if a purchase is returned in perfect condition.

☑ SURVIVAL TIP

Returning Faulty Goods

Under British law, you can return any goods which are faulty to where you bought them and have them repaired, replaced or your money back (you decide) – any time within the six months after your purchase it. You aren't obliged to deal with the manufacturer and retailers cannot override the law with their own terms and conditions.

Sales

Most London shops hold at least two sales a year – in January (the 'January' sales often start on 26th December!) and July – when you can buy certain goods at greatly reduced prices. Old stock and 'ends of lines' (i.e. the stuff no one wanted to be seen dead in) are sometimes marked down by 50 per cent or more, so it's worthwhile earmarking some money from your Christmas and holiday budgets to spend in the sales. Other sales may be held throughout the year, sometimes even just before Christmas if sales have been sluggish (as in December 2007), and some shops seem to have permanent 'sales'.

WEST END

The West End isn't in west London but merely west of the City; it's the heart of the capital's shopping scene, where most of its most famous stores are to be found.

Oxford Street

Oxford Street is the UK's busiest street. At peak shopping times the pavements are almost gridlocked and it isn't uncommon for workers to be late back to their offices after 'popping' to the bank or the pub, having got stuck in a 'people-jam' of purchase-laden pedestrians – most of them tourists. A staggering 9m foreign tourists trudge up and down the street each year, accounting for some 20 per cent of its income, but it's anyone's guess how many are disappointed by what they find.

Until the '60s, Oxford Street was a very smart place to shop, dominated by Edwardian department stores Selfridges, Debenham & Freebody, and Waring & Gillow. Only Selfridges (see below) remains in anything like its original form, and much of modern Oxford Street, particularly the eastern half, is lined with tacky tourist souvenir shops, jeans emporia, record shops, snack bars and employment agencies. However, its Christmas lights still draw crowds, and the police and the Oxford Street Association (a traders' organisation) between them do their best to control shoplifting and pickpocketing through all-seeing CCTV cameras. If you scratch your backside here, it will be recorded for posterity.

Despite the crowds, the crime and the kitsch, Oxford Street is well worth visiting. In the section west of the central crossroads known as Oxford Circus, the mighty department store

Selfridges, 400 Oxford Street (☎ 0800-123400, 💻 www.selfridges.co.uk, Bond Street or Marble Arch tube) has recently undergone a major refit to drag it kicking and screaming into the 21st century. It's still a delightfully eccentric and sprawling place to go browsing, with the largest cosmetics department in Europe and a wide range of fashion clothing, although some departments are drab and unexciting.

Close to Selfridges, at 458 Oxford Street, is the flagship branch of national chain Marks & Spencer (☎ 020-7935 4422, 💻 www.marksandspencer.com, Bond Street or Marble Arch tube). A long-term British institution, 'M&S' (also referred to as 'Marks & Sparks' and simply 'Marks') has been having problems in recent years, which have been blamed on its unexciting fashion ranges. The stores specialise in sensible, classic clothes for both sexes and are the chief purveyors of comfortable and reasonably priced underwear to the nation. This enormous store has the best choice of any branch in London; there's a smaller branch at 173 Oxford Street.

Further east, at nos. 278–306, is the John Lewis department store (☎ 020-7629 7711, 💻 www.johnlewis.com, Oxford Circus tube), which is also part of a national chain. Once again, this is their flagship store and it tends to concentrate on goods that the other stores don't stock. The furniture and haberdashery departments are excellent and in recent years have been enhanced by all kinds of exotica from India and other Asian countries.

Another department store, House of Fraser (☎ 0844-800 3752, 💻 www.houseoffraser.co.uk, Oxford Circus tube), can be found at 318 Oxford Street at the more downmarket, eastern end of the street. Like Debenhams (☎ 0844-561 6161, 💻 www.debenhams.com, Oxford Circus or Tottenham Court Road tube) at 334–338 Oxford Street, it sells the type of mid-range goods available in almost any urban shopping centre.

Like all London shopping streets, Oxford Street is dotted with branches of run-of-the-mill chain stores. Of these, probably the most interesting (or least uninteresting) are the flagship branches of Top Shop and H&M at Oxford Circus, and Miss Selfridge at 40 Duke Street, just around the corner from its parent store. HMV has branches selling CDs, DVDs, computer games and entertainment-linked merchandise at 150 and 363 Oxford Street, and its main rival, Zaavi, is at 14 and 527 Oxford Street.

Oxford Street features two noteworthy shopping malls: The Plaza (☎ 020-7637 8811, 💻 www.plaza-oxfordst.com, Tottenham Court Road tube), a recent development at no. 120, and the smarter West One shopping centre within the Bond Street underground station complex at the western end of the street.

Regent Street

Running at right angles to Oxford Street is the crescent-shaped Regent Street, once an unashamedly upmarket area but looking more down-at-heel since the influx of travel agencies and chain stores. One of its most notable shops is Liberty (☎ 020-7734 1234, 💻 www.liberty.co.uk, Oxford Circus tube) at nos. 210–220. Home of the original Liberty print fabrics, this rambling mock-Tudor department store has a decidedly late-19th century feel and stocks some wonderful women's fashion and jewellery.

Classic English outdoor fashion for weekends in the country can be found at Burberry (☎ 020-7806 1302, 💻 www.burberry.com, Piccadilly Circus tube) at 165 Regent Street, while a classic of a different cut can be found at the Levi's store (☎ 020-7292 2500, 💻 www.levisstore.com, Oxford Circus tube) at nos. 174–176.

If you have children or grandchildren (or you're still a child at heart), don't miss Hamleys (☎ 0844-855 2424, 💻 www.hamleys.com, Oxford Circus tube) at 188–196 Regent Street. Although it isn't cheap, it has a wider range of toys than you'll see anywhere outside an out-of-town branch of Toys 'R' Us. There are five floors and during the pre-Christmas season the shop is a war zone!

Tottenham Court Road

Running north to south at the extreme eastern end of Oxford Street is Tottenham Court Road, best known for its electronics shops, selling hi-fis, computers and cameras, and for its furnishing and interior design stores. Gultronics (☎ 020-8991 9001, 💻 www.gultronics.co.uk, Tottenham Court Road or Goodge Street tube) at no. 52 specialises in laptops and stocks a wide range of computer hardware. You can pick up second-hand equipment at the Computer Exchange (☎ 0845-345 1664, 💻 www.cex.co.uk, Goodge Street tube) at no. 70. For hi-fi, head for Hi-Fi Care (☎ 020-7580 6699, 💻 www.hificare.co.uk, Tottenham Court Road tube) at no. 233 or the oddly named Cornflake Shop (☎ 020-7323 4554, 💻 www.cornflake.co.uk, Goodge Street tube) around the corner at 37 Windmill Street. Jessops (☎ 020-7240 6077, 💻 www.jessops.com, Tottenham Court Road tube), another national chain, has one of the world's largest camera shops nearby at 63–69 New Oxford Street.

Competition in Tottenham Court Road is fierce and most shops will match or beat any advertised price, so this is the place to buy the latest electronic gizmos without wasting pennies.

If you're looking for some new furniture, visit stylish Heal's (☎ 020-7636 1666, 💻 www.heals.co.uk, Goodge Street tube) at 196 Tottenham Court Road or the adjacent branch of Habitat (☎ 020-7631 3880, 💻 www.habitat.co.uk).

Carnaby Street

For many years the pedestrianised Carnaby Street and its satellites offered little but shabby souvenir shops and jeans chains, surviving on the strength of their almost mythical past in the swinging '60s, but lately more interesting outlets have begun to appear again. Carnaby Street itself is still dominated by tatty 'fashion' boutiques and Soccer Scene (☎ 020-7439 0778, 💻 www.soccerscene.co.uk, Oxford Circus tube), 'Europe's leading football store', on the corner with Great Marlborough Street, while at 22a Conduit Street there's Rigby & Peller (☎ 020-7491 4242, 💻 www.rigbyandpeller.com, Oxford Circus tube), corsetieres to HM the Queen. If you're tired of making do with badly fitting, off-the-peg underwear, splash out in royal style and have your 'protruding bits' expertly corralled into shape by friendly, understanding assistants.

Old & New Bond Street

Old Bond Street and New Bond Street (Bond Street or Green Park tube) and their tributaries make up much of the Mayfair district. This is the home turf of the seriously rich and almost every major fashion designer has a foothold in the area. If your credit cards will take it, visit Browns (☎ 020-7514 0052) at 23–27 South Molton Street, Comme des Garçons (☎ 020-7493 1258) at 59 Brook Street, Nicole Farhi (☎ 020-7499 8368, 💻 www.nicolefahri.com) at 158 New Bond Street, Fenwick's (☎ 020-7629 9161, 💻 www.fenwick.co.uk) at 63 New Bond Street, Gucci (☎ 020-7629 2716, 💻 www.gucci.com) at 32/33 Old Bond Street, Joseph (☎ 020-7629 3713, 💻 www.joseph.co.uk) at 23 Old Bond Street, Vivienne Westwood (☎ 020-7629 3757, 💻 www.viviennewestwood.com) at 6 Davies Street or Donna Karan (☎ 020-7495 3100) at 19 New Bond Street – its sister store DKNY (☎ 020-7499 6238, 💻 www.dkny.

com), selling trendier and slightly cheaper clothes, is at 27 Old Bond Street.

For accessories, Watches of Switzerland (☎ 020-7493 5916, 🖳 www.watches-of-switzerland.co.uk) at 16 New Bond Street is worth a visit if you're after an elegant (and, needless to say, expensive) timepiece, while fine jewellery and silverware can be found at Asprey & Garrard (☎ 020-7493 6767, 🖳 www.asprey-garrard.com), the royal jewellers, at 167 New Bond Street, Cartier (☎ 020-7290 5150, 🖳 www.cartier.com) at 40-41 Old Bond Street or Tiffany & Co (☎ 020-7409 2790, 🖳 www.tiffany.com) at 25 Old Bond Street (all Green Park or Piccadilly Circus tube). Slightly less stratospherically priced jewellery can be found at the Electrum Gallery (☎ 020-7629 6325) at 21 South Molton Street, where over 100 designers sell their wares.

Mulberry (☎ 020-7491 3900, 🖳 www.mulberry.com) at 41-42 New Bond Street is the place to go for exclusive leather bags and accessories, or you might prefer the hand-made leather goods at Osprey in St Christopher's Place (☎ 020-7935 2824, 🖳 www.Osprey-London.com). Sotheby's (☎ 020-7295 5000, 🖳 www.sothebys.com), the world-famous auction house, can be found at 34 New Bond Street.

London auction houses are much more than places to buy fine art and antiques, and are a great chance to view a treasure trove of items and experience the excitement of an auction. Members of the public are free to attend auctions to see what's on sale and watch (and join in) the bidding. You must register beforehand if you want to bid and can also leave a absentee bid or bid by telephone or even bid online. There are three main auction houses in London: Bonhams (☎ 020-7447 7447, 🖳 www.bonhams.com), Christie's (☎ 020-7839 9060, 🖳 www.christies.com) and Sotheby's (☎ 0800-813 59681, 🖳 www.sothebys.com).

Piccadilly

Piccadilly (which is a street, not a district) can be said to be part of Mayfair, although it's at the less salubrious end. It's home to several notable shops. The ground floor of Fortnum & Mason is London's food store *par excellence*, containing a cornucopia of mouth-watering goodies from around the world, from truffles to pickled walnuts. Fortnum's food hampers are internationally famous and are despatched around the globe. Fashionable clothes can be found upstairs.

Hatchards at 187 Piccadilly (☎ 020-7439 9921, 🖳 www.hatchards.co.uk, Piccadilly Circus tube) was an independent bookshop for two centuries from 1797, but is now owned by Waterstone's (☎ 020-7851 2400, 🖳 www.waterstones.com), who have their flagship outlet at the former Simpsons store at no. 203–206, reputedly the largest bookshop in Europe.

Near Piccadilly Circus at 24–36 Lower Regent Street, Lillywhites (☎ 0870-333 9600, Piccadilly Circus tube) has six floors of sportswear and equipment, while the quirky Burlington Arcade (🖳 www.burlington-arcade.co.uk, Piccadilly Circus tube) is at no. 7/8. A Grade II listed arcade built in 1819 with a glass canopy and shops with Regency-style mahogany fronts, Burlington Arcade is famous for quality leather goods, bespoke shoes, antique and contemporary jewellery, cashmere and perfumes – and its wealthy clientele – not to mention its patrolling 'beadles' in period costume.

Trocadero

The Trocadero (☎ 020-7439 1791, 🖳 www.londontrocadero.com, Piccadilly Circus tube) at 13 Coventry Street is about as far from the period charm of the Burlington Arcade as it's possible to get. It's a horribly tacky place – a kind of hi-tech amusement arcade with overpriced rides and, at 'Segaworld', six floors of video games designed to turn London's youth into zombies. Elsewhere in the mall you'll find yet more branches of the all-too familiar chain stores.

Zaavi (☎ 020-7439 2500, 🖳 www.zavvi.co.uk, Charing Cross tube) at 1 Piccadilly Circus has possibly the biggest selection of pop music in the capital, including exhaustive rock and indie sections.

St James's

Venture south of Piccadilly and you enter a time warp known as St James's. It's a world of gentlemen's clubs, bespoke tailoring shops and strange little places dedicated to traditional male 'grooming'. If this is your thing, you can order a made-to-measure suit for a modest £2,000 from a tailor such as Gieves & Hawkes (☎ 020-7434 2001, 🖥 www.gievesandhawkes. com, Monument tube) at 1 Savile Row, a made-to-measure shirt from Turnbull & Asser (☎ 020-7808 3000, 🖥 www.turnbullandasser. co.uk, Green Park tube) at 71 Jermyn Street, made-to-measure shoes from John Lobb (☎ 020-7930 3664, 🖥 www.johnlobbltd.co.uk, Green Park tube) at No. 9 and, to complete your outfit, a made-to-measure bowler or top hat from James Lock (☎ 020-7930 8874, 🖥 www.lockhatters.co.uk, Green Park tube) at 6 St James's Street.

While you're there, you may wish to have an old-fashioned shave with a 'cut-throat' razor and a high-class haircut at G. F. Trumper (☎ 020-7499 1850, 🖥 www.trumpers.com, Green Park tube), 9 Curzon Street, or buy gentleman's cologne (and perhaps a floral scent for a special lady) at Floris, 89 Jermyn Street (☎ 020-7930 2885, 🖥 www.florislondon. com, Green Park or Piccadilly Circus tube).

Soho

Nearby, but worlds away from the elegant retro of St James's and smart and expensive Mayfair, is Soho, which with its neighbouring district of Covent Garden houses some of central London's most interesting shops, including grocers' and delicatessens to whet any gourmet's appetite.

Soho is cornered by four tube stations – Tottenham Court Road, Leicester Square, Piccadilly Circus and Oxford Circus – and Soho and Covent Garden are divided by Charing Cross Road, which is the focus of the London book trade; numerous book shops can be found there selling both new and second-hand/antiquarian titles (the latter also buy books from the public). Their future is less certain since the scrapping of the Net Book Agreement in 1995 (not to mention the rise of the internet), as major booksellers can now discount books and there are fears that they will gradually price the smaller independent shops out of the market. Try Blackwell's (☎ 020-7292 5100, 🖥 www.blackwell.co.uk, Tottenham Court Road tube) at 100 Charing Cross Road or the endearingly chaotic Foyles (☎ 020-7434 1580, 🖥 www.foyles.co.uk, Tottenham Court Road tube) at 119 Charing Cross Road, staffed by eccentric assistants who arrange books by publisher rather than author or subject.

If it's second-hand books you're after, try the excellent Henry Pordes (☎ 020-7836 9031, 🖥 www.henrypordesbooks.com, Leicester Square tube) at 58–60 Charing Cross Road and Quinto (☎ 020-7379 7669, 🖥 www.quinto.co.uk, Leicester Square tube) at no. 48a. Specialist bookshops in this quarter include Grant & Cutler (☎ 020-7734 2012, 🖥 www.grantandcutler.com, Oxford Circus tube) at 55–57 Great Marlborough Street, the best bookshop in London for foreign-language books, Murder One (☎ 020-7734 3483, 🖥 www.murderone. co.uk, Leicester Square tube) at 76–78 Charing Cross Road, which specialises in genre books (whodunits, science-fiction, fantasy, horror and romance), Forbidden Planet (☎ 020-7420 3666, 🖥 www. forbiddenplanet. com, Leicester Square tube) at 179 Shaftesbury Avenue, which carries a vast range of adult

2480, Leicester Square or Piccadilly Circus tube) at 52 Old Compton Street, one of London's oldest wholesale merchants, and choose from over 40 coffees. If you're after something stronger, try The Vintage House off-licence (☎ 020-7437 5112, 🖥 www.algcoffee.co.uk, Leicester Square tube) 42 0ld Compton Street. Italian salami, pasta and oils are on sale at I. Camisa & Son (☎ 020-7437 7610, Leicester Square or Piccadilly Circus tube) at 6 Old Compton Street.

There's also plenty of 'glad rags' on offer here: try American Retro (☎ 020-7734 3477, 🖥 www.americanretro.com, Leicester Square tube) at 35 Old Compton Street for themed fashion and quirky bits and pieces, or Paradiso (☎ 020-7287 2487, Oxford Circus tube) at no. 41 for fetish-wear in PVC, rubber and leather! Prowler (☎ 020-7734 4031, 🖥 www.prowlerdirect.co.uk, Piccadilly Circus tube) at 5–7 Brewer Street is a 'gay lifestyle' shop, selling everything from clothes to books and videos. It even has its own travel agency.

comic books and magazines, and Stanford's (☎ 020-7836 1321, 🖥 www.stanfords.co.uk, Covent Garden or Leicester Square tube), the map and travel book specialists at 12–14 Long Acre.

Soho proper – or rather improper – is known first and foremost as the capital of London's sex industry, with public call boxes littered with prostitutes' business cards and walk-up flats advertising the attractions of 'new young models'. There are also sex shows, hostess bars, triple-X cinemas and sex shops aplenty, mostly around the area west of Wardour Street, home of London's film and advertising industries. There's also a thriving gay scene, based around the pubs and bars of Old Compton Street, which has some fine, long-established specialist shops.

Catering to appetites of a rather more sophisticated kind are Soho's many specialist food (and drink) shops. Stop off at the Algerian Coffee Store (☎ 020-7437

Interesting little shops abound in Brewer Street, such as Anything Left-handed (☎ 020-8770 3722, 🖥 www.anythingleft-handed.co.uk, Piccadilly Circus tube), which sells everything from scissors and knives to pens and potato peelers in 'sinister' versions, and the Vintage Magazine Shop (☎ 020-7439 8525, 🖥 www.vinmag.com) at nos. 39–43, selling collectables and memorabilia as well as magazines relating to the cinema and the theatre.

The area around Gerrard Street is London's Chinatown, where you can find some of the best Chinese food shops and restaurants in Britain. Two of the best places to buy exotic ingredients are Loon Fung (☎ 020-7437 7179, 🖥 www.loonfung.co.uk) at nos. 42–44 and New Loon Moon (☎ 020-7734 3887) at no. 9 (both Piccadilly Circus tube).

When it comes to Chinese restaurants, you're spoiled for choice, but for an authentic experience go to one that's full of Chinese rather than 'foreigners'.

Recording studios, music shops and rehearsal spaces are concentrated in Denmark Street, where the biggest and most important shop is World of Music (☎ 020-7836 4656, Tottenham Court Road tube) at no. 21-22. Here you can buy almost anything connected with music – instruments, recording and playback equipment and sheet music. If you're a guitarist, you cannot afford to miss Andy's Guitar Centre and Workshop (☎ 020-7916 5080, 💻 www.andysguitarnet.com) at no. 27, which specialises in electric and acoustic guitars and also does repairs. Nearby Turnkey Soho Soundhouse (☎ 020-7379 6766, 💻 www.turnkey.co.uk, Tottenham Court Road tube) at 114–116 Charing Cross Road stocks studio and computer-based musical equipment.

Soho also has some independent record stores (although not as many as it used to have), so if you're tired of the stranglehold exerted by the mainstream giants, HMV and Zaavi, this is the place to go. There are too many to list here, but some of the best are Ray's Jazz (☎ 020-7440 3205) at Foyles bookshop (see above), Black Market (☎ 020-7437 0478, Tottenham Court Road tube) at 25 D'Arblay Street for hip-hop and rap, and Sister Ray (☎ 020-7734 3297, 💻 www.sisterray. co.uk, Piccadilly Circus tube) at 94 Berwick Street for indie.

Soho has a fruit and vegetable market in Berwick Street (Leicester Square or Tottenham Court Road tube), offering some of the lowest prices in central London. You can also get good fish, cheeses, herbs and spices there. If you're after some superior bangers to go with your mash, head for Simply Sausages (☎ 020-7329 3227, 💻 www.simplesausages. com) at 341 Central Markets.

Covent Garden

On the other side of Charing Cross Road, Covent Garden (Covent Garden tube) has become the home of small, idiosyncratic retailers, although the mainstream is beginning to make itself felt here, as everywhere else. The Piazza, the pedestrianised site of the old fruit and vegetable market near the Opera House, is the place to go if you're looking for upmarket souvenirs, superior toiletries or designer nick-knacks.

You can also browse through the interesting Apple Market in the disused market halls for crafts and clothes, or the Jubilee Market containing cheaper goods aimed mainly at tourists. Both markets change on Mondays, when the stalls are given over to antiques and collectables.

Also pedestrianised, the Neal Street area is the place for anything 'alternative', such as whole food, ethnic arts and crafts and esoterica. The midnight-blue-fronted Astrology Shop (☎ 020-7497 1001, 💻 www. londonastrology.co.uk) at 78 Neal Street has plenty for fans of esoterica, as does Mysteries (☎ 020-7240 3688), one of the best 'new age' shops in the capital, at 9-11 Monmouth Street. Kids will love Benjamin Pollock's Toy Shop (☎ 020-7379 7866, 💻 www.pollocks-coventgarden.co.uk) at 44 The Market, which is full of traditional toys. Kaleido at 11 Long Acre (☎ 020-7836 3444) sells mostly silver jewellery, with some gold and platinum items. If you're into conservation, head for the Natural Shoe Store (☎ 020-7836 5254, 💻 www. thenaturalshoestore.com) at 21 Neal Street, where everything has been produced without cruelty to animals or environmental damage, or go to Birkenstock (☎ 020-7240 2783, 💻 www. birkenstock.co.uk) at no. 37, the only London store to stock the full range of Birkenstock footwear.

Long Acre offers minimalist Japanese store Muji (☎ 020-7379 0820, 💻 www.muji.co.uk) at no. 135 and Stanford's (see above) but is otherwise packed with chain stores and other run-of-the-mill shops.

Southampton Street, which leads to the Strand, has several camping and outdoor shops, while Floral Street is full of independent retailers selling nightlife clothes – try Robot (☎ 020-7836 6156, 💻 www.robotshoeslondon. co.uk) at no. 37 and Agnes B (☎ 020-7379 1992, 💻 www.agnesb.com) at no. 35/36.

Fine foods, cookware and cosmetics can also be found in Covent Garden. Neal's Yard Dairy (☎ 020-7240 5700, 💻 www. nealsyarddairy.co.uk) at 17 Shorts Gardens sells mature farmhouse cheeses, chutneys and breads. For stylish pots and pans, look no further than the Elizabeth David Cookshop at 3a North Row. Finally, to get rid of the London grime, Lush (☎ 020-7240 4570, 🖳 www.lush.co.uk) on the Piazza has environmentally friendly cosmetics and soaps.

WEST LONDON

The West End ends at Marble Arch, where Hyde Park begins. South of the park is an area running down to the river that includes the fashionable shopping centres of Knightsbridge, Kensington and Chelsea.

Knightsbridge

Like Mayfair, Knightsbridge is an upper-crust area servicing the rich of Belgravia. It's here that you'll find the 'world's most famous department store', Harrods (☎ 020-7730 1234, 🖳 www.harrods.com, Knightsbridge tube), at 87 Brompton Road. Harrod's started life as a humble family grocer's in the 19th century; 150 years later (having, like Woolworth's, lost its apostrophe) it's rated the third most popular tourist attraction in London.

Harrods has been owned for some years by the controversial Egyptian businessman Mohammed Fayed, whose son died in the same car crash as the Princess of Wales, and who reputedly rules the store with a rod of iron, turning away customers whose costume is deemed too revealing (don't wear shorts or crop-tops!).

Harrods has a reputation as the 'top people's store' (a clever *double entendre*), where you can buy all the world's best brands under one roof, and it claims to be able to obtain virtually anything. Even if you don't (or cannot afford to) buy anything, the Food Hall is a must-see.

Almost as interesting as Harrods is Harvey Nichols (☎ 020-7235 5000, 🖳 www.harveynichols.com, Knightsbridge tube) at 109–125 Knightsbridge. This is another decidedly upmarket department store, concentrating on fashion and food, although

the fifth-floor bar is known to be something of a pick-up joint.

Like Mayfair, Knightsbridge boasts some of London's smartest fashion boutiques. At its western end, towards Kensington, are all the designer names that you don't find in Bond Street – in Sloane Street, Beauchamp Place and Brompton Road. Check out Jean-Paul Gaultier (☎ 020-7584 4648, 🖳 www.jeanpaul-gaultier.com, South Kensington tube) at 171 Draycott Avenue, Issey Miyake (☎ 020-7581 3760, 🖳 www.isseymiyake.co.uk, South Kensington tube) at 270 Brompton Road, MaxMara (☎ 020-7235 7941, Knightsbridge tube) at 32 Sloane Street and Betty Jackson (☎ 020-7589 7884, 🖳 www.bettyjackson.com, South Kensington tube) at 311 Brompton Road. For beautiful Chinese and Indian designs, visit Egg (☎ 020-7235 9315, 🖳 www.eggtrading.com, Knightsbridge tube) at 36/37 Kinnerton Street, and for exotic underwear that flatters rather than flattens, you need Janet Reger (☎ 020-7584 9368, 🖳 www.janetreger-online.com) at 2 Beauchamp Place or Agent Provocateur (☎ 020-7235 0229, 🖳 www.agentprovocateur.com) at 16 Pont Street (both Knightsbridge tube). If you're a well built chap – either unusually tall or 'well rounded' – you can find clothes to fit at High & Mighty (☎ 020-7752 0665, 🖳 www.highandmighty.co.uk, Knightsbridge tube) at 81–83 Knightsbridge.

Kensington

Kensington has plenty for shopaholics of all persuasions. Kensington High Street (High Street Kensington tube) features a parade of unusual clothes shops, including Kookai (☎ 020-7938 1427, 🖳 www.kookai.com) at no. 125 and the Urban Outfitters (☎ 020-7761 1001, 🖳 www.urbanoutfitter.co.uk) at nos. 36–38. The original Kensington Market has closed but there's a new market on Kensington Church Street. A short stroll away at 1–22 Church Street is Amazon (☎ 020-7937 4692) – no, not a real-world outpost of the famous internet retailer but a clothing outlet selling at cut-to-the-bone prices.

Chelsea

The King's Road, like Carnaby Street, owes much of its cachet to the '60s and '70s. However, unlike the tatty, touristy West End

street (see above), the King's Road (always uttered with the article, though marked simply King's Road on maps) still a living part of London where fashion victims can be seen prancing and preening (especially on Saturdays). When the swingers and hippies departed, the peacock punks moved in and, like a long-surviving pop star, the street has succeeded in repeatedly reinventing itself to move with the times.

The King's Road stretches from the upmarket Sloane Square ('home' of the so-called Sloane Rangers – young, upper class females with traditionally trendy outfits and cut glass accents) at one end to the World's End pub at the other, before becoming the New King's Road and continuing to Putney Bridge.

At the posh end visit the department store Peter Jones (☎ 020-7730 3434, 🖥 www.peterjones.co.uk) in Sloane Square or, if you have fashion-conscious children, at Trotters (☎ 020-7259 9620, 🖥 www.trotters.co.uk) at 34 King's Road, which even has a children's library. Try the CM Store (☎ 020-7351 9361) at no. 121 for trendy club-wear or Steinberg & Tolkien (☎ 020-7376 3660) at no. 193 for quality second-hand togs.

Further down you can visit World's End at no. 430, once the notorious punk emporium Sex, where Vivienne Westwood's outrageous outfits sold by the truckload in the mid-'70s. Despite her recent conversion to *haute couture*, she still sells some of her 'low' clobber from this address. At 49–51 Old Church Street you can find marvellous shoes at Manolo Blahnik (☎ 020-7352 8622, 💻 www.manoloblahnik. com, Sloane Square tube, then take a cab or catch a no. 11, 19 or 22 bus). The nearest tube station for all of the above is Sloane Square.

The King's Road isn't only about clothing. If it's antiques you're after, there's also plenty of choice, one of the most interesting establishments being Antiquarius (☎ 020-7823 3900 💻 www.antiquarius.co.uk, Sloane Square tube) at no. 131–141.

Even further into west London, at 42 Westbourne Grove (Bayswater or Queensway tube), is Planet Organic (☎ 020-7727 2227, 💻 www.planetorganic.com), one of London's best organic supermarkets, with a butcher, fresh fish counter, juice bar and 'miles' of fresh produce and groceries, all produced without the aid of nasty chemicals.

Notting Hill is famous for its carnival and for the Portobello Road Market (💻 www. portobelloroad.co.uk), which has expanded and flourished in recent years and now caters for both the local 'trustafarians' (rich kids living off their trust funds) and the genuinely impecunious. Portobello (Ladbrook Grove tube) is really several markets rolled into one: at the top end it sells bygones and collectibles, including quality antiques at 'reasonable' prices (at least compared with the fancy antique

emporiums in other parts of London); further down, there's a fruit and veg market; and at the bottom end (which disappears under Westway) you'll find clothes, jewellery, books and music. The market starts slowly at around 5.30 each morning, when professional antique dealers trade among themselves. Most traders arrive between 6.30 and 8.30am, and by 10am the street is bustling. Some traders shut up shop after lunch but many stay until late afternoon.

If you're after some cutting-edge fashion, try The Dispensary (☎ 020-7221 9290, 💻 www. thedispensarylondon.co.uk, Notting Hill Gate tube) at 25 Pembridge Road.

CITY & EAST LONDON

City of London shopping is geared to the moneyed yuppies heading for burnout on the trading floors and in the merchant banks of the financial quarter. There's an abundance of fancy shops selling silk ties, flashy accessories, classy shirts and luxury chocolates. However, there's also more down-to-earth shopping, and the redeveloped Liverpool Street Station, with its quality chain stores and food outlets (including an amazing cheese shop), is a good place to start while you're waiting for your train home (but don't buy Stinking Bishop if you have a long journey on a hot day ahead of you).

Harrods, Knightsbridge

If you're choosier, spend your lunch hour at Spitalfields Market in Brushfield Street (Liverpool Street tube), where organic foods are on sale alongside jewellery and clothes. There's also a fashion market every Thursday at which young designers exhibit their wares. On Sundays from 9am to 2pm, Petticoat Lane Market in Middlesex Street (Aldgate or Aldgate East tube) is more of a tourist attraction but still worth a look, while if you're after good household goods go on a weekday pilgrimage to Leather Lane Market (Chancery Lane tube). For unusual and antique jewellery, try Beau Gems

(☎ 020-7929 7060, 🖳 www.beaugems.co.uk, Bank tube) at 33 Leadenhall Market, EC3V.

The East End (more or less as depicted on the interminable TV soap opera, Eastenders) offers a shopping experience of an altogether earthier nature. Try Brick Lane Market (Aldgate East or Shoreditch tube), which sells fruit and veg as well as cheap clothes and household goods from 8am to 1pm. The further east you go from Brick Lane into Cheshire Street, the tattier the market becomes – although if it's East End authenticity you're seeking, you'll certainly find it there. Another East End market worth visiting is Walthamstow Market (Walthamstow Central tube), reputedly Europe's longest street market, with some 300 shops and 450 stalls, open Mondays to Saturdays from 8am to 6pm.

NORTH LONDON

Like the East End, North London has an atmosphere quite unlike the sophistication and glitz of much of the West End.

Bloomsbury

Bloomsbury forms the (unofficial) border between central and north London and is the traditional centre for academic and specialist shops, perhaps because of the presence of the British Museum and much of London University. It becomes more rundown as it stretches north into the seedy red-light district of King's Cross, where prostitutes and drug dealers have traditionally plied their desperate trades, although the area is improving quickly, mainly thanks to nearby St Pancras station becoming the London terminus for the Channel Tunnel Link scheme in late 2007.

Bloomsbury contains many fascinating little specialist book shops, including Bookmarks (☎ 020-7637 1848, 🖳 www.bookmarks. uk.com, Tottenham Court Road tube) at 1 Bloomsbury Street, which specialises in left-wing literature, and Gay's The Word (☎ 020-7278 7654, Russell Square tube) at 66 Marchmont Street.

Towards Euston, army surplus and militaria can be found at the chaotic Laurence Corner (☎ 020-7813 1010, 🖳 www.laurencecorner. co.uk, Warren Street tube) at 62 Hampstead Road, while devotees of African music will enjoy Stern's African Record Centre (☎ 020-7387 5550, 🖳 www.sternsmusic.com, Warren Street tube) at 293 Euston Road.

Camden Town

Further north, Camden Town is a bustling bohemian area full of aspiring actors, musicians, artists and misfits. It's most famous for the Camden Market, which stretches from Camden High Street to Chalk Farm Road (Camden Town tube). It's actually several markets: the covered section (Thursdays to Sundays only) is where you can find rare records and interesting clothes; the fruit and veg market in Inverness Street is open daily except Sundays; at Camden Lock there are arts and crafts, jewellery and clothes, although not all shops and stalls are open or even there during the early part of the week – go between Wednesdays and Sundays for the best choice; and The Stables is the flea market with the cheapest stalls of all, where the Electric Ballroom opens its doors to a jewellery and alternative clothing market on Sundays.

> ☑ SURVIVAL TIP
>
> If you find shopping stressful rather than pleasurable, visit Oddballs Juggling, Kites & Skates (☎ 020-7284 4488, 🖳 www.oddballs. co.uk, Camden tube) at Camden Lock, where you'll find any number of colourful ways to take your mind off it.

Hampstead & Highgate

Hampstead is a sophisticated, well-heeled quarter just north of Camden, where the natives are largely middle-class intelligentsia and media types. When you aren't walking on the still-charming heath or visiting the famous Cemetery, browse along the High Street with its arty little eateries – try the Louis Patisserie at no. 32 for its fabulously sticky cakes – and fashion boutiques. In neighbouring Highgate, stock up on intellectual property at Fisher & Sperr (☎ 020-8340 7244) at no. 46, a second-hand bookshop specialising in books about London.

Islington

Along with Hampstead, Islington is one of the habitats of the 'chattering classes': possessed of too much money and too many opinions. Consequently, many of the shops in the area cater to refined or specialised tastes. If your sartorial preferences veer some way from the mainstream, Regulation (☎ 020-7226 0665, 🖥 www.regulation-london.co.uk, Angel tube) at 17a St Albans Place is reputedly one of the capital's foremost suppliers of fetish-wear and industrial clothing. Or, if you're into taxidermy, try Get Stuffed (☎ 020-7226 1364, 🖥 www.thegetstuffed.co.uk, Angel tube) at 105 Essex Road, where 'petrified' wildlife of every description can be found.

SOUTH LONDON

South London is often portrayed as a cultural and shopping desert but, although parts of its outer suburbs are indeed dull and ordinary, there are some treasures to be found among the dross. Immediately south of the river, the South Bank area has much to recommend it shopping-wise. The Oxo Tower in Barge House Street (Blackfriars or Waterloo tube – and then a good walk) is a complex of retail studios selling 'the best in UK contemporary design' from Tuesdays to Sundays. It has an expensive restaurant (☎ 020-7803 3888) on the top floor with wonderful views across the Thames. Gabriel's Wharf is good for similarly unusual crafts; check out Ganesha (☎ 020-7928 3444, 🖥 www.ganesha.co.uk) at no. 3, which sells vibrant, hand-crafted, Indian textiles and crafts, rugs and hand-stitched wall-hangings.

In the wilds of Waterloo, at 87 Lower Marsh, is Radio Days (☎ 020-7928 0800, 🖥 www.radiodaysvintage.co.uk), with its stock of '50s memorabilia, collectables, books, magazines and posters. At the back of the shop is Masquerade, a shop within a shop, selling second-hand retro clothing. If you're in the area on a Friday or Saturday, don't miss Borough market (London Bridge tube), one of the best – and most popular – farmers' markets in London, where you can stock up on everything from organic cider to French cheeses. In the One World Shop (☎ 020-7401 8909, 🖥 www.oneworldshop.co.uk) at St John's Church, Waterloo Road, you can buy goods from the developing world, including Tanzanian honey, Central American coffee, Lombok pottery tableware and Indonesian silver jewellery, plus crafted toys, T-shirts and Christmas cards.

Greenwich (Greenwich rail) has much more than museums and the Observatory: a tangle of markets tempts the shopper, including a good antiques market on Thursdays in Greenwich High Road, a central covered market selling hand-made crafts (Fridays to Sundays) and a Sunday flea market on Thames Street.

Further south, Brixton Market in Electric Avenue (Brixton tube) is loved by outsiders, but many local residents think it's overrated. Brixton boasts a large West Indian community, and the food on offer reflects this: plantain, breadfruit, strange varieties of fish, exotic herbs and incense. There are also second-hand clothes and bric-a-brac stalls at the east end of the market proper and some interesting shops – check out Alltone Records (🖥 www.alltone.co.uk) for dancehall, dub and reggae. If you like fun retro gifts and clothes, take a look at Joy (☎ 020-7326 5700) on Coldharbour Lane, where you'll find lava lamps, glitter balls, movie star cufflinks and a host of other items of dubious taste.

INTERNET SHOPPING

Shopping on the internet is becoming ever more popular and it's expected that Britons will spend on average of over £1,000 online in 2008. There are numerous shopping site portals, including 🖥 www.shopguide.co.uk, 🖥 www.virginmedia.com, which provides a good directory of British sites, and 🖥 www.shopping.net. One of the best bargain websites is 🖥 www.buy.com, which offers over 10,000 electronic items at discount prices and has forced UK high street retailers to cut theirs. Other useful sites include 🖥 www.onlineclothesshops.co.uk and price comparison sites such as 🖥 www.computerprices.co.uk, 🖥 www.pricechecker.co.uk, 🖥 www.bookbrain.co.uk, 🖥 www.cameratag.co.uk and 🖥 www.pricetracker.co.uk (for video-games).

With internet shopping, the world is very much your oyster and savings can be made on a wide range of goods, including CDs, clothes, sports equipment, electronic gadgets, jewellery, books, wine, computer software, and services such as insurance, pensions and mortgages. Huge savings can also be made on holidays and travel. Small high-price, high-tech items (e.g. cameras, watches and portable computers) can usually be bought more cheaply somewhere else in Europe or (more likely) in the US, with delivery by courier within as little as three days. However, take into account shipping costs, import duty and VAT, which may wipe out much of your savings. Although shopping via the internet is generally secure (see 🖥 http://en.wikipedia.org/wiki/internet_security), research has shown that your credit card details are more likely to be stolen when shopping online than when shopping by phone or mail order.

Buying Overseas

When buying goods overseas, ensure that you're dealing with a bona fide company and that the goods will work in the UK. If possible, pay by credit card when buying over the internet (or by mail-order) because, for bills between £100 and £30,000, the credit card issuer is usually jointly liable with the supplier under the Consumer Credit Act 1974. When you buy expensive goods abroad, always have them insured for their full value during shipping.

VAT & Duty

When buying overseas, take into account shipping costs, duty and VAT. There's no duty or tax on goods purchased within the European Union or on goods from most other countries worth up to £145. Don't buy alcohol or cigarettes abroad, as the duty is usually too high to make it cost-effective. When VAT or duty is payable on a parcel, the payment is usually collected by the post office or courier company on delivery.

12.
ODDS & ENDS

This chapter contains miscellaneous information of interest to anyone planning to live or work in London. Subjects covered include climate, crime, government, monarchy, police, pets, postal services, telephone, television and radio. For further details of these – and of other topics covered in this book – see our sister publication *Living and Working in Britain* by David Hampshire (Survival Books).

CLIMATE

Like the rest of the UK, London has a temperate climate, with few extremes of temperature or climatic excesses, such as tornadoes or hurricanes. It's often damp and the weather can (and frequently does) change rapidly. The least hospitable months are November to February, when it's often chilly and the days are short – it can be dark by 3.30pm. Although temperatures sometimes drop below freezing in winter, particularly at night, it's rarely freezing during the day, and average winter daytime temperatures are around 6°C (43°F). The most unpleasant features of British winters are fog and ice, which make driving hazardous. However, the 'pea-soup' fog that was more often caused by pollution than climate, and which many foreigners still associate with London, is thankfully a thing of the past.

April to September are the best months, with July and August the warmest. Spring is generally the most pleasant time of year, although early spring is often very wet. Summer temperatures average around 22°C (72°F) and sometimes rise above 30°C (86°F). Average daytime temperatures in April and October are 13–14°C (55–57°F).

Rain is fairly evenly distributed throughout the year (many Londoners carry an umbrella at all times), although the wettest month is usually November, with average rainfall between 40mm and 60mm per month. The worst aspect of British weather is the frequent drizzle (light rain) and grey skies, particularly in winter. This has given rise to a condition known as 'seasonal affective disorder' (SAD), which is brought on by the dark, dull days of winter – particularly after the festive Christmas period – and causes lethargy, fatigue and low spirits. However, there's some good news: British winters are becoming milder and in recent years have been nothing like as severe as in earlier decades, although whether this is a long-term change is unclear. In fact, British weather is becoming warmer all round, recent years experiencing some of the driest summers since records began in 1659.

> 2003 saw the highest temperatures on record, exceeding 38°C (100°F) in north Kent (on London's doorstep).

To add some spice to the usual diet of grey skies and drizzle, in recent years the UK has been afflicted by gales and torrential rain (including the infamous storms of 1987 and 1990), which caused severe damage and flooding in many areas. Tornadoes also occur in the UK, but are extremely rare and usually cause little damage.

Weather forecasts are available in daily newspapers, via premium-rate telephone numbers, the internet, and TV and radio (usually after the news). Warnings of dangerous weather conditions, e.g. high winds, fog and ice, are broadcast regularly on BBC national and local radio stations. The most detailed weather forecasts are on BBC Radio 2 and BBC Radio 4, the latter also providing weather forecasts for shipping (good for insomniacs). During the early summer, when pollens are released in large quantities, the pollen count is given on radio and TV weather forecasts and in daily newspapers.

CRIME

Overall, the number of reported crimes has fallen over the last decade in London, where the risk of being a victim of crime is around the European average, although some believe this is because people report less crime, considering it a waste of time (in some areas, 95 per cent of crimes are unsolved). The level of street crime (where men under 30 are most at risk) is higher than official figures suggest – around four times higher, according to some estimates. The number of violent crimes in the UK – and particularly in London, where around 20 per cent of the UK's crime takes place – has increased. There are now around 800 murders a year in the UK (around 150 in London), which is nevertheless fewer per capita than in most other European countries, and you're more likely to choke to death on your food than you are to meet a violent end.

Many crimes are drug-related and committed by and between gangs. The use of hard drugs (particularly cocaine) is a major problem in London, where gangs increasingly use guns to settle their differences. Nearly half of London street crime is committed by cocaine addicts, and some 40 per cent of UK gun crime is committed in London (around 30 people are shot dead in London each year in drug-related incidents). The perceived failure of the government and the police to deal with juvenile crime (parents are rarely held responsible) is one of the most serious social issues in the UK, and particularly in London, where many children are totally out of control by the age of ten or even younger.

Crimes against property are also a problem, particularly burglary, theft of cars and theft from cars. In London, professional thieves even steal antique paving stones, railings, doors and door frames, plus any valuable metals that can be recycled.

Fraud or so-called 'white-collar' crime (which includes credit card fraud and income tax and VAT evasion) in the UK costs billions of pounds a year and accounts for larger sums than the total of all robberies, burglaries and thefts added together.

Although the foregoing catalogue of crime may paint a depressing picture, London is generally a safe place to live, and you can walk around most parts of London day or night, although the police warn people (particularly young women) against venturing alone in unlit and deserted areas at night. If you take care of your property and take sensible precautions against crime, your chances of becoming a victim are small. Note, however, that the crime rate varies considerably from area to area, and anyone planning on living in London should avoid high crime areas whenever possible.

The Metropolitan Police publishes annual crime statistics for each borough, indicating the number of crimes of various types committed each month. These can be found on 🖥 www.met.police.uk/crimefigues/datatable. The table in **Appendix F** shows the statistics for the 12 months to February 2008 in the 32 London boroughs. There are no comparable statistics for the City of London, which has its own police force (see **Police** on page 278).

GOVERNMENT

The UK is a constitutional monarchy, under which the country is governed by ministers of the crown in the name of the sovereign (Queen Elizabeth II), who is head of both the state and the government. However, nowadays the monarchy has no real power and its duties are restricted to a ceremonial and advisory role only, although there are certain acts of government that require the participation of the sovereign, such as the opening and dissolving of parliament and the approval of parliamentary bills. See **Monarchy** on page 274.

Parliament

Parliament is the ultimate law-making authority in the UK (although the Channel Islands and the Isle of Man make their own laws on island affairs) and consists of two houses or chambers, the House of Commons and the House of Lords, which together comprise the Houses of Parliament.

The UK's democratic traditions date from 1265, when King Henry III was forced to acknowledge the first parliament, and Westminster is often referred to as the mother of parliaments, having been the model for many democracies around the world. The present parliament sits in the Palace of Westminster, which was built in the 19th century after the previous building was destroyed by fire (only Westminster Hall survived), and whose clock, known as Big Ben (actually the name of the bell which distinctively chimes the hour), is London's most famous landmark.

The House of Commons is the assembly chamber for the 646 Members of Parliament (MPs), who are commoners (i.e. not titled

people) elected by the people of the UK in general elections, which must be held every five years, unless parliament is dissolved beforehand. Each MP represents an area called a constituency, of which there are 529 in England (74 in London), 59 in Scotland, 40 in Wales and 18 in Northern Ireland.

Voting

All British, Commonwealth and Irish Republic citizens over the age of 18 and resident in the UK can vote in parliamentary elections, provided they're registered voters. To be eligible to vote, your name must appear in a register of electors maintained and updated annually (in the autumn) by councils.

> ### ⚠ Caution
>
> If you're eligible to vote but fail to register as a voter or provide false information, you can be fined up to £1,000.

Voting isn't compulsory and there's no penalty for not voting – but don't complain about the government if you don't! In fact, the turnout for British elections is often among the lowest in the world (although the turnout for general elections has been high in recent years). If you're unable to vote in person, you can do so by post or appoint a 'proxy' to vote on your behalf.

The government of the day is formed by the political party that wins the largest number of seats at a general election. If no party has the majority of seats, a coalition government may be formed between a number of parties. This is extremely rare in the UK as, unlike other countries in western Europe, it doesn't have a system of proportional representation. The candidate in each constituency who polls the most votes is declared the winner (a 'first past the post' system).

All votes cast for other candidates are disregarded, which means that a party such as the Liberal Democrats (the third force in UK politics) often receives millions of votes and ends up with just a few seats. Many people believe this system is outdated and undemocratic (particularly the Liberal Democrats), although it's difficult to see the major parties changing the system voluntarily (Labour went through the motions of investigating electoral reform on entering government in 1997, but then quietly forgot all about it).

Ministers & Members of Parliament

The head of the government is the Prime Minister, who is the leader of the party with the majority of seats (or the leader of the principal party in a coalition) and who chooses a 'cabinet' of around 20 ministers to head the various government ministries, known as Departments (education, defence, employment, foreign affairs, etc.). In addition to the cabinet, the Prime Minister appoints at least 80 'junior' ministers, of which there may be two to five in each ministry. The Leader of the Opposition, who is the head of the largest defeated party (and not part of a government coalition), appoints a 'shadow' cabinet, whose job is to respond to government ministers in Parliament on behalf of his party. MPs who are members of the cabinet or shadow cabinet sit on the front benches (on opposite sides) of the House of Commons. All other MPs are known as back benchers.

The highlight of the week in the House of Commons is Prime Minister's question time, during which MPs can question the Prime Minister, and which often becomes heated when the Prime Minister and the Leader of the Opposition trade insults. The proceedings of both houses are public (except for rare occasions involving national security) and both houses have a public gallery. Television was introduced into Parliament in 1989, although strict rules apply to coverage – primarily in order to conceal the fact that the chambers are often sparsely attended (and most of those in attendance are asleep).

> MPs hold weekly or fortnightly 'surgeries' (like doctors) in their constituencies, when constituents can visit them and discuss their problems. Constituents can also write to their MP and telephone or visit him at the House of Commons.

Political Parties

There are three main political parties in the UK: the Conservatives (also known as the Tories), Labour (or New Labour, as it prefers to be called) and the Liberal Democrats. There are a few smaller parties, most of which contest seats in particular regions or constituencies only. These include the Scottish Nationalist Party (SNP); the Ulster Unionist Party, the Democratic Unionist Party, the Social and Democratic Labour Party (SDLP) and Sinn Fein, all in Northern Ireland; Plaid Cymru (Welsh nationalists); the Green Party and the Communist Party of Great Britain (as distinct from the Communist Party, which is now defunct).

The UK has long been plagued by its predominantly two-party system, with its extremes of left (Labour) and right (Conservatives), and only the Liberal Democrats 'in between' – for whom few people were willing to vote for fear of it being a 'wasted' vote. Now, however, (New) Labour has moved so far to the right that there's little to distinguish the two main parties, the Liberal Democrats having become the left-wing alternative.

Nevertheless, the Conservatives remain – more or less – the party of big business, from which it receives the vast majority of its finances, although the funding of political parties has recently been the subject of considerable controversy and even scandal, with accusations of 'cash for honours' being levelled at both major parties. Traditionally the party of 'the workers' (i.e. the working class) and still receiving most of its funds from the trade unions, Labour has long since abandoned its belief in the public ownership of industry (nationalisation), although it continues to pay lip service to the 'needs' of the common man.

After over a decade in government, Labour still dominates the political scene, although it's currently (summer 2008) lagging well behind the Conservatives in the opinion polls.

House of Lords

The House of Lords is referred to as the 'Other Place' in the House of Commons and is the geriatric ward of the constitution, where retired MPs and a declining number of

Statue of Richard the Lionheart, Westminster

blue-blooded landowners spend their days in retirement. The Lords consists of the Lords Spiritual (archbishops and bishops) and Lords Temporal, who include a fixed number (90) of hereditary peers and peeresses, all life peers and peeresses, and the Law Lords, the precise total depending on the number of life peers the Prime Minister chooses to create to 'replace' those that die off.

Until the beginning of the 20th century, the House of Lords had extensive powers and could veto any bill submitted to it by the House of Commons. It still retains powers to block government legislation, but only temporarily – although this can sometimes have the same result in practice. It remains the highest court of appeal in the UK, with the exception of criminal cases in Scotland, but proposals to replace it with a Supreme Court are under consideration. Members of the House of Lords are unpaid, although they receive travelling and other expenses when on parliamentary business within the UK.

The House of Lords has long been considered an anachronism in the UK and has been partially reformed – until a few years ago all hereditary peers belonged to it – but currently nobody knows quite what else to do with it. It could be replaced by an elected second house (similar to the US Senate) or a completely appointed house, but the likelihood is that it will continue in it's current form for the time being.

Local Government

The administration of local affairs in the UK is performed by local authorities – collectively known as local government. In most areas of England and Wales, services are divided between two authorities, a district council and a county council. In large cities, services are usually provided by a single authority, e.g. the borough councils of London. Services include the police, fire service, libraries and museums, public transport, traffic regulation, magistrates courts, the probation service, waste disposal, highways and road safety, trading standards and personal social services. The UK's ten Strategic Health Authorities, including NHS

London, are funded by central government (see **National Health Service** on page 191).

Local government councils are organised along party political lines, although some councillors are independent. Councils elect a chairman, who in boroughs or cities has the ceremonial title of mayor. The turnout in local government elections is usually even lower than for parliamentary elections (less than 50 per cent). Voting qualifications are broadly the same as for parliamentary elections, but resident EU citizens can also participate. London borough councils hold elections every four years.

Local authority finances come from a variety of sources, including around 25 per cent from council tax (see page 123), a further 25 per cent from the uniform business rate and the remainder from central government. Local councillors are unpaid, although they can claim an allowance for attending council meetings and travel and subsistence allowances.

MONARCHY

The British royal family is the longest reigning monarchy in the world and certainly the most famous – or perhaps that should be infamous. With a brief 'hiccough' between 1649 and 1660, it has reigned continuously for a thousand years. The head of the royal family is the monarch or sovereign, Her Majesty (HM) Queen Elizabeth II, who is married to His Royal Highness (HRH) the Duke of Edinburgh, Prince Philip (son of Princess Andrew of Greece). The monarch is head of state and head of the British Commonwealth, although these are ceremonial titles without any real power. The UK is governed by HM Government in the name of the Queen (see above).

The Queen and Prince Philip have four children: Prince Charles (the Prince of Wales), who is the heir to the throne (despite having remarried a divorcee, the Duchess of Cornwall, after being divorced from the late Diana, Princess of Wales – a move initially believed to be unconstitutional); Princess

Anne (the Princess Royal), also divorced and remarried; Prince Andrew (the Duke of York), divorced from Sarah Ferguson, the Duchess of York; and Prince Edward, Earl of Wessex, who married Sophie Rhys-Jones in 1999 and has yet to divorce her.

The most popular member of the royal family 'proper' was the late Queen Elizabeth the Queen Mother, wife of King George VI, who died aged 101 in 2002. The Queen's sister, Princess Margaret (who was married to the Earl of Snowdon – formerly Anthony Armstrong-Jones), died in the same year. But even the Queen Mother was eclipsed in popularity by Diana Spencer, who married Prince Charles as a timid 20-year-old in 1981, becoming the Princess of Wales in the process, and rapidly became a national and international icon – although not in the eyes of the rest of the royal family. Her death in a controversial Paris car crash in 1997 sent a shockwave around the world.

The Queen's most important functions are ceremonial and include the state opening of Parliament; giving Royal Assent to bills; entertaining foreign dignitaries and diplomats; conferring peerages, knighthoods and other honours; appointing important office-holders; chairing meetings of the Privy Council; and sorting out family squabbles. She also attends numerous artistic, industrial, scientific and

HM Queen Elizabeth II

charitable events of both national and local interest (the Queen and other members of the royal family are patrons or honorary heads of many leading charities and organisations in the UK).

Although she was born on 21st April (1926), the Queen's birthday is celebrated in June, when the weather is usually better (although sunshine is never guaranteed in Britain), with the Trooping of the Colour ceremony on Horse Guards' Parade.

Each year the Queen and other members of the royal family visit many areas of the UK and undertake state visits and royal tours of foreign and Commonwealth countries.

Around 85 per cent of the cost of the royal family's official duties is met by public departments, including the upkeep of royal palaces and the Queen's various modes of private transport. The Queen's public expenditure on staff and the expenses incurred in carrying out her official duties are financed from the Civil List, which is approved by Parliament. Annual allowances are made in the Civil List to other members of the royal family, with the exception of the Prince of Wales, who as the Duke of Cornwall receives the net revenue of the estate of the Duchy of Cornwall. The Queen is estimated to be the richest person in the UK, although a lot of the property attributed to her actually belongs to the state.

The antics of the British royal family are the longest-running soap opera in the world and hundreds of column inches of newsprint are devoted to their 'affairs', both in the UK by the popular press, who delight in printing sensational stories about anyone famous, and abroad. Nonetheless, as the overwhelming public enthusiasm for the Queen's Golden Jubilee celebrations in 2002 showed, despite the vicissitudes of her life, she is still the subject of affection and respect.

PETS

The UK is generally regarded as a country of animal lovers and has over 14m pet owners (including some 7m dog owners). Britons' affection for their 'four-legged friends' is attested to by the number of bequests received by the Royal Society for the Prevention of Cruelty to Animals (RSPCA), which far exceeds the amount left to the Royal Society for the Prevention of Cruelty to Children (RSPCC). It's even possible (and not uncommon) in the UK for people to leave their entire estate to their pets!

The RSPCA (Wilberforce Way, Southwater, Horsham, West Sussex RH12 9RS, ☎ 0300-123455, 💻 www.rspca.org.uk) is the main organisation for animal protection and welfare in the UK and operates a number of animal clinics and welfare centres. The work of the RSPCA is complemented by the Dogs Trust (17 Wakely Street, London EC1V 7RQ, ☎ 020-7837 0006), the UK's largest dog welfare charity, which takes in lost, abandoned and abused dogs, and turns them into healthy, well adjusted pets. No healthy dog is ever destroyed by the Dogs Trust. The most famous animal shelter in London is The Dogs' Home in Battersea (popularly known as the Battersea Dogs' Home), but there are many others, including those run by the Cats' Protection League.

The British are almost uniquely sentimental about animals, even those reared for food. Protests about various forms of commercial cruelty to animals make headline news at regular intervals. Britons are also prominent in international animal protection organisations that attempt to ban cruel sports and practices in which animals are mistreated (such as bullfighting and the production of pâté de fois gras). Many Britons are also concerned about the survival of wild animals and there's even a British Hedgehog Protection Society (BHPS), although no one has yet come up with a way of teaching them to cross roads safely.

Dogs

There isn't a dog registration or licence scheme in England, Wales or Scotland, but after a series of vicious attacks on children, the British government introduced a controversial ban on the ownership of certain breeds of dog. These include pit bull terriers, Japanese tosas, dogo argentinos and fila brazilieros, all of which can no longer be imported into or bred in the UK.

Dogs that were in Britain before the ban was imposed also come under strict rules, and males must be neutered.

All of the above breeds must be registered and muzzled when in public places and if the law is broken or a dog attacks anyone, the owner is liable to a fine and the dog can be destroyed. You can be fined up to £400 (in addition to compensation) if your dog (of any breed) kills or injures livestock and a farmer can legally shoot a dog that molests farm animals.

If you're looking for a dog as a pet, a good place to start is your local rescue centre – see the Dog Pages (www.dogpages. org), the most popular dog rescue site in the UK with up to 40,000 visitors daily. Dog Pages is non-commercial and aims to encourage people to adopt one of the many thousands of dogs looking for new homes in the UK.

Quarantine

The UK has the toughest quarantine regulations in the world, to guard against the importation of rabies and other animal diseases, and has been virtually free of rabies for over 60 years. Apart from those participating in the Pet Passport Scheme (see below), mammals other than specific breeds of horses and livestock must normally spend six months in quarantine in an approved kennel to ensure they're free of rabies and Newcastle disease. Quarantine regulations also apply to guide dogs for the blind and hearing dogs. Around 5,000 dogs and 3,000 cats are quarantined each year in the UK.

If you're coming to the UK for a short period, it may not be worth the trouble and expense of bringing your pet and you may prefer to leave it with friends or relatives.

Before deciding to import an animal, check with the Department for Environment, Food and Rural Affairs (DEFRA, Customer Contact Unit, Eastbury House, 30–34 Albert Embankment, London SE1 7TL, ☎ 08459-335577, 💻 www.defra. gov.uk) for the latest regulations, application forms and a list of approved quarantine kennels and catteries.

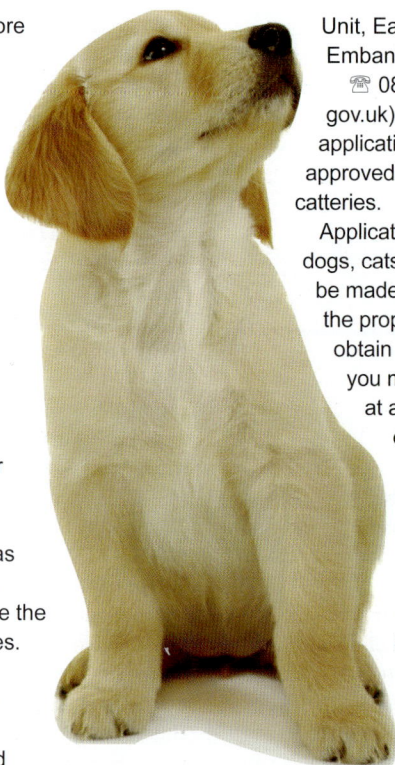

Applications for the importation of dogs, cats and other mammals should be made at least eight weeks before the proposed date of importation. To obtain a licence to import your pet, you must have a confirmed booking at an approved kennel and have enlisted the services of an authorised agent (who will transport your pet from the port to the quarantine kennels). Your pet must arrive at an approved port or airport, be transported in an approved container, available from air transport companies and pet shops, and be shipped within six months of the date specified by the licence.

The cost of quarantine is around £300 per month for a dog, depending on its size (and what it eats), and around £200 per month for a cat. You must also pay for any vaccinations and veterinary costs incurred during your pet's quarantine period. You're permitted – in fact encouraged – to visit your pet in quarantine but won't be able to take it out for exercise.

There are different regulations for some creatures. Birds, for example, serve a shorter quarantine period than animals. Pet rabbits must be inoculated against rabies and cannot be imported from the US. There's no quarantine for cold-blooded animals such as fish and reptiles, but dangerous animals (e.g. poisonous snakes) require an import licence.

Passports & Licences

The Pet Passport Scheme (PETS) enables you to bring your dog, cat, rabbit, mouse, rat, guinea pig or ferret into the UK and avoid quarantine, but only under stringently controlled conditions. Animals must come from certain countries only (and only on certain routes from those countries, and on certain specified flights, ferries or railways), be microchipped, have a 'passport' listing their vaccinations and other necessary veterinary treatments, have had an officially approved blood test not less than six months previously, and have an official PETS certificate from a government-authorised vet. Their owners must also sign a declaration that the pet hasn't been to any country not participating in the scheme (listed below) during the six months prior to their arrival in the UK. Additional demands are made on those travelling from certain countries.

Participating countries include Australia, Austria, Bahrain, Belgium, Canada, Cyprus, Denmark, Finland, France, Germany, Greece, the Netherlands, Iceland, Italy, Jamaica, Japan, Luxembourg, Malta, New Zealand, Norway, Portugal, Singapore, Spain, Sweden, Switzerland, mainland USA, the Vatican and a variety of dependent territories of European countries. However, the list changes frequently and you should check the DEFRA website (🖥 www.defra.gov.uk/animals/quarantine/index.htm) to see whether your country is covered by the scheme and the latest requirements. The site also provides general regulations relating to animal welfare while travelling.

For other domestic animals not subject to quarantine, e.g. most horses, an import licence and a veterinary examination are required. You also need a licence from your local council to keep a poisonous snake or other dangerous animal, which must be properly caged with an adequate exercise area and must pose no risk to public health and safety.

It's a criminal offence to attempt to smuggle an animal into the UK and you're unlikely not to be caught. Illegally imported animals are either exported immediately or destroyed and the owners face (and invariably receive) an unlimited fine and up to a year's imprisonment.

⚠ Caution

There's no VAT or duty on animals brought into the UK as 'personal belongings', but if you import an animal after your arrival, VAT and duty may need to be paid on its value.

Kennels & Catteries

If you don't have a friend or relative who will look after your dog or cat while you're on holiday, you must board it in a kennel or cattery. Ask friends, neighbours or colleagues if they can recommend a kennel or cattery; if they cannot help you, ask your vet. It's important not to take pot luck, as standards vary from excellent to poor. If a kennel or cattery isn't highly recommended, check it personally before boarding your pet and ask what services are charged as extras, such as grooming and medicine. Any veterinary fees incurred while the animal is boarding are charged to the owner. Dogs left at kennels may need to be vaccinated against certain diseases, although the requirements vary with the kennel. If you plan to leave your pet at a kennel or cattery, book well in advance, particularly for school holiday periods.

Vets

It isn't mandatory to have your dog (or any pet) vaccinated against any disease in the UK, although most dogs are vaccinated against a number of them, including distemper, hepatitis, and leptospirosis. After the initial primary vaccinations (fee around £20 to £50), annual boosters are necessary. You'll receive a 'record of primary and booster vaccination' from the veterinary surgeon (vet).

Before choosing a vet, shop around and compare fees. Unfortunately, London is among the most expensive places to keep a pet in the UK. A list of vets can be obtained from the Royal College of Veterinary Surgeons, Belgravia House, 62–64 Horseferry Road, London SW1P 2AF (☎ 020-7222 2001, 🖥 www.rcvs.org.uk) or the British Veterinary Association (BVA), 7 Mansfield Street, London W1G 9NQ (☎ 020-7636 6541, 🖥 www.bva.co.uk), which publishes a series of booklets on pet care. If you cannot afford a vet's fees, the People's Dispensary for Sick Animals (PSDSA), Whitechapel Way, Priorslee, Telford, Shropshire TF2 9PQ (☎ 01952-290999, 🖥 www.pdsa.org.uk) may provide free treatment. Founded in 1917, the PDSA has over 40 PetAid hospitals around the country and cares for over 350,000 pets a year.

POLICE

Britain doesn't have a national police force but 52 regional police forces (43 in England and Wales, eight in Scotland and one in Northern Ireland), each responsible for a county (or a region in Scotland) or a metropolitan area. In the case of London, there are two police forces: the City of London Police, which was formally established in 1839 and covers only the City of London, and the Metropolitan Police, which covers the rest of London. Further information can be found on 🖳 www.cityoflondon.police.uk and 🖳 www.met.police.uk respectively. There are no dedicated traffic or tourist police in the UK, all routine duties being performed by 'standard' policemen (known, officially as police constables or PCs) and policewomen (known as WPCs, for women police constables).

Police forces in England, Scotland and Wales are among the few in the world that don't carry guns (their only weapons are a truncheon and sarcasm), although in recent years an increasing number of policemen have been armed for 'special' duties, such as the prevention of terrorism and when dealing with armed suspects. This is a controversial issue, as a number of innocent people have been shot dead by police marksmen over the past decade. Some police forces have been issued with telescopic truncheons, pepper sprays and tasers, all of which can cause severe injuries if used incorrectly.

> After the deaths of a number of police officers on duty in recent years, there has been an intense debate among the police concerning the carrying of arms. However, the great majority of police officers are against routinely carrying them and many would leave the force rather than do so.

The uniform worn by police forces is generally the same throughout the UK and male police constables or PCs on the beat in England and Wales wear the famous British police helmet. Other police officers (e.g. in cars) wear a flat cap with a chequered black and white band. In addition to full-time police officers, each force has a part-time attachment of volunteer 'special constables'. Traffic wardens, who are responsible for controlling traffic and parking, come under the control of the local police force.

British policemen used to be the most respected in the world, not least by the British people. However, in recent years they've had a bad press and their reputation has been tarnished. According to a number of surveys, many people have lost faith in the integrity and efficiency of their police force. Many are unhappy about police responses when they ring 999 or their local police station, and over half the victims of crime are dissatisfied with the police response. There has been an increase in complaints against the police, many concerning prejudice, harassment, and even brutal and violent treatment. Even more worrying, a public inquiry into the handling of the 1993 murder investigation of a black teenager in London (Stephen Lawrence) found that racism was rife in the Metropolitan Police force. There are few black and Asian officers in the UK (and they're often subject to racial abuse and prejudice from their white colleagues).

The police have consistently refused to allow independent investigations of complaints, which means that successful complaints against the police are extremely rare. Most people don't even bother to complain, as they consider it a waste of time. The Independent Police Complaints Commission claims to be independent, yet its investigations are carried out by police officers. If you're seeking compensation against the police in England or Wales, you must usually seek redress in a county court. To make a complaint against a police officer, you can write to the Chief Constable of the force involved, go to any police station or write directly to the Independent Police Complaints Commission (IPCC), 5th Floor, 90 High Holborn, London WC1V 6BH (☎ 08453-002002, 🖳 www.ipcc.gov.uk).

If the foregoing catalogue of criticism has given the impression of an inherently incompetent, prejudiced and dishonest police force, it would be misleading. The UK still has one of the best police forces in the world and the majority of people rate its performance as satisfactory. What is evident is that the actions of a small minority of officers are increasingly bringing the whole force into disrepute. Unlike some countries, the British public expects its police to be above reproach and, although it may seem old-fashioned in the 21st century, are unwilling to accept anything less than absolute honesty, impartiality and efficiency.

POSTAL SERVICES

What is commonly referred to as 'the post office' in fact comprises three separate businesses: the Royal Mail, which handles letters; the Post Office, which operates post offices; and Parcelforce Worldwide (formerly Royal Mail Parcels), which handles parcels. Of some 14,000 post offices in the UK, only around 500 are operated directly by the Post Office. The remainder are franchise offices or sub-post offices, which don't offer all the services provided by a main post office and are operated on an agency basis by sub-postmasters. There are plans to partly privatise the post office – the government has already been accused of back-door privatisation with the transfer of many post offices from the high street to supermarkets, stationery stores, newsagents' and other shops. And there has been an angry reaction to the decision to close a further 2,500 post offices in 2008, mostly in rural areas where they are a lifeline for local people.

There's a post office in most London districts and suburbs, providing over 100 services, some of them unique to the UK. In addition to offering postal services, the post office acts as an agent for a number of government departments; for example, it sells road tax discs, though it no longer sells TV licences. You can also pay many bills at a post office, including electricity, gas, water, telephone, cable and mail-order bills, council tax, rent payments and housing association rents; you can even pay certain store card accounts. The post office is also a distribution centre for social security leaflets. Main branches additionally provide bureaux de change facilities (although you may need to order foreign currency) and an (expensive) international money transfer

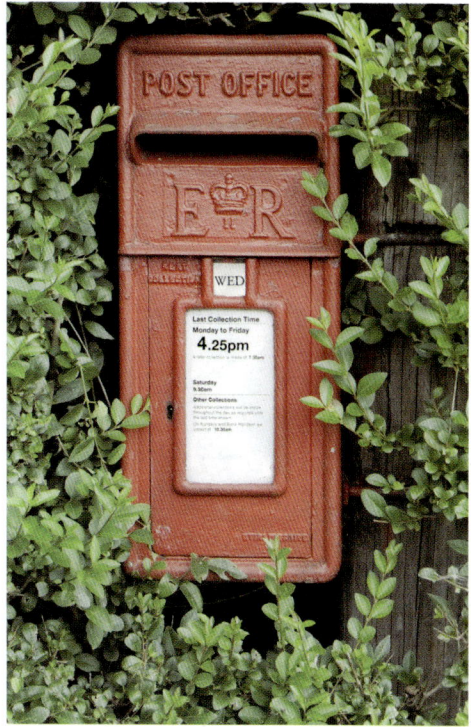

service, in conjunction with Western Union International.

The post office (founded in 1635) is the last bastion of the state-run economy, and like all nationalised companies it's over-staffed and inefficient in some areas. Despite this, it provides one of the most modern (i.e. automated) and efficient postal services in the world. However, overseas rivals are muscling in on Royal Mail services and a number of overseas groups also handle post in the UK.

Post office opening hours are usually from 9am to 5.30pm, Mondays to Fridays, and from 9am to 12.30pm on Saturdays. Sub-post offices usually close for an hour at lunchtime, e.g. 1 to 2pm, Mondays to Fridays, and they may also close one afternoon a week, usually on Wednesdays. Main post offices don't close at lunchtime. Some post offices at airports are open on Sundays and public holidays. Details of individual post offices, including their opening hours, are available from the Post Office (☎ 0845-722 3344, 💻 www.postoffice. co.uk).

If you want to receive post in London and don't have a permanent address, you can

use the *poste restante* service and have post sent to any London post office. Post is kept for a month and an identity card or passport is required to collect it.

Sending Letters

The post office provides a choice of first- and second-class domestic post delivery (further evidence of the British preoccupation with class distinctions). Domestic post covers all addresses in Great Britain, Northern Ireland, the Channel Islands and the Isle of Man. The target for the delivery of first-class post is the next working day after collection and for second-class post, the third working day after collection. Some 95 per cent of first-class post is delivered the next day. It's unnecessary to mark post as first or second class, as any item that's posted with less than first-class postage is automatically sent second class.

To ensure delivery within the UK the next day, first-class post should be posted by 5pm for the local area (e.g. a letter posted in London to another London address) or by 1pm for other parts of the UK, excluding northern Scotland – you'll be lucky if your letter ever gets there.

Airmail letters take an average of two to three days to Denmark, Norway and Switzerland and up to seven days to Italy and some other European countries (which provides a good indication of the relative efficiency – or otherwise – of European postal services). Airmail to other destinations usually takes four to seven days. Surface post takes up to two weeks to Europe and up to 12 weeks outside Europe. Underpaid airmail items may be delayed or will incur a surcharge. Leaflets are published in September, listing the latest dates by which letters and parcels cards should be posted to ensure delivery before Christmas.

Second-class domestic letter post mustn't exceed 750g, but there's no limit for first-class post. This means that packages weighing over 750g must be sent by first-class post. International letters, small packets and printed papers (both airmail and surface) are limited to a maximum of 2kg.

Domestic letters weighing up to 100g now cost 27p second class and 36p first class. The cost of sending a letter weighing up to 20g by airmail is 50p to Europe or 81p to the rest of the world. Postcards cost 56p. The courier industry, particularly in London and other major cities, is growing by some 20 per cent a year and the UK is a major centre for international air courier traffic. Major companies include Federal Express, DHL, UPS and TNT, plus the post office's own Parcelforce service.

The post office produces a wealth of brochures about postal rates and other services, including a *Mini Mailguide* containing information about all Royal Mail products and services. It also has a telephone helpline (☎ 0845-774 0740) and a website (🖥 www.royalmail.com).

Parcel2Go.com (☎ 0844-847 2600 🖥 www.parcel2go.com) is the largest online parcel delivery service in the UK and the only courier website to offer FedEx services along with DHL, City Link, UPS, Home Delivery Network and Royal Mail. Collection and delivery prices start from £6.19+VAT for up to 25kg Economy delivery in the UK; Europe from £17.00+VAT for up to 10kg; and USA, Canada and Asia from £17+VAT for 10kg. These services all come with online parcel tracking, live help and can be paid for online using a credit/debit card or Paypal.

TELEPHONE

Nearly all homes in London have a fixed-line telephone and most Londoners have at least one mobile phone. You can make calls to anywhere in the UK and to most countries in the world without using the operator and a wide range of additional services can be accessed, including an alarm call, call barring, caller display, 'choose to refuse' (which allows you to block certain incoming calls), call diversion, call minder (an answering service), message alert, call return, call waiting, reminder call, reverse charge call, ring back, and 'ring me free'. Some of these are free, while others are quite expensive.

The cost of making telephone calls has gone down sharply in the last decade. Long-distance and international call charges have fallen the most thanks to increased competition among the many service providers.

The general emergency telephone number throughout the UK is 999.

Telephone Companies

The telephone system in the UK is dominated by British Telecom (abbreviated to and universally known as BT), created in 1984 when the state-owned monopoly was privatised. When the telecommunications market was opened to national and international competition in 1991, the UK stood at the forefront of technology in this sector, but other European countries, having subsequently liberalised their own telecoms industries, have now largely caught up. Well over 100 companies are licensed to operate telecommunication services, and competition, although less intense than a few years ago, is still keen, so shopping around to compare rates could save you money.

London users can choose between BT, cable companies (see 🖳 www.cable.co.uk) and a large number of indirect operators. It can be difficult to work out which company to choose, with the increasing number and complexity of schemes and 'packages' on offer, even from the same company (which seem designed to confuse customers). The cheapest option depends on how much you use your phone, when you make most calls, what sort of calls you make (e.g. local, national or international), and how frequently you call mobiles.

☑ **SURVIVAL TIP**

The internet sites 🖳 www.homephone choices.co.uk and 🖳 www.uswitch.com provide tariff comparisons from various providers to help you decide which company offers the best deal. Bear in mind, however, when using comparison sites that they are paid to promote certain companies and deals, and therefore they may not always be independent.

Among the best deal are offered by the Post Office (🖳 www.postoffice.co.uk), Talk Talk (🖳 www.talktalk.co.uk), Toucan (🖳 www.toucan.com), Virgin Media (🖳 www.virginmedia.com) and Yourcalls (🖳 www.yourcalls.net), most of which offer better deals that British Telecom. Most households still rent their phone line from BT, although you can now rent your line from a number of providers (the cost is around the same as BT, £10.50 per month) and transfer both your line rental and calls to another company at the same time and receive one bill for both.

For more information about providers, contact your local telecoms advisory service (see your local telephone directory) or the Telecommunications Users' Association, Woodgate Studios, 2–8 Games Row, Barnet, Herts EN4 9HN (☎ 020-8449 8844).

Installation & Registration

Before moving into a new home, check whether there's a telephone line and that the number of lines or telephone points is adequate (most new homes already have phone lines and points in a number of rooms). If a property has a cable connection, you could decide not to have a BT phone line installed (see 🖳 www.cable.co.uk to check your area). If you move into an old house or apartment, a telephone line will probably already be installed, although there won't be a phone and there may be only one or two connection points.

If you're moving into accommodation without a phone line, you must ask BT or one of the other providers to install one. BT's target for residential line installation is three working days, depending on the area, and the cost is around £125; taking over an existing line is free.

Once you have a BT linebox or master socket, you can install as many additional sockets as you like but you shouldn't connect more than four telephones to one telephone line. You can install additional sockets yourself by buying DIY kits from BT or a DIY shop, or BT can install them for you (although its labour charges are astronomical). BT sells a wide range of extension kits, sockets and cords.

If you're moving to a new address in the same code area, it's usually possible to retain your existing number. For information, call ☎ 0800-800 150.

Using the Telephone

Using the telephone in the UK is much the same as in any other country – with a few British eccentricities thrown in for good measure. All London numbers have the code 020, followed by eight digits, the first of which is 7 for numbers in inner London – an area which, needless to say, doesn't correspond with the geographical concept of inner London (see page 16) – and 8 for outer London. It's widely believed, even by Londoners, that the code for inner London is 0207 and for outer London 0208, but that isn't the case and it's possible to dial a number within the same area without using the 020 code, but not if the 7 or 8 is omitted.

Free numbers, sometimes called 'freefone numbers' by BT, have the prefix 0800. They're usually provided by businesses that are trying to sell you something or, having sold you something, provide a free telephone support service. Numbers with the prefix 0845 are charged at the local rate, irrespective of where you're calling from, and those with the prefix 0870 are charged at the long-distance (national) rate even when you're calling locally, which are increasingly popular with businesses. Premium rate numbers – usually providing specialist information and entertainment – begin 09 and can cost as much as £1.50 per minute. These are beloved by TV and scratch card 'competition' operators, where everyone's a winner, and the 'prizes' are paid for by call charges – the 'message' can last five minutes or more.

When dialling a British number from overseas, you must dial the international access code used in the country from which you're calling (e.g. 011 from the US or 00 from most other countries), followed by the UK's international code (44), the area code without the first 0 (i.e. 20 for London) and the subscriber's number. For the London number 7123 4567, you would dial the access code followed by 44-20-7123 4567.

Telephone numbers are usually dictated one digit at a time on the phone, except for repeated numbers, e.g. 11 or 222, which are given as double one or treble two. Zero is usually read as the letter 'O' (oh).

If you get a bad line, e.g. you're unable to hear the caller or the caller is unable to hear you, or a crossed line where you can hear voices in the background, hang up and redial.

Local & National Call Charges

BT remains by far the largest telephone company in the UK and therefore its rates are shown here as an example of London call charges. This isn't meant as an endorsement of the company, which charges some of the country's highest rates, and you could save a lot of money by using another company (see Telephone Companies above.)

BT charges a monthly line rental fee of £10.50 (including VAT) for a residential line (there's a £1 per month reduction when your is bill paid by direct debit). Like most other providers, BT doesn't price different types of call so that you can see at a glance how much you're being charged, but disguises its call charges in what it calls 'Plans'. These are currently 'Weekend', 'Evening and Weekend', and 'Anytime'. Depending on the Plan you choose and your calling pattern, call charges vary between 3.25 and 5 pence per minute. VAT at 17.5 per cent is levied on line rental and call charges.

International Calls

All private telephones in the UK are on international direct dialling (IDD), allowing calls to be dialled direct to over 190 countries and reverse charge (collect) calls to be made to some 140 countries. To make an international call, dial 00, the country code, the area code without the first zero (with a few exceptions, such as Italy) and the subscriber's number. Dial 155 for the international operator to make non-IDD calls, credit card calls, person-to-person and reverse charge calls (which aren't accepted by all countries). Dial ☎ 118505 for international directory enquiries.

The codes for the major cities of many countries are listed in telephone directories in Section 3: International Information, including the time difference. (One sure way to upset most people is to wake them at 3am!) To find out more about international direct dialling, country codes, BT international services and related topics, visit 🖥 www.bt.com or ring the international operator on ☎ 155.

In mid-2008, BT's standard daytime rates were around 24p per minute to Australia, 18.5p to France and Germany, 15p to Ireland, 10p to Japan and 15p to the US. International charges are listed on the BT website (🖥 www.bt.com). **In contrast, many other companies charge a standard rate for calls to, for**

example, Australia and the USA, which may be as low as 2p per minute!

Using an alternative company to BT (see **Telephone Companies** above) can result in huge savings, even when comparing other companies' standard charges with BT's lowest.

Bills

You're billed by BT for your line rental, phone rental and calls every quarter (three months) if applicable; other providers may have different billing arrangements. If applicable, the telephone connection fee is included in your first bill. BT provides all customers with itemised bills, which state the date and time, duration and cost of each call. Customers can choose to have only certain calls itemised.

BT phone bills can be paid by budget account (to spread costs evenly over the year), quarterly direct debit or cheque using the envelope provided, or at a bank or post office. With a quarterly direct debit, your account is debited 14 days after you receive the bill.

If you don't pay your phone bill within around 14 days of receipt, you receive a red Reminder of Payment, after which you have another 14 days in which to pay it. If you don't pay your bill within this period, your phone is disconnected, usually without any further notification.

If you have a query and cannot obtain satisfaction from your local BT area manager (the phone number is on your bill) or district general manager, you should contact the secretary of your national Advisory Committee (the address is listed in your telephone directory under Code of Practice for Consumers). Complaints about telephone bills dealt with by the Office of

Communications (Ofcom, ☎ 020-7981 3040, 🖳 www.ofcom.org.uk).

Public Telephones

Most public telephones (officially called 'payphones') allow international direct dialling (IDD) and calls made via the operator, as well as domestic and emergency calls. The latest payphones offer internet, email and SMS texting facilities. Many are sterile grey 'vandal-proof' steel and glass booths containing push-button payphones, the iconic red boxes surviving only in some locations of historic interest where they can be kept an eye on (and, curiously, in Malta). Some humbler payphones aren't enclosed and offer little protection from the elements and surrounding noise (although if they remain in working order, most people are happy). A limited number offer wheelchair access and facilities for people with other disabilities.

All payphones are operated by BT and now chiefly accept credit and debit cards – American Express, Diners Club International, Eurocard, MasterCard, Visa and Visa Delta – rather than coins as formerly. Pre-paid phonecards are no longer in use. This eliminates theft because there's no cash in the phonebox to steal, and consequently it's easier than in the past to find payphones that work. Public payphones are to be found throughout London: on public streets, inside and outside post offices and railway stations, and in hotels, pubs, restaurants, shops and other private and public buildings.

Some payphones at airports, ferry ports and main railway stations are reserved for international calls, which is indicated by a sign. Others may display a '999 calls only' (emergency calls only) sign, which means you'll be unable to make an ordinary call but may be able to contact the operator and make a reverse charge or BT Chargecard call. Emergency calls are free from any payphone. Not all payphones accept incoming calls, so check for a sign before asking someone to call you back.

If you need help making a call from a payphone, dial ☎ 100 for the domestic operator or ☎ 155 for the international operator. The BT domestic directory enquiry number is ☎ 118141 (calls cost 60p per minute) from payphones and the international enquiry number ☎ 118505 (£1.50 per minute).

The minimum charge for a call from a payphone is 40p using coins, for which you can make a local or national call lasting 20 minutes (provided there isn't a queue of people outside in the rain). There's a £1.20 minimum charge for credit card calls, in which case all inland calls are charged at 20p per minute thereafter. Operator-connected calls from payphones cost even more than dialled calls and should be avoided if possible. **Payphones should be avoided at all costs when making international calls, as the rates are exorbitant.**

Be wary of using private payphones, e.g. those located in pubs, restaurants, hotels, shopping centres and petrol stations. The rates for these phones is set by the owners, many of whom levy extortionate charges – though charges should be displayed on all private payphones. You should also avoid using hotel room phones, where fees can be astronomical. Some hotels even charge a fee to connect guests to free (e.g. 0800) numbers!

☑ SURVIVAL TIP

With the increased competition and excellent deals available from mobile phone companies nowadays, most people rarely use public phones, which are prohibitively expensive.

Mobile Phones

The UK is one of the world's most prolific users of mobile phone, which once they were reserved as status symbols/fashion accessories for yuppies and the young, but are now an everyday 'necessity' for the vast majority of the population. Mobile phone network providers in the UK include 3G, O2, Orange, T-mobile and Vodafone. There are also a number of providers such as OneTel, Sainsbury's, Talk Talk and Virgin, who buy time from the major operators and run their own services.

Coverage is most limited in the case of the relative newcomer 3G, but there's little discernible difference between the two major companies, O2 and Vodafone. Details about areas of coverage are available on websites such as 🖥 www.mobileshop.org. Some companies have been criticised for the quality of reception offered in some parts of the country (and even worse customer service). Customer service ratings can be found at 🖥 www.onecompare.com/mobile-phone-networks.

You can buy a GSM phone, which can be used in many countries, including much of western Europe, Australia, Hong Kong, South Africa and parts of the Middle East. You used to need a contract with a 'roaming' agreement if you wished to use your mobile phone abroad, but you can now avoid the hugely inflated charges by simply purchasing a foreign or global SIM card. Information can be obtained from 🖥 www.mobilephonemoney.co.uk and 🖥 www.sims4abroad.com. If you're travelling to more than one destination, you will need a separate local SIM for each country.

Phones are sold by retail outlets such as BT shops, specialist dealers (e.g. Carphone Warehouse and The Link), department and chain stores (e.g. Dixons) and supermarkets, all of whom have arrangements with service providers or networks to sell airtime contracts along with phones. You should always deal with an independent company that sells a wide range of phones and can connect you to any network, but shouldn't rely on getting good or impartial advice from retail staff, some of whom know little or nothing about phones and networks.

Retailers advertise almost daily in magazines and newspapers, with constant offers. Phones are even available free if you're willing to sign a contract, which ensures that retailers and network providers can make a big profit through line rental and call charges. Before buying a phone, compare the battery life, memory capacity, weight, size and features (including a camera, internet access and texting), which may include automatic call back, unanswered call store, mailbox, call timer, minute minder, lock facility and call barring. In fact, it's becoming increasingly difficult or impossible to buy a phone which will simply allow you to make and receive phone calls!

Before buying a mobile phone (or pager), check the reviews and comparison tests in surveys conducted by *Which?*, *What Cellphone?* and *W@MOB* magazines. Ofcom (🖥 www.ofcom.org.uk/consumeradvice/mobile/mobileservice) provide independent advice about how to choose a mobile phone provider.

It has been calculated than mobile users in the UK waste an incredible £8bn a year because they're on the wrong tariff.

INTERNET

Broadband internet in the home is available throughout London from as little as £5 per month, which may also include free off-peak calls. If you have a cable or satellite connection you can receive your broadband via these and many providers also offer phone calls and subscription TV in an all-inclusive package.

You can compare broadband packages from a number of providers via the net using Broadband Genie (🖳 www.broadbandgenie.co.uk), Broadband Finder (🖳 www.broadband-finder.co.uk) and Top 10 Broadband (🖳 www.top10-broadband.co.uk). Many websites also allow you to enter your postcode and display information about the broadband packages available from the ISPs operating in your postcode area, e.g. 🖳 www.broadbandchecker.co.uk.

Wifi hotspots cover most of London, but services aren't usually provided free. Many websites list wifi hotspots such as My Hotspots (🖳 www.myhotspots.co.uk/results.aspx?town=london). There are a number of free wireless internet providers in London, although you need to subscribe in order to receive a reliable service, costing from around £3 for 60 minutes up to £10 per month for unlimited access. Online-4-free provide (🖳 www.online-4-free.com) cover in Holborn and along the Thames from Millbank Pier in central London to Greenwich Pier, including a number of key docks and piers. They provide both a free and paid service; the free service allows you to access the internet for free with advertisements or you can choose the paid service with no advertisements.

There are a number of internet magazines published in the UK,

including *Net*, *Internet Magazine*, *Internet User* and *WebUser*.

See also Internet Cafés on page 228.

TELEVISION

British television (TV) is widely considered to be the best in the world – not that this is saying a great deal when you consider the standard of most TV worldwide. Although British broadcasters generate the usual surfeit of nonsense (e.g. inane quiz shows and soaps, otherwise known as 'tabloid' TV) and run a good deal of imported (mostly American) soaps and films to cater for couch potatoes, they also produce many excellent programmes, including nature and culture documentaries, serialised adaptations of novels, bespoke TV films, situation comedies and variety shows, which are sold throughout the world, as well as music programmes, chat shows, sports coverage and news and current affairs programmes – although the presentation of these is increasingly 'showbiz' and newscasters have become 'celebrities'.

Explicit sex and extreme violence are becoming commonplace, even before the so-called watershed time of 9pm (before which programmes with 'adult' content shouldn't be aired). If you find anything offensive, you can make a complaint to the Office of Communications (OFCOM, 🖳 www.ofcom.org.uk), where you can also find details of guidelines.

Broadcasting Standard

The television broadcasting standard isn't the same in the UK as in most other countries, and TVs and VCRs/DVDs manufactured for use in the US (NTSC standard) and continental Europe won't function in London. Most European countries use the PAL B/G standard, except for France, which has its own standard called SECAM. The British standard is a modified PAL-I system (where the audio signal is shifted to avoid the buzz plaguing the conventional PAL system when, for example, transmitting subtitles or other white areas).

If you bring a TV to the UK from the US or the continent, you'll get either a picture or sound, but not both. A TV can be converted to work in the UK, but it's usually not worth the trouble and expense. VCRs/DVDs manufactured for non-British markets are unusable in the UK, and recordings made for the North American market are unplayable on British recorders. Note that it's difficult to purchase VCRs nowadays, although you buy a DVD/VCR recorder. If you want a TV and VCR/DVD machine that will work in the UK and other European countries (including France) and/or the US, you must buy a multi-standard model.

Some multi-standard TVs also handle the North American NTSC standard and have an NTSC jack plug connection, allowing you to play American videos.

Stations

BBC television (🖥 www.bbc.co.uk) has been broadcasting regularly since 1936 and introduced a second station (BBC2) in 1964. There are now several other BBC channels (available only digitally or via satellite or cable), including BBC3 (🖥 www.bbc.co.uk/bbcthree), offering comedy, drama, films and news; BBC4 (🖥 www.bbc.co.uk/bbcfour), for arts, science, history and business programmes; BBC News 24 (🖥 www.bbc.co.uk/bbcnews24) for news; BBC Parliament for political programmes; plus a couple of children's channels.

The first regular commercial programmes began in London in 1955, broadcast by a company originally called Independent Television (ITV, 🖥 www.itv.com), now called ITV1. ITV1 broadcasts regional programmes (there are 15 regions) and national programmes, such as news and soaps. ITV2, 3 and 4 show a mixture of repeats, reality shows, sport and programmes aimed at the youth market, also available on digital television (see below) via satellite, cable and Freeview platforms. Two more terrestrial national commercial TV stations, Channel 4 (🖥 www.channel4.com) and Five (🖥 http://five.tv), were launched in 1982 and 1997 respectively.

All five terrestrial stations (BBC1, BBC2, ITV1, Channel 4 and Five) can be received throughout London. The BBC channels carry no advertising and are publicly funded through an annual TV licence (see below), sales of *Radio Times*, and the trading activities of BBC Enterprises. The other stations have regular 'commercial breaks' (approximately every 20 to 30 minutes). All terrestrial TV stations broadcast 24 hours a day, as do many satellite and cable stations. Programmes on BBC begin at odd times (e.g. 6.20, 8.05), depending on the length of programmes; other broadcasters' programmes usually start on the hour or half hour.

TV Licence

An annual TV licence (£139.50 for colour, £45.50 for the three people who still have black and white sets) is required by anyone who has a TV or video. (Registered blind people are generously offered a reduction of 50 per cent on production of the local authority's certificate for the blind.) If a TV is used for video playback, as a computer monitor or to receive satellite TV only, the licence fee isn't payable. However, your TV must be incapable of receiving terrestrial channels, which means that your TV aerial and tuner circuitry must be permanently disconnected.

The licence fee covers any number of TVs in a home, as well as a TV at a second home in the UK, provided that both TVs aren't used simultaneously.

TV licences can be purchased from TV Licensing, Bristol BS98 1TL (☎ 0844-800

6790, 💻 www.tvlicensing.co.uk) and must be renewed annually. The fee can be paid by direct debit, by credit or debit card, cheque, at PayPoint outlets, via a cash payment plan or a TV licensing savings card. If you're leaving the UK, you can obtain a refund on any unexpired three-month period of a TV licence by applying in writing to Customer Services at the address above.

Digital TV

The UK leads the world in digital television, which provides much clearer and sharper images than standard analogue TV and can broadcast programmes in a widescreen format. Digital TV, launched in the UK on 1st October 1998 by BSkyB (now Sky), offers a superior picture, DVD-quality sound, widescreen cinema format and access to many more stations, as well as interactive services.

Between 2008 and 2012 television services in the UK will go completely digital, TV region by TV region (Whitehaven in Cumbria became the first place to switch to digital in October 2007). The old analogue television signal will be switched off and viewers will need to convert or upgrade their TV equipment to receive digital signals, whether through their aerial, by satellite, cable or via broadband.

If you currently receive just the traditional five UK channels (BBC One, BBC Two, ITV, Channel 4 and Five) on a TV, you'll need to think about your options for receiving digital TV. Every TV set you want to keep watching in your home will need to be converted or upgraded to receive digital TV, which you can receive in four ways: digital cable TV, digital satellite TV, digital terrestrial TV through your aerial or digital ADSL (broadband) TV, each of which is explained below.

> Amazingly analogue TVs are still being (legally) sold in the UK and in mid-2008 retailers were still selling thousands a month, although they will soon be obsolete.

Digital Cable TV: Around 15 million homes in the UK have access to digital cable TV and the digital TV companies are in the process of switching their services to digital, which can also be used for phone and broadband internet access. Features may include a free telephone line (no monthly line rental), internet access via your TV, TV email, digital Teletext, interactive services and games, and digital radio channels. To subscribe to digital cable TV you don't need a TV aerial and you cable TV company will provide you with a set top box and a cable telephone line.

Digital Satellite TV: Digital satellite TV is transmitted via satellite direct to mini-dishes installed in homes and is available to some 98 per cent of UK households. Satellite TV offers the widest choice of channels and service providers; an electronic programming guide (on screen programme information and listings); digital text and teletext; pay per view movies and events; interactive services and games; and digital radio channels. To receive digital satellite TV you require a mini-dish and digibox. The main provider is Sky (💻 www.digital-tv. co.uk/sky-digital) which charge from around £80 for a set-top Digibox and a (digital) satellite mini-dish. Customers must sign up for a 12-month minimum subscription (costing from £26 to £55 per month for digital, depending on the package chosen) and have the connection via a phone line.

Digital Terrestrial TV: Digital terrestrial TV is currently available to around 75 per cent of the UK population, who can receive around 30 TV channels and 16 radio stations free to view (Freeview, the so-called public services broadcasting channels). These include all of the current analogue TV options, plus the BBC's digital services, and you can also access text based services such as BBCi and Teletext. Viewers with suitably equipped set top boxes or IDTVs can also access pay TV services from Top Up TV, which offers elements of ten premium channels for a monthly fee. There are no monthly fees, selected set top boxes can receive Digital Teletext and there's an electronic programming guide (on screen programme information and listings). To receive digital terrestrial TV you need a TV aerial and either an integrated digital TV (IDTV) or a set top box costing from around £10. In areas with poor reception you may require an aerial upgrade. For further information, contact Freeview (☎ 08701-111270 or see 🖳 www.freeview.co.uk).

Digital ADSL TV: ADSL is a way of downloading and transmitting data at high speed over existing phone wires. TV programmes are sold in subscription packages, e.g. films, sports and music, which gives you access to all the programmes in each package which you can watch any time you choose. Features include pay per view, e.g. films, no monthly fees, wide range of subscription packages, video on demand (allows you to pause, stop, re-wind, and fast forward programmes), PC based fast internet access, and the ability to bundle packages with broadband and phone calls. Providers supply a set top box and modem connection to your existing phone socket, and no dish, cable connection, or video recorder is required. One of the major digital TV providers in London is Virgin (🖳 www.virginmedia.com) – to check

you local area see 🖳 www.cable.co.uk/regions/london.php.

For comprehensive information about digital television, see 🖳 www.digitaltelevision.gov.uk and 🖳 www.bbc.co.uk/digital.

Satellite TV

Hundreds of channels are available via satellite TV in addition to the five terrestrial channels, which is also the only choice for those who want to watch foreign-language TV. The UK's biggest satellite TV provider is Sky (☎ 08442-414141 or 🖳 www.sky.com), who provide a wealth of programmes including general entertainment, children's programmes, news, sports (many exclusive sports are shown on Sky and movie channels, plus pay-per-view movies and sports events. You can also receive numerous radio stations via Sky, including most popular stations.

Installation of a satellite mini-dish and decoder costs around £130 and subscription packages from £16 to £45 per month. The Standard Sky Box is installed for £30, the Sky+ box (which allows viewers to pause live broadcasts and schedule future programmes that are broadcast in HDTV) costs £99 and the Sky HD box costs £299 (there's a set-up fee of £30 for the latter two services). These charges are one-off and once you have paid for the equipment it's your property and you don't have to return it to Sky at the end of your contract.

Satellite programmes are listed in most national daily newspapers, general TV magazines and satellite TV magazines such as the *Satellite Times* and *What Satellite and Digital TV*, available from newsagents' or on subscription. The annual *World Radio and TV Handbook* by David G. Bobbett (Watson-Guptil Publications) contains information and frequencies about all radio and TV stations worldwide.

Cable TV

Cable television in the UK was originally confined to areas of poor reception (e.g. due to geographical features or high-rise buildings) or where external aerials weren't permitted. However, there has been an explosion in cable TV over the last decade and millions of homes can now receive cable TV and there are around 3m subscribers (although the UK still has a long way to go to match European countries such as Belgium, the Netherlands and Switzerland, where 90 per cent of the populations have access to cable TV).

The latest broadband cable systems can carry terrestrial broadcasts, satellite and digital TV programmes (see above), and local services. Cable TV is offered by a number of companies on a regional basis. The main provider (having taken over NTL and Telewest) is Virgin Media (🖥 www.virginmedia.com), which offers up to around 150 channels. To find cable TV providers in London and whether a particular area or house has cable TV, see 🖥 www.cable.co.uk/regions/london.php.

There's an initial connection fee of £25 for cable TV, and a subscription of around £20 per month for a basic programme package or up to £45 per month for a package including all the most popular channels.

☑ **SURVIVAL TIP**

One of the main advantages of taking out a cable subscription is that most cable companies offer inexpensive telephone services plus broadband internet access, which can save you enough on your phone bill to pay for your cable TV.

Video & DVD

There are numerous video and DVD hire shops in the UK, which reached (or exceeded) saturation point in the early '90s. The British market is the second-largest in the world, after the US, and the UK has the highest ownership of VCRs/DVD players in Europe (over three-quarters of households). Many video shops are open until 8pm or even 10pm, seven days a week.

To hire a video or DVD, you must usually be a member, for which shops require proof of your address and verification of your signature. If you're under 18, a parent is required to stand as a guarantor. Some video shops have a children's membership scheme with low rental rates for children's films. Members are issued with a card, which is shown when hiring videos or DVDs.

Usually you can take out up to three or four films at any time, which must usually be returned by 7pm the following day. Daily hire charges range from around £1.50 to £4 according to popularity (new top ten films are the most expensive). There's normally no extra charge for weekend hire (e.g. Saturday to Monday) when a shop doesn't open on a Sunday. If you're late returning a film, you're charged an extra day's rental for each day overdue. If you lose or damage a film, you must usually pay for a replacement at retail price. Insurance against loss or damage is sometimes available for a one-time payment, e.g. £5. Videos and DVDs can also be hired from public libraries, where the cost is usually around £1 per night.

Recently released videos and DVDs cost around £15 to buy. HMV, Woolworths and Zaavi stores have a wide selection of the latest videos and DVDs, and major supermarkets also stock a good range. Both videos and DVDs can be bought, often at discount, by mail order from internet retailers such as Amazon (🖥 www.amazon.co.uk) and Mr Benson (🖥 www.bensonsworld.co.uk). Most video and DVD shops also sell second-hand films at reduced prices.

RADIO

Radio reception in London is excellent, including stereo reception (although FM reception isn't always good in cars). The radio audience in the UK is almost equally split between the British Broadcasting Corporation (BBC) and commercial radio stations (although the BBC has been losing listeners to commercial stations at an increasing rate in recent years). Community and ethnic radio is also popular in many areas and a number of universities and colleges operate their own radio stations. In addition to the FM or VHF stereo wave band, medium wave (MW or AM) and long wave (LW) bands are in wide use throughout the UK. The shortwave (SW) band is useful for receiving foreign radio broadcasts.

BBC

The BBC operates five national radio stations (and other digital stations – see below) with easy to remember (if unimaginative) names: BBC Radio 1 (FM 97.6-99.8) for contemporary music; BBC Radio 2, (FM 88-90.2) for 'easy-listening' music; BBC Radio 3 (FM 90.2-92.4) for classical music, jazz and occasionally drama and poetry; BBC Radio 4 (FM 92.4-94.6, LW 198) for conversation, comedy, drama, documentaries, magazine programmes and news; and BBC Radio 5 Live (MW 693, 909) for news, current affairs and sport. There are also around 40 BBC local radio stations, with some 10m listeners.

There's no advertising on BBC radio stations, which are financed by the government and the revenue from TV licence fees, as no radio licence is necessary in the UK.

BBC radio programmes are published in the Radio Times, in national newspapers and listed on the BBC TV teletext information service.

Commercial Radio

Commercial radio is hugely popular in the UK, where it's the fastest-growing entertainment medium, reported to have some 36m listeners or almost 80 per cent of adults. However, there are only some 200 commercial radio stations in the whole of the UK, compared with around 1,000 in France and Italy, and over 9,000 in the US. It's possible to receive dozens of commercial stations in London.

Stations vary from large national stations with vast budgets and millions of listeners, to tiny local stations run by volunteers with just a few thousand listeners. Stations provide national or local news and information, music and other entertainment, education, consumer advice and traffic information, and provide listeners with the chance to air their views through phone-in programmes, emails and text messages. Advertising on commercial radio is limited to nine minutes an hour but is usually less.

Britain has three national commercial radio stations: Classic FM (🖥 www.classicfm.co.uk, FM 100-101.9), which broadcasts 'light' classical music; Virgin Radio (🖥 www.virginradio.co.uk, FM 105.8, MW 1197, 1215) for popular music; and Talksport (🖥 www.1talksport.net, MW 1053, 1089), Britain's first 24-hour, national, speech-only commercial station. London's principal commercial station, and the UK's most popular commercial radio station, is Capital Radio (🖥

www.capitalradio.co.uk), which, with its spin-offs Capital Gold and other regional radio stations, is one of the world's largest metropolitan radio stations, boasting over 3m listeners. It broadcasts mainly pop music.

Digital Radio

Digital radio offers better sound quality and less interference than analogue radio. It's available in around 90 per cent of the UK, including all of London, although you need a digital radio (costing from around £50) to receive it and it can also be received on a PC with a digital card. All national BBC radio stations are broadcast digitally and there are digital-only stations, including BBC Radio 5 Live Sports Plus, BBC 6 Music, BBC Parliament and BBC Xtra. Commercial radio has also gone digital and seven national stations, including FM, Virgin Radio and Talk Radio (see above), are available digitally.

Satellite Radio

If you have satellite TV, you can also receive radio stations via your satellite link. For example, BBC Radio 1, 2,

3, 4 and 5, BBC World Service, Sky Radio, Virgin 1215 and many foreign (i.e. non-English) stations are broadcast via the Astra satellites. Satellite radio stations are listed in British satellite TV magazines such as *Satellite Times*. If you're interested in receiving radio stations from further afield, you should obtain a copy of the *World Radio TV Handbook* by David G. Bobbett (Watson-Guptil Publications).

TIME DIFFERENCE

London, like the rest of the UK, is on British Summer Time (BST) in summer and Greenwich Mean Time (GMT) in winter. The changes are made at 2am on the last Sunday in October (when the clocks go back an hour) and at the same time on the last Sunday in March, when they go forward. In case you forget, time changes are announced in local newspapers and on radio and TV, and are usually indicated on diaries and calendars. The exact time is given by the telephone 'speaking clock' (☎ 123), on the internet and on TVs.

☑ **SURVIVAL TIP**

When making international telephone calls or travelling long distances by air, check the time difference, which is shown in the International Dialling section of telephone directories or via the internet (🖳 www. timeanddate.com/worldclock).

The time in some foreign cities when it's noon GMT in London is shown below.

TIME DIFFERENCE

LONDON	CAPE TOWN	MUMBAI	SYDNEY	LOS ANGELES	NEW YORK
Noon	2pm	5.30pm	9pm	4am	7am

City Hall, Tower Bridge

Gothenburg, moored in West India Quay, E14

APPENDICES

APPENDIX A: USEFUL ADDRESSES

London Embassies & Consulates

A selection of foreign embassies and high commissions in London is listed below. A full list of embassies and consulates in London is published in *The Diplomatic List* (The Stationery Office) and available online from the Foreign & Commonwealth Office website (🖳 www.fco.gov.uk – click on the 'Foreign embassies in the UK' link at the right of the screen), where embassy websites are also listed.

Antigua & Barbuda: 2nd Floor, 45 Crawford Place, London W1H 4LP (☎ 020-7258 0070).

Argentina: 65 Brook Street, Westminster, London W1K 4AH (☎ 020-7318 1300).

Australia: Australia House, Strand, London WC2B 4LA (☎ 020-7379 4334).

Austria: 45 Princes Gate, London SW7 2QA (☎ 020-7584 4411).

Bahamas: 10 Chesterfield Street, London W1J 5JL (☎ 020-7408 4488).

Bangladesh: 28 Queen's Gate, London SW7 5JA (☎ 020-7584 0081).

Barbados: 1 Great Russell Street, London WC1B 3ND (☎ 020-7631 4975).

Belgium: 17 Grosvenor Crescent, London SW1X 7EE (☎ 020-7470 3700).

Belize: 45 Crawford Place, London W1H 4LP (☎ 020-7723 3603).

Bolivia: 106 Eaton Square, London SW1W 9AD (☎ 020-7235 4248).

Bosnia: 5-7 Lexham Gardens, London W8 5JJ (☎ 020-7373 0867).

Brazil: 32 Green Street, London W1K 7AT (☎ 020-7399 9000).

Brunei: 19-20 Belgrave Square, London SW1X 8PG (☎ 020-7581 0521).

Bulgaria: 186-188 Queen's Gate, London SW7 5HL (☎ 020-7584 9400).

Cameroon: 84 Holland Park, London W11 3SB (☎ 020-7727 0771).

Canada: Macdonald House, 1 Grosvenor Square, London W1K 4AB (☎ 020-7258 6600).

Chile: 12 Devonshire Street, London W1G 7DS (☎ 020-7580 6392).

China: 49-51 Portland Place, London W1B 1JL (☎ 020-7299 4049).

Colombia: 3 Hans Crescent, London SW1X 0LN (☎ 020-7589 9177).

Croatia: 21 Conway Street, London W1T 6BN (☎ 020-7387 2022).

Cuba: 167 High Holborn, London WC1 6PA (☎ 020-7240 2488).

Cyprus: 93 Park Street, London W1K 7ET (☎ 020-7499 8272).

Czech Republic: 26 Kensington Palace Gardens, London W8 4QY (☎ 020-7243 1115).

Denmark: 55 Sloane Street, London SW1X 9SR (☎ 020-7333 0200).

Dominica: 1 Collingham Gardens, South Kensington, London SW5 0HW (☎ 020-7370 5194/5).

Ecuador: Flat 3b, 3 Hans Crescent, London SW1X 0LS (☎ 020-7584 2648/1376).

Egypt: 26 South St, Westminster, London SW1X (☎ 020-7499 2401).

El Salvador: 39 Great Portland Street, London W1N 7JZ (☎ 020-7436 8282).

Fiji: 34 Hyde Park Gate, London SW7 5DN (☎ 020-7584 3661).

Finland: 38 Chesham Place, London SW1X 8HW (☎ 020-7838 6200).

France: 58 Knightsbridge, London SW1X 7JT (☎ 020-7201 1000).

The Gambia: 27 Elvaston Place, London SW7 5NL (☎ 020-7823 9986).

Germany: 23 Belgrave Square, 1 Chesham Place, London SW1X 8PZ (☎ 020-7824 1300).

Ghana: 13 Belgrave Square, London SW1X 8PN (☎ 020-7201 5900).

Greece: 1A Holland Park, London W11 3TP (☎ 020-7229 3850).

Grenada: The Chapel, Archel Road, West Kensington, London W14 (☎ 020-7385 4415).

Guatemala: 13 Fawcett Street, London SW10 9HN (☎ 020-7351 3042).

Guyana: 3 Palace Court, Bayswater Road, London W2 4LP (☎ 020-7229 7684).

Honduras: 115 Gloucester Place, London W1U 6JT (☎ 020-7486 4880).

Hungary: 35 Eaton Place, London SW1X 8BY (☎ 020-7201 3440).

Iceland: 2A Hans Street, London SW1X 0JE (☎ 020-7259 3999).

India: India House, Aldwych, London WC2B 4NA (☎ 020-7836 8484).

Indonesia: 38 Grosvenor Square, London W1K 2HW (☎ 020-7499 7661).

Iran: 16 Prince's Gate, London SW7 1PT (☎ 020-7225 3000).

Ireland: 17 Grosvenor Place, London SW1X 7HR (☎ 020-7235 2171).

Israel: 2 Palace Green, London W8 4QB (☎ 020-7957 9500).

Italy: 14 Three Kings Yard, Davies Street, London W1K 2EH (☎ 020-7312 2200).

Jamaica: 1-2 Prince Consort Road, London SW7 2BZ (☎ 020-7823 9911).

Japan: 101-104 Piccadilly, London W1J 7JT (☎ 020-7465 6500).

Jordan: 6 Upper Phillimore Gardens, London W8 7HA (☎ 020-7937 3685).

Kenya: 45 Portland Place, London W1B 1AS (☎ 020-7636 2371).

Korea (South): 60 Buckingham Gate, London SW1E 6AJ (☎ 020-7227 5500).

Kuwait: 2 Albert Gate, London SW1X 7JU (☎ 020-7590 3400).

Lebanon: 21 Palace Gardens Mews, London W8 4RA (☎ 020-7229 7265).

Lesotho: 7 Chesham Place, Belgravia, London SW1X 8HN (☎ 020-7235 5686).

Luxembourg: 27 Wilton Crescent, London SW1X 8SD (☎ 020-7235 6961).

Malawi: 33 Grosvenor Street, London W1K 4QT (☎ 020-7491 4172).

Malaysia: 45-46 Belgrave Square, London SW1X 8QT (☎ 020-7235 8033).

Malta: Malta House, 36-38 Piccadilly, London W1V 0PQ (☎ 020-7292 4800).

Mauritius: 32-33 Elvaston Place, London SW7 5NW (☎ 020-7581 0294).

Mexico: 16 St. George Street, Hanover Square, London W1S 1LX (☎ 020-7499 8586).

Morocco: 49 Queen's Gate Gardens, London SW7 5NE (☎ 020-7581 5001/4).

Mozambique: 21 Fitzroy Square, London W1T 6EL (☎ 020-7383 3800).

Namibia: 6 Chandos Street, London W1G 9LU (☎ 020-7636 6244).

Nepal: 12A Kensington Palace Gardens, London W8 4QU (☎ 020-7229 1594).

Netherlands: 38 Hyde Park Gate, London SW7 5DP (☎ 020-7590 3200).

New Zealand: New Zealand House, 80 Haymarket, London SW1Y 4TQ (☎ 020-7930 8422).

Nigeria: Nigeria House, 9 Northumberland Avenue, London WC2N 5BX (☎ 020-7839 1244).

Norway: 25 Belgrave Square, London SW1X 8QD (☎ 020-7591 5500).

Oman: 167 Queen's Gate, London SW7 5HE (☎ 020-7225 0001).

Pakistan: 34-36 Lowndes Square, London SW1X 9JN (☎ 020-7664 9200).

Papua New Guinea: 14 Waterloo Place, London SW1Y 4AR (☎ 020-7930 0922).

Paraguay: 344 High Street, Kensington, London W14 8NS (☎ 020-7610 4180).

Peru: 52 Sloane Street, London SW1X 9SP (☎ 020-7235 1917).

Philippines: 9A Palace Green, London W8 4QE (☎ 020-7937 1600).

Poland: 47 Portland Place, London W1B 1JH (☎ 0870-774 2700).

Portugal: 11 Belgrave Square, London SW1X 8PP (☎ 020-7235 5331).

Qatar: 1 South Audley Street, London W1K 1NB (☎ 020-7493 2200).

Romania: Arundel House, 4 Palace Green, London W8 4QD (☎ 020-7937 9666).

Russia: 6/7 Kensington Palace Gardens, London W8 4QP (☎ 020-7229 3628).

Saudi Arabia: 30 Charles Street, London W1J 5DZ (☎ 020-7917 3000).

Serbia: 28, Belgrave Square, London, SW1X 8QB (☎ 020-7235 9049).

Sierra Leone: 41 Eagle St., Holborn, London WC1R 4TL (☎ 020-7404 0140).

Singapore: 9 Wilton Crescent, London SW1X 8SP (☎ 020-7235 8315).

Slovak Republic: 25 Kensington Palace Gardens, London W8 4QY (☎ 020-7313 6470).

Slovenia: 10 Little College Street, London SW1P 3SH (☎ 020-7222 5700).

South Africa: South Africa House, Trafalgar Square, London WC2N 5DP (☎ 020-7451 7299).

Spain: 39 Chesham Place, London SW1X 8SB (☎ 020-7235 5555).

Sri Lanka: 13 Hyde Park Gardens, London W2 2LU (☎ 020-7262 1841).

Swaziland: 20 Buckingham Gate, London SW1E 6LB (☎ 020-7630 6611).

Sweden: 11 Montague Place, London W1H 2AL (☎ 020-7917 6400).

Switzerland: 16-18 Montague Place, London W1H 2BQ (☎ 020-7616 6000).

Syria: 8 Belgrave Square, London SW1X 8PH (☎ 020-7245 9012).

Tanzania: 3 Stratford Place, London W1C 1AS (☎ 020-7569 1470).

Thailand: 29-30 Queen's Gate, London SW7 5JB (☎ 020-7589 2944).

Tonga: 36 Molyneux Street, London W1H 5BQ (☎ 020-7724 5828).

Trinidad & Tobago: 42 Belgrave Square, London SW1X 8NT (☎ 020-7245 9351).

Turkey: 43 Belgrave Square, London SW1X 8PA (☎ 020-7393 0202).

Uganda: 58-59 Trafalgar Square, London WC2N 5DX (☎ 020-7839 5783).

Ukraine: 60 Holland Park, London W11 3SJ (☎ 020-7727 6312).

United Arab Emirates: 30 Prince's Gate, London SW7 1PT (☎ 020-7581 1281).

United States Of America: 24 Grosvenor Square, London W1A 1AE (☎ 020-7499 9000).

Uruguay: 2nd Floor, 140 Brompton Road, London SW3 1HY (☎ 020-7589 8835).

Venezuela: 1 Cromwell Road, London SW7 2HW (☎ 020-7584 4206).

Zaire: 26 Chesham Place, London SW1X 8HH (☎ 020-7235 6137).

Zambia: 2 Palace Gate, Kensington, London W8 5NG (☎ 020-7589 6655).

Zimbabwe: Zimbabwe House, 429 Strand, London WC2R 0JR (☎ 020-7836 7755).

Government Departments

Department for Business Enterprise and Regulatory Reform, 1 Victoria Street, London SW1H 0ET (☎ 020-7215 5000, 🖥 www.dti.gov.uk).

Department for Culture, Media & Sport, 2-4 Cockspur Street, London SW1Y 5DH (☎ 020-7211 6200, 🖥 www.culture.gov.uk).

Department for Children, Schools and Families, Sanctuary Buildings, Great Smith Street, London SW1P 3BT and other addresses listed on website (☎ 0870-000 2288, 🖥 www.dfes.gov.uk).

Department for Environment, Food & Rural Affairs, Nobel House, 17 Smith Square, London SW1P 3JR (☎ 020-7238 6000, 🖥 www.defra.gov.uk).

Department of Health, Richmond House, 79 Whitehall, London SW1A 2NS (☎ 020-7210 4850, 🖥 www.dh.gov.uk).

Department for International Development, 1 Palace Street, London SW1E 5HE (☎ 020-7023 0000, 🖥 www.dfid.gov.uk).

Department for Work and Pensions, Caxton House, Tothill Street, London SW1H 9DA (☎ 020-7238 0800, 🖥 www.dwp.gov.uk).

Foreign & Commonwealth Office, King Charles Street, London SW1A 2AH (☎ 020-7008 1500, 🖥 www.fco.gov.uk).

HM Revenue and Customs, Victoria Avenue, Southend-on-Sea, Essex SS99 1BD (☎ 0845-000 0200 🖥 www.hmrc.gov.uk).

Home Office, 2 Marsham Street, London SW1P 4DF (☎ 020-7035 4848, 🖥 www. homeoffice.gov.uk).

Ministry of Defence, Main Building, Whitehall, London SW1A 2HB (☎ 020-7218 9000, 🖥 www.mod.uk).

Tourist Information

English Tourist Board, Thames Tower, Black's Road, London W6 9EL (☎ 020-8846 9000, 🖥 www.enjoyengland.com).

London Tourist Board, 2 More London Riverside, London SE1 2RR (☎ 020-7234 5800, 🖥 www.visitlondon.com).

Visit Britain, Thames Tower, Black's Road, Hammersmith, London W6 9EL (☎ 020-8846 9000, 🖥 www.visitbritain.com).

Transport & Travel

Association of British Travel Agents, 68-71 Newman Street, London W1T 3AH (☎ 020-7637 2444, 🖥 www.abta.co.uk).

Automobile Association (AA), Lambert House, Stockport Road, Cheadle SK8 2DY (☎ 0161-488 7544, 🖥 www.theaa.com).

British Airports Authority (BAA), 130 Wilton Road, London SW1V 1LQ (☎ 020-8745 9800, 🖥 www.baa.co.uk).

National Express, 7 Triton Square, London NW1 3HG (☎ 0845-130130, 🖥 www.nationalexpress.com).

Royal Automobile Club (RAC), RAC House, 8 Surrey Street, Norwich, Norfolk NR1 3NG (☎ 01922-727 313, 🖥 www.rac.co.uk).

Miscellaneous

British Council, 10 Spring Gardens, London SW1A 2BN (☎ 0161-957 7755, 🖥 www.britishcouncil.org).

BBC Television Centre, Wood Lane, London W12 7RJ (☎ 0870-603 0304, 🖥 www.bbc.co.uk).

Border and Immigration Agency, Lunar House, 40 Wellesley Road, Croydon CR9 2BY (☎ 0870-606 7766, 🖥 www.bia.homeoffice.gov.uk).

British Telecom, 81 Newgate Street, London EC1A 7AJ (☎ 020-7356 5000, 🖳 www.bt.com).

Central Office of Information, Hercules Road, London SE1 7DU (☎ 020-7928 5037, 🖳 www.coi.gov.uk).

Confederation of British Industry (CBI), Centre Point, 103 New Oxford Street, London WC1A 1DU (☎ 020-7379 7400, 🖳 www. cbi.org.uk).

Driver & Vehicle Licensing Agency (DVLA), Swansea SA6 7JL (☎ 0870-240 0009, 🖳 www.dvla.gov.uk).

The National Archives, Ruskin Avenue, Kew, Richmond, Surrey TW9 4DU (☎ 020-8876 3444, 🖳 www.pro.gov.uk).

National Association of Citizens' Advice Bureaux, Myddelton House, 115-123 Pentonville Road, London N1 9LZ (☎ 020-7833 2181, 🖳 www.nacab.org.uk).

National Consumer Council, 20 Grosvenor Gardens, London SW1 0DH (☎ 020-7730 3469, 🖳 www.ncc.org.uk).

National Federation of Women's Institutes, 104 New Kings Road, London SW6 4LY (☎ 020-7371 9300, 🖳 www.womens-institute.co.uk).

Office of Fair Trading, Fleetbank House, 2-6 Salisbury Square, London EC4Y 8JX (☎ 020-7211 8000, 🖳 www.oft.gov.uk).

Office for National Statistics, Room 1.015, Cardiff Road, Newport, NP10 8XG (☎ 0845 601 3034, 🖳 www.statistics.gov.uk).

Which (Consumers' Association), Castlemead, Gascoyne Way, Hertford SG14 1LH (☎ 01992-822800, 🖳 www.which.co.uk).

APPENDIX B: FURTHER READING

Books

The books listed below are just a selection of the hundreds written about London (and England). Some books may be out of print, but you should still be able to find a copy in a bookshop or on Amazon. The publication title is followed by the author's name (where applicable) and the publisher (in brackets).

Cycling & Walking

50 Walks in London, Deborah King (AA)

Adventure Walks for Families in and Around London, Becky Jones & Clare Lewis (Frances Lincoln)

American Walks in London, Richard Tames (Interlink Publishing)

Andrew Duncan's Favourite London Walks, Andrew Duncan (New Holland)

City Cycling, Richard Ballantine (Snowbooks)

In and Around London Pathfinder Guide (Jarrold/Ordnance Survey)

London Pub Walks, Bob Steel (CAMRA)

London Step by Step, Christopher Turner (Independent Traveller)

London's Waterside Walks, Brian Cookson (Mainstream)

Off-beat Walks in London, John Wittich & Ron Phillips (Shire)

On your Bike, Guide to Cycling in London (London Cycling Campaign)

Secret London, Andrew Duncan (New Holland)

A Walk Through Charles Dickens' London, Paul Garner (Louis London Walks)

Walking Dickensian London, Richard Jones (New Holland)

History

The Blitz, Vince Cross (Scholastic)

Building London: The Making of a Modern Metropolis, Bruce Marshall (Mainstream)

Derelict London, Paul Talling (Random House)

Everybody's Historic London, Jonathan Kiek (Quiller Press)

Historic London: An Explorer's Companion, Stephen Inwood (Macmillan)

A History of London, Stephen Inwood (Macmillan)

I Never Knew That About London, Christopher Winn (Ebury)

The Little Book of London, David Long (History Press)

London in the Nineteenth Century: A Human Awful Wonder of God, Jerry White (Vintage)

London, Edward Rutherford (Arrow)

London in the Twentieth Century: A City and its People, Jerry White (Vintage)

London: The Biography, Peter Ackroyd (Vintage)

London: A Life in Maps, Peter Whitfield (British Library)

London: A Social History, Roy Porter (Penguin)

The Phoenix: St. Paul's Cathedral And The Men Who Made Modern London, Leo Hollis (Weidenfeld & Nicholson)

Shadows Of The Workhouse: The Drama Of Life In Post-war London, Jennifer Worth (Weidenfeld & Nicolson)

Spectacular Vernacular: London's 100 Most Extraordinary Buildings, David Long (History Press)

St Pancras Station (Wonders of the World), Simon Bradley (Profile)

The Subterranean Railway: How the London Underground Was Built and How It Changed the City Forever, Christian Wolmar (Atlantic)

Thames: Sacred River, Peter Ackroyd (Chatto & Windus)

The 'Times' History of London, Hugh Clout (Times Books)

Tunnels, Towers and Temples: London's 100 Strangest Places, David Long (History Press)

Living & Working

Buying, Selling & Letting Property, David Hampshire (Survival Books)

Guide to Good Living in London (Francis Chichester)

Living and Working in Britain, David Hampshire (Survival Books)

London by London: The Insider's Guide, Graham Pond (Friday project)

The London Jobs Guide: All the Information You Need to Get the Right Job with the Least Stress, Tim Gough (Prentice Hall)

London Living, Lisa Lovatt-Smith & Paul Duncan (Weidenfeld)

London Schools Guide (Mitchell Beazley)

'Time Out' London for Londoners (Time Out)

Where to Live in London, Graeme Chesters & David Hampshire (Survival Books)

Which London School, Derek Bingham (John Catt)

Maps

A-Z Big Street Atlas of London (Geographers A-Z Map Co.)

Geographers' London Atlas (Geographers A-Z Map Co.)

Guy Fox London Children's Map, Kourtney Harper (Guy Fox)

Master Atlas of Greater London (Geographers A-Z Map Co.)

The Penguin London Map Guide, Michael Middleditch (Penguin)

London all-on-one (Quickmap)

Mapping London: Making Sense of the City, Simon Foxell (Black Dog)

The Way Out Tube Map, Roger Collings (Drumhouse)

Miscellaneous

Access in London: A Guide for People Who Have Difficulty Getting Around, Gordon Couch, William Forrester and David McGaughay (Access Project)

The Art & Architecture of London, Anne Saunders (Phaidon)

The Bookshops of London, Matt Jackson (Mainstream)

Focus on London (Office for National Statistics); can be viewed on or downloaded from ▣ www.statistics.gov.uk/london or purchased as a hard copy.

Gay London, Will McLoughlin (Ellipsis)

Guide to Ethnic London, Ian McAuley (Immel Publishing)

Hawke's Eye View: London, Jason Hawkes (AA Publishing)

Holistic London, Kate Brady (Brainwave)

The London Compendium: A Street-by-street Exploration of the Hidden Metropolis, Ed Glinert (Penguin)

The London Encyclopaedia, Christopher Hibbert & Others (Macmillan)

Shops and Services, Ismay Atkins (Time Out)

The Traditional Shops & Restaurants of London: A Guide to Century-old Establishments and New Classics, Eugenia Bell (Little Bookroom)

Pubs & Restaurants

Charles Campion's London Restaurant Guide, Charles Campion (Profile)

Harden's London Restaurants (Harden's)

London Restaurants (Zagat)

London Restaurants: The Rough Guide, Charles Campion (Rough Guides)

The Michelin Guide London (Michelin)

'Time Out' Bars, Pubs and Clubs Guide, Jan Fuscoe (Time Out)

'Time Out' Cheap Eats in London, Tom Lamont (Time Out)

'Time Out' London Eating and Drinking, Guy Diamond & Cath Phillips (Time Out)

Tourist Guides

1000 Things to Do in London, Tom Lamont (Time Out)

Baedeker Guide: London (AA Publishing)

The Best of London, Andre Gayot (Gault Millau)

Blue Guide: London, Ylva French (A&C Black)

Essential London, Paul Murphy (AA Publishing)

Everyman Guide to London (Everyman)

Explorer London, Christopher Catling (AA Publishing)

Eyewitness Travel Guides: London, Michael Leapman (DK Publishing)

Fodor's London (Fodor)

Fodor's Around London With Kids (Fodor)

In and Around London (Pitkin Unichrome)

Let's Go London (St Martin's Press)

London (Eyewitness Travel Guides), Michael Leapman (Dorling Kindersley)

Lonely Planet: London, Pat Yale (Lonely Planet)

Michelin Green Guide London (Michelin)

The National Geographic Traveller: London (National Geographic)

Rick Steves' London, Rick Steves & Gene Openshaw (John Muir)

The Rough Guide to London, Rob Humphreys (Rough Guides)

Time Out London Guide (Penguin)

Magazines & Newspapers

The Big Issue, 1-5 Wandsworth Road, London SW8 2LN (☎ 020-7526 3200 ⌨ www.bigissue.com). Weekly 'street' magazine.

Evening Standard, Associated Newspapers, Northcliffe House, 2 Derry Street, London W8 5EE (☎ 020-7938 6000 ⌨ www.thisislondon.co.uk). London's evening newspaper.

The London Magazine, 32 Addison Grove, London W4 1ER (☎ 020-8400 5882, ⌨ www.thelondonmagazine.net). Bi-monthly literature and arts magazine.

Loot, 3rd Floor, Acresfield, 8-10 Exchange Street, Manchester, M2 7HA (☎ 0871-222 5000, ⌨ www.loot.com). Daily newspaper for buying/selling properties (and just about everything else) privately and property rentals in an around London.

London Gazette, PO Box 7923, London SE1 5ZH (☎ 020-7394 4517, ⌨ www.londongazette.co.uk). Official newspaper of record for London and the UK.

Metro London, Northcliffe House, 2 Derry Street, London W8 5TT, London SE16 7ND (☎ 020-7651 5200, ⌨ www.metro.co.uk). Free daily newspaper (Mondays to Fridays).

Time Out, Universal House, 251 Tottenham Court Road, London W1T 7AB (☎ 0020-7813 3000, ⌨ www.timeout.com). Weekly (Thursdays) entertainment guide.

APPENDIX C: USEFUL WEBSITES

The following list of websites (by subject) is by no means definitive, but includes many sites that will be of help and interest to those planning to live or work in London.

Business

British Business (💻 www.britishbusinesses.com). Online UK business directory.

Business Link London (💻 www.bllondon.co.uk). Includes hot topics and the latest news, plus e-commerce and e-business pages with masses of links to other useful sites.

Business – Visit London (💻 http://business.visitlondon.com). London's official convention bureau.

Londinium (💻 www.londinium.com). London website directory.

Touch London (💻 www.touchlondon.co.uk). London business directory.

Culture

All About English Culture (💻 www.allinfoaboutenglishculture.com). Your key to the fads, foibles and eccentricities of cultural England.

Black Britain (💻 www.blackbritain.co.uk). Jobs and career pages along with helpful feature pages on ethnic issues.

British Museum (💻 www.thebritishmuseum.ac.uk). Houses a vast collection of world art and artefacts.

Ethnic Pages (💻 www.ethnic-pages.co.uk). A useful insight into multicultural Britain, including books, music, arts and crafts, dance and disabilities.

Flavor Pill (💻 http://flavorpill.com/london). Culture site that embraces the high-brow, the underground, the low-brow, and the mainstream, and everything in between.

Icons (💻 www.icons.org.uk). A portrait of England.

London Culture (💻 www.london-culture.co.uk). List of London culture sites.

Pearly Society (💻 www.pearlysociety.co.uk). Dedicated to the community of (Cockney) pearly kings and queens.

Victoria & Albert Museum (💻 www.vam.ac.uk). One of England's most celebrated museums, established in 1857.

We are the English.com (💻 www.wearetheenglish.co.uk/quotes/quotes10.html). A celebration of English heritage.

Wikipedia (💻 http://en.wikipedia.org/wiki/London). The London pages of the free online encyclopaedia.

Education

British Council (💻 www.britishcouncil.org). The UK's international organisation for educational opportunities and cultural relations.

Department for Children, Schools and Families (💻 www.dfes.gov.uk). The DCSF is responsible for improving the focus on all aspects of policy affecting children and young people, as part of the Government's aim to deliver educational excellence.

Education UK (💻 www.educationuk.org). Everything foreign students need to know about education in the UK, from the British Council.

European Business School (💻 www.ebslondon.ac.uk). The EBSL is a leading London business school and the UK's oldest and largest private business school.

English in Britain (💻 www.englishinbritain.co.uk). Online database of over 1,600 British Council Accredited English language courses, at over 300 schools, including many in London.

Learn English (💻 www.learnenglish.org.uk). Learn English online with the help of this free website from the British Council.

London Business School (💻 www.london.edu). Website of the LBS, one of the leading business schools in the world.

Office for Standards in Education (💻 www.ofsted.gov.uk). The government department responsible for inspecting and regulating education and schools in England.

Parental Help (💻 www.parentscentre.gov.uk). A centre for parents and carers with a 'search for a school' facility.

Student Accommodation (💻 www.accommodationforstudents.com). A search engine for students seeking accommodation in and around the UK's major cities.

Entertainment & Tourism

All in London (💻 www.allinlondon.co.uk). A cult entertainment guide.

Beer in the Evening (💻 www.beerintheevening.com/pubs/guide/london.shtml). London pub and bar guide.

British Hotel Reservation Centre (💻 www.bhrc.co.uk). Has been operating hotel booking desks at London airports and railway stations since 1971.

Dirty Dirty Dancing (⌨ www.dirtydirtydancing.com). London hottest night spots.

Enjoy England (⌨ www.enjoyengland.com). The website of the English Tourist Board.

Go East London (⌨ www.goeastlondon.co.uk). Comprehensive tours of East London's most historic areas.

Itchy London (⌨ www.itchylondon.co.uk). Online version of the city guidebook, with reviews of bars, clubs and pubs, and suggestions for places to go out.

Le Cool (⌨ http://lecool.com/cities/london). Hip weekly magazine presenting a selection of concerts, DJs, exhibitions, odd movies, and other cultural events and happenings.

Live in London (⌨ www.liveinlondon.net). Guide to Hotels, Restaurants, Bars, Clubs, Music, Venue, Theatres, Shopping, places to visit, and much more. Also publishes a free magazine.

London (⌨ www.londonby.com or www.londonnet.co.uk). Two of the most comprehensive London websites for both residents and visitors.

London Eye (⌨ www.londoneye.com). Website of London's newest landmark (apart from the gherkin).

London Theatre Guide (⌨ www.londontheatre.co.uk). Dedicated guide to what's on at London theatres.

London Town (⌨ www.londontown.com). One of London's best general entertainment sites with an excellent hotel booking feature (and you don't pay up front!). Also contains articles and restaurant reviews, films and theatre shows, travel bookings and general information.

London Restaurants Guide (⌨ www.londonrestaurantsguide.com). One of London's best restaurant guides.

Mayfair (⌨ www.mayfair-london.co.uk). Interesting guide to London's most exclusive district.

Off to London (⌨ www.offtolondon.com). 'The travellers' guide to London'; one of the better sites packed with information on where to stay, what to do, getting around, shopping, events and more in London.

Restaurant.co.uk (⌨ www.restaurants.co.uk). One of the UK's most comprehensive restaurant search portals.

Secret London Walks (⌨ www.secretlondonwalks.co.uk). Discover the hidden and 'secret' parts of London.

Talking Tours (💻 www.talking-tours.co.uk/index.htm). Offers you the opportunity to walk through time and explore London with a personal commentary that brings the sights and history of the city alive.

This is London (💻 www.thisislondon.com). General information from the *Evening Standard* newspaper.

Toptable (💻 www.toptable.co.uk). Online restaurant booking service, offering deals such as two-for-one offers and tables at hard-to-book London restaurants.

UK Travel (💻 www.uktravel.com). Comprehensive UK travel information.

Urban Path (💻 www.urbanpath.com/london). Good general entertainment guide to London.

Virtual London (💻 www.virtual-london.com). Guided tours of London attractions.

Visit London (💻 www.visitlondon.co.uk). The official website of the London Tourist Board.

Welcome to London (💻 www.welcometolondon.com). London's most widely read online visitor magazine.

Your London (💻 www.yourlondon.gov.uk). Good general website for visitors and residents alike.

Estate & Letting Agents

Countrywide (💻 www.countrywideplc.co.uk). The UK's most largest provider of estate agency and property related finance & professional services.

Estate Agent (💻 www.estateagent.co.uk). Advertise your house for sale free.

Find a Property (💻 www.findaproperty.com). Property for sale in London and surrounding counties; includes a list of London estate agencies;

Fish 4 Homes (💻 www.fish4homes.co.uk). Selection of properties and directory of estate agents around the UK.

Foxtons (💻 www.foxtons.co.uk). London's largest chain of estate and letting agents.

Hamptons International (💻 www.hamptons.co.uk). Specialises in the top end of the property market, i.e. all of central London!

Home Pages (💻 www.homepages.co.uk). Sell your home for £50.

Homes Online (💻 www.homes-on-line.com). Useful information about buying, selling, home improvements and financing a property.

Hot Property (💻 www.hotproperty.co.uk). The Hot Property magazine website, featuring property in London and the south-east.

Houseweb (💻 www.houseweb.co.uk). Independent property website that contains comprehensive advice and tips for the homebuyer.

London Magazine (💻 www.thelondonmagazine.co.uk/estate.htm). Estate agent directory for central London.

New-Homes (💻 www.new-homes.co.uk). Comprehensive database of new home developments throughout the UK.

Prime Location (💻 www.primelocation.com). Consortium of estate agents advertising properties.

PropertyFinder.com (💻 www.propertyfinder.com). Comprehensive property website.

Right Move (💻 www.rightmove.co.uk). Claims to be 'the UK's number one property website'.

Smart New Homes (💻 www.smartnewhomes.co.uk). Search for new homes.

Vebra (💻 www.vebra.com). One of the UK's most visited property sites, run by a consortium of estate agents.

Finance, Mortgages & Property Buying

Charcol (💻 www.charcol.co.uk). Mortgage broker.

Environment Agency (💻 www.environment-agency.gov.uk). Check the occurrence of flooding and other natural hazards in an area.

Home Buyer & Mortgage Advisor Magazine (💻 www.homebuyermag.co.uk). The UK's most popular mortgage magazine. Good general information about buying and selling property.

Home Check (💻 www.homecheck.co.uk). Local information about the risks of flooding, landslip, pollution, radon gas, landfill, waste sites, etc. Also provides general information about neighbourhoods.

Hometrack (💻 www.hometrack.co.uk). Online property reports.

Money Extra (💻 www.moneyextra.co.uk). Financial services, including the best mortgage deals.

Money Net (💻 www.moneynet.co.uk). Financial services, including the best mortgage deals.

Money Quest (💻 www.moneyquest.co.uk). Mortgage brokers.

Money Supermarket (💻 www.moneysupermarket.com). General finance, including mortgages.

This is Money (⌨ www.thisismoney.co.uk). Data and statistics on money matters and useful finance guides.

Up my Street (⌨ www.upmystreet.com). Information about neighbourhoods, including property prices, local services, schools, local government, etc.

Virgin Money (⌨ www.uk.virginmoney.com). The Virgin Group's financial services online.

What Mortgage (⌨ www.whatmortgage.co.uk). Mortgage information and comprehensive advice on buying a property.

Your Mortgage Magazine (⌨ www.yourmortgage.co.uk). A wealth of information about mortgages and all aspects of buying and selling property.

Government

10 Downing Street (⌨ www.number-10.gov.uk). Official website of the British Prime Minister (but don't expect him to answer your emails).

Crime Reduction (⌨ www.crimereduction.homeoffice.gov.uk). A government site providing crime statistics and advice on avoiding and preventing crime.

Directgov (⌨ www.direct.gov.uk). Portal to public service information from the UK government, including directories, online services, and news and information of relevance to specific groups.

Government (⌨ www.direct.gov.uk). Access to the 'good and the great', i.e. the UK's elected officials.

Government Gateway (⌨ www.ukonline.gov.uk and www.gateway.gov.uk). Access to over 1,000 government websites. Government Gateway is a centralised registration service that enables you to sign up for online government services.

Greater London Authority (⌨ www.london.gov.uk). The Mayor of London's website, with information on campaigns, London issues and forthcoming events.

London Boroughs (⌨ www.london.gov.uk/london/links.jsp). Links to all London's borough websites.

Mayor Watch (⌨ www.mayorwatch.co.uk). Check up on what Boris is up to.

National Health Service (⌨ www.nhsdirect.nhs.uk). Gateway to government health information, services and assistance.

National Statistics (⌨ www.statistics.gov.uk). The government agency that produces and disseminates social, health, economic, demographic, labour and business statistics.

UK Government Guide (⌨ www.ukgovernmentguide.co.uk). An easy way to access local UK government websites.

UK Parliament (🖥 www.parliament.uk). Official parliament website.

UK Visas (🖥 www.ukvisas.gov.uk). All you need to know about UK visas.

Webmesh (🖥 www.webmesh.co.uk/government.htm). Links to government departments.

History

Derelict London (🖥 www.derelictlondon.com). Paul Talling's collection of over 1,000 photos of the parts of the city that are coming apart at the seams.

East London History (🖥 www.eastlondonhistory.com). Collection of stories about the East End, focusing on the people who lived there and influenced the area's history.

Greenwood (🖥 http://users.bathspa.ac.uk/greenwood). An interactive map of London in 1827, drawn by Christopher and John Greenwood (website hosted by Bath Spa University).

History (🖥 www.history.ac.uk/cmh/cmh.main.html). A comprehensive history of London, from markets to the city's epidemics.

London City Churches (🖥 www.london-city-churches.org.uk). A guide to City churches, some of the finest ecclesiastical buildings in Europe.

London Remembers (🖥 www.londonremembers.com). A record of all the memorials in London, from blue plaques to fountains.

Pepys Diary (🖥 www.pepysdiary.com). A spoof Pepys diary created by Phil Gyford – fascinating and much more readable than the original.

Port Cities (🖥 www.portcities.org.uk/london). A wealth of information covering all aspects of the capital's enduring relationship with its river.

Living & Working

Accommodation London (🖥 www.accommodationlondon.net). Help with finding a place to live in London, with text in English, French, Spanish, Italian and Swedish.

Get A Map (🖥 www.getamap.co.uk). Free downloadable Ordnance Survey neighbourhood maps.

Gumtree (🖥 www.gumtree.com/london /2553_1.html). Jobs from one of London's best community websites.

Jobcentre (🖥 www.jobcentreplus.gov.uk). The government website for job seekers, with advice on job hunting, training, recruitment and benefits.

Just London Jobs (🖥 www.justlondonjobs.co.uk). Links to jobs from London's top recruitment agencies.

Knowhere (🖥 www.knowhere.co.uk). An alternative look at over 2,000 UK towns.

London Jobs (🖥 www.londonjobs.co.uk). One of London's best jobs websites.

My Village (🖥 www.myvillage.com). Community sites for London and 20 other cities.

Neighbourhood Statistics (🖥 http://neighbourhood.statistics. gov.uk). Contains a wide range of statistics for neighbourhoods in England and Wales.

Proviser (🖥 www.proviser.com). Local property prices and street maps for England and Wales.

Student Accommodation (🖥 www.accommodationforstudents.com). A search engine for students seeking accommodation in London and other UK cities.

UK Online (🖥 www.ukonline.gov.uk). Comprehensive information about local services and neighbourhoods, including schools, health, housing and crime statistics.

UK Visas (🖥 www.ukvisas.gov.uk). All you need to know about British visas.

Up My Street (🖥 www.upmystreet.co.uk). Information about neighbourhoods, including property prices, local services, schools, local government, etc.

Volunteering (🖥 www.volunteering.org.uk). A useful site for those looking for volunteering work, with helpful 'I want a volunteer' pages to help you find a job in London.

Work Gateways (🖥 www.workgateways.com). Organises work for visitors on temporary working visas.

Media

BBC London (🖥 www.bbc.co.uk/london). Excellent, comprehensive website from one of Britain's great institutions – provides local news, sport, entertainment and debate.

British Papers (🖥 www.britishpapers.co.uk). links to the websites of all British newspapers that are online.

Capital Radio (🖥 www.capitalradio.co.uk). the website of London's leading commercial radio station.

Loot (🖥 www.loot.com). Log on to buy and sell virtually anything under one roof.

London Gazette (🖥 www.londongazette.co.uk). Official newspaper of record for London and the UK.

This is England (🖥 www.thisengland.co.uk). Website of *This is England* magazine.

Time Out (⌨ www.timeout.com). Website of London's iconic, best-selling entertainment guide.

The Times (⌨ www.timesonline.co.uk). One of the UK's oldest (est. 1785) and most famous newspapers.

What's On (⌨ www.whatsoninlondon.co.uk). Weekly entertainment guide.

Which? Magazine (⌨ www.which.net). Monthly consumer magazine, available on subscription.

Miscellaneous

Advice Guide (⌨ www.adviceguide.org.uk). Established by the Citizens' Advice Bureau (CAB), with down-to-earth advice, including information about civil rights, benefits and the legal system.

BBC London Weather (⌨ www.bbc.co.uk/london/weather). Provides weather services and maps for temperature, wind, satellite, lighting, pressure and radar.

Britannia (⌨ www.britannia.com/history). The internet's most comprehensive information resource for the times, places, events and people of British history.

British Library (⌨ www.bl.uk). Search the BL catalogues, order items for research, view exhibitions, etc.

British Monarchy (⌨ www.royal.gov.uk). Official website of the British Monarchy.

Cockney Rhyming Slang (⌨ www.cockneyrhymingslang.co.uk). A cornucopia of East End vernacular – helpful in case someone asks if you "saw the wooden pews [news] last night."

Football Association (⌨ www.thefa.com). The Official Website of the England Team, The FA Cup and football (soccer) at all levels in England.

Ginger Beer (⌨ www.gingerbeer.co.uk). London's premier guide to London life for its lesbian community.

Hidden London (⌨ www.hidden-london.com). A website dedicated to the little-known corners of London.

London Architecture Diary (⌨ www.londonarchitecturediary.com). Everything you ever wanted to know about the changing face of London.

London Cycle Sport (⌨ www.londoncyclesport.com). Online resource for anyone looking to take up cycling seriously, with a comprehensive guide to gear, upcoming events and race reports.

London Directory (⌨ www.londondirectory.co.uk). A directory of hundreds of London sites listed by subject.

London is Free (🖥 www.londonisfree.com). Not quite free, but there are many events and activities that cost nothing, listed here.

London Weather (🖥 http://uk.weather.com/weather/today-London-UKXX0085). Provides a ten-day summary forecast, with maps for shorter periods ahead.

Londonist (🖥 www.londonist.com). 'A website about London and everything that happens in it' – news and events, restaurants and bars, happenings and goings-on – looks at the more unusual aspects of London.

Medical Care (🖥 www.med4u.co.uk). The leading UK online medical service. Obtain health advice and a second opinion with ease.

Multimap & Streetmap (🖥 www.multimap.com and 🖥 www.streetmap.co.uk). Invaluable resources for finding your way around if you haven't got an *A-Z*, where you can find any street or postcode in London.

Ordnance Survey (🖥 www.ordnancesurvey.co.uk). Downloadable maps.

Photograph London (🖥 www.photograph-london.com). Photographic view of London.

Premier League (🖥 www.premierleague.co.uk). Official website of England's top soccer league, with links to the websites of London's top clubs.

River Thames (🖥 www.riverthames.co.uk). The definitive guide to everything about the Thames, from sea to source.

Run Riot (🖥 www.run-riot.com). A rundown on London's alternative events, particular those involving the arts.

Sports Link (🖥 www.sportslink.co.uk). Lists sports and leisure facilities throughout the UK.

Untold London (🖥 www.untoldlondon.org.uk). Vast archive of material on the history of London's diverse ethnic and cultural communities.

Walk It (🖥 www.walkit.com/london). A site that attempts to encourage more people to walk around London – the best way to see the city and often the quickest route from A to B.

Wild Web (🖥 www.wildweb.london.gov.uk). A website that aims to encourage people to make the most of London's wild places - exploring them and getting out and experiencing them first hand.

Moving Home

British Association of Removers (🖥 www.bar.co.uk). Association of removal companies offering a professional service, with a conciliation and arbitration service.

I am Moving (⌨ www.iammoving.com). Will inform companies on your behalf that you're moving.

The Move Channel (⌨ www.themovechannel.com). General property website containing everything you need to know about moving house.

Really Moving (⌨ www.reallymoving.com). Comprehensive information about property, including home-moving services and a property finder.

Professional Associations

Building Societies' Association (⌨ www.bsa.org.uk). Central representative body for building societies.

Council for Licensed Conveyancers (⌨ www.conveyancer.org). Council for licensed conveyancers.

Council of Mortgage Lenders (⌨ www.cml.org.uk). Trade association for mortgage lenders.

Federation of Master Builders (⌨ www.fmb.org.uk). Includes a directory of members.

Land Registry (⌨ www1.landregistry.gov.uk). Practical information about registering land and land registry archives.

The Law Society (⌨ www.lawsociety.org.uk). Professional body for solicitors in England and Wales.

National Association of Estate Agents/NAEA (⌨ www.naea.co.uk). The main organisation for estate agents.

Ombudsman for Estate Agents (⌨ www.oea.co.uk). Independent arbitration for property buyers with complaints about registered estate agents.

Shopping & Services

Borough Market (⌨ www.boroughmarket.org.uk). London's oldest food market, established by the Romans and held on its present site for 250 years.

Consumers' Association (⌨ www.which.net). The UK's consumer champion, who publish the monthly *Which?* consumer magazine.

Harrods (⌨ www.harrods.com). London's largest and most famous department store, where it's said you can buy anything.

John Lewis (⌨ www.johnlewis.com). The website of London's (and the UK's) favourite retailer.

London Rate (🖳 www.londonrate.com). Useful resource for Londoners containing a collection of service-industry contacts, which are rated and searchable with prices. Everything from babysitters to builders, computer experts to cleaners, and hairdressers to housekeepers.

Lynku (🖳 www.lynku.com). Designer fashion and furniture sales website for London, offering free weekly update emails and alerts on sales and promotions by category.

Price Runner (🖳 www.pricerunner.co.uk). Compare the prices of a wide range of goods and services.

Shopping Net (🖳 www.shopping.net). The UK's most comprehensive shopping website, which allows you to search thousands of websites for products and services at the best prices.

Street Sensation (🖳 www.streetsensation.co.uk). A virtual tour of London's busiest shopping streets, with photos and links to over 3,500 shops, restaurants and bars.

Travel

At UK (🖳 www.atuk.co.uk). The foremost UK travel search engine and directory.

British Airways (🖳 www.britishairways.com). The website of Britain's largest airline.

Easyjet (🖳 www.easyjet.co.uk). The UK's best budget airline.

National Express (🖳 www.nationalexpress.com). The UK's largest scheduled coach travel company.

National Rail (🖳 www.nationalrail.co.uk). For when you want to get out of London. Timetables, special offers and a journey planner for all the UK's railway services.

Public Transport Information (🖳 www.pti.org.uk). Covers all travel by rail, air, coach, bus, ferry, metro and tram within the UK (including the Channel Islands, Isle of Man and Northern Ireland), and between the UK and Ireland.

Rail (🖳 www.rail.co.uk). The best independent rail information, including timetables.

Transport For London (🖳 www.tfl.gov.uk). Everything you need to know about London's public transport systems.

Travel Britain Guide (🖳 www.travelbritain.com). Travel and tourism deals and resources pages for travel and entertainment resource in the UK.

Travel Line (🖳 www.traveline.org.uk). The UK's premier website for impartial information on planning a journey by bus, coach or train.

Virgin Atlantic (🖳 www.virgin-atlantic.com). The website of Britain's best airline.

Property

English Heritage (🖥 www.english-heritage.org.uk). The organisation responsible for protecting and promoting the historic environment, officially known as the Historic Buildings and Monuments Commission for England.

Into London (🖥 www.intolondon.com). London's longest-running website for flatsharers.

My Property Spy (🖥 www.mypropertyspy.co.uk). Property sale prices in London dating back to 2000 – find out what your neighbour's paid and what your house might be worth.

The Rat & Mouse (🖥 www.theratandmouse.co.uk). In the form of a blog, R&M sifts through the endless conflicting reports on the state of London's property market and attempts to make sense of them. Contains an archive by postcode so that you can find out what people say about your street. (Rat and mouse = 'house' in rhyming Cockney slang – see **Appendix H**).

Property Snake (🖥 www.propertysnake.co.uk). See at a glance whether property prices are up or down in a particular area – and by how much.

Save Britain's Heritage (🖥 www.savebritainsheritage.org). Conservation of historic buildings.

Scoot (🖥 www.scoot.co.uk). Find essential services for homeowners.

APPENDIX D: WEIGHTS & MEASURES

Officially, the UK converted to the international metric system of measurement in 1995 and the use of imperial measures was due to end in 1999. However, many traders insisted on using Imperial measures and the EU finally gave up the battle to ban them in 2007, although products priced in Imperial weights and measures must legally also show their equivalent in metric. If you're confused, the conversion tables on the following pages will prove useful. Some comparisons shown are approximate, but close enough for most everyday uses. You can make conversions online using a variety of websites, e.g. 🖳 www.unit-conversion.info. For information about the metric system, see 🖳 www.metric.org.uk/home.htm.

Women's Clothes										
Continental	34	36	38	40	42	44	46	48	50	52
UK		8	10	12	14	16	18	20	22	24	26
US		6	8	10	12	14	16	18	20	22	24

Pullover's												
	Women's						Men's					
Continental	40	42	44	46	48	50	44	46	48	50	52	54
UK	34	36	38	40	42	44	34	36	38	40	42	44
US	34	36	38	40	42	44		sm	med		lar	xl

Men's Shirts										
Continental	36	37	38	39	40	41	42	43	44	46
UK/US	14	14	15	15	16	16	17	17	18	-

Men's Underwear						
Continental	5	6	7	8	9	10
UK		34	36	38	40	42	44
US		sm	med		lar	xl

NB: sm = small, med = medium, lar = large, xl = extra large

Children's Clothes

Continental	92	104	116	128	140	152
UK		16/18	20/22	24/26	28/30	32/34	36/38
US		2	4	6	8	10	12

Children's Shoes

Continental	18 19 20 21 22 23 24 25 26 27 28 29 30 31 32
UK/US	2 3 4 4 5 6 7 7 8 9 10 11 11 12 13
Continental	33 34 35 36 37 38
UK/US	1 2 2 3 4 5

Shoes (Women's & Men's)

Continental	35	36	37	37	38	39	40	41	42	42	43	44
UK	2	3	3	4	4	5	6	7	7	8	9	9
US	4	5	5	6	6	7	8	9	9	10	10	11

Weight

Imperial	Metric	Metric	Imperial
1oz	28.35g	1g	0.035oz
1lb*	454g	100g	3.5oz
1cwt	50.8kg	250g	9oz
1 ton	1,016kg	500g	18oz
2,205lb	1 tonne	1kg	2.2lb

Area

British/US	Metric	Metric	British/US
1 sq. in	0.45 sq. cm	1 sq. cm	0.15 sq. in
1 sq. ft	0.09 sq. m	1 sq. m	10.76 sq. ft
1 sq. yd	0.84 sq. m	1 sq. m	1.2 sq. yds
1 acre	0.4 hectares	1 hectare	2.47 acres
1 sq. mile	2.56 sq. km	1 sq. km	0.39 sq. mile

Capacity			
Imperial	**Metric**	**Metric**	**Imperial**
1 UK pint	0.57 litre	1 litre	1.75 UK pints
1 US pint	0.47 litre	1 litre	2.13 US pints
1 UK gallon	4.54 litres	1 litre	0.22 UK gallon
1 US gallon	3.78 litres	1 litre	0.26 US gallon

NB: An American 'cup' = around 250ml or 0.25 litre.

Length			
British/US	**Metric**	**Metric**	**British/US**
1in	2.54cm	1cm	0.39in
1ft	30.48cm	1m	3ft 3.25in
1yd	91.44cm	1km	0.62mi
1mi	1.6km	8km	5mi

Temperature	
°Celsius	**°Fahrenheit**
0	32 (freezing point of water)
5	41
10	50
15	59
20	68
25	77
30	86
35	95
40	104
50	122

Temperature Conversion

Celsius to Fahrenheit: multiply by 9, divide by 5 and add 32. (For a quick and approximate conversion, double the Celsius temperature and add 30.)

Fahrenheit to Celsius: subtract 32, multiply by 5 and divide by 9. (For a quick and approximate conversion, subtract 30 from the Fahrenheit temperature and divide by 2.)

NB: The boiling point of water is 100°C / 212°F. Normal body temperature (if you're alive and well) is 37°C / 98.6°F.

Power			
Kilowatts	Horsepower	Horsepower	Kilowatts
1	1.34	1	0.75

Oven Temperature		
Gas	Electric	
	°F	°C
-	225–250	110–120
1	275	140
2	300	150
3	325	160
4	350	180
5	375	190
6	400	200
7	425	220
8	450	230
9	475	240

Air Pressure	
PSI	Bar
10	0.5
20	1.4
30	2
40	2.8

APPENDIX E: TABLES

The tables on the following pages show house prices, rents, crime rates, school league tables, council tax rates and primary healthcare trust ratings in all 32 London boroughs and the City of London.

Average House Prices July 2008 (£000)				
Borough	**Flat**	**Terraced House**	**Semi-det House**	**Detached House**
Barking & Dagenham	149,750	208,250	249,000	365,000
Barnet	249,850	332,600	521,450	1,216,300
Bexley	153,250	216,350	264,150	393,400
Brent	246,400	418,750	395,550	785,300
Bromley	210,450	271,150	338,450	578,700
Camden	477,700	1,299,800	2,235,400	2,680,250
City of London	407,650	n/a	n/a	n/a
Croydon	179,100	245,600	318,550	518,900
Ealing	257,800	364,950	441,300	703,300
Enfield	197,250	270,350	374,500	703,750
Greenwich	221,050	256,500	309,200	1,138,100
Hackney	263,450	490,650	673,000	742,500
Hammersmith & Fulham	448,250	874,850	1,567,750	1,188,300
Haringey	265,800	453,050	738,400	1,482,400
Harrow	234,200	313,900	359,650	698,150
Havering	167,600	232,200	279,800	452,000
Hillingdon	192,450	249,500	293,300	509,600
Hounslow	244,250	352,850	403,250	598,100
Islington	368,750	715,550	1,029,450	1,229,400
Kensington & Chelsea	835,050	2,777,265	3,268,550	5,962,500
Kingston-upon-Thames	246,350	315,600	428,150	646,150
Lambeth	286,950	479,450	631,900	947,700
Lewisham	206,500	291,550	374,700	465,000
Merton	249,200	394,000	562,750	1,599,250
Newham	244,100	250,000	267,150	340,000
Redbridge	214,800	302,250	392,400	728,500
Richmond-upon-Thames	330,400	547,900	655,650	1,224,150
Southwark	299,200	403,500	632,450	824,850
Sutton	195,950	263,600	337,600	557,500
Tower Hamlets	319,950	482,850	417,500	n/a
Waltham Forest	192,450	278,050	332,750	491,550
Wandsworth	353,250	598,200	830,900	2,142,000
Westminster	636,250	1,586,250	3,043,750	n/a

Average Rental Prices Jul;y 2008 (£ pcm)				
Borough	Flat 1-2 bed	House 2-3 bed	House 3-4 bed	House 5+ bed
Barking & Dagenham	950	1,100	1,400	1,750
Barnet	1,050	1,500	2,400	8,650
Bexley	750	1,100	1,550	2,600
Brent	1,200	1,500	2,300	3,250
Bromley	1,000	1,300	1,650	2,400
Camden	1,200	1,500	2,220	4,350
City of London	2,400	3,700	4,250	4,750
Croydon	1,200	1,500	2,050	2,600
Ealing	1,000	1,300	2,400	3,900
Enfield	750	1,100	1,650	2,400
Greenwich	1,000	1,300	1,750	2,800
Hackney	1,000	1,500	1,850	2,150
Hammersmith & Fulham	1,400	1,750	3,250	6,500
Haringey	1,550	2,150	3,250	5,650
Harrow	1,000	1,300	1,750	2,400
Havering	850	1,100	1,550	1,950
Hillingdon	800	1,300	1,750	2,400
Hounslow	1,350	1,600	2,220	2,800
Islington	1,400	1,750	2,250	6,500
Kensington & Chelsea	2,100	3,050	3,700	6,500
Kingston-upon-Thames	1,200	1,750	2,400	3,450
Lambeth	1,000	1,100	1,550	2,150
Lewisham	1,050	1,300	1,750	2,150
Merton	1,450	1,950	2,400	5,200
Newham	850	1,000	1,200	1,750
Redbridge	800	845	1,000	1,000
Richmond-upon-Thames	1,400	1,750	2,600	8,650
Southwark	1,200	1,750	2,300	2,925
Sutton	1,100	1,550	2,150	3,000
Tower Hamlets	1,200	1,500	2,300	3,250
Waltham Forest	800	1,100	1,550	1,950
Wandsworth	1,200	1,750	2,400	3,000
Westminster	2,400	5,400	10,400	11,900

Borough	Total Crimes	Violence	Burglary	Robbery	Motor Vehicle
Barking & Dagenham	19,579	5,018	1,602	625	3,005
Barnet	26,415	5,287	3,950	900	4,689
Bexley	16,672	3,265	2,271	378	2,419
Brent	27,486	6,014	3,357	2,111	3,769
Bromley	25,326	5,215	3,257	797	3,732
Camden	34,385	5,956	3,678	1,061	4,410
City of London*	n/a	n/a	n/a	n/a	n/a
Croydon	30,945	6,702	3,574	1,564	3,826
Ealing	33,574	7,692	4,182	1,473	4,965
Enfield	25,299	4,203	3,713	1,193	4,324
Greenwich	30,311	7,161	3,470	1,230	4,779
Hackney	32,048	7,024	2,775	1,243	4,042
Hammersmith & Fulham	22,865	5,036	2,672	778	3,149
Haringey	28,643	5,373	3,795	1,324	4,538
Harrow	14,235	2,720	2,399	508	2,226
Havering	17,923	3,156	2,279	303	2,892
Hillingdon	25,729	5,904	3,095	778	4,185
Hounslow	23,660	5,423	2,474	813	3,296
Islington	29,273	5,480	3,163	1,172	3,739
Kensington & Chelsea	22,971	3,071	1,705	610	2,857
Kingston-upon-Thames	11,867	2,532	1,066	294	1,273
Lambeth	35,325	7,809	3,721	2,295	3,509
Lewisham	31,573	8,664	2,877	1,575	3,897
Merton	14,955	3,691	1,595	526	1,759
Newham	35,050	7,724	3,291	2,134	6,654
Redbridge	23,236	4,220	2,982	936	4,092
Richmond-upon-Thames	11,646	1,890	1,865	241	1,563
Southwark	40,817	9,149	4,028	2,038	4,687
Sutton	13,399	2,646	1,506	347	2,173
Tower Hamlets	30,476	6,678	2,724	1,214	4,072
Waltham Forest	25,747	5,501	3,146	1,493	4,207
Wandsworth	26,431	5,230	3,013	1,273	4,221
Westminster	62,397	8,335	3,523	1,598	4,338

NB: The Met Police publish monthly and annual figures for each borough, except for the *City of London, which has it's own police force and website ⌨ www.cityoflondon.police.uk/CityPolice.

School League Tables 2007/08			
Borough	Percentage of pupils achieving Level 4 at KS2		Pupils achieving 5 or more GCSEs at grades A* to C
	English	Maths	%
England	80	77	46.7
Barking & Dagenham	77	76	58.7
Barnet	85	82	70.1
Bexley	84	79	62.4
Brent	80	75	64.8
Bromley	84	78	71.3
Camden	78	76	55.9
City of London	96	96	n/a
Croydon	81	75	58.8
Ealing	80	78	62.0
Enfield	78	75	56.2
Greenwich	73	72	47.2
Hackney	73	66	53.7
Hammersmith & Fulham	81	78	66.9
Haringey	76	74	56.2
Harrow	82	79	68.0
Havering	84	81	64.4
Hillingdon	82	77	58.2
Hounslow	79	77	64.3
Islington	77	74	49.3
Kensington & Chelsea	87	83	68.4
Kingston-upon-Thames	85	81	70.7
Lambeth	77	71	56.0
Lewisham	76	74	54.9
Merton	79	77	48.7
Newham	75	73	55.6
Redbridge	84	81	73.6
Richmond-upon-Thames	88	84	57.4
Southwark	73	72	52.7
Sutton	85	82	73.8
Tower Hamlets	81	78	59.4
Waltham Forest	76	75	55.0
Wandsworth	80	77	61.2
Westminster	83	77	55.1

Council Tax Rates (£) 2008/09

Borough	Band G	Band H
Barking & Dagenham	2,210	2,652
Barnet	2,321	2,785
Bexley	2,332	2,799
Brent	2,238	2,686
Bromley	2,105	2,526
Camden	2,219	2,663
City of London	1,539	1,847
Croydon	2,343	2,811
Ealing	2,283	2,740
Enfield	2,306	2,767
Greenwich	2,151	2,581
Hackney	2,180	2,617
Hammersmith & Fulham	1,954	2,345
Haringey	2,452	2,943
Harrow	2,437	2,925
Havering	2,472	2,966
Hillingdon	2,371	2,846
Hounslow	2,334	2,801
Islington	2,080	2,496
Kensington & Chelsea	1,759	2,111
Kingston-upon-Thames	2,633	3,160
Lambeth	2,059	2,470
Lewisham	2,211	2,653
Merton	2,336	2,803
Newham	2,092	2,511
Redbridge	2,294	2,752
Richmond-upon-Thames	2,573	3,088
Southwark	2,037	2,444
Sutton	2,364	2,837
Tower Hamlets	1,959	2,351
Waltham Forest	2,401	2,881
Wandsworth	1,137	1,364
Westminster	1,146	1,375

Primary Healthcare Trust Ratings 2007

Borough	Weak	Fair	Good	Excellent
Barking & Dagenham		♦		
Barnet			♦	
Bexley		♦		
Brent *		♦		
Bromley		♦		
Camden		♦		
City of London *		♦		
Croydon		♦		
Ealing		♦		
Enfield		♦		
Greenwich		♦		
Hackney *		♦		
Hammersmith & Fulham			♦	
Haringey *			♦	
Harrow		♦		
Havering		♦		
Hillingdon		♦		
Hounslow		♦		
Islington			♦	
Kensington & Chelsea			♦	
Kingston-upon-Thames		♦		
Lambeth			♦	
Lewisham		♦		
Merton	♦			
Newham			♦	
Redbridge		♦		
Richmond-upon-Thames		♦		
Southwark			♦	
Sutton	♦			
Tower Hamlets			♦	
Waltham Forest		♦		
Wandsworth		♦		
Westminster		♦		

NB: Primary Healthcare Trusts marked with an asterisk (*) include teaching hospitals.

APPENDIX F: COCKNEY RHYMING SLANG

Cockney rhyming slang is the colloquial language of the East of London. A true Cockney is someone born within the sound of Bow Bells (St Mary-le-Bow Church in Cheapside, London). However, nowadays the term is now loosely applied to many born outside this area provided they have a 'Cockney' accent or a Cockney heritage.

Cockney rhyming slang was invented in the 16th century in the East End of London and was supposedly used by locals to chat without the authorities or informers knowing what they were talking about them. These days it's generally used for fun, although many Cockney expressions have found their way into mainstream English in England and throughout the world.

Rhyming Slang phrases are derived from taking an expression which rhymes with a word and then using that expression instead of the word. For example the word 'look' rhymes with 'butcher's hook'. In many cases the rhyming word is omitted, therefore someone is more likely to say, 'let's have a butchers' instead of 'butcher's hook'.

There are many online sources of Cockney slang including, 🖳 www.cockney rhymingslang.co.uk, 🖳 www.phespirit.info/cockney and 🖳 www.bbc.co.uk/dna/h2g2/A649.

Abergavenny: penny
Adam and Eve: believe
Alan Whickers: knickers
Alligator: later
Apple Fritter: bitter (beer)
Apples and Pears: stairs
April Fool: stool or tool
April Showers: flowers
Army & Navy: gravy
Artful Dodger: lodger
Ayrton Senna: tenner (ten pounds)
Babbling Brook: cook
Bacon and Eggs: legs
Ball of Chalk: walk
Bangers and Mash: cash
Barn Owl (barney): row (argument)
Barnet Fair: hair
Bath Bun: son

Big Ben: ten
Big Dippers: slippers
Billy Goat: coat
Boat Race: face
Bob Hope: soap
Battle Cruiser: boozer (pub)
Bo-peep: sleep
Bow and Arrow: sparrow
Brahms and Lizst: pissed (drunk)
Brass Band: hand
Brass Tacks: facts
Bread and Honey: money
Britney Spears: beers
Brown Bread: dead
Bubble Bath: laugh
Bubble and Squeak: Greek
Butcher's Hook: look
Cain and Abel: table

Cash and Carried: married
Cat and Mouse: house
Cherry Ripe: pipe
Chevy Chase: face
Chew the Fat: chat
China plate: mate
Clothes Peg: egg
Cock Sparrow: barrow
Cream Crackered: knackered (tired/broken)
Currant Bun: sun, son
Custard and Jelly: telly
Daisy Roots: boots
Danny Marr: car
Day and Night: light
Dickory Dock: clock
Dicky Bird: word
Ding Dong: song
Dog and Bone: telephone
Donkey's Ears: years
Drum 'n' Bass: face
Earwig: twig (understand)
East and West: vest
Elephant & Castle: parcel
Elsie Tanner: spanner
Flowery Dell: cell (prison)
Frog & Toad: road
Garden Gate: mate
Ginger Beer: queer (homosexual)
Gipsy's Warning: morning
Gold Watch: scotch
Grasshopper: copper (policeman)
Greengages: wages
Ha'penny Dip: ship
Half Inch: pinch
Ham and Eggs: legs
Hank Marvin: starving (hungry)
Harry Lime: time

Hit and Miss: kiss
Irish Jig: wig
Isle of Wight: light, right
J. Arthur Rank: bank, wank
Jack and Jill: hill
Jack Tar: bar
Jam Jar: car
Jimmy Riddle: piddle (urinate)
Joanna: piano
Khyber Pass: arse, glass
King Lears: ears
Lady Godiva: fiver (five pounds)
Lee Marvin: starving
Left in the Lurch: church
Lemon and Lime: crime
Lemon Squeezy: easy
Loaf of Bread: head
Lollipop: shop
Loop the Loop: soup
Mickey Mouse: house
Mince Pies: eyes
Moby Dick: sick
Mork & Mindy: windy
Mother Hubbard: cupboard
Mutt and Jeff: deaf
Mystic Megs: legs
Nanny Goat: boat, coat
Ned Kelly: telly
Nellie Dean: queen (homosexual)
Noah's Ark: lark
North and South: mouth
Oedipus Rex: sex
Oily Rag: fag
Oliver Twist: pissed
One Time Looker: hooker
Pat Malone: alone, own
Pen and Ink: stink
Peter Pan: can (prison)

Pick and Mix: sticks (countryside)
Pig's Ear: beer
Pinch (steal): half Inch
Plates of Meat: feet
Pony: £25
Pony & Trap: crap
Pork Pies (porkie pies): lies
Rabbit & Pork: talk
Radio Rental: mental
Rat and mouse: house
Rhythm and Blues: shoes
Robin Hood: good
Rosie Lee: tea
Round the Houses: trousers
Ruby Murray: curry
Saucepan Lid: kid
Septic Tank: Yank
Sexton Blake: fake
Sky Rocket: pocket

Steam Tug: do something stupid (steam tug = Mug = Fool)
Sweeney Todd: flying squad (police)
Syrup of Figs: wig
Tea Leaf: thief
Tick-tock: clock
Tit for Tat (titfer): hat
Todd Sloane: alone, own
Tom Foolery: jewellery
Trick Cyclist: psychiatrist
Trouble and Strife: wife
Turtle Doves: gloves
Two and Eight: state (of anguish)
Uncle Dick: sick
Vera Lynn: gin
Weasel & Stoat: coat
Whistle and Flute: suit
Widow Twanky: hanky

Maybe it's Because I'm a Londoner
(words & music by Hubert Gregg)

Maybe it's because I'm a Londoner, that I love London so.
Maybe it's because I'm a Londoner that I think of her wherever I go.
I get a funny feeling inside of me just walking up and down.
Maybe it's because I'm a Londoner that I love London Town.

INDEX

Survival Books

Essential reading for anyone planning to live, work, retire or buy a home abroad

Survival Books was established in 1987 and by the mid-'90s was the leading publisher of books for people planning to live, work, buy property or retire abroad.

From the outset, our philosophy has been to provide the most comprehensive and up-to-date information available. Our titles routinely contain up to twice as much information as other books and are updated frequently. All our books contain colour photographs and some are printed in two colours or full colour throughout. They also contain original cartoons, illustrations and maps.

Survival Books are written by people with first-hand experience of the countries and the people they describe, and therefore provide invaluable insights that cannot be obtained from official publications or websites, and information that is more reliable and objective than that provided by the majority of unofficial sites.

Survival Books are designed to be easy – and interesting – to read. They contain a comprehensive list of contents and index and extensive appendices, including useful addresses, further reading, useful websites and glossaries to help you obtain additional information as well as metric conversion tables and other useful reference material.

Our primary goal is to provide you with the essential information necessary for a trouble-free life or property purchase and to save you time, trouble and money.

We believe our books are the best – they are certainly the best-selling. But don't take our word for it – read what reviewers and readers have said about Survival Books at the front of this book.

Order your copies today by phone, fax, post or email from:
Survival Books, PO Box 3780, Yeovil, BA21 5WX, United Kingdom.
Tel: +44 (0)1935-700060, email: sales@survivalbooks.net,
Website: www.survivalbooks.net

Buying a Home Series

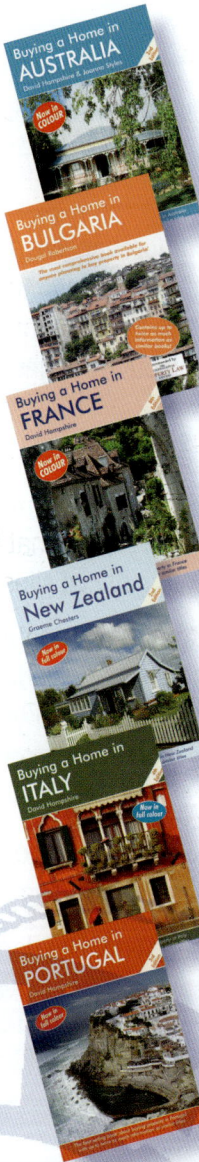

Buying a home abroad is not only a major financial transaction but also a potentially life-changing experience; it's therefore essential to get it right. Our Buying a Home guides are required reading for anyone planning to purchase property abroad and are packed with vital information to guide you through the property jungle and help you avoid disasters that can turn a dream home into a nightmare.

The purpose of our Buying a Home guides is to enable you to choose the most favourable location and the most appropriate property for your requirements, and to reduce your risk of making an expensive mistake by making informed decisions and calculated judgements rather than uneducated and hopeful guesses. Most importantly, they will help you save money and will repay your investment many times over.

Buying a Home guides are the most comprehensive and up-to-date source of information available about buying property abroad – whether you're seeking a detached house or an apartment, a holiday or a permanent home (or an investment property), these books will prove invaluable.

Living and Working Series

Living and Working in
AMERICA
David Hampshire

Living and Working in
CANADA
Edited by Graeme Chesters

Living and Working in
FRANCE
David Hampshire

Living and Working in
NEW ZEALAND
Edited by David Hampshire

Living and Working in
SPAIN
David Hampshire

Living and Working in
SWITZERLAND
David Hampshire

Our Living and Working guides are essential reading for anyone planning to spend a period abroad – whether it's an extended holiday or permanent migration – and are packed with priceless information designed to help you avoid costly mistakes and save both time and money.

Living and Working guides are the most comprehensive and up-to-date source of practical information available about everyday life abroad. They aren't, however, simply a catalogue of dry facts and figures, but are written in a highly readable style – entertaining, practical and occasionally humorous.

Our aim is to provide you with the comprehensive practical information necessary for a trouble-free life. You may have visited a country as a tourist, but living and working there is a different matter altogether; adjusting to a new environment and culture and making a home in any foreign country can be a traumatic and stressful experience. You need to adapt to new customs and traditions, discover the local way of doing things (such as finding a home, paying bills and obtaining insurance) and learn all over again how to overcome the everyday obstacles of life.

All these subjects and many, many more are covered in depth in our Living and Working guides – don't leave home without them.

The Expats' Best Friend!

Culture Wise Series

Our **Culture Wise** series of guides is essential reading for anyone who wants to understand how a country really 'works'. Whether you're planning to stay for a few days or a lifetime, these guides will help you quickly find your feet and settle into your new surroundings.
Culture Wise guides:

- Reduce the anxiety factor in adapting to a foreign culture
- Explain how to behave in everyday situations in order to avoid cultural and social gaffes
- Help you get along with your neighbours
- Make friends and establish lasting business relationships
- Enhance your understanding of a country and its people.

People often underestimate the extent of cultural isolation they can face abroad, particularly in a country with a different language. At first glance, many countries seem an 'easy' option, often with millions of visitors from all corners of the globe and well-established expatriate communities. But, sooner or later, newcomers find that most countries are indeed 'foreign' and many come unstuck as a result. **Culture Wise** guides will enable you to quickly adapt to the local way of life and feel at home, and – just as importantly – avoid the worst effects of culture shock.

Culture Wise – The Wisest Way to Travel

The essential guides to Culture, Customs & Business Etiquette

Other Survival Books

Investing in Property Abroad: Essential reading for anyone planning to buy property abroad, containing surveys of over 30 countries.

The Best Places to Buy a Home in France/Spain: Unique guides to where to buy property in Spain and France, containing detailed regional profiles and market reports.

Buying, Selling and Letting Property: The best source of information about buying, selling and letting property in the UK.

Earning Money From Your Home: Income from property in France and Spain, including short- and long-term letting.

Foreigners in France/Spain: Triumphs & Disasters: Real-life experiences of people who have emigrated to France and Spain, recounted in their own words.

Making a Living: Comprehensive guides to self-employment and starting a business in France and Spain.

Renovating & Maintaining Your French Home: The ultimate guide to renovating and maintaining your dream home in France.

Retiring in France/Spain: Everything a prospective retiree needs to know about the two most popular international retirement destinations.

Running Gîtes and B&Bs in France: An essential book for anyone planning to invest in a gîte or bed & breakfast business.

Rural Living in France: An invaluable book for anyone seeking the 'good life', containing a wealth of practical information about all aspects of French country life.

Shooting Caterpillars in Spain: The hilarious and compelling story of two innocents abroad in the depths of Andalusia in the late '80s.

Wild Thyme in Ibiza: A fragrant account of how a three-month visit to the enchanted island of Ibiza in the mid-'60s turned into a 20-year sojourn.

For a full list of our current titles, visit our website at www.survivalbooks.net

WHERE TO LIVE IN LONDON

An important new book and the only publication dedicated to where to live in London. Essential reading for newcomers planning to live in London or existing residents thinking of moving to a different neighbourhood. Containing detailed surveys of all 32 boroughs plus the City of London.

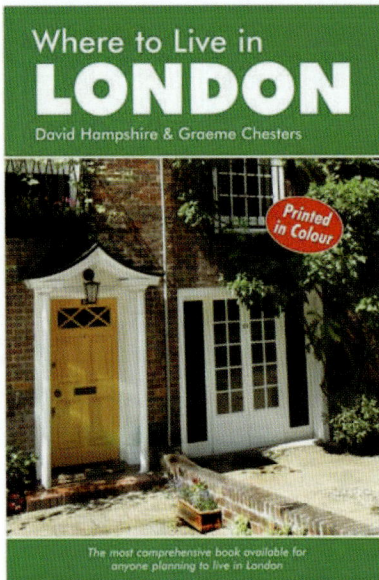

PRINTED IN COLOUR!

Topics include:

- ♦ Orientation - finding your bearings
- ♦ Getting around London
- ♦ Choosing where to live
- ♦ The London property market
- ♦ Buying or renting a home
- ♦ Property prices & rental costs
- ♦ Schools & higher education
- ♦ Health services & hospitals
- ♦ Crime statistics
- ♦ Leisure & sport facilities
- ♦ Detailed surveys of all boroughs with maps, and much more.

Written by David Hampshire, author of *Living & Working in Britain* and Graeme Chesters, co-editor of *Living & Working in London*. *Where to Live in London* provides a comprehensive insight into life in the many diverse areas of London.

Buy your copy today at www.survivalbooks.net

Survival Books – The Experts on Living in London

BUYING, SELLING & LETTING PROPERTY

Buying, Selling & Letting Property is essential reading for anyone who owns or is planning to buy a home in the UK, and is designed to guide you through the property maze and save you time trouble and money! Most importantly it is packed with vital information to help you avoid the kind of disasters that can turn your dream home into a nightmare!

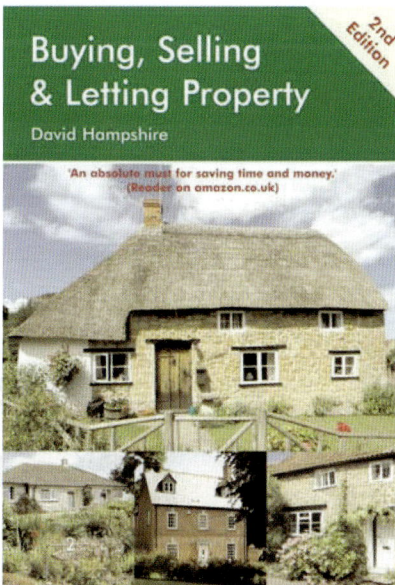

Topics include:

- ◆ Choosing the location
- ◆ What to buy
- ◆ The buying process
- ◆ Mortgages
- ◆ Moving house
- ◆ Home improvements
- ◆ Letting
- ◆ Selling your home
- ◆ Useful addresses, publications & websites
- ◆ Comprehensive glossary, checklists and much, much more.

Buying, Selling & Letting Property is the most comprehensive book about buying property in the UK.

Buy your copy today at www.survivalbooks.net

Survival Books – The Homebuyers' Friend

CULTURE WISE ENGLAND

The Essential Guide to Culture, Customs & Business Etiquette

Travellers often underestimate the depth of cultural isolation they can face abroad, even in a country where English is spoken. *Culture Wise England* will help you understand England and its people and adapt to the English way of life. Most importantly, it will enable you to quickly feel at home.

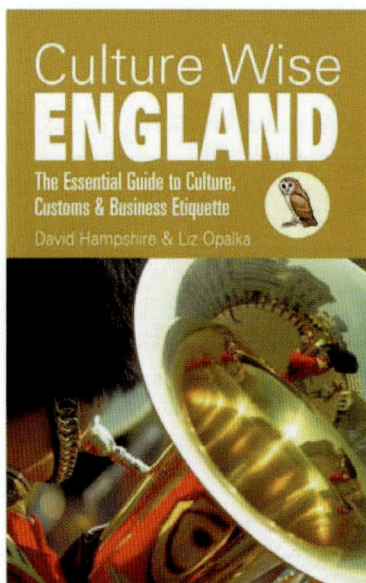

PRINTED IN COLOUR!

Topics include:

- How to overcome culture shock
- The historical and political background to modern England
- English attitudes and values – at home and at work
- Do's, don'ts and taboos
- How to enjoy yourself in English style
- Business and professional etiquette
- England's spoken and body language
- Getting around England safely
- Shopping the English way

Culture Wise England is essential reading for visitors and residents who want to understand how the country really works. Whether you're planning to stay for a few weeks or a lifetime, it will quickly help you find you feet after arrival, settle in smoothly and integrate into your new surroundings.

Buy your copy today at www.survivalbooks.net

Survival Books – The Wisest Way to Travel

LIVING & WORKING IN
BRITAIN

What's it really like Living and Working in Britain? Not surprisingly, there's a lot more to life than castles, cricket and crumpets. This book is guaranteed to make your life in Britain easier and more enjoyable. Regardless of whether you're planning to stay for a few weeks or indefinitely, *Living and Working in Britain* has been written for you.

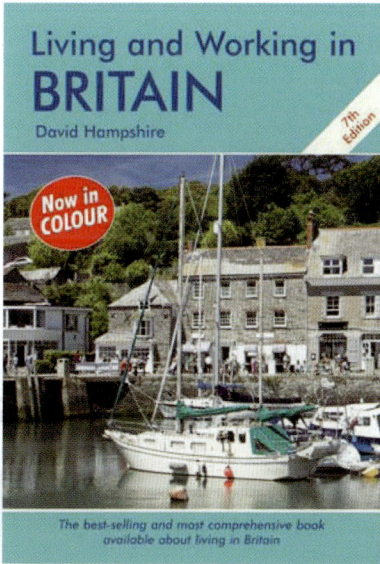

Living and Working in
BRITAIN
David Hampshire

7th Edition

Now in COLOUR

The best-selling and most comprehensive book
available about living in Britain

PRINTED IN COLOUR!

Topics include:

◆ How to find a job with a good salary and conditions

◆ How to obtain a residence or work permit

◆ How to avoid and overcome problems on arrival

◆ How to find your dream home

◆ How to make the most of post office and telephone services

◆ How to get the best education for your family

◆ How to make the best use of public transport and much, much more.

Living and Working in Britain is the most comprehensive and up-to-date source of practical information available about everyday life in Britain. It's packed with 400 pages of important and useful data, designed to help you avoid costly mistakes and save both time and money.

Buy your copy today at www.survivalbooks.net

Survival Books – The Expatriates' Best Friend

📷 Photo Credits